Digital Critical Editions

TOPICS IN THE DIGITAL HUMANITIES

Humanities computing is redefining basic principles about research and publication. An influx of new, vibrant, and diverse communities of practitioners recognizes that computer applications are subject to continual innovation and reappraisal. This series publishes books that demonstrate the new questions, methods, and results arising in the digital humanities.

Series Editors
Susan Schreibman
Raymond C. Siemens

Digital Critical Editions

EDITED BY

Daniel Apollon, Claire Bélisle,
and Philippe Régnier

University of Illinois Press
URBANA, CHICAGO, AND SPRINGFIELD

First Illinois paperback 2017
© 2014 by the Board of Trustees
of the University of Illinois
All rights reserved
1 2 3 4 5 C P 5 4 3 2 1
♾ This book is printed on acid-free paper.

This book has a special web page at
www.digitalcriticaleditions.com.

The Library of Congress cataloged the cloth
edition as follows:
Digital critical editions / edited by Daniel Apollon,
Claire Bélisle, Philippe Régnier.
pages   cm. — (Topics in the digital humanities)
Includes bibliographical references and index.
ISBN 978-0-252-03840-2 (hardback)
ISBN 978-0-252-09628-0 (e-book)
1. Editing—Data processing.
2. Digital media—Editing.
3. Criticism, Textual—Data processing.
4. Transmission of texts—Data processing.
5. Document markup languages.
6. Scholarly electronic publishing.
7. Humanities—Data processing.
I. Apollon, Daniel, 1951– editor of compilation.
II. Bélisle, Claire, editor of compilation.
III. Régnier, Philippe, 1952– editor of compilation.
PN171.D37D54   2014
808.02'70285—dc23   2013048565

PAPERBACK ISBN 978-0-252-08256-6

Contents

Preface

This book originated in a French-Norwegian project co-financed by the Aurora program in 2005. Several workshops and brainstorming sessions brought together a team of Norwegian specialists in textual criticism and *tekstteknologer* (experts in digital text technologies) from the Universities of Bergen and Stavanger, the Text Technology Research Group at Aksis, Unifob in Bergen (now Uni Computing, a division of Uni Research AS) and a Lyon-based team pooling together, *dix-neuviémistes* (experts in the analysis and editing of French nineteenth-century literature) and digital text experts from LIRE (CNRS, Centre national de la recherche scientifique) and École Normale Supérieure (ENS de Lyon).

The idea was to investigate how the transition from the print-based humanities to various forms of *digital remediations, reexpressions,* and *presentations* affected the way scholarly editors were dealing not only with the practicalities of critical text editing but also, in a deeper way, with various conceptions about the nature of texts and their transmission. To take the bull by the horns, we decided, given our combined experience as philologists, text critics, text encoders, scholarly editors, and analysts of the digital turn, to set the searchlight on the future of philology's inherited crown jewel—scholarly editing.

Hence, the chapters in this book cover in a non-exhaustive manner a wide range of issues, offering the reader a sweeping view from ancient Alexandrian philology to cutting-edge issues in text markup, from the Lachmannian revolution in textual criticism to visions about user-supported online critical editing, and from narrowly distributed peer-directed products to community-oriented broad products endeavoring to bridge between the expertise, partially hermetic, of philologists and new kinds of reading practices in cyberspace.

In order not to dwell on arcane theoretical issues nor on highly technical text markup considerations, and in order to give a helping hand to readers who may find the challenge of developing new hybrid skills a daunting task, this book offers its idealized reader, actual or potential digital editors wondering how to plan their next e-edition, a sober description of state-of-the-art techniques and standards of text-encoding grammars and transformation mechanisms. To also avoid the danger of splendid isolation in philology's traditional authoritative "texts," this book attempts—(mis)quoting Michel Houellebecq's novel—to "extend the domain of fight" to new kinds of texts and collections. In retrospect, the perils of such an exercise, of which the present editors and authors are fully aware, may reside in the attempt to combine sociohistorical, technological, and user perspectives.

Unless mentioned otherwise, all Internet links were accessed in March 2013. All translations into English of quotations in French or German were made by the editors unless stated explicitly.

Acknowledgments

We thank the Norwegian Research Council, the Norwegian Royal Ministry of Foreign Affairs, and the French Ministry of Foreign Affaires and Égide for the initial Aurora grant that helped us transform ideas into a real book.

Thanks to Unifob AS in Bergen and École Normale Supérieure (ENS de Lyon) and the CNRS LIRE team on Avenue Berthelot in Lyon for hosting several workshops, brainstorming sessions, and editorial meetings. A special thanks to Isabelle Treff and her LIRE team for managing the logistic support at CNRS LIRE in Lyon; to Alexandra Saemmer and Eliana Rosado for brainstormings in Lyon; to Stéphanie Dord-Croulé for sharing with us her early efforts to design a digital critical edition of *Bouvard et Pécuchet,* a book in its making that was interrupted by Gustave Flaubert's death; to Catherine Volpihac-Auger, Jill Walker Rettberg, Hilde Corneliussen, Silje Hommedal, Daniel Jung, and Eldbjørg Gunnarson; and to many more people in Lyon and Bergen. We thank those who took part in early brainstorming sessions at Aksis in Bergen in May 2005: Ludovic Frobert, Serge Heiden, Stephen Shimanek, Annette Lundeby Gjerde, Rune Kyrkjebø, and Gisle Andersen. We thank also *Henrik Ibsen's Writings'* general editor, Vigdis Åse Ystad, and Chief Text Encoder, Christian Janss, for their hospitality. We also thank the many participants in the worldwide Studia Stemmatologica community and the University of Helsinki for precious insights gathered during the workshops held during the two last years of this book project.

We have, finally, a special warm thought for the greatly missed Bärbel Plötner–Le Lay (1957–2007) of CNRS LIRE for all the kind support she offered while editing early versions of this book at ENS in Lyon.

Introduction

As Texts Become Digital

DANIEL APOLLON, CLAIRE BÉLISLE,
AND PHILIPPE RÉGNIER

As the world becomes digital and new generations consider computers, mobile appliances, and the Internet as extensions of their body that are essential for living and being today,[1] the future of the traditional forms of culture, knowledge, and scholarship appears to be at risk. The very status of texts, heirs to a long tradition of manuscript and printed books, is evolving with multimedia writing, constantly developing technologies, and new reader expectations. Dynamic creation of new spaces and media for knowledge is gradually superseding the authority of secular cultural objects.

Many scholars in the humanities and the social sciences have been working for some time now with digital tools and are actively engaged in demonstrating how new functionalities made possible by these tools enrich their critical work. However, recent digital technologies for encoding texts are still enigmatic black boxes for most researchers working in the field of philology and textual criticism. After nearly fifty years of combined efforts and production of significant digital editions, decisive issues have come up that raise questions about the future of critical editions and about researchers' capacity to integrate the specialized digital tools that have been developed for philological and critical edition work.

It is worthwhile to restate here rather naively that the notion, practice, and techniques of "critical editions" as well as the role of the "scholarly editor" both antedate the age of information processing and the Internet by centuries. The comparative study of critical and scholarly edition, in its various forms, reveals an intricate maze of historical, geographical, and sociocultural processes linked with philological micro-practices. These processes may be treated as forces that act upon the publisher-editor-reader triad and bring forth specific products. For example, one may meditate on the considerable variation between critical apparatuses in modern critical edition.[2] However, a full treatment of a possible functional relationship between the above-mentioned external forces and concrete editorial practices falls beyond the horizon of this book. More modestly, while keeping an eye on these external forces or regimes, the various contributions included in this book undertake to describe important transitional problems and new emerging editorial horizons.

After a brief presentation of the approach adopted, the context of knowledge society, and the readership addressed in this book, attention is drawn to four evolutionary forces that have particularly important consequences for scholarly edition: (1) the exponential development in the production and accessibility of documents; (2) the emergence of specific tools for scholarly work; (3) the new political regime of editing; and (4) the expectations and positioning of readers as users who are organizing their paths in the texts and thus increasingly becoming actors of their reading itinerary. For each of these "forces acting on critical and scholarly edition," decisive questions are identified and discussed. The introduction ends with abstracts providing an overview of the eight chapters.

A Wide-Ranging yet Practical Approach

The chapters in this book cover a wide range of issues from the markup of texts, to critical editing, to the reading practices that these texts motivate and request. The different approaches outlined in these pages may apply to a wide spectrum of text-critical products—for example, contextual editions combining primary texts and secondary contextual material (e.g., *Woolf Online: An Electronic Edition*, *Les Saint-Simoniens* project), genetic editions (e.g., *Wittgenstein's "Nachlass": The Bergen Electronic Edition*), traditional philological establishment of the scholarly "best" text (e.g., Chaucer, James Joyce, Kierkegaard projects), or a hybrid approach (e.g., the digital text archives and forthcoming e-edition of *Henrik Ibsen's Writings,* which combines the establishment of an authoritative text with critical apparatus enhanced by rich, fact-oriented commentaries).

This approach to digital edition is not meant to eclipse theoretical and epistemological considerations that may affect editorial practice. However, only such theoretical aspects that appear to have direct bearing on editorial practices in general and on the digital context in particular are covered in these pages. So, rather than discoursing on "What is a text?" the authors answer questions like "Which kind of text is produced?" "How is this text produced?" and "Why is it produced in this particular way?"

Underlying assumptions and "embedded paradigms" of particular editorial practices and traditions are also described and discussed. The reader should be aware that one does not need to assume the existence of some kind of unified, coherent practice underlying the whole critical editorial process. On the contrary, one could choose to look at the whole process of scholarly edition as a collection of loosely interconnected procedures beginning with the selection of sources and compilation of material and ending with screen-based reader interaction. New tools, such as the rich set of text-encoding techniques and transformational mechanisms available today, while offering a unified technical approach, may assemble quite heterogeneous parts.

Over the past five decades, a complex, diversified, and possibly fragmented interpenetration process of information technology and critical editorial practice has been taking place. Although early speculations on the announced "death of the book" and its replacement by some new paperless artifacts have failed, the increased impact of information and communication technologies (ICT) on editorial practice seems to be irreversible. Nevertheless, the production of printed critical editions is under growing pressure from increasingly pervasive information technologies. The relationship between institutionalized century-old scholarly editing practices and the relative novelty of information technology by no means constitutes a homogenous phenomenon that may be addressed en bloc. On the contrary, one may replace the term "confrontation" with the softer terms "interpenetration" or "progressive confluence." The slow intrusion of digital architectures into traditional editorial territories formerly reserved to books and managed by established institutions (publishing houses, governments, universities, and academies) has created a new state of affairs that both advocates and critics of online editing may need to address systematically.

Developing networks have accelerated the obsolescence of closed computer systems (which had been used since the 1960s to establish text archives and corpus bases). The sudden global diffusion of Internet access has created a de facto pressure and demand not only to provide "computer-based" online editions but also to embed a strong user-oriented communication dimension into the editorial process. The novelty of the situation is the result of a rapid transition from an early formative period (roughly 1960–1993) that was dominated by traditional pre-Internet computer systems, which were almost exclusively closed information-processing devices, to the networked information society (see the fundamental texts of Manuel Castells 1996, 1997, 1998, 2004). As more and more communication, expression, sharing, and collaboration tools emerge, Internet-based architectures are becoming predominantly communication-processing architectures that exploit underlying information-processing mechanisms. They can offer a complete chain of textual and multimedia production from content gathering to user-driven content transformation and reuse in user-oriented productions.

Part of the ambition of this book is to relate a set of editorial practices and epistemological projects to a set of technological practices. The term "editorial practices" refers to a wide array of procedures, rules, and micro-regimes that are activated by the editor(s) and form a chain of production, which is organically linked with a corresponding chain of editorial decisions. The term "technological practices" refers to the choice and combination of particular mechanisms. To clarify the picture, these mechanisms may be ordered into four categories: (1) content gathering and preprocessing, such as collating, adjusting, or aligning sources; (2) generation of intermediary or internal representations by means of encoding; (3) transformations of these representations by means of algorithmic mechanisms; and finally (4) output of presentation by means of an ultimate transformation.

However, the different chapters do not provide a blueprint of various ways of producing critical editions on paper (only) nor include a ready-to-use kit offering all-encompassing computer-based online solutions. As a matter of fact, straightforward solutions may simply not exist, since neither "critical edition," nor the role of the "scholarly editor," nor "online" or "computer techniques" are unambiguous concepts. The main reason may be that even before the onset of computers and the Internet there was no consensual or unified print-based approach to critical editions. On the contrary, the historians of critical editions tend to emphasize the variety of preconditions, programs, and epistemological frameworks that have guided critical editors over time. Even within the realm of relatively restricted application fields, such as nineteenth-century European literature, it may be difficult to operate with a unified concept of critical editing. The main reason undoubtedly lies in practical as well as more ideological divergences amplified by fragmented academic cultures, by the inherited policies of publishing institutions, as well as by individual preferences. Considerations and limitations that are linked exclusively to the nature of the material to be edited must also be taken into account. When producing a critical edition, decisions on what constitutes a text or a collection of texts worthy of being edited, controversies on what constitutes the object of description (e.g., focusing on the sole authoring process versus a sociocultural contextual approach), various representations or their absence of the targeted readers, and other issues have an impact on the editorial project, whether it is online or in printed form.

This book has been conceived as a reflection on all of these questions in order to deepen them and to start answering some of them. It originated in a French-Norwegian collaboration between research teams coming from different editorial traditions. For those scholars having had the experience of working with digital tools, it had become obvious that the introduction of digital tools and media rather profoundly upsets the editorial activity and that these disruptions could only be dealt with collectively. Moreover, they were looking for an in-depth rethinking allowing an extensive appreciation of the complex network of historical, social, and economic forces that could impose on scholarly editorial practices new organizational, presentational, and representational regimes.

With a complex web of historical, sociological, and economical forces impos-ing *representational* and *presentational* regimes on editorial practices, there was a definite need to describe and understand the theoretical and practical impact of information technologies and the Internet for scholarly edition. Questions ranging from "Why should I opt for online digital edition?" to "How can I design and implement an online critical edition?" or "How should I encode my texts?" needed to be answered.

This book's modest aim does not include interpreting the diverse digital editorial practices as reflections of diverse textual ideologies. It does intend, however, to plead for a reasonable amount of standardization in the presenta-tion of the critical apparatus and of transparency in critical editorial work, in order to make it both more accessible to and more understandable by a greater number of persons. Consequently, whenever the connection with digital edito-rial practices was deemed relevant, historical, sociological, or political economy considerations were taken into account.

Lastly, there was an acknowledged necessity to take some distance from the *production* side of the editorial process and concentrate on the consump-tion or reception side by looking at the needs and perspectives of the reader. Assuming that critical editions, both on paper and online, are planned, as-sembled, and shaped, implicitly or explicitly, with some intended readership in mind, the shift from the book medium to online editions challenges the traditional representation of "readership." While the term "reception," which refers mainly to readers of printed texts, makes perfect sense when applied to reading material like paper-based fiction or poetry, it may be less adequate for covering the online user experience. Accordingly, this book explores how new ways of presenting critical editions within digital environments may indeed fulfill the expectations of readers to use and interact with the content in such a way that these readers may become actors. Indeed, a digital online critical edition may introduce a strong notion of transfer of power from the producer to the user or reader.

The future of digital critical works could be imagined through Robert Darn-ton's thought-provoking pyramidal book vision. In an article titled "The New Age of the Book" (1999) Darnton provides an understanding of the electronic book as a structure of "layers arranged like a pyramid": at the top level, one finds a concise presentation of the content, such as in a pocketbook; a second level gives access to enriched versions, and they themselves provide links to different aspects, without any dominant story line, up to versions containing specific historical, theoretical, philosophical, or pedagogical approaches. "Far from being utopian, the electronic monograph could meet the needs of the scholarly community at the points where its problems converge. It could provide a tool for prying problems apart and opening up a new space for the extension of learning" (Darnton 1999, 77). Even though this approach was formulated more than a decade ago, it can nevertheless be considered as prospective, since e-books are still without a dominant form or technology, and it can undoubtedly inspire the passage of critical edition from paper to digital.

Critical editions that are already online attest to the great diversity of presentation modalities and interactive tools that are available for scholars' editing work. The relative newness of digital critical edition partly explains the profusion of technical solutions and presentation mode. This wild digital sprouting illustrates also the instability and the volatility of the emerging new literacy. Nevertheless, it is also possible to anticipate a diversification of the underlying episteme.

The work in critical edition is in some ways, again, as in the sixteenth century, at a crossroads: in danger of being marginalized, and sometimes even ostracized, in research institutions because such work is considered to be too small-scale. Scholars today are confronted with a technicist vision of efficiency and high-yield investments that seems at odds with their objectives, their needs, and their competences (an extensive coverage of the theme of scholarly communication in the digital age is given by Borgman 2007). This book uncovers how the development of critical and scholarly editing in a digital environment opens a new field for the elaboration and finalized presentation of texts and information, thus reconciling informational diversity and complexity with reading devices, goals pursued, and readers/users.

A Knowledge Society Context

Digital technology has become inevitable in societies that are increasingly based on knowledge. Although still in infancy, the present technologies have propelled into homes unbelievable quantities of texts, pictures, and films, not only providing people with entertainment but also making accessible to them the world's knowledge and cultural treasures through libraries and dedicated websites. Never before has access to ancient or modern, common or rare, writings been so widespread and developed as in this emerging "knowledge society."[3] Today a document is created with digital tools, edited on multimedia platforms, disseminated electronically on digital networks, and stored in digital archives. Digital technology can be found at each step of the document life cycle, facilitating the editorial workflow because it allows integration of all the stages in a flexible combination of processes and tools.

Information and communication technologies, which could be conveniently renamed "intelligence and knowledge technologies," play an important role in the growing standardized formatting of knowledge in a society characterized mainly by the development of "knowledge intensive" sectors. This double movement of a growing codification of knowledge, with its standardization and transferability, and the rediscovery of the central role of tacit knowledge, acquired through personal experience and social interaction, could very well favorably describe the underlying processes of critical editing. With the digitization of great quantities of texts and images, the development of digital libraries, the integration of web tools and services in universities and research centers, and the growing importance of virtual networks, the practice of critical editing is undergoing changes as deep and drastic as those that are overtaking journalism, education, or product distribution.

Even though the digital context eminently concerns the future of the scholarly critical edition practice and is recognized as fundamental in the relationship to knowledge, numerous aspects of the ongoing transformation in the relationship of digital context to knowledge are more or less unheard of, and the interest of humanist scholars in the subject remains insignificant. The integration of new technological tools for research and editing in literature research entails new requirements and competences that scholars have not always had the chance to acquire. But most important, this development of innovative tools requires the identification of new challenges and the development of pertinent intellectual strategies for the use of the tools. It is also important to recognize that, as an important American scholarly association, the American Council of Learned Societies Commission on Cyberinfrastructure for the Humanities and Social Sciences has done that which must be stressed today are "the institutional innovations that will allow digital scholarship to be cumulative, collaborative and synergetic" (Welshons 2006).

For Whom Is This Book Written?

The emergence of norms, standards, and user-friendly tools opens new horizons both for "classical" critical edition practices (e.g., historical, genealogical, or typological) and for the new approaches of textual criticism and analysis (e.g., textual genesis, automatic classification, presentation of textual corpus in their documentary environment, or *Umwelt*). This book is intended for those who are interested by all the different forms of textual criticism, whether they are researchers, editors, engineers, students, or simply readers who wish to fully exploit the potential of digital media. The information presented here primarily concerns the new possibilities offered to practitioners of critical editing as well as the problems and obstacles that impede the realization of new ambitions.

More specifically, three types of actors/readers may be particularly interested in this book: stakeholders who earn their living with critical edition; users, students, teachers, researchers, and humanist readers; and technological actors such as designers, developers, distributors, and archivists.

Stakeholders and Main Parties Concerned
with Digital Critical Edition

Literary production is considered today as a cultural heritage that societies and nations are expected to share. Digital critical editions require considerable work, significant costs in investment and production, as well as the collaboration of an increasing number of various actors. Consequently, it is crucial that the financial challenges already familiar to stakeholders be balanced with the decisive scholarly and technological challenges along with the means needed to secure successful outcomes of editorial undertakings. Stakeholders must arrive at consensus and agreement in order to honor their growing role in the production of projects, such as online collaborative editorial projects, that nevertheless assure a financial viability.

PUBLISHERS   Publishers are looking for systematic field-proven approaches to deal with the transition from purely paper-based editions to hybrid or online editions. While publishers today exploit many sophisticated ICT-based tools in the production chain of paper-based editions, considerable indecision, and even resistance, can emerge when dealing with the prospects of online editions. This book therefore offers prospective online publishers—for example, a publisher of a critical edition of Flaubert's writings—an introduction to the steps to be taken from early text collation to final online distribution.

CRITICAL EDITORS AND RESEARCHERS   This book is also intended for scholars who are experienced as, or in the process of becoming, critical editors and who want to systematically exploit the potential of information technology, and possibly of the Internet, to produce high-quality digital critical editions of texts or collections of texts. Such scholars may have a fully recognized expertise in critical edition but lack an overall view of digital approaches and techniques. The aim of the different contributions is precisely to build a bridge between the art of critical editing and the current technologies available. By combining a "confirmed practice" with new tools, in an evolutionary perspective, traditional scholarly editors may become new architects of online critical editions or of hybrid digital/paper editions.

LIBRARIES AND OTHER RESOURCE CENTERS   Producing critical editions is based on resources often held by libraries and intended for readers who are usually also library users. With the development of the digital world and instant connection from homes to more and more online resources, not only have new access problems appeared, but also the privileged role of libraries in providing access to knowledge and cultural resources is increasingly challenged. Already largely physically bypassed by students, except for using the facilities as quiet work areas and Internet access spots, libraries are forced to redefine their professional goals and their role in providing access to textual and multimedia resources.

Readers as Users

The readers/users of critical editions, such as teachers, students, and other interested persons, will find valuable material in these pages, which they may also exploit to enhance their interaction with traditional and online products. Readers of this text are introduced to the fundamental changes taking place and obtain an enriched overview of the current digital context and of the new possible uses of texts, augmented with critical apparatus, annotations, comments, and so on. This information is also particularly relevant for the technology-aware persons who are developing new digitally based forms for interacting with texts, writings, and all types of documents, as this book may provide them with a broader view of the context and of their own work.

Technological Actors

This book is also intended for all the technical actors—that is, the specialists and experts who take part in the technological process. The book will also be of interest to the designers of programs, tools, and user environments; the developers who transform innovative ideas into operational devices; as well as the specialists of interfaces (GUI, or Graphical User Interface) and human-computer interaction. Because the production of digital critical editions is in its early stages, the needs are immense and the interest for cultural heritage grows every day.

But a new category of professionals will be particularly concerned: the distributors of digital content. It is becoming more and more obvious that putting textual content online, even for free, is not sufficient to induce reading them. Online content needs to generate a readership and communities of users. Thus, there is good reason to expect the emergence of a new profession that will attend to this new type of need and will invent the paths and information channels that will allow critical editions to find their readers on the web. Developing digital critical editions of ancient texts and documents will require the appearance of a new type of editor/entrepreneur. If the humanist scholars have done a remarkable job of exploring and developing tools, means, and solutions so far, it has now become urgent to find this new type of entrepreneurs, as was the case of printers/publishers, a craft that the invention of printing incited for its development in the fifteenth and sixteenth centuries in Europe.

Finally, the development of digital critical editions also doubly addresses archivists' work: first, because it is their responsibility to put into place the preservation of new types of media and documents, but also because the development of critical editions creates new uses of archival documents. Thus there is good reason to think that archival access will be forced to become more transparent, more open, and more effective in the coming years.

The Explosive Growth of Texts

The exponential development in the production and accessibility of documents is the first of four important evolutionary forces considered here as weighing significantly on scholarly edition. In a world that is becoming digital, one of the most important disruptions concerns the textual universe. Libraries all over the world are digitizing their heritage collections and making them available online. Thus, ambitious initiatives emerge, such as the European digital library known as Europeana,[4] which brings together digital resources from the national libraries and cultural heritage institutions of the twenty-seven member states of the European Union; Google Scholar, a digital service of Google that is intended for researchers in order to facilitate their access to scholarly literature;[5] and Wikipedia, a collective production of an online general encyclopedia based on spontaneous public contributions, with the possibility of constant updating and modifications. The processing, storage, and diffusion of texts has definitely reached a level of quality, quantity, and rapidity never before experienced. Not only are the writings and past treasures a mouse click away but also, and more important, the production of new textual and other information each year is such that the annual output of textual variants and duplicates already surpasses the existing computer storage capacities. It has therefore become urgent for publishers, editors, curators, and others to completely rethink their relationship to archives, tradition, and storage of cultural memory.

Going from the Gutenberg era, the printed book, and the paper culture to the digital world implies obvious technological transformations but also less visible changes, which are more opaque and difficult to appreciate and which involve the role of texts and editorial work in our societies.[6] It is a fact that a digital environment transforms knowledge in quantity, quality, and diversity. Never before has information been acquired so rapidly, with processes so powerful, and with such gigantic storage capacities. Digital technology, including the Internet, offers an overabundance of tools to interact with texts and, more generally, with all types of documents.

Of course, today we lack a minimum of historical hindsight that would be needed to fully assess the consequences of the fact that the world has become digital. The expression "all things, at all times, and in all places" (or "anything, anywhere, and any time") roughly characterizes this new situation. Digital technology abolishes in different ways the waiting time, the delay that time for transportation involves, and arouses a demand for immediacy. Moreover, the new networked information regime (Castells 1998) holds out the possibility of encoding everything or nearly everything (all existing books and motion pictures), and it seems normal that all that has been written, filmed, or taped should be available and directly usable. Finally, digital technology is not confined to specific locations but imposes itself everywhere (ubiquity), and the drastic reduction in time and transmission costs of contents is also lived as the abolition of geographical as well as cultural distances.

The Consequences of Ubiquity: Continuation or Disruption?

The mix of helplessness and great expectations of the general public, condensed in the well-known motto "all things, at all times, and in all places," is also found in those actors who, as editors, text scholars, or document experts, try to grasp and master this new environment imposed on them. In retrospect, the time involved in producing a manuscript or a printed text can be deemed slow, whereas the evolution of the digital technology functionalities and of cultural interaction models is already perceived by the present generation as proceeding at meteoric speed. Digital technology seems to respond to two logics: (1) a logic of continuity, linked to the need to reinvest in traditional and familiar practices such as table of contents, indexes, and page layout, and (2) a logic of opportunity, introducing innovative tools that answer new user needs, like full text search, automatic indexing, conceptual maps (e.g., Topic Maps software and computer ontologies), and dynamic annotation. The logic of opportunity can indeed be destabilizing with the abundant use of dynamic visualization tools, summary generators, or automatic translators.

Three types of attitudes toward digital technology, hardly compatible in daily practice, become manifest: on one hand, digital technology is sympathetically received as a continued coming about, allowing consolidation and enhancement of past assets and knowledge; on the other hand, the two attitudes described below, which are more sensitive to the split that digital technology introduces, stand in opposing directions:

- On one side, the advocates of this split, for whom the web constitutes a historic opportunity to put an end to the elitist modes of knowledge management and communication, considered inefficient or representative of a certain cultural power; this fracture fosters an often utopian vision of a culture being disseminated, shared, and knowledge being built by all persons and for all persons;
- On the other side, those preoccupied that such a disruption entails a real loss

of competence, cultural assets, know-how, and results in a superficial and
ignorant world.

It is almost impossible to express an unbiased position, for each one is compelled
in his or her everyday activity to permanently experiment the advantages and
limits of this unending digitization. The anxiety of literary circles is obvious with
regard to the number of reports, books, and other manifestations that herald
the "end of humanism" (Robert Redeker,); "the death of books" (Benoît Ivert[7]);
"the decline of reading" (Bernadette Seibel); "a civilizational split" (Pierre Nora);
or, more bluntly, "the exhaustion of European culture" (Jean-François Mattei).

Quite naturally, different interpretations try to account for the present situation; for those who see in the digital world a reproduction, a conservation,
and an amplification of the Gutenberg-era resources, this represents an exceptional opportunity to move to large-scale and ambitious editing projects.
In this perspective, digital editing is considered more as a series of recognized
transformations and transpositions of practices, know-how, and processes than
as a radically innovative action. Difficulties encountered along the way would
be of only a practical, logistic, or industrial nature, digital technology being
perceived more from a utilitarian point of view than from an ideological one.
Digital editing becomes a prosthetic instrument, filling more or less the same
magnifying role as the microscope or the telescope. If digital editing should ever
replace paper editing, it would not be because books have inherent deficiencies
or shortcomings but because of production and diffusion costs and of institutional pressure. In a way, the digital world would constitute a new territory for
the expansion and expression of written texts. Whereas books and texts have
undergone for the last centuries a linear evolution, the dynamics of the digital
world follows, as Paul Virilio (1997) prefigured, a logic of acceleration and abolition of distance.

However, without neglecting the eventuality of a permanent breach, going
from Gutenberg to the Internet can also be seen as a series of transpositions and
transformations aiming to produce meaning. When one takes as a starting point
the intention to create, communicate, manage, and consume meaning, it becomes
possible to decipher the new digital tools and practices in a different manner.

The transition from one literacy mode to another seems to point toward
two dynamic forces. On one side, a conservative dynamics would secure the
transmission and reproduction of conceptual tools, schemas, competencies, and
practices stemming from the Gutenberg Galaxy (McLuhan 1962). Electronic
editing therefore can be described broadly as an activity that recapitulates, reproduces, and points to paper-based written texts. On the other side, a dynamics
of rupture, innovation, or phase shift would force us to become aware of the
differences present in this new medium. Whoever takes the time to examine

the presentation and the dissemination of contents on the Internet can identify a multitude of innovations, form, and content hybridizations that frequently leave an impression of proliferation and rhizoid development.

Consequently, one of the main concepts being questioned is that of property. Since the eighteenth century, literary property has been based on a perpetuated identity of works that are recognizable in whatever form they are transmitted. What becomes of literary propriety in a world where texts are mobile, adaptable, and open? Walter Benjamin's (1936) views about the effect of the work of art's reproducibility on its loss of aura seem even more confirmed with the advent of the ubiquitous access to information and to the digitized work of art. The relationship between the digital tools (transformation, marking, diffusion, annotation, and analysis), the "works" (in a traditional or recent acceptance), and the combined aura of the work and the specialist of the work has become problematic in a threefold manner. The loss of aura, authority, and inherited expertise seems combined to a radical reconfiguration of the relation between expertise and critical analysis, between the expert's authority and the accessibility to the expert tools.

An insistence is made here on the term "recapitulation": by this word we intend to describe a legacy of processes, ways of doing, historical schemas, and conceptual tools that we bring together under the notion of "technologies of the intellect" in reference to Jack Goody (see Goody n.d., 1986; Goody and Watt 1963). However, "recapitulation" is not a synonym for "reproduction." In the same way that an animal fetus recapitulates the history of the evolution of living beings, the cyber world recapitulates, compresses, and amplifies, but in so doing it succeeds in distinguishing itself innovatively from the typographic system of the Gutenberg Galaxy. "Recapitulating" connotes here a dynamic force of reconfiguration, recycling, compression, and recontextualization of inherited literacies. Such a dynamic, and in some ways disconcerting, situation seems to characterize the periods of formation and stabilization of the new "technologies of the intellect." However, the aim of this book is not to offer the reader an in-depth discussion of the cultural impact of digital technology; consequently, we limit our intentions to situating digital scholarly editing within the context of this double dynamic force.

Thus advocates of a continuity model can be reassured with the integration in the digital world of multiple content representation and presentation modes that originate essentially from models developed by the Gutenberg Galaxy. This is also true for audiovisual media, such as television, films, or radio, all of which precede the digital era and have inherited forms and molds from the printed world, including even audiovisual content. In the same way that audiovisual mediality draws from novels, the printed press, theater plays, the circus, and mostly film art, digital hypermediality draws indiscriminately on audiovisual productions and on the representation modes of Gutenberg-era contents.

Decisive Questions Following the Explosive Growth of Texts

DOES THE EXPLOSIVE GROWTH OF THE TEXTUAL DOMAIN IMPLY THE EX-
TENSION OF THE CRITICAL EDITION DOMAIN?   The explosion of the textual domain does not necessarily imply that so-called old or traditional texts have become obsolete and must be relinquished as remnants of a bygone era. It also does not mean that we should draw a line on the paleo-textual problems and on the reconstruction of lost original texts. The conjecture and reconstruction as well as the establishing of a reference text, all activities that can be beneficially computer assisted, will always have their raison d'être, and a really good future, provided they are updated. This is likewise true for the value judgment of experts of a textual tradition, based on tangible and material contacts built up over the years and without which critical editing would not exist.

But the contemporary phenomena of production, propagation, and redu-plication of texts; their contents and the mechanisms they bring into play; and their combination with graphics and multimedia has a breathtakingly futurist character and requires raising the problem of extending the domain of textual criticism and that of critical editions.

This extension raises two types of questions. Some questions focus on the multimedia contexts into which more and more texts are interwoven. Can the tools used specifically for the analysis, comparison, and selection of texts be extended to map new semiotic and semantic combinations? Another type of questions deals with standardizing the processes of scholarly editions in order to establish firmly its presuppositions, to codify the main mechanisms, and to multiply the uses of such editions. Would it thus be possible to make more ac-cessible and transmissible this art of judgment and "informed reading" that is the work of the critical editor?

The extension of the domain of critical editing could be envisioned in three directions: by applying new methods and techniques to "old" texts and "old" problems, by applying "old" methods and "old" problems to neotexts, or by applying new methods to neotexts.

1. The potentially gigantic and nightmarish undertaking of digitizing of heri-
    tage libraries—in reference to the Google Library project, with the controver-
    sial settlements of Google with authors, book publishers, and libraries, and to
    the developing European digital library Europeana—is a good illustration of
    the role that scholarly critical editing could and should hold in the world of
    rapid digitizing.[8] The risk inherent to projects is that "old" texts may be digi-

tized and diffused in expeditious fashion without benefiting from the contribution of the methods and norms of scholarly editing. There is the risk that this problem, already exposed in paper scholarly editions, will become worse in digital editions.

2. The tradition and principles of scholarly editing will have to be updated as much because of our textual heritage (e.g., Alexandre Dumas, Ludvig Holberg, the Koran, or Scandinavian sagas) as because of the new textoids. We propose here the words "textoid" and "neotext" with the intention of stimulating the imaginations of researchers and critical editors who are faced with more fluid, more dynamic, and more evanescent productions. These textoids or neotexts—which could very well, but not necessarily, challenge certain generally accepted definitions of what a text is and of the extensibility of the textual world—constitute a new approach to criticism and editing. They also should not elude old methods and old editing norms—for example, the current swarm of extimist[9] literature of blogs on the Internet, giving rise to a generalized infatuation, or the textual genealogy systems that are auto-constructing themselves in the Wikipedia organization.

3. Neotexts open new perspectives on old problems, such as the textual limits, intertextuality, textual genesis, the reconstruction of the textual tradition, Vorlage, etc.[10] In fact, any "classical" problem can be transposed into the world of neotexts.

WHAT WILL BE THE CONSEQUENCES OF EXTENSIVE HASTY DIGITIZING WITHOUT APPLICATION OF THE BASIC PRINCIPLES OF CRITICAL EDITING? Textual criticism, text philology, and scholarly editions such as they are known and practiced since the nineteenth century, even with their shortcomings, constitute the essential basis on which new constructions will be established. Otherwise, if this basis is ignored, digital editions run the risk, despite all the mass digitizing capacity that one can dream, of giving birth to texts and corpuses of very doubtful quality.

The experience of documents already online testifies that quality is not always guaranteed. Numerous initiatives have been launched without abiding by the essential editorial choices and possible textual conjectures that may be required prior to making heritage texts available on the Internet. If the development of printing has had a beneficial effect in drastically diminishing copy and interpretation errors, these have never completely disappeared, with a greater or lesser tolerance depending on the editions. The development of the Internet constitutes a sort of repetition of history, with this major difference: that the mass of texts is not the same.

The possible alliance between the precision requirements of text criticism, the experience of scholarly editors, and the "digital toolbox" opens new fertilization perspectives for our science, which is also an art. "Toolbox" refers here to the potential offered by text encoding, parsing, and automatic classification techniques along with representation modes for digital texts and the navigation and reading tools. The edition of *Henrik Ibsen's Writings* illustrates this type of alliance.

The Emergence of Tools and Digital Networks for Critical Editing

A second evolutionary force that must be taken into account is the emergence of specific tools for scholarly work. The impact of digital technology on critical editing can be seen at several levels, from the initial transcription work up to the diffusion and valorization strategies of the work done. Even though digital critical editions have been produced in Europe over the past fifteen years, results are still barely known or disseminated and not easily accessible. Recent initiatives in France—such as the ESF (European Science Foundation) Young Researchers Forum in 2011 on "Changing Publication Cultures in the Humanities"; the "Report on Digital Humanities" published by the Observatoire Critique; or, at a more institutional level, the setting up of the TGE (Très Grand Équipement) Adonis and the different Digital Resources Centers for Research, by the Research Ministry and the CNRS (National Scientific Research Centre) in France; or the work of the different Digital Humanities Teams within the INKE (Implementing New Knowledge Environments) framework in Canada—attest to the will to inform about ongoing actions and to bring French research teams up-to-date in the field.

The situation is quite different in the United States, where American teams have benefited, with the start of large library digitization programs in the 1990s, from sizeable means and support for the integration of digital tools in critical edition. This has resulted in an important breakthrough that is visible with the centers of excellence in scholarly edition, the mastery of digital tools by a significant number of researchers, and the online presentation of exemplary critical editions of heritage works. Nevertheless, there is no guarantee that critical edition has a future, and these pioneers have met with numerous obstacles, the development of specific tools not being the least.

Critical editing is a research activity based on a historical method that is both rational and experimental, which has as its aim the establishment of texts in their latest state as willed by the author or according to whatever criteria provides an authoritative version of the text. This activity, which is scientific, ingenuous, and small scale, had gained renewed credibility and dynamism during the Renaissance, when it developed the humanist approach to knowledge. It specifically overcame the crisis that arose when written works went through the hands of illiterate printers who were unknowingly corrupting the language and the texts. As a consequence, the great humanist Henri Estienne feared that "printing would relegate to a position of secondary importance, if not in oblivion, manuscripts and the never ending comparison of variants that make for a living tradition" (Jehasse 1976, 5). While printing allowed the development of critical editing, it also threatened its survival. As Jean Jehasse reports, "In fact, researching manuscripts, collating variants, and confronting texts attained an unequaled scientific value, and printing allowed a series of innovation that created modern editing" (70). But at the same time, the danger of contaminating texts and of inserting errors has never been so great: "Printing universalizes and somehow perpetuates a text often faulty in its information, if not in its formulation too. Again, the risk is for barbarism to spread, the more so since typography finds itself reduced from its rank as an eminent art to the level of a subsidiary and mercenary technique; [. . .] from now on, here comes the reign of 'illiterate' merchants accumulating their fortune with the work of ignorant apprentices" (5).

These remarks have acquired a new relevance because the digital world is creating a similar situation. Again, text presentations are often made by persons who are very knowledgeable in digital technology but often ignorant of the critical tradition. Consequently, numerous books have been digitized and made available to readers without any critical justification or enlightenment as to which edition had been selected nor any serious revision of the digital transcriptions by competent people.

Any publication of documents is usually combined with an editorial activity that involves dating the text, decrypting it, collating different versions, choosing variants, interpreting, providing information, and so on; it also includes laying out the texts, the illustrations, the tables, the charts and other items, as well as addressing the typographic and compositional elements. This editorial activity, particularly important for ancient texts, is a matter of scholarly competency that, until recently, was generally found in libraries and research units. Now, with the development of digital libraries and a generalized access to cultural heritage collections, new readers have begun to become involved in the field.

Technological choices, although more difficult to interpret, can also influence or make perceptible an implicit bias for certain conceptions of contents or of certain processes that have brought about such contents. For example, the practice of marking up the text witnesses (e.g., manuscripts) could theoretically impose de facto a notion of text closure and lock the text into a fixed interpretation. Alternatively, choosing a specific markup could impose a "supertext" that would have the effect of a straitjacket. That is why the more explicit the relations between the editorial practices and the technological choices, the more it will be possible to exploit such a product at its true worth.

The Complex Relations between Editing and Digital Technology

The relevancy of digital technology in the scholarly editing process and the production of final results cannot be seen as a simple yes or no problem. The digital editor of the future must navigate in an environment of options that can be incompatible or self-contradictory. The digital dimension can be integrated in different degrees in the editorial process. A critical edition will be considered digital if it attests to a consequent digital implication at several stages. Peter Robinson's (2006) proposal that "a digital edition should be based on full-text transcription of original texts into electronic form, and this transcription should be based on explicit principles" seems a useful minimal definition. It must be noted, however, that "transcribing" is not editing in the full sense of the term.

Beyond transcribing with digital markup of the editorial content (which can imply contents other than texts), several algorithmic tools open analytical perspectives that until now have been impracticable for small-scale textual criticism: automatic classification of witnesses; lexical and soon semantic filtering of pertinent traits in contents; massive information cross-checking; parallel corpora alignment; and ad libitum (and often ad nauseam) variations of representation forms, to give only a few examples. However, these tools, even though very effective, do not spare the editor from working with a holistic view of his editorial activity. On the contrary—and this is the underlying thesis of the authors of this book—the technological choices tend to bring out the critical editor's "textology."

There is no doubt that computer means available in the last decades and new standards and encoding practices allow the processing of colossal amounts of texts. However, this new horizon of massive processing encounters the seminal obstacle (but is it really an obstacle?) of the inherent slow progression of the critical editing process. Therefore, the digital potential is based on the hope that time, human resources, and intellectual space will be liberated. The possibility of producing editions, critical at different levels, of massive textual contents, homogeneous (such as authors' texts and "avant-textes"[11]) or heterogeneous (texts and other contents coming from similar environments or eras), however, implies mobilizing new human resources and combining new knowledge and know-how. The sociological dimension of critical editions is also of primary importance: traditional scholarly editing does not happen in an institutional, economic, and political void. The new order that to a certain extent is implied by the systematic integration of digital technology in scholarly editing must deal with different structural and institutional obstacles.

While traditional scholarly editions have clearly identified production modes, intermediaries, and target readers, digital scholarly editions, particularly when online editions are concerned, have the potentiality to deeply influence critical editors' conceptions, the editing process components, and the nature and distribution of the readership targeted by the new products. As Robinson (2006) implies, even if he does not describe the object nor the effects of the possible modifications he refers to, that the very act of critical reading could be modified by the digital environment: "The new technology has the power to alter both how editors edit, and how readers read."

Text transcription, critical apparatus, and variant codification have been practiced according to norms of workmanship that are specific to a particular school or to a particular scholarly editing conception. This transparency could disappear with systematic digital encoding for content transcription, with a real danger of ending up with cryptic contents—or worse, contents that are indecipherable except for a few initiated persons. The elaboration, use, and systematic documentation of recognized encoding standards have become imperative. For even in the case of an ideal conformity to universal norms and standards (e.g., XML [Extensible Markup Language], XSL [Extensible Stylesheet Language], and TEI [Text Encoding Initiative]), the risk of being hermetic remains prevalent. That is why the focus of interest, beyond the markup operating modes, is the critical editor's underlying praxis.

Peter Robinson's five propositions to define digital critical editing give us the outlines of what could be called a "continuity minimal model."[12] These five theses refrain, however, from extending in any way the critical editing notion to new objects of study, as Dino Buzzetti and Jerome McGann (2006) do on the same website (Burnard and O'Keeffe et al. 2006), while still defending the original critical project: "The basic procedures and goals of scholarly editing will not change because of digital technology. True, the scale, range, and diversity of materials that can be subjected to scholarly formalization and analysis are all vastly augmented by these new tools. Besides, the emergence of born-digital artifacts opens up entirely new critical opportunities, as well as problems, for librarians, archivists, and anyone interested in the study and interpretation of works of culture. Nonetheless, the goals of the scholar remain unaltered—preservation, access, dissemination, and analysis/interpretation—as does the basic critical method, formalization."[13]

This cautious opening does not however go as far as including the ambitions of the "nouvelle critique" (Cerquiglini 1989a, 1989b) nor even probably the alternative approach represented by textual genetics (Ferrer 2002, 2008) and even less New Criticism's largely debated positions.[14]

*Decisive Questions about the Potentialities and Limits
of a Radical Change Approach*

DOES TECHNOLOGY CALL INTO QUESTION TRADITIONAL PRACTICES?   Taking an active interest in critical editing implies being confronted with a multiplicity of traditional editing practices and their scholarly variant, critical editing.

These practices are dealt with more specifically in the first part of this book. The aim here is to emphasize the underlying questioning that has incited both the seminars and discussions and the production of a work such as this one.

What comes out of the exchanges at the very outset is that the concept of traditional textual practices perhaps does not exist. Every researcher knows that there is a plurality of practices, with little or no defining borders, that effectively belong to the artistic exercise of scholarly editing and that are eminently individual practices. Researchers who devote themselves to these practices are either solitary scholars or academics caught in career constraints where evaluations value only individual productive work.

Walter Benjamin's (1936) vision, with mechanical reproduction (and all the more so with digitized production and dissemination) liberating the work of art from its parasitic dependence on rituals, takes us way beyond the continuity minimum model outlined earlier. Paul Valéry's premonitory lines taken from *La conquête de l'ubiquité* ("The Conquest of Ubiquity" [1928]), with which Walter Benjamin opens his famous essay, can be applied to this new situation providing "Beaux arts" is replaced by "editorial practice" and "antique industry of Beauty" by "critical edition":

> Our fine arts were developed, their types and uses were established, in times very different from the present, by men whose power of action upon things was insignificant in comparison with ours. But the amazing growth of our techniques, the adaptability and precision they have attained, the ideas and habits they are creating, make it a certainty that profound changes are impending in the ancient craft of the Beautiful. In all the arts there is a physical component which can no longer be considered or treated as it used to be, which cannot remain unaffected by our modern knowledge and power. For the last twenty years neither matter nor space nor time has been what it was from time immemorial. We must expect great innovations to transform the entire technique of the arts, thereby affecting artistic invention itself and perhaps even bringing about an amazing change in our very notion of art.[15]

WHAT HAPPENS TO "CRITICAL EDITING"?   The contributions in this book illustrate two different forces affecting existing practices:

- *Primo*: a centrifugal force exploiting the new computer-based tools' efficiency to reinforce and enrich the procedural aspect of traditional practices and to amplify, by extension, the underlying norms of a critical edition classical project (e.g., genealogical approach, error-correction search, and best text search).
- *Segundo*: an exocentric force that from now on, since nothing except tradition forbids it, allows extension of the critical editing notion to new critical practices and norms that are less focused here on the true or best text than on its social, cultural, or historic function. Thus "critical editing" would mean

not only to collect, to select, to reconstruct, and to establish but also to systematize a work's contextualization in a vaster environment (e.g., by creating hyperstructured multimedia collections).

WHAT PROOFS ARE THERE THAT USING DIGITAL TOOLS AND MEDIA FACILITATES CRITICAL EDITING?   Many researchers who now involve themselves in digital technologies have stressed the important investment in time and attention that is necessary in order to achieve a mastery of the technology. Nevertheless, such a competence has proven to be an absolute requirement for these pioneers to be able to create new software tools that are capable of taking on key critical edition processes. For example, at first sight it would seem that publishing in extenso would be an ideal solution in the case of different versions of the same text, a solution that is hardly conceivable on paper. But in the long run it turns out that such a large quantity of texts in itself does not facilitate reading. The same applies to hyperlinks or pop-up windows that allow notes and commentaries to be shown or hidden. There again, quantity rapidly becomes a problem to manage at both the level of display as well as the level of codification, and solutions that could be applied generally have yet to be identified. Markup tools, developed in order to automate text reading and exchange such as the TEI, have rapidly proven to be too complex for most researchers and editors to manage with regard to the results expected. Finally, the development of multiple tools to deal with specific processes such as the transcription of ancient types, collation, annotation, and analysis has resulted in almost no possibility of interoperability, because the tools belong to different proprietary systems.

DOES DIGITAL MEDIA MAKE CRITICAL EDITIONS MORE ACCESSIBLE AND THEREFORE MORE DEMOCRATIC?   Printed scholarly editions are rarely best sellers, and they usually do not get distributed outside the limited circle of researchers and libraries. And yet establishing texts is a crucial pivotal step in knowledge production. One can find on the web tentative endeavors trying to make known to interested readers the underlying editorial decisions by making available all the documents (original edition, facsimiles, transcription, notes and comments contextualizing the work, etc.) that allow one to have an in-depth understanding of the different editorial steps such as collation, textual analysis, textual genetic study, and so on. Nevertheless, these approaches turn out to be complex, largely unknown, and not very visible on a system like the web, and attempts made to disseminate the underlying editorial methodology remain insufficient to be truly productive.

DOES THE QUALITY OF CRITICAL EDITIONS INCREASE WHEN THEY ARE PRODUCED WITH DIGITAL TOOLS?   Using tools that allow analysis of great quantities of texts, comparisons of the different versions, and historical align-ment according to authoritative criteria would seem to guarantee an improved research process. It is precisely one of the gains of knowledge societies to have largely developed the codification of a good part of existing knowledge in order to allow more powerful processing with software tools. Can the possibility of working on large quantities of data with digital tools bring about progress in research? Can new research processes that allow for significantly improved results be expected?

The Political Economy of Scholarly Editing

A third evolutionary force is centered on the political economy of scholarly editing. The authors of this book do not limit their contributions to a narrow internal mapping of digital scholarly editions nor, worse, to producing a col-lection of basic recipes and formulas. We consider it worthwhile to inscribe the different technical, editorial, and to a certain extent epistemic characteristics of critical scholarly edition in the larger framework of historical, cultural, and institutional forces that exercise a structuring power on the evolution of criti-cal edition practices before and during the digital era. In order to avoid a too rigid approach of notions about unchanging parameters and to allow a more dynamic reading of the variable forces weighing on critical editorial practices, we endorse in this work the notions of "political economy" and "regimes."[16] Thus the reader will find an outline of old and new regimes that would impose a series of varying editorial norms. These adaptable editorial norms result from centuries-old efforts and govern at various levels as much the ambitions as the technical practices of critical editing.

Two Key Notions: "Political Economy" and "Regimes"

These two key notions allow the authors to present a critical discussion of the modes of transition of critical editing from paper to various digital products. The recurrent themes in the ongoing debate concerning continuity versus rupture in the passage from print to digital (we take as an example the case of the critical apparatus and the critical edition of documentary collections) are addressed not only from the perspective of the continuity of certain ancestral regimes but also from the more current perspective of regime conflicts and the issues at stake. Thus, there is a variety of products emerging on the expanding market of digital critical edition, including complete or "exhaustive" editions, "analytical" projects that enable scholarly interpretation and comments of textual genealogical reconstruc-tions, as well as more ecological endeavors that aim to present texts or collections in their environment. These various products are approached in this book not only as expressions of the opportunities offered by new open technologies but also as the expression and the reproduction of antagonistic positions between different norms and practices and, more deeply, between epistemes. Some authors also establish links between these ruptures and the conflicting issues at stake at the economic level. The two themes of the inversion of offer and demand and of the progressive blurring of the distinction between editor and user within the invitational and participatory concept of online communication (Gulbrandsen and Just 2011) illustrate the economic issues at stake.

This more organic vision, one that it is hoped is more useful than a vision solidified in technical determinism and subject to a particular academic tradition, will stimulate the reader to better appreciate his own practices as user, researcher, editor, and, basically, reader.

Decisive Questions Linked to the Notion of Authority

IS TEXTUAL CRITICAL EDITION BOUND TO BECOME MARGINAL AND RE-
SERVED FOR A HANDFUL OF SPECIALISTS, OR, ON THE CONTRARY, DOES ES-
TABLISHING THE AUTHORITY OF A TEXT REPRESENT A CRITICAL COMPETEN-
CY THAT SHOULD BE FOSTERED AMONG ALL CITIZENS OF OUR KNOWLEDGE
SOCIETY?   A growing number of recent and ancient texts that have recently been made available through the Internet have been digitized with minimal precautions and with no "quality assurance" that would allow identification and authentication of their origin and of the state of the documents, and even less the recording of the different traces of their evolution and dissemination in time and space. There follows in this web era a growing uncertainty about the status of texts in our societies and the eventuality of a rupture of the transmission chain. These findings are all the more disconcerting because the perspective of a loss of genealogy and authenticity more deeply affects the mass-produced recent texts than the classical texts. Must one conclude that editing has become quite commonplace, a normal and justifiable evolution in the perspective of a mass diffusion of literature? Or, on the contrary, are we witnessing a degeneration that reveals a loss of editorial competence that needs to be attended to urgently? Humanities researchers undoubtedly have a new and important role to play in a networked knowledge society. It could be their responsibility to reintroduce a discourse on the authority of documents and on the issues at stake in digital critical editing. One of the guidelines adopted by the authors of this work is that digital technology neither solves nor eliminates the recurrent problem of textual authenticity and authority; rather it only recontextualizes ancient problems and relates them to new problems, rupture lines, and evolutions that are intimately linked to the dynamics of a networked society (see Castells).

HOW CAN THE PRESENCE OF LITERARY TEXTS AND OF A HUMANIST PERSPEC-
TIVE BE SECURED IN THE DOMINANT CULTURE?   The preceding question
dealt with texts and documents in general. Here the challenge that confronts
scholarly editors of literary texts consists of inventing economic strategies
for a smooth transposition of critical practices and norms stemming from
the long history of printing and progressing into the cultural and economic
realities of the networked digital world. A critical view of the minimum model
of continuity outlined above, considering digital technology as only a tool
for amplifying and accelerating preestablished practices, has the major disadvantages of not actively taking into account cultural, social, and economic
dynamics as distinctive features of networked society and not being aware
of the already exploited or still latent potential of the new architectures of
digital information.

This introduction limits itself to introducing a few of the characteristics that
should have decisive influence on the becoming of online literary critical edition
in reference to Manuel Castells's diagnostic (generally, 1996, 1997, 1998 and, more
specifically, 2004) that underlines the distinctive traits of a networked society
as opposed to a pre-digital world: auto-reconfiguration capacity, adaptability,
scalability, interoperability, competition, cooperation, and distribution. The contributions in this work reinsert humanist perspectives within the framework of
the inherent dynamics of digital networks within which innovative practices and
nonconforming cultural ideals emerge. Consequently, it is out of the question
of creating survival niches for critical editing within a cyberspace that would
be ignorant of this exception zone, but, on the contrary, one would wish to
inscribe the humanist perspective at the heart of a textual system that involves
production, transformation, diffusion, and transaction practices, whose scale,
retrospectively, would astronomically surpass all that the pre-digital civilization
has produced in the past.

WHAT TYPE OF PRESENTATION WILL GUARANTEE THE PROPER LEVEL OF
APPRECIATION FOR LITERARY TEXTS? DO CRITICAL EDITIONS BELONG TO
THE FIELD OF ACADEMIC SCHOLARSHIP AND SCHOLARLY PRACTICES, OR
SHOULD THEY COME UNDER THE CULTURAL AND HERITAGE MANAGEMENT
ATTENDING TO A WIDESPREAD PUBLIC OF USERS?   The reader of this book
will discover as he or she goes through the pages that even if it is perfectly pos-
sible to reproduce in a classical printed form a critical edition of literary texts,
the forces that affect the digital field impose major shifts and ruptures.

Actors of the pre-digital classical system were characterized by a trichotomy
between stakeholders, producers, and consumers. Producers include scholarly
editors, literary experts and critics, and publishing houses. Stakeholders, as
illustrated in Philippe Régnier's contributions, frequently sided with political

power. Consumers, well-advised readers or students, participated in an absorption and reproduction system of cultural values.

The networked knowledge society implements a rupture with this trichotomy: the distinctions between stakeholder and consumer, between producer and consumer, and between stakeholder and producer are becoming obsolete and must be replaced by a new perspective in which each actor of the system combines different roles. The most prominent trait is the user/contributor, who consumes and contributes to the products and new ideals of a shared construction and increasingly undermines the control of literary products by the accredited title holders. This phenomenon, linked to the inversion in the offer and demand of cultural goods, increasingly subverts the validity of textual products hailed as representative of canonical practices, such as classical university scholarly edition. Although not proposing definitive solutions, the various contributions of this book provide several opportunities for further thought and illustrate how diverse technical approaches—in particular, encoding techniques—make it possible to reconcile traditional concerns with ambitious diffusion to larger publics.

FINALLY, IS THERE AN IN-DEPTH TRANSFORMATION OF EXISTING PRAC-TICES? It is a hypothesis generally accepted by researchers that this integration of technologies in text and document production deeply modifies the different editorial activities, their sequencing from production to reception. It is thus a profound mutation that is developing in the research fields of critical edition and scholarly reading and that is slipping out of the hands of researchers. Consequently, the emerging concept of "dynamic editing," which resorts to a series of technologies, processes, and cultural norms, is a good illustration of the changes under way both in the present and future of scholarly edition and in editing at large. If such is the case, researchers need to not only become familiar with these developments but to also meet and organize exchanges based on their respective competences and their ongoing experiences in order to work jointly at solving the problems that come up. New tools and innovative technological solutions need to be appreciated and integrated appropriately in research work.

New Modalities for Interacting with Texts

The development of computer tools and of the web has considerably modified the conditions for interacting with texts and constitutes a fourth evolutionary force. In the last few years, books, journals, and other magazines have undergone important evolutions in presentation, layout, choice of paper, and even the writing mode. If most digital books, especially scholarly editions, still show a great similarity to one another, with a major part of the surface devoted to texts, the same does not apply for magazines and newspapers, which can easily have whole pages dedicated to graphical or photographical illustrations. Computers have introduced a mobility and a variableness that have become the basic conditions of digital writing. In standardizing sign representation, digital technology has facilitated the availability of not only alphabetical signs but also visual and sound signs. Thus digital cameras integrate more and more professional know-how, making the production of photographs (and eventually their editing) quite easy.

Having gone from a stable, permanent, quite elaborated and aesthetically finely worked presentation, in the production of digital critical editions we have experienced very basic presentations at the beginning, often of inferior visual quality and with poor navigational functionalities. Today we are confronted with very complex presentations, with pictures, graphics, and visual animations. The use of hyperlinks, at the heart of the web since its beginning in the '90s, makes it possible to organize the presentation of information according to its complexity and with precision levels that accelerate search and navigation within great loads of data.

Readers as Navigators/Editors

It follows from the split of the traditional triad of stakeholders, producers, and consumers described above that a new relation between production and reading—or, better, between production and use—needs to be explored. Below are the main characteristics of these new interaction modalities with texts in networked digital environments that may lead to a recontextualization of scholarly edition:

- Users' relationship with perused or stored texts is no longer limited to traditional reading, understood as the meticulous absorption of statements, but includes a variety of transactions and manipulations (see Bélisle 2004a, 2004b, 2001). This implies a diversification in reading modalities, which in a majority of cases are not symmetrical to the writing and publishing modes.
- The notion of reception that expressed the relation of immersion in the work and its absorption by the reader no longer adequately describes the distribution-diffusion-access-reuse cycle practiced by the new cultural actors of digital space.
- Several remixing aspects seem to abolish even more the distinction between producer and consumer, editor and reader: even if at the beginning the digitally distributed work is received passively (that is, "read"), there is more and more frequently a use for other ends, themselves followed by reuses that are poorly controlled, recyclings, autonomous creations, and various remixings and compressions.

- In many cases the user of textual goods does not find himself in the role of reader, but directly (if, for example, this or that digital edition allows it) or indirectly (through the bias of recyclings and remixings) has a co-editor activity that can eventually be perceived as a threat for the original product.
- The potential users of digital scholarly editions represent groups that do not necessarily share the same scholarly, cultural, and political interests. Thus the new digital products may less often be based on a preconceived definition of the potential users and even less often manage or control the readers.

This outline of the reorganization of the production-reading relation implies an imperative evolution of the necessary publishing and editorial expertise and will require an overhaul of university courses in this domain. It is clear that current students already work completely within the new relation outlined above. The supremacy of written texts over multimedia survives only in a few privileged sectors of Western cultures. University students have developed a strong multimedia literacy that is significant in terms of the way they relate to critical editions and their validity.

New Text Interactions

WHAT TYPE OF READINGS CAN BE OFFERED TO USERS/READERS OF CRITICAL EDITIONS?   The relationship to written works, especially with their integration in multimodal writing (text, but also graphics, images, photographs, and even animation), has evolved such that the familiar linear presentation that is dominant in printed works has become clearly insufficient. The author/editor needs to offer new possibilities for circulating and navigating in the presented work and in the critical and cultural supplements that he wishes to make available to his readers. If this new requirement can initially appear as a constraint, it is also a tremendous opportunity to invent new paths for discovering works and critical editions. The editor will thus have to explore what might best interest the potential reader, what issues will pique his curiosity, and what activities he would like to accomplish in interacting with texts.

In this way a critical or scholarly edition could present a range of possibilities—from the scholars' professional reading, and including journalists' browsing and skimming, intellectuals' transversal or diagonal reading, text amateurs' skimming reading, school children's intensive reading, dilettantes' poaching reading, and doctoral students' in-depth reading, up to the reading games aimed at readers who are expecting to be entertained. It will be the editor's responsibility to imagine what historical, philological, linguistic, cultural, cognitive, or semantic aspects will be most helpful for each specific reader in providing access to a work's specificity, depth, and richness.

MUST A MORE DEMOCRATIC APPROACH TO INTERPRETING PATRIMONIAL
TEXTS BE EXPECTED, WITH PROVISION OF NEEDED COMPLIMENTARY INFOR-
MATION?   What will result from facilitating the access to works and critical
and scholarly editions by creating their digital presentation? Can it be expected
that critical thinking and interest in the production conditions of literature, its
ecological context of diffusion, will grow in readers at large? In the history of
mankind there have never been such great quantities of cultural resources put
at the disposal of everyone. Even if disparities exist and many persons still do
not have digital access, it is possible to foresee that in the same way that the
availability of electricity has gradually spread over the entire surface of the earth,
digital access will follow the same path.

It is not impossible that a genuine demand for access to critical editions from an
important number of readers will emerge. It can be expected that such a demand
will not be for linear reading but for an interactive access to series of historical,
cultural, geographical, biographical, bibliographical, as well as philological information, with provision of research, visualization, and storage tools.

These are examples of questions that are currently arising with the first varied
and instructive uses and online publications. The different chapters of this book
should help editors to find their marks in this moving field.

Horizon and Structure of the Book

This work offers a general survey of critical editing confronted with the digital
world. It is organized in three complementary parts. To begin with, part I describes the historical context and the main challenges that researchers, teachers,
and the public at large of readers/users meet with the integration of digital tools
and medium in the activity of critical edition. Part II details how critical edition
deals with the technical constraints it faces in order to explore new presentation modalities of heritage texts. Finally, part III offers a concrete outlook on
critical edition practice through examining cases that range from data capture
and layout to the institutional and organizational conditions for production.

In chapter 1 Odd Einar Haugen and Daniel Apollon offer a historical overview
of critical editions since the nineteenth century from three angles: a historic
perspective, a contextualizing perspective, and an intrinsic perspective. The
historical perspective is based on the important development of Karl Lachmann
and Gaston Paris, who have introduced a rigorous formalism coupled with a
logical approach that is still present in "philological science" and includes the
first tryouts in using computers to improve, extend, and diffuse scholarly editions. A vast overview of the evolution and the diffusion of the different paradigms and practices is developed by the authors. This chapter also addresses
questions of content and authority.

The issues at stake in digital scholarly edition constitute chapter 2. Its author, Philippe Régnier, identifies, classifies, and comments on the main challenges and opportunities that the use of digital technology, computers, and dynamic schemas in online publication of critical editions entails. He also emphasizes how the new digital environment can modify and perhaps extend textual criticism's scope and reach. Special attention is paid to societal, epistemological, and cultural factors that can influence the evolution of the discipline; to the rapid change and transformation rhythm; to the inherent instability of new digital environments; and finally to the multiplicity of the varied representational frameworks that can compete within a digital structure.

In chapter 3 the difficult question of the different characteristics of critical edition is presented by Daniel Apollon and Claire Bélisle. A global view of the processes and key components of digital critical edition is illustrated with examples of problems and concrete solutions. The aim here is to show how "traditional" components of critical edition—for example, the critical apparatus, the page layout, indexes, and different types of reference systems—can be combined, through digital technology, with tools for analysis and dynamic organization under the reader's control. Through concise examples of online productions, the authors show how the historical modes and conventions are reformulated in a digital environment and how digitally specific modalities can renew critical edition projects.

Critical edition digitization ambitions, from the conception and aims of editors to the expectations of readers, are treated in depth in chapter 4 by Terje Hillesund and Claire Bélisle. The first part of the chapter deals with issues and questions raised by the digital trend in scholarly text editions as they migrate from one media to another. The authors explain through the concept of remediation how the traits and configuration of editions that are present in print technology live on in digital technology, even though text creation and dissemination have profoundly changed. Digital remediation of text is taking place within a digital context impelling new reading habits. Exploring these new emerging reading practices, coupled with a probing of readers' expectations, forms the object of the second part of the chapter.

Digital critical edition supposes a mastery of markup systems. Consequently, in chapter 5 Claus Huitfeldt presents an overview in the form of an inventory of standards, and of markup, presentation, and archiving techniques. He describes the state of the art with a focus on key architectures and key techniques considered as the basis of digital critical edition.

Focusing on the aims of digital critical edition, Alois Pichler and Tone Merete Bruvik present in chapter 6 an organized inventory of tools that can help with collation, edition, research, reading, and conservation. Building on the inventory and discussion of the previous chapter, the authors offer an overview of the tasks and aims that express the ambitions of digital critical edition. Readers can discover a classified inventory of tools and techniques used at different levels of data collection, transcription, edition, research, consultation, and archiving. The description and discussion of these techniques thus provide readers with a natural progression from collection to edition and from edition to use and to conservation. Special attention is paid to tools and techniques that enrich traditional critical editions and facilitate scientific decision making, as well as facilitate, stimulate, and amplify readers' traditional and new access to edited materials.

In chapter 7 Odd Einar Haugen revisits the long history of the practice of text criticism and scholarly editing and looks into the recent development of more objective methods based on mathematical techniques. He discusses how various qualitative and quantitative methods have been used in modern editions and proposes a typology of editions based on three dimensions: the reproduction of the source, the rendering of the process lying behind the text, and the selection of sources for the actual edition.

Critical edition of heterogeneous documents is addressed by Sarah Mombert in chapter 8, which is focused on critical edition of hybrid materials: heterogeneous documents, facsimiles, pictures, sounds, and videos. Through a few concise examples, she illustrates how and why different collections, although "critical," do not attain the usual ambitions of critical editions (Greek authors, the Bible, canonical authors) but address another conception of "critical" and "edition." Mombert explores the implications of critical projects when reconstructions of the given texts' original states are of less or peripheral interest. She shows through examples how thematic and diachronic collections of materials pertaining to a common theme, author, or period, or similar themes, authors, or periods, raise new critical issues: the focus on the "state of the text(s)" shifting to the context and the immediate cultural environment deemed capable of casting new light on the collection. Consequently, the term "critical" is used principally to connote the construction of a context amplified through comments, intersecting links, and thematic indexation. Nevertheless, one must decide on the authenticity and the relevance of each item in such a collection and on the relative pertinence of the choices made. These collections share with standard critical edition common tools and techniques that help the scholarly editor in the production of a digital critical collection: markup, conceptual maps, and extended research modalities.

The political economy of digital critical editions and the development of research networks constitute the object of chapter 9, written by Philippe Régnier. The aim here is to describe and discuss the ecological environment and the concrete human resources in digital critical edition. In the first part, building on the scope of scholarly editing's "political economy in a pre-digital era," Régnier describes and discusses the human resources context that has followed the migration of critical edition to the digital world. The impacts of collaborative work, human networks, open software ideology, and resource sharing on the new political economy of digital scholarly edition are reviewed. Special attention is given to the role of institutions such as publishers, research organizations and universities, and scientific networks in this new production environment.

In addition to publication information for the references found in the text, the bibliography includes a list of online sources and software tools that might be of interest for readers.

Notes

1. The expression "as the world becomes digital" refers indirectly to the title of the conference lecture "Pourquoi et comment le monde devient numérique" (Why and how the world becomes digital) at Collège de France held in 2007–2008 by Gérard Berry (see Berry 2008).

2. The critical apparatus is the complimentary source and reference material that the author of an edition of a text provides, usually in footnotes. The reader will find a definition and broader discussion of the term "critical apparatus" in chapter 3.

3. The expression "knowledge society" seems to have been inspired by the writings of Daniel Bell (1973, 1980), a sociologist, and Jean-François Lyotard, a philosopher (see, particularly, Lyotard 1984 [1979]), even though neither one uses this expression. Rooted in knowledge management and social welfare management, the concept of a knowledge society is based on two previous concepts: "information society" and "post-industrial society." The origin of the expression "knowledge society" dates back to publications of the 1980s. (Gernot Böhme and Nico Stehr [1986] are the first to map down a conceptual content for the expression. For a history of the use of the expression "knowledge society," see chapter 1 in Stehr 1994.)

4. In answer to a request coming from several European countries for a virtual European library that would open Europe's cultural heritage to everyone, a cross-domain, cross-border, user-centered service named Europeana was launched in 2008. As of July 2016 it provides contextual information about more than 54 million digital cultural objects stored in different types of European heritage institutions and allows access to the original sites that hold the digital contents. Europeana has a general public portal (http://www.europeana.eu) and a professional portal (http://pro.europeana.eu), which is an important source of technical information, information on metadata standards, and updates on associated projects.

5. In line with its self-proclaimed mission of organizing all the information of the world and making it universally accessible and useful, Google is negotiating with publishers and libraries to provide a specific access to books; magazines; and scientific, disciplinary, and research publications.

6. A creative exploration of the ways technology may alter the production of texts and meaning is offered by Bergmann and Fraistat 2002.

7. Benoît Ivert is president of the French National Centre of the Book, or CNL (Centre National du Livre).

8. The Europeana website address is http://www.europeana.eu/portal.

9. This term has been coined by Serge Tisseron: "I propose to call 'extimity' this tendency that brings someone to expose aspects of one's private life, be it physical or psychic intimacy. This inclination has gone unnoticed even though it is essential for a human being. It consists in the desire to communicate about one's inner world" (2001, 29).

10. The German term *Vorlage* refers to the known or unknown text or document, such as a manuscript or heterogeneous collection of textual fragments, that is supposed or known to have been used by the author, editor, or translator of a work.

11. The French *avant-texte* may be translated into English with "pre-text" or "foretext." Many English-speaking literary critics choose nevertheless to use the French term. See Ferrer 2010.

12. See http://www.tei-c.org/Activities/ETE/Preview/robinson.xml on the TEI site. Peter Robinson's five propositions for "electronic textual editing" are:

1. The use of computer technology in the making of a particular edition takes place in a particular research context.
2. A digital edition should be based on full-text transcription of original texts into electronic form, and this transcription should be based on explicit principles.
3. The use of computer-assisted analytic methods may restore historical criticism of large textual traditions as a central aim for scholarly editors.
4. The new technology has the power to alter both how editors edit and how readers read.
5. Editorial projects generating substantial quantities of transcribed text in electronic form should adopt, from the beginning, an open transcription policy.

13. Buzzetti and McGann (2006); Lawall (1988); Wellek (1955–1993); and Wellek and Warren (1949, 20–28).

14. The terms "New Criticism" and "New Critics" refer to the American movement of literary criticism that gained a wide influence in the '50s. It should be kept distinct from the French Nouvelle Critique, sometimes termed "French New Criticism."

15. Our translation from Paul Valéry (1960, 1283–1287). This work was originally published in *De la musique avant toute chose* in 1928.

16. Such a new regime, called "metareading," is described by Patrick Bazin (1996).

PART I

History, Challenges, and Emerging Contexts

1. The Digital Turn in Textual Scholarship

Historical and Typological Perspectives

ODD EINAR HAUGEN AND DANIEL APOLLON

Three Perspectives

This chapter is written under the assumption that the history of textual scholarship from its very beginnings to the digital age can be understood from three perspectives. These perspectives are not the perspectives of the historian who tries to grasp the development of textual scholarship, but rather the perspectives held by the practitioners of the art and science of editing texts, for scholars who edit, comment, and analyze texts written by other people. This chapter assumes that editors may choose to look backward, outward, or inward.

First, looking backward means to search for the origin of the text and to trace its development through time. When dealing with classical and medieval works, the editor has to track the process of copying, starting with the original text and then moving on from one copy to the next. When dealing with post-Gutenberg texts, the editor needs to trace the development from the first drafts made by the author until the end product, usually a printed edition. Second, looking outward means to view the text as a product situated in a sociohistorical context. This implies that its contents, its use, and its organic relationship to other texts and sociocultural realities is of greater interest than its origin and material transmission. Third, looking inward implies viewing the text as an individual expression of its own right, as a self-contained document, to be read and understood on its intrinsic merits. One of the characteristics of texts and literature, highlighted by the New Criticism in literary studies in the 1950s, is the existence of multiple layers of meaning and of a wealth of interpretations.

The approach defended in this chapter reflects the belief that the self-contained nature of texts, as advocated by this New Criticism (looking inward), and the awareness of the organic relationship of texts to their world (looking outward) can benefit from a historical approach to the text and its transmission (looking backward). The purpose of this chapter is to show how these three perspectives may shape digital text scholarship.

The tripartite view outlined above is, of course, a simplification, and it is not intended to be a scheme in a Hegelian sense for the actual history and development of textual scholarship. It includes, rather, three aspects that have been differently weighted in the practice of textual scholars over the years, to the extent that these perspectives can be seen as competing but not mutually exclusive points of orientation. Any scholar who primarily looks toward the origin of a text and tries to chart its development will understand and acknowledge the fact that each stage of the text also has a contemporaneous setting and interpretation and will indeed exploit such contextual knowledge. Any scholar focusing on the setting of a text, on its *Sitz im Leben* (German: literally, its "setting in life"), or its uses is well aware that the text also has a material history and a physical aspect.[1]

This chapter takes a broad look at the history of textual scholarship with these perspectives in mind. While the history of textual scholarship is commonly traced back to the birth of Western philology in the Hellenistic age, shaped and cultivated in the Library of Alexandria, the starting point here is the methodological foundation of textual scholarship in the early nineteenth century. This does not mean that the long history of textual scholarship in antiquity, in the Middle Ages, or indeed in early modern times should be disregarded as "prescientific," but that major approaches to textual scholarship, in print and online, can be exemplified and discussed with reference to scholars of the nineteenth and twentieth centuries.

Looking Backward: The Formalist Approach

The conception of modern textual criticism is commonly thought of as belonging to Karl Lachmann (1793–1851) and his generation of editors in the first half of the nineteenth century. Lachmann's work covered all three major fields of editorial philology—classical philology, Bible philology, and medieval philology—and thus has become a point of reference in all of these fields. Lachmann expressed clearly the basic tenets of a scientific textual criticism very early in his career in a critical review published in 1817 of Friedrich von der Hagen's edition of *Der Nibelungen Lied* (1816). Lachmann claimed that the editor should search for the original version of the text, or, if that was unattainable, for as close an approximation to the original as possible: "On the basis of a sufficient number of good manuscripts, we should and we must build a text which reflects all of these, a text which either would be the original text or a text which would come very close to the original."[2] This position found support in the contemporary

historical source criticism, or *Quellenkritik*. In fact, textual criticism and historical criticism, following Lachmann's reasoning, should be seen as two aspects
of the same approach. Only when younger and less authoritative witnesses had
been removed through a strict analysis would the editor (or historian) be able
to understand the text in its true context.

Later in the nineteenth century this program was enthusiastically adopted
by the German Romanist Gustav Gröber (1844–1911) and the French Romanist Gaston Paris (1839–1903). The first contribution in this field was Gröber's
analysis of the manuscripts of the story of the Saracen knight Fierabras (1869),
but the most important and consequential work proved to be Paris's edition of
the Alexis legend (1872), published together with the French scholar Léopold
Pannier (1842–1875). This edition contained a thorough analysis, a recension,
of all manuscripts of the Alexis legend as well as a complete text based on the
results of this analysis. The introduction gave a clear and concise discussion
of the principles for the recension of manuscripts, from a theoretical point of
view as well as from a practical one. This edition became a paradigm for French
editorial philology for more than half a century.

The position of Karl Lachmann and Gaston Paris is one of strictness and
formalism. The recension of manuscripts is, in the memorable words of Paris,
an almost mechanical operation, "une opération pour ainsi dire mathématique"
(Paris and Pannier 1872, 13). Recension also implements a highly reconstructive
approach, since it strives to trace the text to its origins. After the original author
had finished his work, textual deterioration was likely to set in. The task of the
textual critic was to remove as many corruptions as possible from the text in
order to restore it to its former glory. This perspective is certainly not new; it
was already an integral part of the Homeric scholarship of the Alexandrian age
(as shown by Honigman 2003 and Niehoff 2007). The practice of indicating corruptions by a dagger sign, the obelus, was probably introduced by Zenodotus
of Ephesus, the first librarian (ca. 325–ca. 234 BC), and *Echtheitskritik* (German:
"criticism of authenticity") has been part of textual scholarship ever since. The
novelty of the Lachmannian approach resides in its systematic exploitation of
corruptions, or errors, as a means of establishing the filiation or derivation of
a text. Looking for errors became not only a part of the examination of the
text but also the very foundation of its recension and its genealogical analysis.
Gaston Paris emphasized the basic fact that copyists very seldom make the
same mistakes at the same places (1872, 10). From this observation it follows
with logical necessity that the filiation of a text can be established on the basis
of the errors in the manuscripts.

When Joseph Bédier (1864–1938) edited the medieval text *Le Lai de l'Ombre*
in 1890, it was, as he himself observed, under the sign of Lachmann ("sous le
signe de Lachmann"), or, he might have said, under the auspices of Gaston

Paris, the ever-present editor of the journal *Romania*. The introduction to the edition concluded with a stemma showing the relationship of the manuscripts and continued with a text constituted on the basis of this stemma. The story might have ended here, and Bédier might have moved on to other fields of study and left the *Le Lai de l'Ombre* edition as a youthful exercise. However, he felt uneasy with his recension and returned to the text over the years. After revising his edition in 1913, he published in 1928 an article in *Romania* in which he discussed the recension of *Le Lai de l'Ombre* and the methodological conclusions to be drawn from it. In this article Bédier draws no less than eleven different stemmata for the text, all equally valid and possible as explanations of the transmission of the manuscripts. Rather than moving from uncertainty to certainty, as the 1890 edition with its single stemma would seem to indicate, Bédier had indeed moved from certainty to uncertainty. Above all, he suspected any stemma construction of being heavily biased. Leafing through the volumes of *Romania,* he noticed that the overwhelming majority of stemmata published in this journal had only two major branches. That was indeed a strange forest, a *silva portentosa,* and rather than reflecting a historical fact, Bédier suspected that it reflected a weakness in the method and its usage. So after almost four decades of struggling with the manuscripts of *Le Lai de l'Ombre* and a growing uneasiness with the Lachmannian method, Bédier concluded that the method had to be suspect. There was simply too much bifidity in the recensions—that is, too many stemmata in which there were only two main branches. Bédier provocatively claimed that the best answer still was that of the old humanists: to choose the best manuscript in the tradition, the *codex optimus*, and rely on that, save for obvious corruptions (Bédier 1928, 356). Editions of this type are usually referred to as *best-manuscript editions*, and in spite of the seemingly unscientific selection procedure, these are still recognized as a major type of edition (see, e.g., Foulet and Speer 1979, 38, and elsewhere in this book).

In spite of—or possibly as a consequence of—Bédier's fundamental criticism and doubt about the genealogical method, the study of manuscript traditions has continued to be the object of logical or mathematical approaches. Along this line can be placed people like Henri Quentin (1872–1935), Walter Wilson Greg (1875–1959), and Dom Jacques Froger. Quentin was very critical of the use of common errors, "*fautes communes,*" which were so central in the Lachmannian tradition. He would accept only variants and nothing but variants (1926, 37): "I do not recognize errors or common mistakes, neither good nor bad readings, only the variant forms of a text, on which I by a method of the strictest statistics first delimit the families, then the classes of manuscripts within each of these, and finally the families within these classes."[3] In spite of this criticism, Quentin should be regarded as a formalist and thus a textual critic who basically shares Paris's conviction of the regularity and analyzability of manuscript evidence. In fact, Quentin claimed that he had been able to formulate an iron rule, "une règle de fer" (1926, 37), that would remove all subjectivism from manuscript recension.

Already in 1963, dealing with the rich inventory of New Testament manuscripts, Ernest Colwell and Ernest Tune advocated to carry out a statistical comparison of each manuscript with all other available manuscripts witnessing a given text. While it would be difficult to disagree with this program, the development of the necessary tools took some time. However, when the Centre National de la Recherche Scientifique (CNRS) summed up the status of modern textual criticism in the conference report "La pratique des ordinateurs dans la critique des textes" (Irigoin and Zarri 1979), there was a large array of methods available. However, considering the rapid spread of software tools and the increase of computing power, progress in this area seems to have been slower than anticipated. Indeed, the emergence of powerful methods of multivariate data analysis contributed to strengthen the awareness of practitioners that universal and irrefutable methods allowing the editor to infer filiation from incomplete textual sources may not exist. Since 1979 the list of multivariate techniques has been extended with biplot methods, such as correspondence analysis (see Apollon 1985), and in more recent decades graph-oriented methods, such as phylogenetic analysis, a methodological pillar of evolutionary genetics, have emerged as a new contender. Peter Robinson and colleagues have argued that phylogenetic analysis can come a long way toward solving the chronological problem inherent in any recension (Barbrook, Blake, Howe, and Robinson 1998). Recently, a Finnish research group tested a number of quantitative techniques using an artificial data set and concluded that phylogenetic analysis is indeed a strong contender, but not the only serviceable technique nor possibly the best one in the field (Roos and Heikkilä 2009). Unfortunately, we do not have any complete manuscript filiations from antiquity or the Middle Ages; we have only fragments of unknown proportions. The "true" filiation of a text can thus never be ascertained, but only approximated. These recent methodological advances have the seemingly paradoxical side effect of confirming the position and role of editor at the center of the editing process.

While the basic tenets of the genealogical method have not been questioned since the time of Lachmann, and the method, ideally, should still be regarded as valid, it is not always practicable. A manuscript filiation can indeed be modeled by analyzing the distribution of errors over time, but only if the recension is uncontaminated—that is, each copy has been made from a single exemplar. If there have been multiple sources along the line, the method breaks down quickly. Against contamination no remedy has been found, Paul Maas concluded— "Gegen die Kontamination ist kein Kraut gewachsen" (1960, 30). The depressing fact is that so few traditions are uncontaminated. In classical Latin literature,

Karl Stackmann, for example, believes that only the works of the most important authors were transmitted without contamination (1979, 252). In vernacular
medieval literature, texts were often copied quite freely, blurring the distinction
between the copyist and the redactor. In short, the genealogical method remains
a valid method, but only for a minority of manuscript traditions. There is no
such thing as a "genetic tracer," any textual equivalent of mitochondrial DNA,
that may help the editor and readers to irrefutably identify an original text.

What a mathematical analysis can offer is a way of mapping the distribution
of variants of a text. While this has been envisaged for a long time (see, for example, the bold statement by Henri Quentin quoted above), it is only in the last
decades that this has been made possible in practice. Mathematical models do
have their limitations, however. They can undoubtedly help the critic to establish
a focal text, in the sense that they can identify clusters of variants and thus the
likely centers in the transmission of the text. It is less certain that they can help
in establishing an archetypical text—that is, a text in which the diachronic axis
has been revealed, and thus showing which variants belong to an earlier stage
of the text and which belong to a later stage.[4]

Rather than dethroning the editor, early computer-assisted textual criticism
has confirmed his or her central position, adding tools and enlarging his or her
decision space. Given the wide array of document-encoding tools and standards
available nowadays, as described elsewhere in this book, and the general availability of presentational tools and easy access to online publication, the digital
text scholar may choose to offer all elements of the inward perspective to a wide
array of readers and users.

Looking Outward: The Ecology of Texts

The backward-looking perspective described in the section above endeavors
to establish a text that is as irrefutably as possible and as close as possible to an
original prototype. Only to the extent it is deemed necessary and only when
material criteria are not available are external aspects taken into consideration.
Therefore, exploiting external aspects, such as sociocultural, psychological, or
institutional knowledge, occurs mainly on a case-by-case basis. And indeed
when such external aspects are exploited by the textual critic, the genealogical
method practiced does not encourage the critic to fully integrate these aspects
and exploit some kind of overarching theory about the relationship between
the text and its environment.

The first turn from an exclusively backward-looking perspective toward an
outward-looking perspective exploits the awareness that a text or document is
authored or at least put together by a human compiler or editor with a particular
intention. One assumes that the originator of such a text exhibits a minimum of

linguistic, literary, or historical consistency, reflecting a more general practice that is typical of his or her time and environment. The German biblical redaction criticism schools (*Redaktionskritik* or *Redaktionsgeschichte,* see Reinhard and Merk 1997) offer an example of a careful transition from a strictly backward-looking perspective to a more open perspective focusing on the authoring or editing activity that is thought to subtend and effectively produce the literary and philological form of the text. Since critics in the German *Redaktion* tradition investigated biblical texts, they had to emphasize the predominant role of an editor (*Redaktor*) in the genesis of the text. By doing so, they had to take into consideration the literary and ideological habitus of the editor and exploit a partly attested, partly hypothetical contemporary political, linguistic, and religious context in order to describe this habitus. They assumed that even when dealing with a significantly edited product, which synthesized oral and written material from diverse sources, periods, and contexts, the Redaktor intentionally compiled, recomposed, and reformulated significant portions of the text handed down to us. The history of the text-critical and redaction-critical treatment of the biblical Genesis offers a good illustration of the impact of redaction criticism (see, e.g., Kratz 1997, Perrin 2002). Indeed, the critical edition of the *Epic of Gilgamesh* (George 2003), one of the oldest known literary narratives, functions as a redaction-critical comparison between the cuneiform texts available as well as numerous other Sumerian, Babylonian, and Hittite fragments.

The main difference between the redaction-critical and the contemporary textual genetic school (discussed in greater detail in chapter 3 of this book) is that the former deals with ancient text traditions without known authors nor access to preliminary material, and the latter deals with well-documented authored contemporary literature. Textual genetics sets out to trace with considerable accuracy the authorial process with material proof in hand (e.g., the various drafts of Flaubert's *Madame Bovary*). However, both schools described here remain text-centric, tied to the inscriptional nature of text, carefully avoiding treating such texts as historical sources among others, or witnesses to a much larger environment, encompassing other documents and artifacts.

As a first conclusion, one may start to distinguish between varieties of a text-centric perspective and an environment-centric perspective. In the following, we briefly discuss some outward perspectives with no intention to cover all instances. To point out that a text has a context, that it has a *Sitz im Leben*—or to use a more recent metaphor, an ecology—is as near to a tautology as one may wish to come. A text is, after all, a weave, a product of many strands, which presumably are not cut along the borders of the text itself but continue outside and tie the text to other texts and to society at large. On the other hand, exploiting the contextual dimension and transforming it into an editorial strategy remains a daunting challenge. It involves among other things shaping a theory, which must describe how the diverse strands of the text, such as the linguistic, literary, and ideological characteristics, express a functional relationship to historical, social, ethic, religious, and other characteristics of an environment. The more theoretical the approach is, the more refutable it becomes. One then has to deal with a variety of competing approaches involving the text and its world. If the perspective of the editor is still governed explicitly or implicitly by the desire to reconstruct and establish an authoritative text, the whole enterprise might become rather perilous. If, however, the perspective of the editor is more eclectic, less committed to reconstruction, and more committed to contextualizing exposition and interpretation, then the variety of outward perspectives may turn into structuring various forms of text ecologies. For such an "ecological editor," text-centric perspectives, such as the redaction-critical or textual genetic approach, may be combined with other, sociocultural approaches, such as classical-reconstructive or even environment-centric approaches. At the end of the nineteenth century, Gustave Lanson (1894) introduced elements of a socio-critical model, outlining a rather deterministic functional relationship between a social environment, the authorial process, and the "text." However, Lanson did not elaborate on his approach, nor did he abandon a strict biographical approach, but he chose to focus on text-centric, detail-oriented close reading (*explication de texte*).

One has to wait until the end of the 1980s to see a renewed and more principled attempt at removing historical bias in textual scholarship and refute some of the basic tenets of the genealogical method by invoking the environment within which texts were produced and disseminated. Bernard Cerquiglini in his book *Éloge de la variante* (1989a) intended to deliver the fatal blow to a genealogical method that was already severely shaken by new critics on both sides of the Atlantic. To do so, he demonstrated how medieval texts reflected conditions of production that were qualitatively different from those presupposed by the genealogical school. Distinguishing longitudinal variants (emerging within a given text and due to repetition) from lateral variants (emerging from the existence of several diverging copies of the same text), Cerquiglini showed how recent editing practices resorted to harmonizing and repairing these problems, thus "correcting" the imprecision, redundancies, and joyful excesses of medieval copyists. With printing spreading as a technology guaranteeing faithful copies of texts, the negative attitude of text critics toward textual variation implied a strong belief in the unique and true copy (see Eisenstein 1979 and 2005; see also Menzer 2001). Furthermore, the slow emergence of intellectual ownership and copyright strengthened the need to stabilize not only contemporary texts but old traditions as well. Cerquiglini argued that the straitjacket of such a restrictive approach could not do justice to the production principle of medieval writing (Cerquiglini 1989b), which was governed by the principle of "joyful excess."

This medieval textual exuberance fundamentally challenged nineteenth- and twentieth-century critical editors, because the possibility that a diversity of "original" texts might exist was always there. The "modern" response to what was perceived as a possible mess was to force the scientific straitjacket of textual standardization, using the method of philological reconstruction. In his fourth chapter of *Éloge de la variante*, "Gaston Paris and the Dinosaurs," Cerquiglini overtly criticizes the ideological underpinnings of the reconstructive approach defended by traditional editorial philology (mainly Lachmann, Paris, and Bédier, who were discussed above in the section on the backward-looking perspective), accusing their main figures of succumbing to a desire for origins and actually rewriting the text in the name of science. The main value of Cerquiglini's contribution lies in its radical and refreshing reappraisal of textual variance. It also shows that the backward-looking perspective cannot confine itself to the Lachmannian approach, but must take into account the cognitive, literary, and technological environment of a text, as failing to do so will lead to anachronistic rewriting. Therefore, while fundamentally different from redaction criticism, Cerquiglini's new philology actualizes the necessity to relate the critical editorial process to the world of the text.

On American soil the "new philology" (or, rather, "renewed philology" or "new materialism") was heralded in an issue of the journal *Speculum*, edited by Stephen G. Nichols (1990b), in which the study of the medieval manuscript in its materiality was seen as a product of interaction with a cultural context (1990a, 1997a, 1997b). At this time "philology" had almost become obsolete in English, and if it was still used, it referred to pre-Saussurean comparative linguistics (Sampson 1980, 13ff). The *Speculum* issue talks about a new philology, proudly reintroducing the concept into the English language. It should be pointed out that English seems to be the odd man out in this context; philology had remained as a field of study in other European languages, most prominently in German and subsequently in the Nordic languages. In French, *philologie* also has a wide meaning and usage and includes all linguistic, literary, hermeneutical, and historical methods applied to written records.

Since the 1960s the wide diffusion and immense popularity of competing structural, semiotic, psychoanalytic, and Marxist methods led many literary critics of philology to widely reject it as being a fossil science and fundamentally irrelevant to the exploration of texts. These new approaches sought their inspiration in various disciplines that combined, often rather freely, very different perspectives, such as Russian formalism (Propp 1927), structuralist linguistics (Ferdinand de Saussure, Roman Jakobson), early manifestos from the French Nouvelle Critique (Maurice Blanchot, Roland Barthes, Michel Foucault),[5] and psychoanalysis (Sigmund Freud, Jacques Lacan), to mention just a few. The most significant thrust to the post-philological movement was the discovery or invention of intertextuality (a term coined by Julia Kristeva in the 1960s), emphasizing study and interpretation of the interaction between multiple layers, strands, and links that weave a given text or text tradition to other texts, artifacts, or representations. As a consequence, textual analysis, as practiced by structuralists and others, became more concerned with mapping relations and echoes between texts, with no ambition of tracing the "origin" of the various items involved in such analysis. The lasting contribution of structuralist and various brands of new critics does not reside primarily in the strict and much criticized application of reductive methods borrowed from linguistics and mathematics. Their main success was to establish a large interdisciplinary consensus that texts are integral parts of a continuous discourse. Social text theories criticized, as one would expect, the inwardness of structuralist and semiotic methods. Both Marxist and socio-critics like Marc Angenot (1985; see also Angenot and Robin 1985) endeavored to demonstrate the social roots of such a general discourse in "grand narratives" (*grands récits*). The resulting opinion was that texts should be analyzed and edited not as monadic structures but as parts of a much larger discursive space.

All of these ideas and programs showing that what was inside the text was also outside and vice versa were already formulated several decades before the invention and spread of the Internet. Although they generally lacked a technological vision (with Cerquiglini as one noteworthy exception), and although they were in many aspects fundamentally incompatible, they nevertheless contributed to preparing the ground for later hypertext theory.[6] They also contributed indirectly to opening an intellectual space that allowed scholarly editors some decades later to imagine online text editions weaving primary material (e.g., author's drafts) into a much larger navigable space and, as paradoxical as it may seem, allowing them to reinstall philological textual criticism as one textual dimension among other possible dimensions as part of a wider critical space.[7]

Looking Inward: Defining a New Philology

In 1968 Roland Barthes, in the wake of Maurice Blanchot (Blanchot 1942, 1955), who had redefined writing as the "absence of the author," announced the "death of the author," followed by Michel Foucault's question "What is an author?" (Foucault 1969). The French Nouvelle Critique rejected a long tradition epitomized by Charles-Augustin Sainte-Beuve's biographical method and Gustave Lanson's historical determinism (close reading, or French: *explication de textes*). The much-criticized biographical method insisted that the reader or critic needed to gain an understanding of the author's life and thought in order to interpret and edit the text correctly. To make it worse, the *nouveaux critiques* voiced a fundamental distrust in the notion, utility, and even reality of the concept of "author" and claimed a correspondingly fundamental interest in the reader, announcing that "the birth of the reader has to be paid by the death of the author."[8] The text should no longer be restrained by the creator but should be allowed to lead its own life, attain new meanings, and enter into new contexts. From the theme of the death of the author in the French Nouvelle Critique, it is possible, obviously, to draw a direct line to the theme of the death of the archetype in textual studies. No longer should the text be judged by its closeness to a supposed original version, nor should this Holy Grail, the pristine product of some original genitor of the work, be considered the ultimate prerequisite for interpreting texts. Each writing, to paraphrase Barthes (1968), should constitute thereafter a work of its own. Barthes's author, reduced to an abstract representation of the reader's mind, appears more as being constructed by the work than the work by the author. The work is no longer to be approached as an extension of the author. Barthes and his followers programmatically removed the author as the origin of the text and replaced him or it with language (French: *langage*) or discourse. So if it still makes sense to speak of critical editions after Barthes and Foucault, the focus has moved from reconstructing a true copy of the author's hand and mind to an exploration of the polysemic universe of texts.

As pointed out in the previous paragraphs, the impacts of semiotics and socio-criticism have modified the vision of what is to be considered "inward" and "outward." In many cases the boundary has become blurred, leading to endless debates. The new philology may be seen as an attempt to bridge these two perspectives, avoiding falling into the traps of reconstructive genealogy on the one hand and extreme socio-criticism on the other. Any text should be allowed to be appreciated as an individual expression that is valid and representative for its time and setting. In a sense this view somehow reflects a social democratic vision of conditions required for the production of texts: the habitus of an individual is seen as being shaped by the upbringing, not by the genes. Texts are functionally related to some general social and cultural ethos. Some new philologists have taken this position and, understandably, proposed an alternative to philological reconstruction. The strict recensions of the nineteenth century and the *eliminatio codicum descriptorum* meant that many late manuscripts were simply disregarded as corrupted late products. If it could be proved that they were nothing but late copies of other known manuscripts, their only merit would be to add new errors to the tradition. When looking single-mindedly backward toward the (most often hypothetical) original, it was meaningful to declare such manuscripts as manuscripts of "no critical value." In some cases this meant the baby was thrown out with the bathwater. Even if the text contained in a manuscript could be considered as a derivative product from a diachronic point of view, such a manuscript could also be of considerable interest from a synchronic point of view, offering a valuable witness to the time and locale of its production. For this reason, new philologists have made a case for rehabilitating a number of late manuscripts. Indeed, it may be useful to adopt a less principled approach to the material original of texts and to rehabilitate the contemporary settings of all manuscripts in order to see their details more clearly. Hence, disregarding the filiation of the manuscript can indeed constitute a valid procedure as an interim act of focusing on the totality of a text tradition as we know it.

However, empirical facts are difficult to refute, even if they are inconvenient. No one will dispute that manuscripts have been copied from one another, and at the end of the line there is an original, a first version of the text as it has unfolded through the filiation. In almost all classical and early medieval text traditions, the original has been irrevocably lost. What remains are later copies, distant by several centuries and stages of copy from the original. The scholarly editor has to deal with traditions where a majority of the once existing manuscripts have been lost through damage, neglect, fire, shipwrecks (many saga manuscripts were lost on the perilous sea voyage between Iceland and Norway, for example), through the *auto-da-fé* of Jewish and Islamic manuscripts of the Spanish Inquisition, during the Wars of Religion, or through the widespread destruction of papist literature during the Reformation. For this reason, not only the original but a major part of the whole manuscript tradition as well may have disappeared forever. Only an educated approximation of the original is possible, based on an analysis of the earliest surviving textual witnesses. This is the concept of the archetype, as defined by Paul Maas in his austere "Textkritik" (1927 and later editions). The archetype, to avoid misunderstanding, is not a physical source but, rather, a theoretical concept, and as such it is not prone to any death, but is no final proof of the existence of an original and is not irrefutable. The archetype simply reflects the labors of reconstructive efforts made by textual critics. As a concept it is strictly neutral. The text of the archetype is not a priori "better" than that of later manuscripts; it is at best one of the least refutable hypotheses of the original state of the text. Only when the original reading of a text is deemed to be of higher value than secondary readings can the archetypical text be said to be the better text.

Although new philologists have succeeded to a certain degree in reconciling the material witnesses of a text tradition with their historical environment, they may have introduced a problematic relativism. If all manuscripts (or any material source, physical or digital, for that matter) are regarded only on their intrinsic values, their genealogical links will be severed. It will then no longer be possible to assign a given manuscript a precise position its own genetic history. Such mapping can only be done using a diachronic approach, by looking backward, however faulty the results of the genealogical or similar methods may be. As a consequence, the new philology may eventually fall into the same kind of extreme posture as the pure synchronic analysis of a linguistic stage, which dives into the study of idiolects, the language spoken in a family, or even by an individual, at a certain point with no or little consideration for macro trends through time. In geology or evolutionary genetics, such simplifications would amount to failures.

There are also highly pragmatic reasons for looking backward. Some texts have been copied in very large numbers. In a wealth of manuscripts it is a pressing question to know where a particular manuscript is situated within its tradition. Does it belong to a representative core, retaining most of the presumed original readings? Is it peripheral, typical of only an era or a geographic locale? Is it an *Einzelgänger*, a loner, with few or no immediate relatives?

Unless new philology intends to evolve into a pure idiographic science, it needs to reflect and take into consideration the diachronic axis of a manuscript tradition. This is why, in our opinion, there should be no opposition between the diachronic approach of the "old" philologists and the synchronic approach of the "new" philologists. It is a matter of perspective and of priority.

The Resilience of a Two-Dimensional Spatial View

The introduction of printing by movable type in the fifteenth century[9] is often seen as a revolution and a main turning point in human history. However, looking at textual scholarship, and especially at textual editing, the most outstanding trait of early printed books is the close mimicking of manuscript codices of the day. Johannes Gutenberg's Bible looks like a well-executed manuscript in its overall design of pages with two columns, in the frequent usage of colored initials, and in the illuminations in the margin. Even the Gothic type was carefully copied from handwritten script.

The papyrus roll and the codex have two dimensions. The column of the roll and the page of the codex define the space for the text, and the margins of the page add a separate but not unrelated field for comments, additions, and illuminations. This geometry has been carried over into the display of digital editions. Like Gutenberg in his age, digital editors want to communicate with their users, to present their texts in a format that is as familiar as possible. The screen displays a two-dimensional image, exactly like the codex and the book. The text is contained within columns and set off with margins. The display in most cases is oriented toward printouts. Texts of some length are still being read on paper, and it is thus practical to make the display on-screen as printer-friendly as possible. The presentation of writing and text, on parchment, paper, or online, relies on several thousand years of accumulated intellectual technology, a fundamental visual literacy that may be as difficult to eradicate as alphabetic script.

With the Internet, the World Wide Web, and hypertextual writing space, this has changed. Digital texts have moved away from their page-bound confinement in two dimensions. Social media have also deeply influenced how individuals look at texts and how standard narratives are constructed. There are, however, two important factors that have contributed to retaining, for a while at least, the two-dimensional page layout paradigm in new media. The first is the inherent mimicking conservatism of new reading appliances that are intended to replace the book in many contexts. So far it seems that the metaphor of the printed page is quite resilient, using and even expanding its visual toolbox, including lines, columns, margins, text blocks, headers and titles, and other visual aspects. In fact, the increasing number of PDF (Portable Document Format) files based on this conservative model demonstrates the immense popularity of the paginated book. The second and more fundamental factor is the nature of writing itself. Writing—or script—is inherently two-dimensional, linear, and sequential. The direction of writing may vary from left to right, as in Greek, Latin, and Cyrillic script; from right to left, as in Arabic and Hebrew script; from top to bottom, as in traditional Chinese writing; or from bottom to top, as in most ogham inscriptions of Old Irish. In all cases writing remains linear: it has a starting point and an end point (however, reading may become highly nonlinear). It is hard to see any realistic alternative to alphabetic script in our societies for the nearest future. There may be a drift from the logographic scripts of China, Japan, and Korea toward alphabetic scripts, but alphabetic, two-dimensional script remains an integral part of written culture. The orthography may be simplified and made more regular, new typefaces will continue to be drawn, the use of nonalphabetic icons may increase, but the alphabet as such is not likely to change. If this holds true, the display of texts will basically remain two-dimensional. For obvious reasons it cannot be reduced to one dimension, and there does not seem to be any immediate advantage in trying to make script truly three-dimensional. Braille is probably the only exception to this rule; because it is a tactile script, it must be rendered in three dimensions. Book lovers might add that the slight impression of lead type on paper, recognizable by touch and by the faint shadows of each letter, is an added dimension to alphabetic script, but as we know from offset printing on glossy paper, such impressions are a side effect rather than an integral part of the script.

Script is an intellectual technology for representing human language. The success of alphabetic scripts lies in the fact that, in the words of André Martinet (1965), they copy the double articulation of the spoken language. The phonemic units of the spoken language are represented by the graphemes (i.e., the letters) of the alphabet, as far as possible in a one-to-one relationship, and these units, by themselves meaningless, on the next level constitute words, phrases and sentences of distinct meanings. Some would object that multimedia—mixing text, graphics, moving pictures, sound, and real-time processes—invalidate the paradigm of the alphabetic script. It seems more likely, however, that online material will continue to be assimilated into the two-dimensional textual representation. The resilience of the two-dimensional spatial model versus the possible adoption by a large public of more dynamic, nonlinear texts, as well as the emergence of a new literacy will be at the center of debate in the years to come.

The thrilling fact is that all aspects of scholarly editing and textual criticism discussed so far—ideologies and methods—are eminently applicable to new texts. Indeed, the contemporary concern for trust, positive identification of authorship, and countermeasure against content falsification on the Internet may draw on the experience of genealogical method and text genetics.

The Emergence of New Texts

Perhaps the most significant contribution to textual studies of the digital age is loss-free copying. The fallible act of copying has indeed been the rationale of textual studies for well over two thousand years. At the time of the Alexandrian philology, the Homeric texts had been handed down over several hundred years and, through the process of copying, a number of textual variants had arisen. Removing these errors became one of the first objectives of textual scholarship, and this has continued to be of prime importance, especially for what has been termed the formalist approach. Indeed, the genealogical method of Lachmann and his contemporaries can be summed up as a method of common errors (German: *Methode der Fehlergemeinschaften*). However, what are erroneous readings in a manuscript from one point of view may be seen as innovations from another point of view. In a treatise on textual criticism, Martin L. West points out that instead of talking about "errors," he would prefer to talk about "readings of secondary origin," thus distancing himself from the most prescriptive interpretations of the formalist tradition (1973, 32n3).

The main, perhaps even exclusive, focus of critical editors is on texts that have been produced and handed down before the modern techniques of loss-free copying. The major divide is still between texts written and filiated in the age of the manuscripts and texts written and reproduced after the invention of printing—in other words, a divide between the pre-Gutenberg and the post-Gutenberg periods. The genealogical method described in this chapter is primarily concerned with the study of manuscript traditions and is of less relevance for printed texts. The editing of printed texts has a different focus, since these editions so often have focused on the end product, the *Ausgabe letzter Hand* (the edition of the author's final version), rather than the origins, the *Ausgabe erster Hand* (the edition of the author's first version). What this branch of philology shares with manuscript philology is the awareness of change and errors—both changes in the drafts by the author himself and changes throughout the process of printing. In the age of lead typesetting, new runs of printed books were often set anew. In most cases type used for the previous run had been used for new jobs. Thus, within the story of a printed book, errors were introduced by the typographers. Changes were sometimes made after consultations with the author or the publisher (especially if the text contained sensitive matters of religious or political contents). Other changes were made inadvertently, on the judgment of the printer, or after the author's death.

As suggested above, modern digital texts may change the traditional divide between pre-Gutenberg and post-Gutenberg editorial philology. First of all, loss-free copying has made it impossible to reconstruct the filiation of many texts. Moreover, the life expectancy of many modern digital texts is much shorter than for any printed text. SMS (Short Message Service) messages, Twitter flux, instant messaging on Facebook, or Snapchat messages that disappear a short time after they have been viewed, to mention a few new textual usages, may be deleted a few minutes after they have been received. E-mails, blogs, and chats are also living on the margin. A great number of texts simply vanish each year, probably to a much higher degree than what has ever been the case for printed texts. The widespread adoption of social media may indeed shorten the life cycle of such texts more brutally. The future scholarly editor of such post-Gutenberg textual traditions may have to resort to the whole armada of textual scholarship and invent new ways to deal with short-lived documents.

The Digital Philology

Digital philology is both a revolution and not a revolution. It has brought new tools, efficient data handling, and a wholly modern outlook to philology. Yet the texts studied and edited remain grossly the same, and the questions asked by digital philologists do not seem to be qualitatively different from the questions asked by pre-digital philologists. Indeed, online editions have been produced mainly within the philological paradigm. Surprisingly, projects favoring the intertextuality more than the quest for authenticity and origins, or socio-criticism endeavoring to demonstrate the functional links between content and sociocultural realties, have produced few if any online critical projects. What remains to be seen is whether digital tools will change the direction of philology not so much because of internal preferences but because of the alluring possibilities opened up with such tools. It should be added that in many cases digital tools are not new. They are simply more efficient; tools have become so fast and fail-proof that investigations that were once too huge to contemplate now have become possible to implement. In the following pages we outline a few characteristics of critical online editions.

Dissemination: Still an Issue

There exists an impressive physical infrastructure for disseminating printed books. Shops and libraries can be found in almost any city, and new and used books can be ordered over the Internet from a growing number of vendors. Physical and digital distribution of books are slowly merging, but not without problems, including resistance from traditional publishers. Price may be an argument, but not always, at least when it comes to scholarly editions. For scholarly editions on paper, prices can be fairly high, especially for gentlemen's editions like *Íslenzk fornrit* for Old Norse texts, *Henrik Ibsen's Writings* (2006–2009), or the many learned editions of *La Pléiade*. Digital editions are in their infancy, and pricing versus open access is still a question that must be decided.[10] Some products are simply free (Woolf Online), while others are quite expensive—for instance, the CD-ROM of Chaucer's *General Prologue* (Solopova 2000) costs as much as several cloth-bound tomes. As for the dissemination of these products, many editions, especially those containing facsimiles or other large files, are still stored and sold on solid media such as CD-ROM or DVD (e.g., *Wittgenstein's "Nachlass": The Bergen Electronic Edition,* published by Oxford University Press [2000], which as of October 2012 was priced at US$2,500). This means that digital editions are subject to the same legal, commercial, and institutional restrictions as printed editions.

Display and View: Unresolved Tensions

A printed edition has a single display, typically a single column per page, sometimes with line numbering on alternate pages and a critical apparatus at the bottom of the page. Having more than one display means adding wholly new pages, perhaps another volume, to the edition. This is costly and not done without good reason. The display of the printed text is sometimes a compromise of several options. The editor may wish to display the text at more than one level—for example, at both a diplomatic level, close to the source, and a regularized level, where the orthography has been adjusted. This is especially helpful when dealing with vernacular texts in which a detailed rendering is needed for a linguistic analysis. Representing the text on more than one level in a printed edition is usually out of the question, and the editor has to either go for one level only or resort to an original, complex, and less generally accessible layout (e.g., the synoptic editions of the Greek New Testament). Moreover, when a text is available in more than one manuscript and the variation between the manuscripts has a bearing on the text, the editor usually uses a critical apparatus to represent and summarize this variation (see chapter 3 for an in-depth coverage of the critical apparatus).

A digital edition usually displays the text in a similar manner, as pointed out above. In fact, digital editors often invest much time in having the edition look "right." This is not necessarily a sign of conservatism or lack of inventiveness; it is, rather, to let the text come into the foreground and be displayed in a manner that does not draw attention to the digital medium. Awkward fonts, wrong margins, and misplaced apparatuses are all examples of a display that goes wrong and turns the attention away from the text. Even if a good electronic display can be very unassuming, it all too often happens that the edition has a nonintuitive interface. The digital scholarly editor might be drawn between the need to preserve and reproduce the original textual look of the work or corpus published online and the need to exploit as much as possible the navigational dynamics of a web-based environment and the various tools and viewing mechanisms available.

If the typical display of a digital edition strives to become a look-alike of a traditional printed edition, it may underexploit the capacity of the digital medium to offer its users alternative views of the same material. There are therefore a great number of digital editions that offer more than one view of the text. In the present volume, two editions of this type are discussed. The Bergen Electronic Edition of Wittgenstein's *Nachlass* displays the text on two levels, a diplomatic level and a normalized level, while the Medieval Nordic Text Archive offers three levels, adding a facsimile or record-type level to the diplomatic and normalized level (see chapter 6).

Searchability: A Constantly Evolving Opportunity

The alphabetic index is the printed edition's strong technology. A good index can be most helpful, especially when words and names in the text have various and sometimes unpredictable spellings (which usually is the case in older texts). A good subject index is produced as the result of a thorough analysis of the book's contents.

Simple free text searching may serve as the digital edition's poor man's index. It can sometimes elicit more information from the text than a standard index. However, to equal the quality of a good index, the digital edition must be marked up with information about its document structure and contents. There are no technical problems with carrying out a thorough markup of a text. The guidelines of the Text Encoding Initiative (TEI) offer a plethora of elements to be used, and any new elements can be added thanks to the flexibility of XML (Extensible Markup Language) and similar markup schemes. While a printed edition without a good index looks naked (and there is no way of hiding this embarrassing state), the quality and amount of markup in a digital edition is much less visible. Questionable markup may hide many erroneous preconceptions or plain typographical, conceptual, or factual mistakes and still deliver a list of search results to users who are unaware of the shaky foundations of the product. The amount of work involved in producing a high-quality markup may be considerably underestimated by the project promoters. As a consequence, indexing and cross-references can easily be left to a later stage and never completed.

The idea of a concordance is usually traced back to work being done on Hebrew Masoretic texts around the tenth century, but the first full concordance did not appear until 1230. That was the concordance of the Latin Vulgate Bible by Hugo de Saint-Cher and a team of no less than five hundred other Dominicans (*Concordantiae Sacrorum Bibliorum*). Until recently, the production of concordances has been the exacting and manual work of going through a source text word by word and linking every running word (perhaps with the exception of the most frequent words, like "and" and "the") to a headword. The most spectacular example is the lifelong work of Gerhard Lisowsky, *Konkordanz zum hebräischen Alten Testament* (3rd ed., 1958). Getting the context for a particular word required leafing through the edition and inspecting visually every word. The Key Word in Context (KWIC) concordances were one of the first offers of digital text tools, and their effectiveness has rendered printed concordances obsolete, or if concordances still are printed, they can be produced from a digital text.

Until recently, digital search tools offered only simple lexical searches, enhanced by technologies such as regular expressions, allowing users to combine several searches in a single instruction. Recent advances in conceptual modeling, propelled by the vision of the Semantic Web,[11] have opened new avenues for conceptual search, as illustrated by computer ontologies, topic maps, and tools like WordNet.[12] However, no method can replace the fundamental contribution of the scholarly editor.

Analyzability: An Evolving Possibility

In addition to search tools and concordances, digital editions may offer new tools that blur the frontier between pure presentation and viewing on the one hand and analysis and knowledge production on the other. Some online editions have evolved by gradually integrating more functions, tools, and views. The explorative editions of Chaucer's *Canterbury Tales* by Peter Robinson and his colleagues are a case in point. The CD-ROM edition of *The Wife of Bath's Prologue* initially contained diplomatic transcriptions of all manuscripts containing the prologue as well as digital images of them (Robinson 1996). However, at this stage of the project there was no critical text. Establishing the text was left to the academic readers. It was a kind of do-it-yourself edition, a text archive rather than a proper edition. In the subsequent edition of the text's *General Prologue*, diplomatic transcriptions as well as digital images of the manuscripts were offered (Solopova 2000). Moreover, the edition contained tools for collation and phylogenetic analysis of the texts. Most important in this context, however, is the fact that there is also a critical text based on the whole textual tradition. While the editors of the *The Wife of Bath's Prologue* in a sense had abdicated, they made their presence known in the *General Prologue*. In the latter edition, readers can access the whole material and are still allowed to constitute their own text, but this time with the systematic advice of the editors and with the help of a number of tools.

Cumulativeness: For Experts and the Public Alike

When a printed edition has been published, it is closed in the sense that additions and corrections have to be offered to the readers as additional publications. In the past the death of the editor or simply a lack of funds often made such maintenance work impossible. Digital texts are a different kind of beast. They will often grow over the years. In the case of editions, the editor may want to add new information, update references, and correct any mistakes in the text. New contributors may add additional layers, such as biographical information. In user-modifiable editions, informed readers may want to add markup for names, grammatical information, or the like as is done with Wikipedia. There is thus a sliding border between the mere act of copying and the creation of a new edition. There is also an increasingly blurred boundary between the editor and user contributions.

Even if the digital edition is made from scratch, directly from the primary sources without any existing edition intervening, the edition may not be final and may profile itself as being under perpetual construction. The success or failure of such an editorial policy may depend on the economical sustainability of the enterprise and on the commitment of a dedicated community of users. Someone else, such as the general public, might want to add information or analysis to the text. In a TEI-conformant file, such activity will be documented in the header. It is not unlikely that future digital editions will contain a long list of additional editors, contributors, and critics. One editor may have been responsible for the actual transcription, another for the markup of personal and place names, yet another for grammatical information, and so on.

User Participation: Possible, but Practicable?

The printed edition is a final statement. It can be read, digested, and thrown away. There is no real feedback from the readers, save academic reviews, and no way of modifying the printed pages, save producing a new revised edition—but at what price? Such limitations are technically removed in a digital edition. The digital edition can present more than one text on more than one level of representation. For a classical or medieval text it can present transcriptions and facsimiles of all manuscripts, and it can display each transcription on more than one level (e.g., on a diplomatic and a regularized level). For a modern text it can provide all drafts and versions by the author (to the extent that these are known) and all printed versions. The user can then piece together the text for him- or herself and add annotations, emendations, or even conjectures. One person's edition can thus become different from another person's edition. The Bergen Electronic Edition of Wittgenstein's *Nachlass* has already seen this happen. A digital edition has the potential of being an *editio continua*, no longer constrained by the editors, as argued by Alois Pichler and Odd Einar Haugen (2005). Some have commented positively on this; others have been more skeptical. What is not a matter of controversy is that digital texts are much more difficult to constrain than printed texts. It remains to be seen if the tension between experts (the analyst, the editor) and the users of the edition (experts and nonexperts) will generate higher-quality products. Although user annotation is fully realizable technologically and has been mainstreamed in social media, one may still ask whether the resources between experts and readers are still unevenly distributed. While many academics bash Wikipedia for its unreliability, the considerable success of the project across many languages and cultures should augur a new era for user-annotated digital editions.

New Tools, Old Directions?

The view taken in this chapter is that the digital revolution essentially is the introduction of more efficient tools. It is not the introduction of new scientific methods or critical ideologies. It is not the introduction of new points of view. In fact, the first stage of the digital revolution, before the wide adoption of social media and the relative victory of the user-sharing ideology over the centralized content-production ideology, was very similar to the introduction of printing by movable type half a millennium earlier. That was a brand-new tool that suddenly made it possible to produce books in large quantities and thus spread knowledge to a much larger section of society. The contents of the book, however, were not new. The design was a true copy of the time-honored codex. The main agent of change today, allowing digital media to convey new modes of productions and possibly initiate a new kind of literacy, may turn out to be online collaborative media where the roles of producer, diffuser and consumer tends to merge (see, e.g., Bruns 2005).

Returning to the three perspectives outlined at the outset of this article, they all seem to be neutral with respect to digital technologies. Looking backward reflects a historical interest, an interest in explaining synchronic variation as the result of diachronic development. There are new and more efficient tools for investigating the filiation of a text, but the rationale for doing so (to repeat our claim once more) lies beyond the technology. Looking outward is as important as ever, and the methods are sometimes identical to those used for diachronic studies. Advances in display will also be important for the actual dissemination of texts; the facsimile edition and the text edition can close ranks and become cheaper and more available. And those who prefer to look inward, toward the structure of the text itself, will find many digital tools helpful, such as concordance tools, markup schemes, and methods for pattern recognition.

The outcome of this discussion is a healthy skepticism toward messianic prophecies for the digital age. Textual scholarship has a long history, and it will not change overnight with advances in digital technology. However, new technology may lead to the development of new methods, and it will most likely lead to a change of priorities. One early example in the brief history of digital philology is the idea that the editor should present the whole material and then, almost in a positivist manner, take a long step backward, leaving the choice to the users. *I am not the keeper of the text. Make your own edition!*

However, such a position, as democratic as it may seem, may be a step in the wrong direction. The editor should not succumb to the temptation of the unlimited helpfulness of the digital medium. Presenting the material in its wealth is so temptingly easy. And it is the accessibility of this option that may lead the editor or expert to forget that editorial judgment is still what the editor has to offer, no matter what tools are available. The editor's voice should come over strongly. In the wealth of textual variants, which may appear to the user as huge informational noise, the editor's critical advice is as important as ever. The challenge is to evolve a new kind of digital accountability allowing the user to track these decisions and possibly reject them on ideological or factual grounds.

The digital age has redefined the practice of textual scholarship, but so far this redefinition has in no way led to any revolution in our fundamental understanding of texts. What it has revolutionized is our way of working with texts, because it has given us new and extremely versatile tools in organizing and analyzing texts and their history. Moreover, in many cases digital editions have become dynamic and interactive by moving the focus from the editor to the users, from the editor as a controller of the text to users as re-creators of texts. In short, digital editions have the potential of being truly dynamic in a way that a printed, paper-based edition never can be. Yet no revolution lies in the tools as such, but rather in the extent that these tools are being used in ways that lead to a new understanding of texts, to new questions being raised. Whether that will happen remains an open question. This view echoes, though distantly, some central themes in contemporary cognitive archaeology, which heavily emphasizes the links between evolving usages of materials and technologies, as witnessed by artifacts, and the shaping of human cognition. The purpose of this book is to try to sketch some answers to the question of whether new digital tools augur a new kind of textuality.

Notes

1. The term *Sitz im Leben* goes back to the theologian Hermann Gunkel (1967, 1998) but has since spread to other literary disciplines, among other contemporary text pragmatics (see Wagner 1996).

2. "Wir sollen und wollen aus einer hinreichenden Menge von guten Handschriften einen allen diesen zum Grunde liegenden Text darstellen, der entweder der ursprüngliche selbst seyn, oder ihm doch sehr nahe kommen muss" (Müllenhoff and Vahlen 1876, 82).

3. "Je ne connais ni erreurs, ni fautes communes, ni bonnes, ni mauvaises leçons, mais seulement des formes diverses du texte, sur lesquelles, par une méthode qui s'appuie sur des statistiques rigoureuses, je délimite d'abord les familles, puis je classe les manuscrits dans l'intérieur de chacune d'elles, et enfin les familles entre elles" (Quentin 1926, 37).

4. The use of various quantitative methods is discussed in somewhat more detail in chapter 8.

5. The term "Nouvelle Critique" should be kept distinct from the term "New Criticism." The first term describes a postwar literary movement in France initiated by Roland. The second term describes an American literary movement that stretched from the interwar period to the 1950s in the United States.

6. See, for example, Bolter (2001); Landow and Delany (1991), Landow (1992); Delany and Landow (1994); Aarseth (1996 and 1997); and Landow (2006).

7. Woolf Online (www.woolfonline.com) illustrates such reintegration of genealogical and genetic aspect in an outward perspective.

8. "La naissance du lecteur doit se payer de la mort de l'auteur" (Barthes 1984, 69).

9. In order to avoid eurocentric biases, it should be mentioned that mobile types *also* were invented by Bi Sheng in China in the eleventh century and in Korea during the thirteenth century.

10. One example is the commercial policy of the digital edition of the complete works of Pierre Bayle (*Corpus des œuvres complètes de Pierre Bayle*), published in the Classiques Garnier Numérique collection.

11. "The Semantic Web is not a separate Web but an extension of the current one, in which information is given well-defined meaning, better enabling computers and people to work in cooperation" (Berners-Lee, Handler et al. 2001).

12. See http://wordnet.princeton.edu.

2. Ongoing Challenges for Digital Critical Editions

PHILIPPE RÉGNIER

As observed in this beginning of the twenty-first century, the reality of "digital critical edition" is still too embryonic and too unstable, even though it is developing, to be considered only in its present state and to be adopted without wondering about its future. It is indeed a strange situation where one has the impression of leaving the familiar and well-established world of printed books for the adventure and the risks of a medium commonly described as immaterial, in perpetual evolution, and without rules. Let us dare state up front that the issue at stake is neither external nor temporary: philology, this old lady born of the marriage of humanism and printing, is from now on definitely confronted with the question of its media mutation.

In facing this opportunity for modernization—which stands a good chance of increasingly often imposing itself as a necessity—philology finds itself at a crossroads of rather diverse choices, with the moral obligation, however, whatever the path chosen, to remain loyal to its fundamental values. Briefly said, philology must reassess its strategy to take into account digital technology. It can no longer remain apart if it does not want to be paralyzed or isolated. It can no longer remain a passive user if it does not want to find itself confined in inadequate frameworks. Philology needs to be endowed with a vision of its future.

But thinking about prospects of the future, as one knows, is similar to the utopian method invented by Thomas More, which consists of examining, criticizing, and especially interpreting what exists at the moment of writing in order to imagine what could or should exist tomorrow or the day after tomorrow. By definition, thinking prospectively involves taking risks that are justified by the hope of gains superior to those guaranteed by daily routine. Also by definition, it is a cause of dissent. That is why very divergent opinions coexist among philologists, even within the same specialized fields, within the same groups, and often in the same heads. The enthusiasm of some philologists is equaled only by the grimness of others.

This is not astounding, considering, as recalled in the preceding chapter, that the theoretical advances of printed philology, its norms and presentation techniques result from two centuries of discussions that were much more strenuous than commonly imagined, without having ever reached a unique and definite model. The contrary would be surprising, one is tempted to say, considering the diversity of schools of thought and practices.

Focusing on digital edition, it would seem fit to assess the issues at stake, and, considering the precedent printing effects, to dismiss no hypothesis—neither the strongest ones nor the wildest—in trying to find the most stimulating one, the one that would have digital edition at the heart of a general process of change.

Quantitative Change or Qualitative Mutation: Cultural Catastrophe or Progress?

A common opinion consists in denying the problem formulated as a question in the header above. Digital technology is considered neutral. The question retained is not the improvement of or change in editing but how to edit more, much more, and more rapidly, for the immense number of readers who now have overdeveloped reading capacities.

Let's take, for example, a thirty-year-old precedent: text processing and computer-aided publishing. These major inventions seem to have corresponded exclusively to increases in productivity and quickly fallen into oblivion and indifference as their use became generalized and their access available to most persons writing and publishing. In the same way, computer-assisted editing and reading tomorrow could result in nothing more than an increase of existing capacities. Has anyone seriously contended that the forms of the printed book would have directly provoked any type of scientific revolution?

On the other hand, however, would anyone contest the obvious fact that both inventions have completely reformatted our very way of thinking? And, more deeply still, that they have definitely brought about a new humanity? The passage from print to digital could eventually turn out to be as decisive as the passage from Stone Age to the Bronze Age or the one from manuscript to print.

For the time being, current daily experiences with digital texts often involves using websites where the site authors are sparingly identified, if at all, and there is usually no information concerning where the site is located or when it was set up: looking for a quick answer, users arrive through the guidance of a generalist and commercial web search engine. For example, one might wish to find the

Cours de philosophie positive d'Auguste Comte. Searching for the text through Google leads one directly to the picture, rather stimulating for bookworms, of the front panel of the old binding of the Stanford University Library copy of the original edition, published in 1838.[1] Besides this quasi simulation, capable of partly restoring for the reader a library atmosphere, the textual content is integrally accessible in image mode, with full text search functionalities. But volume 3 is only volume 3. It does not equate the totality of the volumes that make up the work, beginning with the first. As for the New York Public Library copy listed in the top search results, it corresponds only to volume 6.[2] One of the links presented points to the complete digitization of the work on the Gallica website of the Bibliothèque nationale de France (Comte 1830a). Here also it is possible to download the totality of the *Cours* in PDF, a format that is not very convenient for turning pages and that allows only very slow reading. While awaiting the promised possibility of full text search, navigation takes place by rowing, as it were, like in galley times—without sails, much less steam engines.

To come back to Google, probably one could accept as a "table of contents" a selection of "best extracts" (along criteria similar to those of the Science Citation Index), "references to other books," "references from web pages," "academic references," and the mention of "books on closely related subjects." This could be seen as the beginning of a new type of critical apparatus built by algorithms and robots. But it is an apparatus that is constituted according to criteria so quantitative, so scantily and badly organized, so foreign to the world on paper, so inadequate to the requirements of a philosophical and academic mind, that it is tempting to describe it, depending on one's mood, as a bazaar or as a curio cabinet, a terra incognita to be explored or an inextricable undergrowth to be avoided. It may be even more expedient to go to the closest library or bookstore to locate the desired text. Finally, the user in this thought experiment, to be spared further pain, would slip over the link to the Comte page of the French commercial cultural daily news website evene .fr, and also of the purely pedagogical formula of the University of Quebec in Chicoutimi website based on the small "Classiques Larousse," dated 1936 and supported by annexed documents.[3]

Such experiences, which are actually very frequent, give the impression of an overwhelming offer as well as the impression of regressing to a pre-philological era of incredible miscellanea that were handed out in antiquity and during the Middle Ages. In parallel to an extraordinary expansion of the sphere of well-read persons, there is something akin to a global deconstruction process of textual heritage by the third industrial revolution. And this process, the control of which is beyond the reach of the knowledge organization and conservation specialists who are librarians and document researchers, arrogantly ignores philology and philologists.

However, to circumscribe the problem, let us suppose that the reorganization of the incoming chaos falls within the competence of librarians and document specialists and not of philologists. A close examination of more elaborated digital publications nevertheless leads to similar thoughts at the basic level of textuality itself.

Let us begin, as an introduction, with the example of the 2001 online publication of a literary monument whose philosophical dictionary nature seemed predestined to a digital transposition—that is, the *Dictionnaire historique et critique de Bayle*. Useful whatever the case, the digital version provides easy access to a major text that previously was available only in libraries. It results from the work, among others, of a Franco-American project for a treasury of French language (*Trésor de la langue française*) known as the ARTFL Project (American and French Research on the Treasury of the French Language), conceived and carried out by a team from the Analyse et Traitement Informatique de la Langue française (ATILF) of the Centre National de la Recherche Scientifique (CNRS) on the French side and by the Division of the Humanities, the Division of the Social Sciences, and the Electronic Text Services (ETS) of the University of Chicago on the American side.[4] Due to its display in facsimile on the screen, Bayle's digitized dictionary has retained its very special page layout. The reader can read the text by scrolling page by page. The reader can also read the text by using a table of contents endowed with hyperlinks, navigating from article to article, from volume to volume, much more rapidly than would be possible with the heavy physical volumes laid on one's table, following the complex routes provided by Bayle and his collaborators, who needed to outsmart censors and in order to allow one to make out the coherence of the instigating ideas. But with the exception of a few succinct pages explaining the project and describing the text and its characteristics, there are no comments to guide the nonspecialist reader neither within articles nor in his course from article to article. In the light of philological norms, however, the greatest flaw is that the e-editors do not provide access to what would have been the main interest of a genuine edition: the large-scale reorganizations and enrichments from which stems the text they have chosen—that is, the last authorized edition (Amsterdam, 1740). Even more radical comments have been voiced against the two digitized versions of Diderot's *Encyclopédie*.[5] By being digitized, this sun of the Enlightenment era has become, according to Philippe Stewart, a "fragmented galaxy." The digital machine, he explains, is incapable of following the semantic road of correlations between articles that produces all the subversive quality of the textual system: it only knows discrete words, quantified in bytes (2002, 190). The general argument is completely obvious: these e-editions of philosophical dictionaries are not critical editions; they are databases. To sum up, it seems that two observations can be made: (1) that there exists a tension, perhaps already a rupture, between the procedures and norms of modern critical edition and the digital critical edition trials carried out since the '90s, and (2) that the restructuring of texts into database forms is jeopardizing textuality itself by barbarously atomizing it.[6]

Proof that a point of no return had been reached is the fact that no one has imagined printing these digitized texts in a book form that could put them in the ordinary category of critical editions, a status they were not claiming anyway. What would be the purpose? In fact, there is little doubt that such digital editions did not answer specialists' refined needs. But by the very fact of their availability, and whatever the elementary character of the intellectual operations that they facilitate (lexical studies, checking a quotation, curiosity exploration, and so on), they have a utility and an efficiency that nonspecialist researchers are apt to appreciate. They probably open the way for digital critical editions of monuments whose size constitute an invincible challenge. This is even truer since commercial publishers of living dictionaries, such as the *Larousse,* the *Robert,* or the *Universalis Encyclopedia*, have committed themselves to the production of digital versions and, consequently, are now contributing to the development of more complex software and to formatting solutions in answer to users' demands.

Moreover, it is not entirely a coincidence if the majority of initiators and authors of the experiences referred to above do not come from the field of French literature, a discipline that, within established role sharing, should have presided over their conception and their elaboration, and where the above-mentioned objections come from. It is because of its technical incompetence, which is not without remedy, that this discipline has been confined to watching the evolution of linguistics and informatics, or more exactly, language engineering and computer engineering.

Such a phenomenal interdisciplinary takeover by sciences that are sometimes derogatorily qualified as "technosciences" is certainly not to be understood in terms of a decadence of traditional humanities. The history of science and techniques needs to point out more than one transition achieved through interdisciplinary transfers. It is commonplace for the importing discipline that such transfers result from temporary compromises on norms. If the discipline survives the ordeal, its redeployment in a second phase can lead it to respond by inventing theories, methods, and norms that will assure it a new life. Philosophy and literature benefited from such an experience during the '70s when they assimilated the concepts and methods of linguistics and semiology.

It must be pointed out also that, as opposed to first-generation digital editions that exhibit their database structure, the editions that followed and that we will be evoking here have chosen to be applied not to dictionaries but to continuous texts. These editions can thus present themselves as principally hypermedia systems with the ambition to reinvent and even to maximize the potential of the connotative and labyrinthic. In other words, they function in a reticular mode that characterizes literary thinking and in which the Internet claims to have its roots.[7] This is all the more reason for estimating that interdisciplinary cross-breeding between the humanities and the sciences and techniques of information and communication has a great future ahead.

The Meaning of a Lexical Renewal

Let us now move to technical issues and the associated lexicon. Is it really so difficult for philology to adapt to the words and forms that come from the Internet? The media changes between paper and screen, between ink and electrons, have well-known predecessors that have been properly analyzed by writing and book historians as genuine transfers, not from discipline to discipline this time, but specifically from one technical era to another technical era.

Simplified character fonts have replaced calligraphic writings. Labels and concepts of title, author, and editor have replaced the copyist's signature, amounting to, in short, a generalization of punctuation (period, comma, and their complex derivatives, beginning with the semicolon and the question mark). The numbered page has become the basic reading unit (without columns or, preferably, with only one column, which is the etymological meaning of the word "page"). Division occurs in "volumes," "parts," "chapters," and "paragraphs." Structural abstractions, such as the "table of contents" or "summary," function as reading guides. Marginal and bottom page "notes" (in replacement, notably, of interlinear notes or of "chains" encircling the text as a fruit encircles its stone) and so forth invite the reader to focus on specific portions the text. All of these small mechanisms of our textual functioning that seem natural and as old as writing itself, today are, as a matter of fact, rather recent and fundamental inventions.[8] Expressions and practices based on new information and communication technology that are ordinarily perceived as purely technical take on a quite different scientific and cultural dignity when referred to in the frame of long-term history.

Very few scholars have taken the risk of going beyond observing and of making such an acknowledgment.[9] But some time from now, maybe as soon as the end of the twenty-first century, some modern scholar will be able to stand back and write the history of how humanity went not from the volumen to the codex, and from the codex to the printed book, from the printed book to periodical press, and of their long cohabitation, but the passage from the printed world to the digital world—in other words, from the book to the "database," from the "web page" to the "website," from the "home page" or "web page" as such to a still unknown standardized reading unit (a "screen" defined in inch format and in a number of visible dots?). Likewise, this scholar will also have to explain how we have organized the migration of bottom page notes (and even still marginal ones) to a hypertextual note system. Because digital text notes are notes of a different nature, of different levels, and of different sizes,[10] they must be distinguished by new display codes (e.g., underlining or color codes in replacement of the still unfixed code of traditional diacritical signs and of digital diacritical signs that perhaps will have been chosen among the "special signs" functionality of current word-processing software). In the end, in the same way that a Gutenberg-era reader succeeds in mastering, more or less, the book by excellence, which is in fact a collection of ill-assorted books, a small library in itself, a Bill Gates–, Larry Page–, and Sergey Brin–era reader who is confronted with the virtual library of all the libraries humanity has produced will be able to navigate the boundless and constantly renewed infinite course of the web.

But he will also need to learn to dive—to continue this now lexicalized metaphor—in stages, each stage corresponding to an additional mouse click. Many authors, beginning with Ted Nelson, the pioneer of hypertextuality, have drawn attention to the fact that computer writing, as it is developing now, is creating a new way of writing and reading that is radically different from the linearity and tabularity inherited from the use of papyrus (for writing) and from the use of parchment and from the book (for reading). Databases and hypertexts both obey a logic (in the etymological meaning of the word: an organization of the *logos*) that is not the dominantly sequential and horizontal one of reading and writing on paper, with texts disposed in lines and blocks, but the dominantly nonsequential, vertical digital organization, with fields or headings, by association and by strata arranged in levels of depth.[11] Hence we have the "pull-down menus," "tool bars," and "links" by which we gain access to these depths. He or she who has not been involved in the development of a database and a website, who has not had the opportunity to be confronted with the obligation to think in terms of fields and to organize an arborescence, cannot understand nor measure the problem. We must reconcile ourselves with this idea that we are dealing with something absolutely new—and the sooner the better. Are we not witnessing the emergence of expressions such as "research hypertexts" and "hypertextual editions"?[12] We can lament more simplistic technology as we trample the laboriously produced "sites" and "databases" that make up most of the existing projects and endeavors. Scientifically, they also have the inconvenience of shunting the references, which are still more or less explicit in works that include the "critical" dimension of a philologico-philosophical quest for authenticity and for the accuracy of an essential discourse. For it is this quest that is the strength of critical editions in their nineteenth-century acceptance. Perhaps it is to preserve such a dimension that a precious resource such as the complete digitization in full text of the first and last authorized edition of Balzac's *La Comédie humaine* is still labeled a "critical online edition." But this labeling turns out to be simply promotional. The digitization process is limited to reproducing a printed edition and in no way recalls the manuscripts nor provides any annotation apparatus.[13] The digitized version is useful in that it allows full text search and comprises presentation notes, biographical elements, and different documents with information on the organization of the work.[14]

An enlightening example of the difficulty of finding proper labels is the Heinrich-Heine-Portal as described by that website's editor, Nathalie Groß (2005, 60–73). This publication, begun in 2002, is defined by Groß as a "digital edition" of the works and the correspondence of the writer. Practically, the main objective is to provide online access, while occasionally adding corrections, to the two printed critical editions of the complete works of Heinrich Heine that were already published conjointly in former East Germany and West Germany. But to this objective of scientific (without fusion) reunification of the two editions has been added an (immaterial) reunification objective between the philological productions and the original texts themselves, as the Heinrich-Heine-Portal offers access in image mode to manuscripts and editions, as well as press articles, published during the author's lifetime. In addition to these components, there are other *disjecta membra poetae*, engravings, and contemporary portraits, with a forthcoming general bibliography. There is also information on current research activities about Heine. Consequently, Groß (2005) describes the project as that of a "complete platform" for the study of this author. Incidentally, the German title of the article is worded in terms that effectively refer to something completely different from a critical edition and translates as "Digital Heine—An Internet portal offering an integrated information system." In taking up and continuing the masterly "critical editions" in order to transform them into something better and different, presented as a kind of digital reincarnation of the author, the Heine portal "surpasses" them all in reference to the subtle Hegelian meaning of the *Aufhebung,* implying simultaneously both abrogation and perservation, by its integration into a greater whole built on the more general information principle rather than on a principle of edition.

Forging new words turns out to be all the more difficult when the words are not imposed by the universal newspeak of computers, because the subsumed products are themselves quite diverse, they are composites, and they correspond to a variety of quite diverse scholarly projects. It is nevertheless a first step toward the consecration of newness as such.

Hybridizing Old and New: Toward Novel Kinds of Editions

A phenomenon such as this conflict between old and new, "Antiques against Moderns," is obviously far from being original. Still, it is necessary to appraise it each time and learn to distinguish what is the newness coming out of the old limbo.

It would, however, be counterproductive to pretend being able to identify within the philologist community a line of fracture between two kinds of editors: on one side, traditional editors, who would be lingering behind with the traditional critical-book editing, and, on the other side, editors who, having opted for the digital solution and gone ahead, have won the right to not be accountable to their colleagues for the specifically philological quality of their work. This would result in not only freezing each one in positions that are bound to evolve but also situating the debate at the superficial level of tendencies, if not fads, and not in the field of the science of texts. The decisive question is this: Are there specifically scientific effects to be expected from the use of digital technology? And if so, which ones?

If one wants to risk a forecast, then it must begin with a brief analysis of the state of the domain. Depending on the era (antiquity, Middle Ages and classicism, or modern and contemporary periods) of the texts they are presenting, depending on the cultural region they belong to (Anglo-Saxon world, German and Scandinavian worlds, francophone and French world, etc.), depending upon the original material they are dealing with (manuscripts, books, correspondence, newspapers or journals), and depending on their aims (historical, philosophical, aesthetic, etc.), academic editors are mainly interested in the following:

- The reconstruction of a lost archetype
- The establishing and commenting on a text that was initially poorly edited and/or is now unobtainable
- The genetic process of intellectual and artistic creation
- The historical, political, social, ideological, and aesthetic context
- The evolutions apparent through the successive illustrated, popular, scholarly, bibliophilic, etc. rewritings and editions, whether authorized or not
- The generic and media transfers of protean text narrations (from serialized novels to book novels, from theatrical plays to films, from poems to songs, from separately published articles to a posthumous authorized anthology, etc.)

In parallel, the observer cannot escape noticing that the various focuses of interest listed aboved are linked with many external factors: the market and the uses envisioned, the expected free or paying outlets, the decisions made by the various actors implied (researchers, engineers, research teams, etc.) and by the institutions they are addressing to go for either the printed or the digital version or both in a complementary, concomitant, or successive manner (with a widely variable and rarely announced "moving wall"). To complicate matters, these actors may choose a CD-ROM solution at times and an Internet one at others;[15] they may also prefer sometimes websites, sometimes databases, and sometimes websites with databases, sometimes portals; they may either stick to black and white or use color. As a result, some editions may be solely textual while others may be multimedia, or even hypermedia. Some editions may leave the visitor/user totally free to explore as he or she wishes, or they may either impose a specific path or offer a choice between paths or a range of choices that are adapted to the type of interest or professional identity the user communicates to the system. They may choose fixed formats or dynamic ones. Finally, some editions may use use proprietary software while others use open software. The combination of all these scientific and technical variables results in an indescribable diversity, much more wide-ranging than the small selection of formulas developed in the printed world.

The ultimate question that comes up is the much more extensive one of whether the fate of the digital world is to completely absorb the printed one like it has itself absorbed the manuscript culture, or whether both will coexist in a competitive, complementary, and interpenetrating relationship along the lines of the coexistence in the nineteenth century of books and periodical press. Without delving into pointless speculation and science fiction, it is worth meditating on the unprecedented fact of the multiplication of possible outcomes: it opens the door to an extraordinary flexible adaptation to contents.

Coming back to the Auguste Comte case, the works of Comte would surely deserve a HyperComte system conceived along the ambitious model promoted by Paolo D'Iorio of the website HyperNietzsche.[16] However, for lack of such a solution, would it not be wise for the community of positivism specialists to provide, at least to begin with, a concurrent use of the volumes of the complete works, annotated with the creation of a website where the raw texts digitized in full text could be visualized or downloaded?[17] The access and search facilities provided by such an option, even though still basic, would represent a considerable achievement. Of course, in this type of option, printing remains the norm and reference. And the passage to digital technology equates here, at least provisionally, to putting into brackets the critical edition ideal.

A more complex evolutionary stage, to use the language of natural science, is one where the critical edition ideal, unchanged as elaborated for the printing world, is fully renewed by a digital reproduction with eventually a few supplementary functionalities. This second option is best illustrated by the series of editions developed under Arcane, a multifunction software conceived and developed by an engineer, Éric-Olivier Lochard, to answer the needs of a network of eighteenth-century literary scholars.[18] The order received was for a "computer-assisted critical edition" software that would also be a collaborative tool for a geographically dispersed community. Arcane retrieves all the presentation forms that correspond to philological norms and effectively allows the edition work to reach the ready-for-printing stage with important gains in time devoted by the researchers to their discussions and to compiling and writing. This good computer genie, less unpredictable than Aladdin's, continues to evolve and is a general-purpose editorial tool capable of also meeting the needs of a complete editorial chain. During the production phase, like in a database, it stores and manages the files sent by the collaborators, beginning with the established texts up to the notes, comments, and presentations. Once the production is over, the software attends to the page layout, as desktop publishing software would, taking into consideration the constraints of the publishing house that will bring out the critical edition. Parallel to the published work there exists a database that offers specific functionalities for helping researchers (lexical statistics, locating co-occurrences, searching for quotations, thematic indexing, graph statistics, network mapping) that can be constantly enriched and can be available online depending on further developments (and the authorization by the commercial publisher).

A third option, which diverges fundamentally with the norms and uses of printed critical edition, is that of the William Blake Archive.[19] Its architecture, specific yet exemplary in allowing many other possible developments, can be explained partly by the remarkable characteristics of this British creator's work. Blake's twofold literary and graphic production actually transgresses so much the limits between poetry and literature and extends so far beyond the current cultural and material frameworks that in order to function as the multimedia system that it is, it seems to have been awaiting the creation of the hypermedia database. The site was created in 1994 and has been accessible for some years at the highly symbolic website of the Library of Congress.[20] The originality allowed by digital technology here is precisely not the perfection of a critical edition (in Blake's case the printed book has attained that), but the bringing together of texts and images. The inclusion of a biography, a glossary, and a chronology, as well as critical articles and a kind of discussion forum, and putting specific tools at the disposal of visitors, make this "archive" at once a scholarly edition, a special library collection, a museum, and a research center. The term "knowledge site," coined by Peter Shillingsburg (2006), is probably too extensive and generic an expression, but it is beginning to catch on to signal this new type of computer production, distinguishing it both from critical edition *stricto sensu* and the mass of commercial sites and others. Be that as it may, the William Blake Archive has been validated by the Modern Language Association of America (in 2003) and even distinguished by a prize awarded by this same society (in 2005), under the canonical category of "scholarly edition."

New formulas, sometimes qualified as hybrid, are emerging between the classical formula of copying from one support to the other and the romantic or utopian formula for the invention of a new genre of scholarly edition. Frequently seen solutions are books whose bindings have been arranged so as to allow the insertion of discs containing the digital version or complementary elements and, more rarely, books that direct their readers to a companion site.[21] Inversely, an online publication of textual data can rely on the publication of a printed critical volume.[22]

It is true that the cultural and scientific hierarchy among the objects to be edited themselves partly prescribes the choice of the means to be committed. But the more or less polymorph nature of these texts and the specificity of their intended uses are in all likelihood expected to be more and more decisive. In comparing the accomplishments and the prototypes, and in outlining their specific differences along with their common evolution and tendencies, one is inclined to imagine that in the future there could be not just one model of scholarly edition but a whole constellation of models according to the types of objects to be edited.

The far horizon, as outlined in many projects, however, is the post-Gutenberg option, where digital technology replaces and evacuates printing, similar to how the book is said to have killed the popular and religious art of architecture as expressed by one of Victor Hugo's characters in *Notre-Dame-de-Paris*.[23] To a certain extent, this is the age that the University of Bergen announced with the electronic edition of Wittgenstein's posthumous *Nachlass* manuscripts on CD-ROM,[24] as well as Rouen University's online publication of Flaubert's manuscripts of *Madame Bovary*:[25] the digitization of the originals in image mode accompanied by their transcription in full text and search functions. Digital technology takes over from printing because in this latter medium it would be impossible to present materially and economically, and to provide reading and managing facilities, for such huge masses of such multiformed documents. But this post-Gutenberg stage is even closer to the one that HyperNietzsche had prophesized and had begun to configure by the end of the '90s. What we have begun to see with the Heinrich-Heine-Portal is what NietzscheSource, last avatar of the successive HyperNietzsche versions, extends with the production of a consolidated version:[26] an integrated, open platform that brings together a great quantity of textual and non-textual data, indexed and organized in a hypertextual system, based on a preceding solid-paper critical edition that it transforms, and that tends to exploit as much as possible the evolutionary and interactive nature of the Internet. Only the multi- and hypermedia dimensions are still missing. But tomorrow is another day.

Between today and tomorrow, let's bet that the diversity of electronic scholarly editions will remain significant and bewildering. But let us also ask ourselves if this last model of an integrated platform has not set, by its paramount ambition, the new critical frontier to be reached.

The Future of a Few Antinomies

Even advanced technology cannot be a substitute for theory. It is therefore necessary to look at the scientific principles. How do these experimentations connect with the main philological doctrines? What effect are they likely to have on the renewal of the existing positions?

The Lachmannian method, which for a long time has had the monopoly of the reference model role, is an approach based on purification and decontamination, conceived to correct the corrupt texts handed down by the antique and medieval worlds. In modern philology this is also the case, particularly in France, with the dogma of the last authorized version, based on the same half-scientific, half-religious cult of the creative origins, or, if one prefers, with a belief in the authentic spirit and the exact letter. In both cases it is a question of going back to the original text or restoring it by removing all the errors, additions, and interpolations that have been agglomerated to the original text. However, the opposite tendency exists, resulting from the digital offer itself, but extends, revives, and accelerates a fundamental tendency of printing. It is this propensity to include more and more elements, be they diverse, massive, more or less prior, or external or foreign to the considered text. This tendency confirms the legitimacy of these elements based on the fact that they exist. It proposes to take them into account and to interpret them inasmuch as they are the indisputable remnants of the semantic investment of copyists, exegetes, and editors standing on the shoulders of original authors.

Without even evoking the expansion of the canons of philology and the inclination toward their abolition that represents the scholarly republication of so-called illegitimate texts (because they are popular, anonymous, outside of the established categories, etc.), we observe that printed critical editions of modern texts have not ceased since their beginnings and are constantly revising their doctrinal basis in continuously pushing back the sacrosanct notions of author and authority:

- From edition of works published by authors during their lifetime up to the posthumous editions of the fragmentary and disordered drafts, even those never meant for publication
- From the edition by an author of his own letters addressed to a specific person up to the exhaustive posthumous edition of his active correspondence, even his general correspondence
- From the edition of unpublished and/or unfinished works to the publication of unprocessed manuscripts (through facsimiles and diplomatic editions), personal diaries, notebooks, rough copies, genetic files, reception files

The widely practiced whistleblowing on the interest allegedly manifested for Baudelaire's and Nietzsche's laundry bills summarizes the problem and the misunderstandings. The publication of such textual snippets, considered sacred because they are linked in some way to the creator's body of works, is actually only a servile imitation of an evolution determined by a sort of economic and intellectual tug-of-war. This bid to outdo others has pushed and continues to push scholarly editors to quasi-exhaustiveness, motivated by a fetishism confining idolatry.[27] It is necessary to emphasize that successive editorial theories have not anticipated this evolution, nor thought it out, not as a denial of their specific logic but in order to put into perspective the role it plays in the etiology of the actual evolution. The truth is that theories have more often followed this evolution and accompanied it, even if it meant having to come up with justifications after the fact. One finds here, along with scientific paradigm changes, radical taste and aesthetic changes. Writers themselves—beginning with Victor Hugo (in France) or Louis Aragon in the twentieth century, with the subtly expressed will to go further than his illustrious predecessor—have opened the way by conserving and making it a point of bequeathing all (or almost all) of their manuscripts and other papers, the first to the national library, the second to the Centre National de la Recherche Scientifique (CNRS). Explicitly made responsible by the donator of the mission of producing a research on Aragon's texts and avant-textes, promoters of textual genetics and the research unit that are considered the main carriers of this mission have never made a mystery of the correlation between their theory and the refined reading pleasure they wish to procure nor of their intention to participate in the promotion of an aesthetic revolution.[28]

Thus the digital world, maximizing its power since it has integrated audio-visual technology to become "multimedia" and manifested its Semantic Web ambition, opens a perspective of more than complete and definitive editions: almost unlimited and in permanent progression; perfectly heterogeneous (texts, still images, animated images, and sound); virtually capable of being interconnected by an infinity of links intentionally created by editors or automatically generated by machines. This raises the question of limits or absence of limits. Within the sole (fluctuating) limits of economic constraints and legal conditions, it is now conceivable to assemble and manage together the following:

- The image (preferably in color) of all of an author's papers and known manuscripts, all of his work manuscripts up to the copy given to the publisher, and the image of all the published editions during his lifetime from the original edition to the last authorized edition, including the illustrated editions and the stored proofs
- The image, also in color, of all posthumous editions, including all the critical editions
- All the presentations, annotations, and, even more unthinkable, all the commentaries of all the specialists concerned by all the specialties
- The sources, the intertexts, and other co-texts
- Work tools such as the primary and secondary bibliography, the author's dictionaries or dictionaries of his work, his biography, or a fine chronology of the era
- The intellectual, visual, and musical universe of the creator—that is, his

"personal library as a writer," his "imaginary museum," the musical works, the monuments, the sceneries, the interior decorations having constituted his audiovisual environment

- Reception files comprising impressions, reactions, discussions, and other traces of reading by all the contemporary critics and all the readers, renowned or obscure or nobodies, who have left traces in essays, articles, correspondences, or discussion forums
- Public readings or recitations recorded by the author or by actors
- Theater plays inspired by the text, including their stage productions as they have been or could be recorded
- Pictorial and graphic transpositions in general, including digitized plastic art ones
- Television or cinematographic adaptations
- Depending on the case (poem, novel, historical narration, etc.), music adaptations or transpositions in musical shows (operas, operettas, musical comedies, etc.)
- Counterfeits, pastiches, imitations, continuations
- Translations in all languages
- Published monographic researches
- Past and ongoing activities and publications by specialized scholarly society or societies
- Tapings of expositions and conferences
- Ongoing research and discussions (collaborative dimension of website)
- Copied extracts and personal comments when reading with a pen in hand, as in olden times
- Pedagogical tools (textbooks, course outlines, lecture notes, exercise models)
- Impressions, reactions, and information requests from readers and visitors

All of this should be considered while putting in the foreground, last but not least, the textual data, indexed, structured, classified and organized, presented and annotated, from the basic level of the word up to the level not only of the "complete works" but also of the entire production, for which there does not currently exist a specific word. The concerned production could even include, as might be the case for Alexandre Dumas and for Victor Hugo, among others, the writer's house and its interior decoration.

Digital presentations have a tendency to accumulate, amalgamate, and continuously grow, and this seems to be inscribed in the very principle of their conception. Probably such a list will appear as a utopia or a monstrosity capable of exploding not only the quantitative limits but also and above all theoretical frameworks and the norms in use. Here again, history can help us remain confident.

From antiquity to the sixteenth century, cultural habits were to conserve only the works and to destroy all drafts, manuscripts, and correspondences. The fact that the manuscript era did not produce handwritten critical editions of the manuscripts it was (re)producing is not entirely fortuitous. It is also not entirely fortuitous that printing, to succeed in producing critical editions of modern texts, books of books, in a way, experienced the need to base such editions on . . . manuscripts. The multiplicity of material supports, their hierarchy, their newness or outdatedness, their succession or their cohabitation are the cause and the matter of philological activity: beyond the very quest itself for the inaccessible original text, this is precisely what philology is in charge of managing. Why wouldn't the digital era have to invent its own manner of recovering and managing texts, text derivatives, and the textual environments of the printing era? It is this immense construction endeavor that the Google, Amazon, and Europeana projects are launching. It's a shame that there is no awareness of the urgency of thinking it out and of conducting it not only at the macro level of libraries but also at the micro level of the works.

For antiquity specialists or medievalists, the formerly unthinkable, and consequently, self-censored, liberty of displaying, besides the text reconstructed in its most ancient and reliable conjectured state, the multiple variations that have deformed or enriched and transformed it can only increase tension between, or bring closer together—in the same confrontation logic (productive and dispassionate, one may hope)—Lachmannian philology, dedicated to its quest for archetypes, and the "new philology," more interested by the proliferation and the creative infidelity of copies than by the authenticity and the purity of originals.[29] Since the material and technical possibilities exist, how could it be possible to provide the restored state that is estimated to be the most probable without also offering the different states that have value by their very existence and, vice versa, to exhibit and legitimize the evolutional states without also proposing the hypothetical generative state to which they refer? His scientific community and society expect the philologist to send a clear-cut opinion on the text and its states as much as they would less and less understand—since, again, he is no longer limited to a book or a series of books—that he imposed a unilateral vision and denies them a direct and integral access to all the textual materials and all the debate arguments. To bring medieval manuscript literature into the era of indefinite and universal reproducibility is not a utopia. Thus, while awaiting translations, stemmas, variant studies, annotations, and so on (a critical edition is not produced in a day, not even in a few small years), an example of what is offered can be found on the Internet with the prestigious manuscript located in Lyon of *La Quête du Graal* text and illuminations, while disposing, on the same screen of a new transcription, folio by folio (*Edition "en ligne" de la Queste del saint Graal*).[30]

As far as they are concerned, modernists and contemporaneists are divided by a similar opposition between partisans of the author's supreme authority (and often of the last published edition during his lifetime) and partisans of the work's autonomy, as it develops intrinsically (from the draft to the first original edition, even disavowed, up to the same last authorized edition, but taking into account all the intermediary steps). Specialists of the eighteenth, nineteenth, and twentieth centuries also have to deal with the ambient rejection of their monopolistic power, if not their scientific censure. It is also hard to imagine that they could take the liberty of not delivering everything.

Their other great quarrel is the one that has the holders of the text closure and immanent criticism battling against the supporters of the historical inscription and its contextualization. To say it in grossly simplified words, the first orientation brings together structuralism and formalism in general, among which are the École de Genève (Geneva School),[31] gender poetics, and textual genetics. The second orientation encompasses Marxism and sociologisms in general, including sociocriticism and literary history.[32] Without being fully applicable to philological problems, this line of division notably applies in the cleavage between German historical criticism (*die historische-kritische Ausgabe*) and French genetic criticism. The first one tends to put texts in communication with an unlimited historical material, while the second, less removed from the École de Genève than it will acknowledge, adopts the Saussurian principle of the epistemological break. In other words, unlike historical criticism, genetics does not content itself with tending toward putting history between brackets. It traces insuperable frontiers between literature and non-literature, between texts, their successive states, their preparatory files, the writer's immediate bookish environment (what we know or have kept of his library), on one hand, and, on the other, all the external textuality. One might ask how these theoretical controversies concern the theory of digital critical editions. The most important way is that each of these two orientations can benefit from digital technology to develop their fundamental intention.

There is no doubt that digital technlogy is useful for historicism, where scholars' erudition and need of exhaustiveness now have at their disposal an unlimited intertextual space in which to deploy.[33] As far as textual genetics is concerned, its early interest in hypertextuality and its eagerness to exploit the multi-window system, in the manner of synoptic editions, and to display simultaneous manuscripts and their transcriptions demonstrates its early and clear awareness of the rich future offered by machines and computer screens.[34] But other critical schools, still, are likely to join the movement. Thus, critics who have not been particularly interested until now by editorial practices, and who have been inspired by the Geneva School, could themselves find it to their advantage to use hyperlinks to propose thematic paths that are more or less guided, such as in-depth reading paths for vertical reading, speleological reading, and reading according to the paradigmatic axis of the Ariadne threads that they are talented enough to develop in their essays. In any case, some linguists who are specialized in discourse analysis do not hesitate in predicting the rapid expansion of "digital philology" with applications up to the intratextual research domain.[35]

But independently of the centrifugal stimulations that each one already finds in digital editing to reinforce his differentiation, there is a centripetal evolution that these scholars will have problems eluding. In fact, the book form and the corresponding academic uses seem to oblige a scholarly editor to follow only one method, inasmuch as the book (or the series of volumes) is what identifies him and gives existence to his work, whereas the Internet forms seem to invite grouping, inasmuch as the extent of the surface occupied is the best guarantee for success in the competition for visibility. The previously recalled evolution of HyperNietzsche is significant in this respect: the project, formed within textual genetics, has developed and become a European project only at the expense of an attention expanded way beyond this discipline's ordinary objects. As a general rule, an equilibrium will need to be established between the exhaustiveness norm of the material presented on a philological site or portal and the necessary pluralism of proposed methods and paths that will condition visitors' consulting of diverse horizons and interests.

Let us resist vertigo. For, besides the cumulative effect of the conflict between specialists and schools to be exposed in a unique and single place, the sometimes enormous growth of the total number of researches and annexes liable to be grafted directly onto a work's text will lead even more to a general and growing disproportion, perhaps unbearable eventually, in the ratio of critical apparatus to work. This is the last antinomy we would like to draw attention to, but it is not the least.

As old as criticism itself, a reproach that is usually addressed to editors and exegetes is that they often overburden the text with their commentaries and interpretations, substitute their representation of the text to that of the author, and intervene between the author and reader. Such a reproach applies even more to digital critical edition: one only has to look at the monstrous list of possible components outlined above. Consequently, readers/visitors of critical platforms (let's risk a neologism) should be allowed to go directly to a bare and practically reliable text.

It is impossible at this point not to reaffirm that the philologist's work is to show that this is a naive ideal. The edition of a work, even printed, is never the work itself, even if only by the fact of the typographical recomposition, changes in the material medium (cover, paper, binding, etc.), the particular symbolic status involved in a "scholarly" edition, and the temporal distance between the original work and its scholarly edition. It is obviously a quite different situation to read the *Roman du Graal* on a parchment manuscript and with illuminations in the Middle Ages and to read it today in a paperback format, or to discover *Madame Bovary* in 1857 as a serial in the *Revue de Paris* and to take it up in the twentieth century in the Pléiade collection. The change is at least as noticeable with digitized text, where presentation and graphical choices—one cannot overly insist on this aesthetic issue—have to be recreated. Let's leave aside the austere, minimalist settings of the presentation of *Madame Bovary* on Wikisource: even if this digitization in full text can offer other functionalities and may be more laden with historicity than the image-mode digitization of the Charpentier edition on the site of the Bibliothèque nationale de France, its reading display lacks any attractiveness.[36] How, then, can we not bemoan the chilling austerity, the deterrent complexity, and the technical absurdities (the site being incomprehensible without instructions for use and without a practical initiation) of most of the interfaces of the digital prototypes already referred to? It is true that the printed literature formats, like those of the "series" that have become familiar in the different countries, were not invented in a single day. The major issue at stake with the ongoing experiences is in creating and stabilizing the standards of digitization to provide users with a stable environment so that, when going from one platform to the other, they will not be obliged to have to learn again each time how to use the platform.

Under these conditions is it not philologists' honor to clearly claim their scientific and cultural mission if they do not want to find themselves cloistered and retreated in a paper world? This is a threefold mission. It is still philologists' responsibility to take sides—that is, to provide a coherent version of the text from the standpoint of their knowledge and their criteria.[37] There are no material limits forbidding them to propose several solutions, presented, for example, as entries and distinct paths included in or indicated on a unique portal: each one must be based on an explicit argument, and this should be sufficient. Unless they intend to abuse their scientific authority, twenty-first-century philologists must also explain how they have worked, how the text has been written and edited in its original context—in other words, how it developed and then how it was reedited, altered, or reestablished—and, in the end, and independently of any value judgment, how it has been enhanced by its transmission. Finally, philologists can also be held responsible for the functional and aesthetic quality of the digital framework to which they entrust their work and that results in a new text avatar. To put it plainly, they have to collaborate on the invention of digitized text standards in the same way that their remote ancestors progressively created standards for pagination, tables of contents, and all the display referred to above, for the printed text. It is at the cost of all these tasks that they participate in a kind of continuous creation.

Let us put forth a suggestion to loop the loop: would it not be appropriate to throw a bridge over these thoughts concerning the co- and post-authorial role of the scholarly editor and the various theories that praise the legitimacy and the creativity of copies and variants, even those that are unauthorized, but that leave the last editor, himself often the theorist personified, in a sort of non-reflective blind zone? It is well known that these theories are dominant in the Anglo-Saxon world under the influence of the specific problems of the Shakespearian philology (which has to deal with texts that lack the author's manuscripts but have been staged even during the lifetime of the author, based on more or less re-elaborated copies).[38] They have been intensified in Germanic countries, in particular by Hans Zeller, who considers a text to be the totality of its manifestations and its attested intentions,[39] and by Hans Walter Gabler, who has aroused passionate controversies in reconstructing Joyce's *Ulysses* from his unpublished manuscript rewritings up to making a completely new version, said to be closer to Joyce's intentions than even the one published by Joyce.[40] This most recent modernity is reminiscent of the practice of copyists in antiquity, who allowed themselves interpolations (without feeling the need to point them out) with the commendable aim of providing a better and more complete text. We are only too well aware of that. Will we ever try to rediscover the contemporary meaning of their interpolations after having denounced them for so long as a falsification practice? Taking into account such practices and the provoking pretension to be more Joycian than Joyce at least has the virtue of drawing attention to a certain textual plasticity and to the dynamics of their growth. Would it not be better to try to accompany and guide this process, comparable to that of a snowball that grows as it rolls down the hill, rather than try in vain to stop it? In the general tendency to accumulate and amalgamate the greatest number of illegitimate elements around the original textual kernel, just as in the methodological proliferation generated by the diversity of textual realities, there is plenty to render obsolete the current segregation between critical edition, historical-critical edition, and genetic edition.[41]

Because its material base and technologies legitimize a will to go to the end of an evolution that has been ongoing since the '70s, tomorrow's digital scholarly edition will probably make of this ambition its rule: aim at both a maximum of completeness and a plurality of approaches. We will thus establish a relation of continuity and excellence concerning as much critical editions as complete works such as we know them—each one, finally, very organically tied to printing.[42] In fact, scholarly "platforms" or "infrastructures" already offer a storage capacity and data structuring and management techniques that are so superior to those of books that editors will not indefinitely restrain themselves from imitating books and maintaining themselves in such a framework in order to present and communicate their works. This acknowledgment strongly encourages predicting a philology as hypercritical as it will be hypertextual, respectful, indeed, of history and of the evolution of texts, but up to this ideal stage of not wanting to choose and impose a unique "configuration": a non-dogmatic philology for a boundless textuality.

Notes

1. The experience began in April 2008. On May 26 of the same year, the link remained unobtainable after a ten-minute search, and the first link (http://books.google.fr/books?id=HisCAAAAQAAJ) given by the search engine was now the first volume, a digitization of the copy from the Bodleian Library in Oxford (Comte 1864). On May 28 the Google search engine, having updated its ranking hierarchy, or responding differently to a more specifically formulated query ("Cours de philosophie positive Stanford"), again gave the top ranking to a link pointing to the Stanford copy of the first volume (see Comte 1830b). This time the third volume, identified not by the volume number but only by the publishing date, was ranked in the third position, after volumes 4 and 6. Repeated in 2013, the same experiment yielded different and equally unsatisfactory results: the same seemingly random confusion of volumes and editions made worse by the insertion of opportunistic mentions of reprints. This last expression characterizes the production and diffusion of on-demand digitized reproductions offered by some publishers who think they are smart enough to quickly seize the opportunity to exploit abundant and free-of-charge raw material and, until further notice, benefit via Google from free advertisement. This is but one small example of the current instability and "disorder" in accessing online books as compared nostalgically with the permanence of medieval books, chained to their classification shelves, to the catalogs (even digitized), and to the card files of "real" libraries.

2. Google points to volume 4 (see Comte 1839, link accessed last January 28, 2013).

3. See http://www.evene.fr/livres/livre/auguste-comte-cours-de-philosophie-positive-1893.php. Electronic edition of Auguste Comte, *Cours de philosophie positive* (1re et 2e leçon). Paris: Librairie Larousse, janvier 1936. 108 pages. Collection Classiques Larousse. 12e tirage. Cours de philosophie positive 1re et 2e leçon (1830–1842), downloadable at http://classiques.uqac.ca/classiques/Comte_auguste/cours_philo_positive/cours_philo_positive.html.

4. Special thanks to Catherine Volpilhac-Auger for having drawn our attention to this electronic version of the ARTFL Project: *Dictionnaire de Bayle* and for having communicated the analysis from which we freely borrowed here. See [Bayle] and ARTFL in bibliography.

5. The Éditions Redon CD-ROM and the online database, but with reserved access, of Institut National de la Langue Française (INALF) and ARTFL. See full reference to the ARTFL Encyclopédie Project in the bibliography with URL history.

6. The claim that texts are being denatured by their digital segmentation has a familiar ring in significantly calling to mind the passionate and reactionary hostility expressed in 1911 by the so-called Agathon against the German method of index cards practiced by a famous French literature historian, Gustave Lanson, and at odds, argued his opponent, with the continuity characteristic of the reasoning in French-style essays. (Agathon 1911, 38, qtd. in Espagne 1990, 153).

7. See, for example, Gérard Genette's well-known introductory considerations on "transtextuality" (including what he himself names "hypertext") in *Palimpsestes* (1982).

8. See, for example, the excellent work of Adalbert-Gautier Hamman (1985) that ends precisely with the invention of critical edition norms.

9. Even in France, Roger Chartier, a recognized book and reading historian, is about

the only one. This was precisely the central focus of his inaugural conference held at the Collège de France in 2007, "Écouter les morts avec les yeux" (Listening to the dead with our eyes; see Chartier 2008). This recognition approach, analogously inspired by the historical precedents, is more common outside of France. We have been confirmed in this approach by Christian Vandendorpe (1999) and Peter Shillingsburg (2006).

10. Let us try to specify its typology: other versions or variants, author's notes, those of the first editors, translator's notes, those of the scholarly editor. Among these latter are notes concerning the text, intellectual commentary notes, and historical commentary notes. Without neglecting the references within the notes, limited to their bibliographic description or containing an extract of the referred text (or a link to the complete text if it is available online). And in all cases there is the need to inform the reader of how long he will be distracted from his central object, the reading of the main text. The note accessed can have the dimension of a regular book annotation, or it can be a comment on the size of an article, or it can itself be a text of the same type, if not a complete corpus that invites the reader to make a substantial detour before returning to the main text.

11. See Vandendorpe (1999).

12. The first tryouts and scholarly explorations in France on this subject came from L'Institut des Textes et Manuscrits Modernes (ITEM), pioneered by Jean-Louis Lebrave (see the historical account he provides in Lebrave 1997, 143, in part. n1). See also Lavagnino 1995 about the notion of "hypertext editions." These terms are now superseded by the terms "electronic editions" or "digital editions."

13. In this case, the first and last editions authorized, as published by Furne.

14. See Mozet, undated. In her introduction, Nicole Mozet, the scholarly editor of this "critical online publication," seems to limit her ambitions, using the expression "electronic edition."

15. Because of publishers' reluctance and ongoing unsolved technological problems, e-books do not seem to have yet reached a sufficient maturity to be promising products.

16. See D'Iorio 2000a, 2000b, 2002a, and 2002b.

17. Such projects exist with copyrights.

18. See Lochard and Taurisson 2001. Arcane's leading paper production is the *Correspondance de Pierre Bayle* (see Labrousse and McKenna 1999–2005). For a presentation of the database behind it, see McKenna and Leroux 2003.

19. The endeavor follows directly that of the *The Complete Writings and Pictures of Dante Gabriel Rossetti: A Hypermedia Archive* (McGann 1992). Stauffer 1998 describes how the Rossetti Archive was tagged.

20. The production conditions, the innovations, and the contents of the online William Blake Archive are analyzed by Aurélia Chossegros (2007).

21. See, for example, Berne 2005. This book accompanied by a DVD was published for the "Sartre" exhibition, presented by the Bibliothèque nationale de France (BnF), Paris, from March 9 to August 21, 2005. It was also, at the same time, published online as part of a *Sartre* virtual exposition accessible at the BnF (see full reference in the bibliography under the title *Sartre*). We do not know of any other instance of the use of the three media.

22. This is what is about to be finalized in support of the online publication of *L'Écho de la Fabrique* and *Les Journaux d'Alexandre Dumas* (see references in the bibliography),

the Lyon teams directed by Ludovic Frobert and by Sarah Mombert, respectively. See more treatment of these online editions in chapter 8.

23. More about the symptoms of this fear can be found in, among others, Le Men 2002.

24. This edition is referred to later in this book.

25. For a description of this project, see Girard, Leclerc et al. 2004–2008.

26. Maybe this version will be available online when this book comes out.

27. For a historical anthropology of philology, see Espagne 1998.

28. L'Institut des Textes et Manuscrits Modernes (ITEM), http://www.item.ens.fr. See Grésillon 1994, 205ff.

29. See Cerquiglini 1983 [English translation 1989a] and Nichols 1990b.

30. The novelty of this online edition is not absolute and follows the facsimile published by Albert Pauphilet in 1923.

31. Regarding this school of literary criticism inaugurated and named by Georges Poulet, and that cannot be reduced, of course, to the "formalist immanentism" that his friend Marcel Raymond himself criticized, see Jeanneret 1995 (part. 59).

32. Peter Shillingsburg (2006, 60), wiser from his experience as editor of Thackeray, comes to the same conclusion regarding Anglo-American criticism.

33. See Ricklefs 1999, 1ff.

34. See Lebrave 1997, 143n.38, and Grésillon 1994, 199n.53.

35. See Viprey 2005.

36. See full links to the online Wikisource and Gallica editions in the bibliography.

37. On this point, as for many others, we share Peter Shillingsburg's views, for whom it would be inconceivable that a digital edition would be limited to giving access to the different editions of a text and refrains from being a critical edition in the proper meaning (2006, 156).

38. The last and most meaningful theorization in the United States, since the '60s, is the concept of eclectic text developed by Fredson Bowers and those following him. For a basic view of the evolutions and tendencies of Anglo-American philology, see the article "Textual Criticism" updated on May 15, 2008, in Wikipedia, and the skeptical souvenirs of Peter Shillingsburg (2006, 152f).

39. See Zeller 1975.

40. See Gabler 1993 and 1995.

41. Antoine Compagnon expressed this idea as early as the '90s: "everywhere, the role of the computer is perhaps rendering obsolete the distinction between critical edition and genetic edition" (Introduction to the colloquium on genetic criticism organized by Almuth Grésillon at Columbia University, New York in 1994 [see Compagnon 1995, 400]). See also Grésillon 1995.

42. See Sgard and Volpilhac-Auger 1999.

3. The Digital Fate of the Critical Apparatus

DANIEL APOLLON AND CLAIRE BÉLISLE

The adoption of digital technologies has upset our relationship to texts and confronts us with the long history of critical edition underlying this relationship. The advent of the printing press had already put an end to the erratic fluctuation of texts that were subject to the hazards of physical or mechanical hand-copying. Many medieval manuscripts are assorted with maledictions issued by the author or the scribe against future counterfeiters, threatening them with leprosy or burning in hell. These curses illustrate well how the old scribal culture based its conception of the intrinsic uniqueness of the text on prescriptions and prohibitions inherited from religious, popular, and legal traditions. Text was to acquire its reproducible identity with manufacturing, although this is a later phenomenon. With the development of printing technology and the improvement of the organization techniques of distribution, new horizons were opened up.

Printing, making mechanical reproduction possible, offered the prospect of a more durable, even permanent transmission of works and, eventually, a greater stability of texts. The increased mechanical reproducibility of works contributed to reinforce, industrialize, and modify a much older conception of the uniqueness of texts. Within a few centuries, a new form of "textual positivism" emerged and brought together traditional philology, scientific positivism, and historicism, thus consolidating representations of the uniqueness of texts based on rights of ownership and privileges in order to exploit works. Gradually, privileges—sometimes revocable, sometimes irrevocable—were granted to printers, publishers, or authors and acquired a specific legal dimension. The ruling power guaranteed the uniqueness of the work, imposing various restrictions on how the text could be reproduced. The printer and, gradually, the author would obtain a letter of privilege, provided they enjoyed some higher protection. Later on, accepting that the authenticity of the text builds upon a faithful reproduction of the author's intentions became a common belief. Despite the progressive installation of the author in his or her work (limpidly described by Cerquiglini 1989a, 25, quoting Michel Foucault; see also Cerquiglini 1989a, 57ff), this form of textual positivism, equating textual identity with the inertia and fixedness of the inscription as a token of the ownership of the author, hid a more complex empirical reality characterized by a greater fluctuation and instability of texts and their transmission. The distinction made by the critical editor between scribal and authorial variants (Cerquiglini 1989a, 119) became all the more important.

The fact that digital tools propel us into a state of greater editorial fluctuation should be no surprise. This age-old fluctuation, being an inherent characteristic of the transmission of ancient texts antedating print technology, imposes itself today as the norm of digital writing. Such a generalized textual variability in the digital era is neither accident nor fate. It reflects both how easily modifications and updates can be produced in a digital environment and how knowledge increasingly can be shared by various means of collaboration. It is within this new context that when migrating to digital medium, critical editions of texts and documents have been forced to redefine their ambitions about textual truth, scholarship, and sharing. This chapter outlines the contours of the scholarly project and the ambitions of such critical editions as they begin to take shape in contemporary digital media.

Although textual variation is an interesting phenomenon by itself, it also reflects a human dimension within culture.[1] This is why each scholar who establishes a critical edition operates with a set of presuppositions or assumptions that are bundled with the work they have interpreted. Hence, one can speak of the epistemic program of a scholarly community being implemented by the author of a critical edition. Such a program reveals itself through the scholar's intention to apply it knowingly to a documentary mass. While texts undoubtedly still function as social organizers, especially in legal and commercial matters, visions about the transparency of the text are no longer a matter of scholarly interest. By denying traditional philology any significance for critical and cultural studies, various postwar academic and cultural currents have given this shift needed legitimacy. Accordingly, the above-mentioned textual positivism, which is rather naive in many respects but also quite useful as a social bond in other respects (see Lucien Febvre's remarks as quoted in the opening pages of Cerquiglini 1983), is being ever more relegated to a few increasingly marginalized disciplines (classical studies, romance philology, biblical exegesis, and textual criticism). Scholarly edition today is characterized by a diversity of hardly matching textual visions that link the production of meaning in a work, sometimes to the author's intentions, sometimes to a functional relationship between the text and its sociocultural environment, and sometimes to the tension between the work and the expectation of the readers. Not only does variability affect texts and their transmission, but it also affects textual epistemologies.

From the perspective of traditional philology, synchronic and diachronic textual variation may occasionally be considered as an enriching factor. More frequently it is considered a shameful decadence, a degradation of the text subject to losses, scribal errors, mixtures of variants, and contamination. The result is the dramaturgy of the reconstruction of the work's uniqueness corrupted by time or by unlucky scribes. Time, the scribe's hand, counterfeiting, shameful compressions, and expansions of a much-sought-for original text act as antagonists the critical editor needs to oppose using a toolbox of methods, or, if necessary, calling upon his "taste." Driven by the perspective of loss and regeneration, critical editing aims to restore the initial state of the text. The genealogic approach dominates philology in the nineteenth century and the first half of the twentieth century and is applied to diverse antique, religious, and medieval works (see Roques 1995). However, all of these often gigantesque efforts require an almost inhuman minuteness, resulting frequently in failures, according to Birger Munk-Olsen:

> The edition of a text is double-sided. On one side, there is an exciting task which involves studying manuscripts, penetrating the language and thought of the author, establishing the text by means of ingenious conjectures or by selecting wisely between the variant readings offered by the different text witnesses. On the other side, when the text is long and the manuscripts numerous, there is a fastidious task made of pure routine be carried out, collating textual versions and untangling among a myriad of variants the genealogical links between manuscripts. Sometimes, the scholar has to devote an entire life to this task. Hence, the results are often disappointing: editions with a text and critical apparatus full of mistakes and imprecision's, uncompleted editions due to the death or exhaustion of the editor, announced editions never published because some philologists, initially enthusiastic, underestimated the extent and the difficulty of the undertaking. (1969, 94)

It is understandable that from a utilitarian and instrumental perspective, automatic processing of philological material may offer fresh opportunities to delegate demanding and human-resource-intensive tasks to computers (e.g., collating variant readings, aligning parallel text witnesses). It should be emphasized, however, that such expectations about computerizing textual criticism do not actually challenge the epistemological status of critical edition, which may be conceived of as a pure genealogical reconstruction (or, later, under the auspices of the French school of textual genetics, as retracing the authorial process through the avant-texte, see Biasi 1996; Deppman, Ferrer, et al. 2004). Likewise, the early efforts of Dom Jacques Froger are steered by the logics of genealogical reconstruction and show parallels with the introduction of computational methods in reconstruction of biological evolution (e.g., using cladistics to infer phylogenies; see Felsenstein 2004). Strong expectations were encouraged by the prospects of ever-increasing computing power during this pioneering period of computer-assisted textual criticism shortly before the emergence of the personal desktop computer and, about a decade later, the Internet. These expectations, displaying affinities sometimes with Karl Lachmann, sometimes with Joseph Bédier, are still central in contemporary projects (e.g., the Canterbury Tales Project, directed by Peter Robinson since 1998).

Yet every philological project, in addition to having empirical interests, implicitly or explicitly includes a hermeneutical, even philosophical or cosmological dimension. This profoundly affects the status of the text that is considered as the object of critical edition. After the Second World War, the conjugated effect of several literary and academic currents, mutually opposing and ignoring one another but agreeing to reject genealogical philology, succeeded in relegating traditional philology to niche disciplines such as classical, biblical, and medieval studies. The French Nouvelle Critique; the Anglo-Saxon New Criticism; and the combined impact of the works of critics such as Michel Foucault, Jacques Derrida, Roland Barthes ("any text is eternally written here and now. [. . .] The birth of the reader must be paid by the death of the Author" [1984; our translation]), to name only a few emblematic figures of these currents, contributed to throw suspicion on every attempt to link the work and its texts to a unique prototype. Bernard Cerquiglini (2000) stresses the opposition between the new and the old philology: "Thus, despite the magnificence of its positive knowledge, and its occasional refinement, old philology appears to be linked with an outdated episteme, being anachronistic in its approach [to medieval concepts], and has probably little relevance as a method for editing" (note the diverse criticism of this position in Busby 1993a, 1993b, and Dembowski 1996).

One may observe nowadays that both the general public and departments of literary studies in universities have abandoned demands for original textual truth. Scholars and publishers have forsaken "authoritative text" in favor of variations, derivations, detours, and the wealth of unforeseeable connotations. As a consequence, the context of interpretation and the intentions and expectations of readers have received increased attention. This shift reflects the opposing paradigms of old and new philology (we reproduce quite freely below the comparative table from Cerquiglini 2000):

Textual authority (traditional, authorial etc.) vs. textual sharing
Printing technology (books) vs. Internet (hypertext)
Textual genesis seen as a hierarchical tree vs. textual genesis seen as a network
    or rhizome of various elements
The author vs. the disseminator or the reader

Uniqueness, authority vs. variation, expansion
Contempt for copies and praise of the original vs. positive reception
Verbal essence vs. materiality and usage
Decontextualization vs. contextualization and recontextualization
Reconstruction and conjecture vs. deconstruction, simulation and derivation
Autarchy, uniqueness vs. comparison, family resemblance
Writing seen as oral residue and trace vs. synergy between oral and written
Unique signification vs. overflow of sense
Entireness and closure vs. fragmentation, disintegration and reintegration
  of the text

Whichever theoretical approach is chosen by a scholarly publisher or critic—traditional, contextual, or oriented toward reception—any philological project possesses an instrumental and material dimension, being conditioned by practical constraints. In the same way as the textual production tools partly determine the shape of the work, the modes of organization and of technical reproduction, adopted or imposed, define the contours of a critical edition. Since any literacy can be considered as a particular intellectual technology (see Goody n.d., 1986; Goody and Watt 1963; Olson 1994; Olson and Cole 2006; and Ong 1986, 1997, 2002), then, any critical apparatus can be conceived of as the material and technological expression of a given philological project. As such it may reveal the positions taken by scholars and publishers relative to the various dimensions described above.

Finally, it is generally admitted these days that reading and understanding a text is partly a result of how the reader himself represents this text and how he thinks signification emerges. As a consequence, even a critical edition that builds upon the norms of old philology should take into account the intended or, at least, expected reader. As a matter of fact, critical edition on print could easily identify a scholar's potential readership as being his peers, limited numerically to a few researchers in the same domain with the addition of his students. This is no longer possible when dealing with online digital critical editions. In this case, not only does the potential readership escape any assignment to disciplinary boundaries, but, in addition, the diversity of possible presentations available to scholars induce them to target a readership composed of individuals possessing very diversified competencies and exhibiting various levels of proficiency.

This chapter, after addressing some conceptual landmarks, raises questions about three key aspects of critical editions:

1. Questions pertaining to the targeted public: for whom are critical editions produced nowadays?
2. Questions pertaining to the critical apparatus: how much of an editor's reflection and criticism does he or she share with the readers?

3. Questions pertaining to the digital medium: how does the digital medium influence the implementation of a critical edition?

Conceptual Landmarks

A walk through the different sections of a university library usually suffices for discovering a diversity of scholarly editions. While paging through these works, the reader may experience an impressive editorial landscape of techniques and layouts, being able to distinguish at first glance if she is holding a "critical," "scholarly," or "learned" edition.

"Critical," "Scholarly," or "Learned" Editions

Although these three terms are not completely synonymous, in order to simplify terminology in these pages, we intend to use the term "critical edition" to refer to a whole spectrum of editions of texts, documents, and collections that offer well-defined and structured information relating to a clearly identified content. Thus such a definition accepts both those editions that concentrate on producing commentaries and notes as well as computer-based resources that exploit databases and complex text markup. The term "critical edition" is preferred to the term "philology," which belongs more to linguistics and textual stemmatics. "Critical edition," then, refers to the specific study of texts with the intention to secure their transmission as faithfully, authentically, and completely as possible, including information about the processes that have made it possible to establish the selected and published text. By extension, "critical edition" can refer to efforts to establish (or restore) the possibility of interpreting a work as closely as possible to the intentions of the author (traditional version), to its immediate context (historicizing version), or to its uses during transmission through time and space. More recently "genetic critical editions" have taken their distance from the "final" text (e.g., the *editio princeps*) in order to document the diverse phases, items, traces, and residues left by the authorial process (this process is summarized by the term "avant-texte"; see Lebrave 1997, 2006).

Using different presentation methods, these various editorial products express a shared effort to provide readers with tools that may be used not only to help them to refine their judgment on the authenticity and the genesis of texts, document, and contents but also, quite simply, to help them to evolve a broader and deeper understanding of the roots and environment of the text, thereby opening reading to new horizons. More prosaically, a critical edition is traditionally thought to comply with an editorial standard that adds to the established text information on significant variants and provides a critical apparatus that may also include explanatory notes. To continue simplifying terminology, the term "text" here refers to the primary object of critical editions. The reader of these pages should feel free to use as a substitute to this term others such as "documents," "items," "images," or any other convention that may be more relevant in a given context. The secondary object of critical editions covers all kinds of formal or discursive metadescriptions that point to the text.

The problem that critical editions need to solve are various, depending on whether the original documents are papyrus rolls, codices, paper books, or inscriptions on diverse materials, facsimiles, photographic pictures, or more recent digital texts. When a document can exist only as a single item or as a few copies with important or minimal variants, the challenge resides in producing the most authentic edition that communicates the initial meaning of the text or document. As one may guess, each of the following elements—the established text, the significant variants, and the initial meaning—reflects editorial and even epistemological choices, pointing to what is a text, what is the meaning of a text, and what is reading a text.

Accordingly, the term "critical edition" may refer as well to learned editions targeting a general public of informed readers (e.g., *La Pléiade* in France). It can also refer to a comprehensive scholarly edition intended to provide a community of scholars with a state-of-the-art text-critical platform (e.g., the Stuttgartiensa edition of the Hebrew Bible). The distinction is between *minimalist products,* which provide the reader with very few but supposedly crucial clues on the history, interpretation, or historical context of the published text, and *maximalist products*, in which the amount and complexity of information coded and stored about the text exceeds by far the text's own magnitude (see Brossaud and Reber 2006).

Éditions, Éditeurs, *and* Publication

Each language, through its vocabulary, operates with a particular semantic mapping, which may sometimes generate areas of confusion for translators. Possible confusion may arise about which roles are being referred to when using the French terms *éditions*, *éditeur*, and *publication*. For example, the distinction introduced in English when using two different words—"editor," referring to the expert establishing the text to be published as authoritative, and "publisher," designating the person or commercial company responsible for producing and distributing the work of the editor—has no counterpart in the French term *éditeur*. In French *éditeur* is a term that needs to be completed in order to remove all ambiguity and make it possible to make a distinction between the specific editorial work that aims to establish the text and the production of material artifacts (see Catach 1988a, 22ff; see also 1988b). Similar precautions are needed to understand the distinction made in various languages between, for example, in French, *éditeur* (e.g., scholarly editor) and *rédacteur* (technical editor); in Norwegian, *redaktør* (scientific or technical editor) and *utgiver* (publisher); and in German, *Herausgeber* (scientific editor), *Redaktor* (usually some copyist in the early history of the text), and *Verleger* (publisher).

A wise solution is to focus on the roles and functions underlying the various uses of the terms *éditeur* and *édition*. Moreover, the French term *publication* may be defined as being both "the action consisting in making public, letting everybody know" and "the result of this action" (ATILF, laboratoire CNRS Analyse et Traitement Informatique de la Langue Française). One finds in this double definition the overlapping of the two functions and the two roles identified by Christine Ducourtieux (2004) as a key characteristic of electronic edition: "The work of the scholarly editor and the follow-up of the commercial publisher with the aim of formatting the product are both at the core of the definition of edition: author, composer, printer, etc. the editorial chain is taking shape" (our translation).

Digital environments upset this editorial chain: the scholarly editor has the possibility to become also the online publisher, making his editorial work public. Therefore, in this chapter we apply the words "to edit," "editor," and "edition" to all the processes that are implemented, stretching from the establishment of the text to online publishing. Moreover, the term "editor" can be interpreted literally, as a flesh-and-blood person, or sociologically, as an organization or institution, such as a particular academic school of thought or community of practice that actually produces and possibly documents the set of decisions, which contribute to the establishment of the text.

We use the term "edition" here to describe all kinds of distributable materializations of a work on any medium acknowledged by the reader, whether it is a codex, a printed book, or a computer file. Editions can even point beyond these well-known mediums and refer to less easily recognizable collections of online artifacts—for example, a unique dynamic presentation of a special perspective on the text produced for me here and now.

Critical editors establish the texts they edit by adding different types of information. These editors use critical apparatus to display this mass of information with various purposes, according to different traditions, presuppositions, and targeted readership. One may identify four characteristics shared by such editors:

- Critical editors are operating within an articulated or reasonably consistent epistemological horizon.
- Critical editors exploit know-how or techniques based on restricted or shared knowledge that justifies the decisions applied to texts.
- Critical editors implement a set of procedures that produce and document these decisions.

- Finally, critical editors exploit a toolbox of conventions, symbols, and spatial arrangements that offer the possibility to mark, independently of the texts, the traces of editorial decisions, thus allowing their readers to assess and exploit for their own objectives the editorial process that has been applied to the texts.

Because the field of electronic edition is in its very beginning, and is witnessing frequent and important innovations, the characteristics listed above may prove to be useful indicators.

Readers and Readership

The reader of a critical edition constitutes also a little researched evolutionary phenomenon. We will use the terms "reader" and "readership" to describe the public targeted by the editor, knowing well that for the time being the primary public of online critical editions is mostly composed of students and peers. However, an editor may have discovered that online publishing actually may open his or her work to a new and previously unknown readership with different requirements not only for presentation and complementary information but also for the type of content offered. Accordingly, it is not unthinkable that these new readers may have new demands for gaining access to the collation process, emendations, and even updates of the texts. Just as textual genetics has made an alternative and interesting exploration of the writing process, gaining access to editorial processes could allow readers to rediscover the social factors that condition the shape of texts, their historical evolution, and their epistemological function.

Analogous to the previous definition of the term "editor," it is possible to think of the reader as being either a real person with a targeted competence, a hypothetical reader who has not yet materialized, or part of a general readership—that is, any user of the text. Moreover, "reader" may have a more metaphorical reference, such as to search engines or any algorithm exploring texts. In this twilight zone, the editor, the reader, and the "processing agent" may merge into a unique role.

Textual Variation as an Ongoing Challenge

Variation is the basis of the need for all types of critical editing. How the variations are considered and processed depends on the objectives aimed at by each critical editor. The very notion of critical edition is irrevocably bound to the need to map, codify, and assess the potentially unbounded variations of such elements that are deemed to constitute a text, collection, or hypothetical "family" of documents.

Fundamentally, from the perspectives of the editor, the publisher, and the analyst, a text may be viewed as a collection of items, which may vary considerably or modestly in time and place. The variational perspective applies to all kinds of text, documents, and heterogeneous collections. It applies equally to ancient texts, such as the *Odyssey*, the *Gilgamesh Epos*, biblical accounts, or Nordic Sagas, and recent texts, such as novels, electronic literature, blogs, or press material. To complicate matters, variation applies to the genesis of reasonably homogeneous products such as modern novels as it does to short-lived collections of heterogeneous items, as is increasingly the case in cyberspace these days.

The awareness that texts, documents, works, or collections, like any other human artifacts, do vary in time, space, and memories constitutes a fundamental insight from which one may derive a rich set of theoretical perspectives, editorial practices, and techniques. The use of varying concepts like "the *text* of Plato," "the *works* of Ibsen," or even the "Song *of Roland,*" or any related expression, can lead to various degrees of imprecision. Most readers and users may not perceive such imprecision to be a pressing matter, except when fundamental doubts arise as to the authenticity of, say, a document or a novel. Public debates on the authenticity of a document—for instance, the debate on the false diaries of Adolph Hitler or controversies on the Essenian origin of the Dead Sea Scrolls—may catch the attention of many readers, while other types of content may evade such scrutiny. Meanwhile, specialized and systematic interest in textual variation as a primary object of study (e.g., for establishing an authoritative text of Montesquieu) or as a means to highlight more general issues (e.g., to gain access to the authorial activity of Flaubert or Ibsen) remains predominantly the academic focus of a small group of experts and the concern of a minority of publishers and editors, nowadays as ever before.

It may be convenient at this point to stress that the awareness of textual variation does not remain confined to a particular school of textual critics or scholarly editors. Assumptions about variation seem to underlie nearly all flavors of textual criticism. Variation as a research theme and editorial challenge does indeed cover the whole spectrum of schools from classical text criticism as we know it from the nineteenth century to more recent attempts to break partially or totally loose from the straitjacket of philology. The decisive turn away from philology happened with the rebuttal of author-bound interpretation as witnessed, for example, since the interwar period by the Anglo-Saxon New Criticism and, after the war, the French Nouvelle Critique. Thus, the huge postwar effort to shift focus from the material text, to the authorial activity, to various intertextualities (Kristeva 1969) or dimensions of transtextuality (Genette 1982) does not do away with textual variation, but expands it, reappraises it, and recontextualizes it. The differences, say, between classical genealogical text criticism (Lachmann, Paris, Maas, Bédier, and others), more recent brands of textual genetics (Ferrer, Lebrave, Pichler, Gabler,[2] and others) and textual ecology (e.g., collections situated in their contemporary historical or cultural environment) do not reside in the acceptance or rejection of variation itself but compete on variational aspects that are thought to be productive. Even the most sociological approaches, such as Gustave Lanson's notion of close reading (French: *explication de texte*) and, more recently, even socio-criticism (French: *la sociocritique*) (Angenot and Robin 1985; Markaryk 1993a, 1993b), are not throwing variation overboard but concentrate on reintegrating the "work" into a wider social discourse. It is therefore no surprise that most if not all postwar approaches to textual and literary criticism happen to nourish a fundamental disinterest for, say, reconstructing text from ancient manuscripts and actively endeavor to replace what they think is retrograde intellectual fixation with fresh analyses of literature as products of social or other interaction. As a consequence of the new intellectual climate in literary studies, the gap between "critical studies" and "critical edition" is wider than ever.

Textual States

Any kind of textual analysis or critical editorial activity refers explicitly or implicitly to one or more states of the text. However, opposing views of textual states compete to express the theoretical tensions described above. The first approach, as defended by textual genetics, privileges the various states of the avant-texte and the emerging text as witnessed during the writing process, while the states of the text created after the first published editions are not taken into account (see Lebrave 1997; Lebrave and Grésillon 2009). The second approach, being rigorously genealogical, privileges the concern of the textual critic and scholarly editor who possess nothing but "after-texts" to identify and authenticate a hypothetical prototypical "text" by exploiting and filtering, where it is deemed feasible, the various witnesses attesting this text. The third approach regroups critical schools, occasionally defending incompatible positions, for which the state of the text refers to a functional relationship linking the diverse linguistic, graphical, discursive, and other components of a text with the socio-historical, economical, or psychological environment that conditions it. Hence, text is bound by its inseparable coupling with its environment. There exists no text without its environment, and no genuinely critical activity may occur without taking into account diverse dimensions of trans-textuality (Genette 1982). It is the environment that produces successive textual states. Thus the term "textual states" tends to cover the diverse shapes, modes of expression, and evolution of trans-textualities.

Textual Criticism and "Critical Editions"

The three approaches outlined very briefly in the last section allow us to apply the notion of textual criticism and critical edition not only to supposedly homogeneous texts (for example, Balzac's novels, Ibsen's *Peer Gynt*, the *Song of Roland*) but also to collections of texts, pictures, sounds, and diverse items that may express the heterogeneous nature of the documents that constitute the work. The online archives of the double work of Dante Gabriel Rossetti aggregate texts, drawings, and paintings, juxtaposing several layers of collations and interpretation, an operation that would have been difficult to carry out on paper. In the online Rossetti Archive, priority is given to the intertextual and trans-textual dimensions. It is precisely in this domain that digital tools make it possible to innovate more radically, not only allowing one to escape from the material constraints of print technology and from the boundaries of the book page but also opening new horizons for more eclectic projects that offer the possibility to "tag texts in several dimensions" (McGann 2004). Woolf Online, a pioneer of its kind, publishes a multilayer online edition that associates a genetic edition of Virginia Woolf's novel *Time Passes* with a comprehensive virtual contextual space. The major avant-texte of Woolf, the "Initial Holograph Draft," is presented using various aligned and synchronized synoptic layouts, allowing the reader to follow the evolution of Virginia Woolf's writing process step-by-step. This avant-texte, being linked structurally to the "text" of the first printed editions of the novel, is associated item by item with a vast contextual space that covers the sociohistorical dimension (newspaper pages, film news, radio programs, testimonies from friends and public figures, history of the strikes mentioned in the novel), geography, and biography (private journals, letters, and photographs).

These two instances of an online critical edition illustrate briefly how digital tools make it possible to bring textual criticism and critical editions out of their strong isolation. Paradoxically, digital tools already enable one to combine diverse visions, treatments of the states of the text, and methodologies that were difficult to bring together in the age of printed editions. It is perfectly possible today, as already demonstrated by Woolf Online, to associate a clearly philological edition, in all accepted meanings of the term, with other layers that map contextual, intertextual, and hermeneutical dimensions. Already in 1984, well before the appearance of the first online critical editions, Nina Catach (Catach 1988a) exploited the findings of a survey to provide an inventory of the multivalent use of the terminology of critical editions (e.g., "variant," "text edition," "editor"), exploring their underlying presuppositions and disparate treatment in order to defend the hypothesis of the multiplicity of critical edition. Digital tools nowadays enable one to make explicit such multiplicity that remained hidden in hard-to-document former practices. We may be back in a situation that resembles diverse forms of learned commentaries that were in vogue long before historical positivism, mentioned in the beginning of this chapter, appeared on the scene.

For Whom Are Critical Editions Made Today?

The important amount of work required to produce a critical edition suggests that its public should be of equal importance. As a matter of fact, the readership of a critical edition depends on the editor's ambition for his or her work. Since the nineteenth century, critical editions have been produced primarily for the peers of the editor, such as philological experts or experts in a particular domain. This is probably the reason why critical editions of today that conform to traditional standards still rely on a system of competencies with a rather restricted vision of their public, considering any critical reader as a being a quasi clone of the editor. However, in addition to this rigorous conception of the editor's work, other less positivistic and more ecological types of critical editions appear that demonstrate a greater concern for describing the text in its phases of production, reproduction, or reception.

Critical editions are traditionally written and presented using an allusive and hermetic style. Reading such works with ease requires much practice of this form of writing and reading. Such a selective academic approach could be justified in the past when one considers that texts printed on paper used to enter a long life cycle and became reference materials, which publishers used to produce editions stripped of their notes. Such editions were relatively easy to access for a larger public of readers, for whom the proposed text appeared as a unique text that was handed down from the identified author. Only learned people and scholars reading these texts were likely to realize that certain parts of the texts were the result of conjectures, philological investigations, and, sometimes, tough discussions between experts.

The problem that today's online critical editors have to solve is to find the means to undertake a more complex research enterprise while producing modular presentations adapted to various publics. As a matter of fact, thanks to the fact that computer-based research tools for collection, analysis, and comparison are much more powerful and rapid than the handwork of research in book libraries, a researcher today can quickly acquire knowledge on the content of texts, their organization, and chronology, having constant access to a wealth of contextual geographical, historical, linguistic, and cultural information. Not only can the researcher produce richer and more exhaustive results, but she can also exploit a whole toolbox in order to communicate these results to various audiences. Being freed from the limits imposed by the area of the printed page, the researcher can now give wings to her imagination, inventing new reading paths adapted to the types of readers who are targeted.

However, one must admit that researchers who produce critical editions today still primarily target their own peers. This implies that critical editors preferably take into account very specific practices and expectations. Hence, a survey carried out as part of the Public Knowledge Project and presented at the 2008 International Digital Humanities Conference by Caroline Leitch, Ray Siemens, and their colleagues (Leitch and Siemens 2008, 145–46) produced evidence of a diversity of sophisticated reading strategies among learned readers.[3] The results of this study showed that learned readers tended to valorize online tools, which complemented and augmented reading strategies that were already practiced by these readers (see the detailed report of the initial study by Siemens, Willinsky, et al. 2006, followed by Siemens, Leitch, et al. 2009, and more recently Siemens, Timney, et al. 2012a and 2012b). The predominance of peers in the targeted readership can be explained in part by academic challenges and by the institutional setting that conditions this kind of work. In order to establish a text, to produce an edition containing a varied and well-justified critical apparatus, one needs to invest much time and expertise.

Hence, it is normal that a scholar seeks to draw personal benefit by drawing on the impact of the publication on the same public that evaluates and allows him to advance professionally. In other words, for a whole generation of university scholars who had been gaining access to knowledge primarily by means of printed books, what most greatly signifies the scientific and academic value of a peer is being the author of such a visible monument of science as a paperbound critical edition. A number of critical editions are available online, but the editor who addresses mainly his peers keeps a presentation very close to print. Such is the case of, for example, critical text editions like the *Piers Plowman* Electronic Archive and SEENET (Society for Early English and Norse Electronic Texts),[4] whose editors already in 1995 wanted to react against the invasion of electronic editions of low quality and to "combine exploitation of the full capacities of computer technology with preservation of the highest standards of traditional scholarly editing. We want not only to publish reliable machine-readable texts but we want them accompanied with highly competent introductory materials, glossaries, annotations, and apparatus. We want our texts to bear all of the virtues of traditional print editions and at the same time to begin to create the new kinds of text enabled by computer technology" (Duggan 1994).

Another example is the Canterbury Tales Project, presented at length by Elisabeth Lalou (2004). According to her, the authors of the project want to produce "a truly scholarly edition which uses all the advantages offered by electronic edition" using the renowned text of Geoffrey Chaucer "preserved in not less than 82 manuscripts and four editions from the fifteenth century." This

CD-ROM edition is produced by seven different authors using different sources. Such critical editions comply with strict standards for academic excellence that are enumerated as part of the short presentation of the criteria for a scholarly edition on the site of the Centre for Textual Studies at De Montfort University. More detailed recommendations, emphasizing the practice of text markup, have been formulated by Dino Buzzetti and Jerome McGann (2006).

At first glance, even if one partly drops the requirements that were mentioned in the recommendations cited above, it may be difficult to imagine how this type of publication could possibly correspond to the practices and expectations of any public—that is, any person who is interested in documents that belong to a literary or cultural heritage. Yet it is this last hypothesis that underlies the establishment of electronic libraries and the vast human efforts deployed since the beginning of the 1990s. The aim is to gradually give any Internet user access to the whole literary and cultural production of the humanities, adding, when possible, information allowing non-scholars to reconstitute texts and to gain access to information needed in order to analyze the meaning of a text or document.

Some online editions do not define themselves as being "critical editions" or "scholarly editions" and are presented as targeting the largest possible public. That is the case of the Tout Molière site, where it is written: "This site, conceived in a spirit of scientific rigor, targets a large public: students in universities or high schools who are looking for information relative to Molière; curious readers, theatre enthusiasts who are interested in our playwright, and scholars who will find here a number of useful tools for their work" (Tout Molière; our translation).

Generally, one can think that the presentation of a critical edition overestimates the time that the reader needs to understand and follow a line of thought. The critical editor, mastering a lot of information, usually wishes to enlighten the reader by helping him to get into the complexities of the interpretation of the text. Therefore it will be difficult for the editor to accept that the reader derives a meaning using the sole words that are present in front of his eyes. As a consequence, the specialist will find it necessary to provide the reader with contextual, historical, and academic pieces of information that will help him to go into the "deep," real, and exhaustive meaning of the text. This attitude mirrors the suspicion against letting "profane" interpreters, "non-scholars," use texts that a scholar has spent weeks, even years, to decrypt and establish. Still, it is difficult to decide whether such assistance is indispensable when many items of information are linked with a text, or if it is simply a strategy designed to distinguish oneself, thus allowing the specialist's erudition and the excellence of his work acknowledged among his peers.

The generalized distribution of an increasing amount of information, an activity that in earlier days was believed to require special training, is taking place today, more democratically, as "web publishing." This situation forces one to think of critical editions not only as monuments that are accessible to a few insiders but also as cultural challenges to be shared. Several authors have begun to take on this challenge, as evident in the nonexhaustive list that follows: Woolf Online; the Rossetti Archive; the integral printed and electronic edition of Henrik Ibsen's Writings; African-American Women Writers of the 19th Century; Decameron Web; Le Cartulaire Blanc of the Abbey of Saint-Denis; eMunch, an electronic archive of Edvard Munch's written material; Biblioteca Virtual Miguel Cervantes; the Perseus Project; the Sternberg Project; and the World of Dante.

The Critical Apparatus

The critical apparatus can be identified as the typical visible characteristic of a critical edition. It is therefore important to try to define what is meant by this term, not necessarily with the intention of establishing some canonical standards, but rather in order to map its multiple meanings and uses, while searching to identify some core aspect of the critical work around which the critical apparatus of the scholar is defined and built. The critical apparatus, having the double function of demonstrating the erudition and seriousness of the scholar and of helping the reader to understand and appreciate the text or the document that is presented, offers a codified system of layered competencies that link the competence of the editor to the competence of the reader. As such, the critical apparatus may be an unavoidable device if one wishes to place oneself within the framework of critical editions and a philological perspective.

So where does the authority of a text and the trust placed in it come from? Accessing all kinds of texts on the Internet has brought (again?) into the open the age-old problem of the trustworthiness of texts, of the criteria needed to assess the value, authenticity, and validity of any text presented on a medium. Already, Wikipedia, an ongoing collaborative encyclopedia, has clearly highlighted the problem of the relationship between disseminated knowledge and source knowledge. While, on one hand, critical editions pursuing a genealogical ambition require a knowledge process that involves backtracking information in order to restore truth, on the other hand, collaborative writing of information on the Internet envisions textual truth as a goal that needs to be reached by means of a number of contributions and shared emendations. For example, the freely readable "View history" tab version of Wikipedia articles can be thought of as a rather unique historical case of collaborative critical apparatus in that it allows the readers of Wikipedia to follow the traces left by a text in perpetual evolution. In addition, the same readers can contribute to the elaboration of the text. Is the trustworthiness of texts a product of the positivity of their content, of the controlled establishment of the text, of their interpretation as a production of meaning, or as an emergence from the successive approximations of collaborative work? As a consequence, the role played by the critical apparatus in the production of textual meaning points to an epistemological position.

Before presenting the critical apparatus in depth, it may be important to identify the main visions of critical edition and philology that one may invoke.

The Critical Apparatus and the History of Scholarly Editing

A critical apparatus is always the result of the concrete activity of text experts or specialists who also inherit the institutional, epistemological, and technological constraints and possibilities of their time. Consequently, a critical apparatus always somehow reflects the environment and the different influences and forces, material or immaterial, that interact and play on those who exercise the craft. The evolution of critical apparatus can be observed in a series of phases in the history of critical edition, which we conveniently might summarize into five successive periods.

The early phase, starting in late antiquity, coincided with the wide distribution of Christian and Jewish writings and involved the gathering, collation, and comparison of various manuscripts in order to authorize one particular version of an oral tradition through a few manuscripts that witnessed it. The scribes did not use critical apparatuses as such during this first phase, but relied on some basic sociocultural and political approaches to tradition, which made it interesting and important to scrutinize written accounts in order to assess their authenticity. This phase corresponds roughly to the situation characterized by Walter Ong as the state of residual and secondary orality, where both conservation and elimination of oral features, such as repetition and parallelism, occur. The phase ended roughly when graphical annotation techniques became standardized in manuscripts, particularly codices, exhibiting an increasing wealth of annotations—for example, colophons, early systems of links between parts of the text or words, remarks, and so forth—which may be considered as early versions of a critical apparatus. This phase also saw what may be called the emergence of systematic meta-annotation or information with exclusive reference to a given text or body of documents. One may study pre-medieval Christian and rabbinical texts as late examples of this first phase.

During the second technical phase, local or area-wide standards and collections of symbols emerged that increased the notational efficiency of the copyists. This early standardization can be seen in the textual tradition of the Church fathers and in the manuscripts of the elaborate commentaries of rabbinic literature, where such annotation and link systems (one could be tempted to use the term "hyperlink") were increasingly refined into consistent techniques and where professional practices were taught and disseminated through schools or scriptoria. This second phase was almost exclusively associated with the work of theologians. It remained very much centered on efforts to produce authoritative revisions or recensions of texts, such as the Byzantine recension of the New Testament. There might be forerunners like the work of the translators who produced the *Septuagint* between the third and second century BC in Egypt. Such works of translation from Hebrew into Greek must necessarily have involved extensive critical comparison of Hebrew manuscripts. Earlier, the highly hypothetical Torah Redactor (R) of the Hebrew Pentateuch may be considered an early collator and critical editor of mixed written and oral sources.

Starting during the Carolingian period in Europe, a third phase, involving a renewed interest in antique literature, encouraged the transfer of the editorial practices developed for religious texts during the second phase to secular texts. This period reached its apex during the Renaissance with massive copying and distribution of the writings of Greco-Roman authors. Frequently, commentaries and annotations were added to pre-Christian Greco-Latin texts. The end of this third phase, coinciding with the late Enlightenment period and the early industrial revolution, saw the ideals of natural science increasingly pervading the ambitions of textual criticism.

The fourth phase emerges with the convergence of science and philology, as evidenced by the paramount importance of genealogical reconstruction of text prototypes from variants that spread in all European universities during the nineteenth century. The parallelism of conjectures about ancient species and the archaeological reconstruction of ancient cities is striking. This was the golden age of textual positivism and historicism (with the development of historical-critical analysis). The detailed critical apparatus function became vital for the whole reconstructionist undertaking, as a visually retrievable database legitimizing the reconstruction of textual prototypes.

The fifth and still ongoing phase is more atomized and witnesses a departure from the univocal, narrow ambitions outlined above. New literary and "critical" schools, such as textual genetics (see above), that are more interested in what happens before the publication of a text, around the text, and in the minds and environment of the authors (the auctorial process) reveal new ambitions that operate on a partial or total break with the past. The efforts deployed by new currents or schools of thought such as the new philology are typical of this eccentric dynamics. Diverse variants, which may be labeled ecological, emphasizing the relations of the text to a contemporary social cultural environment, contribute to open the notion of textual criticism or liberate the notion of textual criticism from its ties to reconstruction positivism.

Each of these five phases corresponds to typical producers and users of such textual products. Likewise, each of these periods has seen some processes of institutional embedding or disembedding of the practices described. It is therefore natural to expect fundamental changes in the way experts throughout history formalize their critical activity.

At the Roots of the Critical Apparatus: Philology

The history of textual studies is marked by important shifts, inaugured by the development from the sixteenth century of the critical mind—of lucid, objective, and reasoned analysis of texts in opposition to dogmatisms and authority principles—and culminating during the nineteenth century in an alliance between textual scholarship and positivistic scientific methods. Moreover, philology, considered as "the scientific study of language through the critical analysis of texts" (following the French definition of the online version of *Dictionnaire Le Robert*), not only has numerous roots and traditions but also depends on the epistemological stance and presuppositions of scholars as to the nature of texts and the place (or absence of place) that interpretation and reception can occupy in the elaboration of meaning.

A critical apparatus that accompanies a text aims to highlight and complement the text by providing additional information to the reader. The aim of the editor who provides such information is to allow the reader to evaluate and possibly to verify the authenticity and the scientific quality of the text that he reads or studies. The editor always addresses her peers through the critical apparatus. The form and content taken by this apparatus is the result of the scholarly editor's philological approach or general vision of critical edition.

According to the TLF (Le Trésor de la Langue Française), a critical edition is an "edition that restores the contents of a text (and possibly its successive states) and is equipped with an explanatory commentary"; the "critical" dimension amounts to carrying out a reasonable examination of the sources. The term "learned edition" is used for an edition with notes and grammatical, historical, and literary comments. It is important that the notes do not draw away the attention of the reader but instead offer guidance during his or her journey through the text.

Critical examination of the text conceived as outlined above is the essential task of philology. The method used is an objective and reasoned examination using more or less systematic criteria in order to discriminate between different texts, different versions or variants of a same text, and to exercise a judgment that leads to the establishment of a text. The philological work allows one to restore a text and possibly its variants, depending on their importance and the targeted readership by the editor.

There are three main conceptions of the scholarship work underlying the publication of a critical edition:

1. "Purist" philology inspired by the exegesis of religious texts and applied later to secular texts. In this case the work of the philologist amounts to proposing a reconstruction of an original that may be deemed reliable and authentic (from the hand of the author), or to establish a reference text, building upon a large number of textual witnesses when they exist. Establishing the authenticity of an original textual state builds upon the hypothesis of a first text (or of a formative state mixing oral and written tradition) that supposedly has been perverted by various copies, glosses, and printings, and that needs to be reconstructed by comparing the variants. This philology produces diplomatic editions as faithfully as possible to the original and brings modifications to punctuation and orthography in only limited cases, preferring to let the reader experience problems with understanding the text rather than distorting the intention of the author. Another scientific approach to purist philology ("scientific" meaning rigorous and demanding) is stemmatic analysis, which flourished during the nineteenth century thanks to the work of Karl Lachmann, Joseph Bédier, and later Paul Maas and Jacques Froger, among others. The study of variants collected while comparing different witnesses encouraged these and other scholars to look for the "good text," meaning a unique original text, by exploiting close and remote family ties to ultimately propose a stemma, a genealogical tree of a text, using, if necessary, mathematical tools. However, often one has to admit that an ancient text has reached us only through multiple text families, none of which can pretend to represent the prototype of the other.

2. The second approach to philology is commentary, exposition, inventory, and learned periphrastic expansion with possible encyclopedic aspects. This type of philology, drawing heavily on various rhetoric traditions, is already present in Patristic and Talmudic literature and is further evolving and still attested today in legal texts. The hermeneutical function aims to provide an exploration and an interpretation of the textual space, which, depending on a larger context, cannot be obtained by limiting oneself solely to the linguistic dimension of the text. Thus, exposition of the textual truth will evolve toward a critical commentary dealing with the relation between the text and its environment, exploring its boundaries. This kind of philology culminates in Lanson's methods (French: *explication de texte*, an expression related to later developments of the notion of close reading), biblical redaction criticism, and other forms of critical exegesis. Various conflicts regarding limits to the interpretation of the text impinge on the choices made by editors who choose this second approach.

3. It is possible to identify, using the term "transgressive philology," the new approach to textual criticism that has developed in the wake of the French Nouvelle Critique; of the New Criticism; and, paradoxically, in the wake of the French school of textual genetics, although some still consider it a step backward. Announcing the demise of the text as an ultimate foundation

of truth and questioning the status of the author, a new critical dimension evolved during the 1960s under the joint influence not only of scholars and writers such as Roland Barthes, Michel Foucault, Jacques Derrida, and Julia Kristeva but also of surrealism, psychoanalysis, Marxism, and semiotics. The text is viewed more as an instance of the world, a snapshot or confluence that becomes interesting by situating it within the flux that surrounds it. A text functions simultaneously on several literary, cultural, social, and other levels that critical editions need to take into account. Such is the case of poststructuralist perspectives that stress the multiplicity of methods, deconstruction, decentering of the literary work, and the many modes of function of a work. Hence, any digital edition may be viewed as a medium that amplifies already existing practices and allows one to include various perspectives on text analysis. The result is that historical positivism can be transgressed in various ways. The first transgression is obviously linked with the impact of the Nouvelle Critique on philology. The second type of transgression, which is more difficult to identify, draws on "material philology" inspired by Cerquiglini (1983), who dreams of restoring the materiality of the text in all of its splendor (indirectly, this theoretical stance opens interesting future perspectives to understand "dematerialized" online texts).

Matthew Driscoll (2010) undertakes to explain how this "material philology" constitutes a new deal for critical edition:

The principal innovation in the area of editorial theory in recent years has been the so-called "new" or "material" philology, the call to arms for which was the publication in 1990 of a special issue of *Speculum,* edited by the romance philologist Stephen Nichols of Johns Hopkins University in Baltimore. The immediate inspiration for this new philology came from Bernard Cerquiglini's polemical essay *Éloge de la variante* from 1989 [originally published in 1983], which marked a clear turning point in the history of medieval textual studies by arguing that instability ("variance") is a fundamental feature of chirographically transmitted literature: variation is what the medieval text is "about." [. . .] Literary works do not exist independently of their material embodiments, and the physical form of the text is an integral part of its meaning; one needs therefore to look at "the whole book," and the relationships between the text and such features as form and layout, illumination, rubrics and other paratextual features, and, not least, the surrounding texts. These physical objects come into being through a series of processes in which a (potentially large) number of people are involved; and they come into being at particular times, in particular places and for particular purposes, all of which are socially, commercially and intellectually determined; these factors influence the form the text takes and are thus also part of its meaning. These physical objects continue to exist through time, and are disseminated and consumed in ways which are also socially, commercially and intellectually determined, and of which they bear traces. (90–91)

Thus, "philology," a "word loaded with a disturbing reputation of fallacious transparency," points at diversified theoretical positions, which need to be made explicit by the critical apparatus.

The Production of a Critical Apparatus

The critical apparatus, being defined by tradition exclusively within the framework of specialized scholarly practice (e.g., within domains such as classical antiquity, Latin texts, biblical exegesis, medieval texts, eighteenth-century literature, etc.), functions as a tool that legitimizes the authority of the editor and provides the learned reader with a concrete opportunity to acknowledge the quality of the work of the editor. The critical apparatus prevails from the sixteenth century in scholarly editions with the rigorous work of Jean Bolland (*Acta Sanctorum*), Daniel van Papenbroeck (or Daniel Papebroch, the precursor of historical criticism), and, especially, Jean Mabillon, who in his treatise *De re diplomatica* described a strict method for distinguishing the textual source of bad quality from authentic sources. These genuine scholars force the publishers of ancient documents to take into account the production history of the different manuscripts and the criticism of variants in order to allow one to distinguish what is genuine from what is legendary, incorrect, wrong, or false. The term "critical apparatus" is applied to all learned annotations that an editor adds to an original text. Critical edition, originating in ecclesiastical environments, develops further among secular scholars, plays a major role within philological science, and imposes itself in academic traditions and in editorial practices in ancient classical literature.

In Hubert de Phalèse's online *Dictionnaire de l'édition* (Phalèse, undated) one finds the two French terms *apparat critique* and *appareil critique* (the two terms are synonymous, but the last one is generally considered as being out of fashion). Understood strictly, a critical apparatus is a technique that involves a system of annotation and a method for tracking variants and editorial decisions. The critical apparatus provides the information that is needed to establish the text. Also, if we follow another definition (found in the TLF), a critical apparatus is a "collation of textual variants and conjectures placed in general at the bottom of a page in a critical edition." The critical apparatus provides the reader with information that allows him or her to control the trustworthiness of the text. These definitions assume a meticulous and manual approach. Taken in a wider meaning, however, the term "critical apparatus" may be part of an approach that is less preoccupied with detailed textual variants than with redactional aspects in a historical and cultural perspective or with the close contextual environment.

Thus, it appears that the inclusion of notes and editorial comments in the critical apparatus is not subject to consensus and that it is bound to vary relative to the philological stance of the editor. The choice to include these items (or not) betrays the epistemological project of the editor. According to some, these items are not part of the critical apparatus but belong to a more general discourse about the world. A shift occurs, then, to a form of textual criticism that amounts to a conscious production of discourse that from the point of view of these critics moves away from the primary knowledge object of critical edition: the original state of the text. In offering new possibilities for presentation, digital tools have the potential to change analytical practices by allowing, organizing, and presenting different procedures pertaining to production, interaction, and transactions between the various actors involved.

The three main components that constitute a critical apparatus (we limit the description, as an example, to the case of traditional critical edition) are the following: The first component is the *selection of sources*, including the textual witnesses and the explanation for and justification of editorial decisions. Usually any critical edition needs to provide a register of all the source symbols and scribal abbreviations that will be displayed in the critical apparatus (such symbols are usually termed in the plural form "sigla"). Depending on the magnitude of the edited textual tradition, the editor can either establish his own nomenclature (e.g., in the case of an isolated work) or borrow from well-established conventions (e.g., in biblical textual criticism). Depending on whether the manuscript text witnesses are few or many, the editor will have to decide to carry out either an exhaustive or a selective collation of representative variants. In the last case, he will have to justify the selection criteria that have been applied (for example, in the critical editions of the New Testament, few if any of the readings of minuscule manuscripts are quoted, much less selected, while most if not all variants in the papyri are quoted). In a digital environment the choices are more open: the critical editor can avoid making such decisions, first, by carrying out an exhaustive collection of textual data (digitizing texts using text encoding) and then, in a second phase, by developing a set of rules, which the editor or user may use in order to select more relevant sub-views. By adding mechanisms that exploit various search, parsing, and classification algorithms, it will be possible to make automatic and reversible selections, a situation unthought of just a few decades ago.

The *collation of variants* exploiting the selection of sources can be either exhaustive, at the risk of registering graphical and orthographical variants without relevance for the ongoing project, or more or less selective, giving priority to "readings" that are deemed important. These variants, now registered and linked to their source, allow diverse decisions and conjectures that may ultimately allow a reconstruction of the text that, hopefully for the editor, is close to the hypothetical original. Additionally, the textual critic can exploit these variants in order to reconstruct the transmission history of the text to modern times.

Within a digital environment, exploiting the data resulting from the collated variants can be partially automated.

The *notes and comments* considered as a supplement of information allows documenting the genesis, context, and historical kinship of a text. The critical apparatus can be very scant, either because the textual tradition that is studied attests to few significant variants (as is the case in several works of Ibsen), or because the editor or publisher wishes to spare his or her readers the cognitive overload that a sigla-rich textual apparatus may cause. Diverse layout strategies allow the editor to facilitate the access to critical notes: the most common method involves splitting the critical apparatus into several layers in order to distinguish, for instance, purely orthographic variants from so-called significant variants. Likewise, commentaries that cover factual or material information can be allocated a specific form and a distinct layer within the critical edition. It is obvious in a digital environment that a strategy that aims to reproduce the book world as faithfully as possible may grossly fail to tap the available hypertextual dynamics. Hence it is perfectly imaginable that an online critical edition does not offer its users any system of layered notes under the text, but offers diverse perspectives and "views" (e.g., synoptic layout of various sources, parallel reading displaying synchronized facsimile, diplomatic and normalized views, or local interaction using pop-up windows).

The *identity of the project* is revealed through the choices of the types of commentaries or remarks that are included in a given critical edition. The topic area of these commentaries and annotations depends on the epistemic horizon of the critical edition. These commentaries thus can address different parts of the work:

- The avant-texte, in order to understand the early state of the text, its genesis, its formative dynamics, and perhaps to better grasp the intention of the author or the nature of the forces that have influenced the early stages of the text
- The *infratext*, in order to understand and reconstruct, using material witnesses, the first stage of the meaning of the text conceived as the succession of words that may have formed the early state of the text. The goal here is not to get behind this prototype but to establish it. Lachmann's approach and Bédier's "best text," together with the "new philologists'" renewed interest for variants, operate essentially at this level of analysis. This does not, however, hinder profound disagreements between these approaches. Therefore, in spite of their visual resemblance, critical apparatuses as they have been used by Lachmann and Bédier may serve diverging ambitions (aiming in Lachmann at reconstructing a lost prototype by means of conjecture; aiming in Bédier at choosing the best text).
- The *intratext*, in order to identify or analyze the internal structure of the text treated as a (closed) world, such as in a classical structuralist approach (e.g.,

structural semantics) or, less strictly, in the perspective of "material philology" (Driscoll 2010).

- The *intertext*, in order to document the ties between the text and other external texts. The goal here is to explicate all references made by one or several
witnesses of a text to known or unknown external texts or artifacts (known if
one has access to at least one physical instance). If the work is a collection of
texts—a corpus—the goal of the annotations will be to highlight the already
existing cross-references between various items of this collection. The value of
this undertaking depends, of course, on the relevance of such a collection. Yet
another perspective, more influenced by the Nouvelle Critique, can include
a systematic coverage of allusions, the term "allusion" taken here in a very
broad sense, to non-explicit textual phenomena (expressing the intertextual
dimension inherent to all texts). Nothing hinders one from extending these
intertextualities to pictorial references or any other non-manuscript witnesses
that belong to a wider, unexplored context.
- The *metatext*, in order to highlight the text as a point of access to the world, as
a source, as a witness to the world (of particular relevance is Marc Angenot's
notion of "grand stories" [*grands récits*]; see Angenot 1985, Angenot and
Robin 1985).
- The *aftertext*, in order to highlight the transmission and possibly the reception of the work. By relating explicitly information available within the text
with information within the world, the critical editor takes part in an operation aiming to reveal the world to the readers.

Any critical editor will have to distinguish, within the intellectual constraints
of his academic and sociocultural environment, between hardly objectionable
comments, such as remarks that soberly paraphrase the author's usage or explicit
thought, and comments that point toward salient features of the text, such as
synthetic remarks on the state of the text or linguistic and semantic information
linked to other parts of the text exploited to prove some pattern. The boundary
between "objective" and "subjective" annotations is always fluid and depends
strongly on the theoretical stance taken by a critical observer.

New Horizons for Critical Editions?

The new digital opportunities to establish and structure critical editions and to
flexibly present critical apparatuses open new horizons. Hence, digital critical
editions have been credited with the possibility of stimulating a more fruitful
approach to textual work, representing a new species of "editio sapiens" (Cazalé and Mordenti 1997; see also Meschini 2007), "hypertext savant" (scholarly
hypertext, D'Iorio 2000b), or "Electronic Knowledge Sites" (Shillingsburg
2006).[5] Another scholar who since the 1980s has integrated computer tools
in his editorial work is Peter Robinson, who in 2004 dared to point at a more

important challenge for future editions—namely, the need to produce what may be called fluid, cooperative, and distributed editions that are elaborated not under the auspices of a single person ("the editor"), but under the auspices of a community of scholars and of readers working together. Because they are the result of the work of many, such online critical editions will be the property of everybody.

On one hand, editorial work is changing. Electronic critical edition encourages one to take into account and present more material, to offer more tools and versions, thus facilitating the work of reading peers who want to follow hypotheses that may diverge from the stance taken by the editor/publisher of the site. Moreover, by taking into account new objects of study, such as blogs, wikis, or visual animations in electronic literature, the scholar may be forced to go beyond the immediate context of plain texts and books as part of his or her editorial undertaking. As Shillingsburg writes, beyond all the focus on the permanent evolution of software and hardware, "we need more people thinking deeply about ways in which texts translated into new mediums lose old functions as they acquire new functions and how interactions with texts in the electronic world differ from interactions with print editions" (2006, 145).

On the other hand, critical edition tends to impose itself as a cultural norm. A new intercultural epistemic vision allowing a wider distribution of critical information emerges from online work. Hence, it is not unthinkable that the notion of edition, conceived as the production of a stable, established, and legitimate version of a text, indeed can explode under the pressure exerted by the digital environment. A negative consequence is that textual stability may disappear. A positive consequence is that online editions may allow a greater diversity of commentaries. Another possible consequence in continuity with the traditional philological vision is that, contrary to the disruptive trend mentioned above, the development of online critical editions can lead to the following:

- More editorial reverence toward the text than has been seen in the past, because computers allow more exact and more exhaustive collations and the editor can be caught by the game
- More trustworthy representation of sources, because the software tools increase accuracy at various levels and encourage automatic verification
- Exhaustive collection of information, because the intrinsic logic of data collection encourages the editor to collect everything within reach
- The systematic inclusion of apparently less crucial textual witnesses, for the same reason as above
- A transfer of the ultimate power from the editor to the user with regard to the choices of presentation
- An increasing mixture of critical apparatuses freeing themselves from the constraints of the layout of the printed page

- An increasing mixture of critical apparatuses existing side by side but mirroring hardly comparable epistemic projects
- An increasing hybridization of the critical approaches such as are currently seen in a still primitive form in the "critical apparatus" of Wikipedia. The three Wikipedia tabs "discussion," "edit this page," and "history," with the addition of possible footnotes and cross-reference in the article, offer one of the first historical cases of participative hybridization of production and consumption in a critical edition process. In Wikipedia the "true text" is always somewhere ahead of the critical process.

To what extent can the new forms and dynamics outlined above influence editorial practice and force a new technological vision on critical edition? Three possible scholarly approaches may be envisaged:

- A fundamentally utilitarian and pragmatic approach that strives to avoid as long as possible the full transition to collaborative digital environments, or, as a solution of last resort, seeks to reproduce as faithfully as possible the book mode within a digital environment. Such an approach can blend, paradoxically, technophobia (hiding behind book fetishism) with technophilia (strong belief in the power of algorithms). It seems to operate, consciously or unconsciously, according to a mechanistic conception of information technology (following the argument that "ultimately information technology is a dead but quite useful tool").
- A more visionary, utopian approach that welcomes the replacement of the Gutenberg civilization and the book by a global digital-sharing culture and acknowledges the benefit brought by these new technologies as being the decisive solution to the chronic problems of critical edition.
- An approach that is firmly rooted in a vision of technological determinism, where digital environments are to various degrees autonomous agents that enforce a new politics that requires systematic quality control, operationalization of former informal practices, and the replacement of an institutional value-driven academic bureaucracy owning canonical knowledge into a goal-driven productivist technological bureaucracy.

These three approaches can be illustrated to various degrees by three examples, respectively:

- The first approach is illustrated by the electronic edition of the Canterbury Tales Project directed by Peter Robinson. The computer-based techniques used in this project (started in 1989–1990) knew little of collaborative distributed digital environments, but serve primarily as powerful amplifiers of traditional textual criticism and offer efficiency, exhaustiveness, constant quality improvement, the possibility of accessing all textual data, and other benefits. This pioneering project has tested and produced new analytical tools and implemented diverse innovative work methods that are now adopted by other projects. In its present form, this product still ignores the social and cultural dynamics of Internet-based collaborative criticism. It remains essentially a pre-Internet project stressing production more than communication and reception.

- The second approach produces online critical editions that are usually distinctly multilayered and show a strong will to federate somewhat heterogeneous projects by allowing them to converge toward a common content. Nontextual contents are added in order to highlight contextual issues. The already mentioned projects Woolf Online and the Rossetti Archive reflect this second approach.
- With the third and last approach, one can spot innovative efforts to transgress the presuppositions, ambitions, objects, and canonical methods and prescribed contents of traditional critical edition. Several disparate texts may be linked together in a hypertext structure, occasionally with timelines added to facilitate a global understanding of the material. The project PhiloSource not only houses texts from diverse European philosophers but also adds a large number of secondary audiovisual sources, thereby creating an encyclopedic dimension.

Digital Environments and Critical Editions

The implementation of the editor's critical activity in a digital environment has consequences at different levels. The creation of a critical apparatus always depends on the transformation of observations (human or automatic) into processable constitutive elements (data) that exist in various states depending on the technologies used:

- A *system of linkage* (usually variants of entity-relationship models) that allows one to establish a link (hyperlink) between an item of meta-information referring to a portion of a text or contents and a location or region within this text or content. The human and machine costs of the activity depend on the type and variation of information that refers to various text locations.
- A *lexicon*, in the wide sense of the term, that is a list of symbols that refer to a classification deemed important, such as the use of conventional sigla for designating manuscripts and the use of fixed Latin expressions to express a technical function—for instance, the term *conjectio* for a conjecture, or *emendatio* for emendation, or *lectio difficilior* for "most difficult reading to prefer." More generally, a particular mental classification can be transformed into a lexicon with entries that may be linked to the text.
- A *partitioning* between various lexica that point at different systems of classification. For example, some symbols and links may serve as material descriptions of manuscripts attesting to particular variants, while other lexica and classifications refer to redactional, historical, or linguistic aspects. Online environments allow any degree of separation or, conversely, merging between

lexica. Computer ontologies and topic maps allow one to integrate all classifications that underlie any editorial activity.
- A *material technology* that allows one to operationalize classification and
dynamic linking procedures on real contents (accessible as "data") and to produce an accessible memory (online publication) with an optimal life expectancy. The printed page and the hypertext structure constitute such material
technologies.

Strictly speaking, both print/handwriting technology and digital environment
share all but the last item in the list above. The main difference between the two
is that the latter technology skips the materialization step and replaces it with
an informational architecture that can be manipulated and reconfigured at will.[6]

The New Frontiers of Digital Critical Edition

Because of practical constraints, philologists and critical editors in the pre-digital
age concentrated their work on a restricted number of texts and witnesses. These
specialists had to operate with rather closed worlds and were tempted to dig
into minute details at the expense of wide coverage of large and unmanageable
text collections. Nowadays one may just refer to the astronomical quantities of
texts involved within the Wikipedia environment, the steadily increasing size
and ambitions of electronic corpuses, and the number of reference bases and
analytical tools available.

Quantity itself becomes a kind of new frontier for textual science. Scholars and
publishers are now facing the opportunity to carry out analytical and dissemination work addressing not only hundreds or thousands of pages but also literally
billions of pages in many languages. One may even imagine the possibility of
digitally harvesting all the texts produced in a society throughout a generation
and making the ultimate result the object of textual science and of a new kind
of critical edition. This new perspective precludes dealing with too many details,
such as the meticulous case-by-case observation of glyphs and punctuation in
medieval manuscripts. It encourages new kinds of global, sweeping approaches
that are more related to the way geneticists and bioinformaticians now work
with human genome decoding, or how archaeologists handle massive amounts
of artifacts collected during excavations, or with what is commonly labeled in
computer science as data mining.

The second frontier is also related to quantity but addresses more qualitative
issues or the possibility of addressing significantly more complex relationships
in any content that has been digitized. Many functional relations between variants or text items that were impossible to map by normal human standards can
now be gathered, checked, represented, and analyzed by means of systematic
algorithms that may reveal new patterns of interest. This will affect not only

the practical aspects of editorial work but also the nature of the decisions to be made by the editors and ultimately what critical edition is about.

The third frontier is related to the cross-fertilization of information structuring and emerging modes of distributed communication. It is best exemplified by referring to the possibility of merging the process of critical edition and informed reading by calling upon readers to contribute to or even modify an edition. This implies a new acknowledgment of the potential of these readers and users to contribute, individually or collectively, in order not only to improve and complement a critical edition but also to add original contributions using textual data made available online.

The fourth frontier is multiplicity: no longer is the choice limited, for example, to producing either strict genealogical editions or more ecological editions, such as highlighting external information. Widely different epistemological projects, formerly incompatible, can now cohabit and interact by means of layered markup within a common digital environment. One example is Woolf Online, where extracts from films, pictures, newspaper excerpts, and a wealth of biographical documents are linked to the published novel and its avant-texte, although without putting up obstacles to the establishment of a text that adheres to traditional critical standards. Such products may well herald the advent of a new text epistemology, bridging over old controversies and, as one might expect, generating new ones.

The Choice of the Presentation: Recent Solutions and New Challenges

The various choices of presentation, in print or online, are not only motivated by aesthetics and ergonomics. Any kind of online and on-paper presentation also actualizes the epistemological project that is inherent to a given critical edition. The spatial and dynamic layout accessible on a computer screen expresses in diverse ways some knowledge to be shared.

We have argued in the preceding pages that it is possible to implement online critical edition projects that express widely different ambitions and visions simultaneously. Hence, such online projects can vary between two opposites. At the first extremity one finds general-purpose projects that may be synthetic, multilayered, ecological, and so on, offering to resituate texts in their historical, cultural, and literary environments. In these projects the editor and, if possible, the readers are not searching for the "true" text (although this question may not be rejected as such) but are more interested in using the text regardless of its state in order to open a window on a world to discover. At the other extremity one finds online critical edition projects that operate within the strict perspective of traditional philology. Such projects have a declared ambition to give as faithfully as possible an account of the author's intention, as is the case when the editor believes he possesses the first textual state of the work, or when the same editor chooses to engage in a potentially infinite comparison between, say, the "final" manuscript of the author (if it exists) and later editions. This last position matches well the established, elitist historical positivism described earlier in this chapter.

Hence, the choices made for presenting the critical apparatus actualize the epistemological stance and communication strategy of the editor. The diverse possibilities offered by information technologies will concretize these choices.

Critical editions on paper, since they do not allow variable layout, make the text fixed in its mold and freeze it in its new state. The paper-and-book tool imposes the absolute boundary of the frame of the page and thus puts severe restrictions on the presentation of the critical apparatus. It could materialize as occasional short notes or, inversely, as a critical apparatus/text ratio that is clearly in the favor of the critical apparatus (as illustrated by Moshe Goshen-Gottstein's monumental and prematurely interrupted critical edition of *The Hebrew University Bible Project*). The paper culture implicates a hierarchy that gives prominence to text over image, the notion of critical edition being applied in practice mostly to texts and very seldom to images (although all principles inherited from critical philology may apply to, say, cinematic work). From the nineteenth century, for industrial and ergonomic uses, publishers prefer increasing the number of pages rather than increasing the size of the page. The appearance of the photographic facsimile allows more details to be displayed— for instance, in spite of the size restriction of the book page, one could read facsimiles of uncials and minuscules. During the twentieth century, while an airy layout makes its appearance in editions targeting the general public, allowing more blank areas and making the text easier to read, critical editions stick to pages crammed with text and sigla and deliver critical apparatuses at the limit of readability.

Online digital presentation offers new possibilities for concretizing the relationship between the critical apparatus and the work. A number of constraints imposed by the surface of the printed page disappear. The page area will have to be reconfigured within the frame of the display and satisfy new readability requirements. However, whatever size it may have and whatever visual comfort it may offer, a display is far from being a universal panacea for all woes caused by printing technology. Organizing and presenting information architectures with an increasing underlying complexity poses serious challenges to online critical edition. In the wake of interactive possibilities that are proposed to the users, new cognitive problems appear. For example, the disappearance of the traditional critical apparatus in favor of user-selected visualizations encourages a continuous switching between various points of views on the texts. However, while the perfectly aligned and synchronized synoptic visualization of three normalized versions of an Ibsen text may be reasonably readable for an expert reader, any comparison of, say, more than four sources adds to the risk of bringing the user into a state of a visual and, as a consequence, cognitive chaos. One needs to realize that the cultural acquisition of symbols, conventions, and dynamic access mechanisms within digital environments is only in its infancy and that the former functional coupling of critical editor–academic reader remains to be reinvented for online scholarly editions. Sooner or later the critical editor will need to add to her purely academic role the additional roles of redactor, mediator, and online publisher in order to facilitate wider public use and to contribute to the product in a rewarding manner.

Conclusion

It would be tempting to see in the contributions of the Nouvelle Critique and of the new philology an ideology offering durable solutions excellently matching the potentialities already present in the new digital environments. Hence, the possibilities to encode texts and corpora ad infinitum, to shape new critical editions using multilayer architectures and semantic techniques, encourage an approach that combines precision (e.g., exhaustive collection of variants) with contextualization of the work within its world. Even if admittedly overlapping and synergies occur, one should avoid operating a simplistic and opportunistic confusion allowing an epistemological project to be directly derived from readily exploitable functionalities in a digital environment. Such an approach would reflect a simplistic techno-determinism treating the "digital" as a compact, unique phenomenon behaving as an autonomous actor who acts on editorial practices. As Alvin Kernan (1987, 181) underlines, "Knowledge of the leading principles of print logic, such as fixity, multiplicity, and systematization, makes it possible to predict the tendencies but not the exact ways in which they were to manifest themselves in the history of writing and in the world of letters."

Notes

1. The cultural value of source and witness criticism was admirably exposed by Marc Bloch (1995).

2. See particularly Gabler 2003 and 2010.

3. Digital Humanities 2008, University of Oulu, Finland, June 24–29, 2008, was the twentieth joint international conference for the Association for Literary and Linguistic Computing and the Association for Computers and the Humanities as well as the first joint conference of those two organizations with the Society for Digital Humanities. See Digital Humanities 2008, http://www.ekl.oulu.fi/dh2008.

4. "The long-range goal of the *Piers Plowman* Electronic Archive is the creation of a multi-level, hyper-textually linked electronic archive of the textual tradition of all three versions of the fourteenth-century allegorical dream vision *Piers Plowman*." [Plowman].

5. We reproduce here the list given by Meschini 2007.

6. See exploration of the transition from classical to digital thinking in editing by Rehbein 2010.

4. What Digital Remediation Does to Critical Editions and Reading Practices

TERJE HILLESUND AND CLAIRE BÉLISLE

In migrating their editorial work on literary resources from print to digital technology, researchers have heeded new challenges and ambitions for scholarly editions. This chapter addresses these objectives by looking at designs, aims, and uses of existing scholarly editions as they migrate from one media to another. The first part deals with issues and questions raised by the digital trend in scholarly text studies and with the shift in how historical texts are recorded, presented, and studied. Confronting the optimistic promises of added value that digital editions will bring to scholarly works, we explain through the concept of remediation how traits and configurations of editions that are present in print technology live on in digital technology even though text creation and dissemination have profoundly changed. Underscoring both the fragility of digital information, as compared to the long-lasting paper document, and the extreme versatility of its representation, which makes it capable of answering a wide variety of scholarly reading expectations, we conclude that changes expected in scientific aims and methods are still to come. Digital remediation of text is taking place within a digital context that is impelling new reading habits. Exploring these new emerging reading practices, coupled with a probing of readers' expectations, forms the object of the second part of the chapter. Having observed how reading evolves with digital technology, we explore the enduring uses and the disruptive changes that organize the new ways readers relate to texts and documents mediated by digital technology. Finally, a brief overview presents the challenges that textual scholars will face if they choose to attend to the new expectations of readers as the digital medium becomes the main work area for reading and working with critical editions.

Digital Remediation of Critical Editions

The terms "digital libraries" and "digital scholarly text editions" indicate a shift in how historical texts are recorded, presented, and studied. Without trying to provide definite answers, this chapter presents issues and questions raised by the digital trend in scholarly text studies, using the British Library's online gallery as an example of digital libraries and the Canterbury Tales Project as an example of digital scholarly editions. Is digital technology simply a new means of gaining access to materials existing in another medium, or does it bring radical changes in the representation of texts and documents? Jay David Bolter and Richard Grusin addressed this issue in their groundbreaking study of the differences between media by coining the concept of "remediation." Remediation refers to the refashioning that each new technology introduces in its presentation when a medium tries to represent another medium. "Like their precursors, digital media [...] will function in a constant dialectic with earlier media, precisely as each earlier medium functioned when it was introduced" (Bolter and Grusin 2000, 50). As remediation involves a claim of improvement, it can be under-stood as a process of cultural competition between consecutive technologies that present scholarly editions. But does digital technology entail more, as the "endless crescendo of enthusiasm and expectations with which Western culture is greeting digital media" (267) would let one believe? The chapter examines some of the scholarly implications of the ongoing digital remediation of text. As a starting point, it looks briefly at an earlier shift in the history of text: the transition from manuscripts to printed books.

From Manuscripts to Print to Digital Media

Recuyell of the Histories of Troye was the first book ever to be printed in English. The story was translated from French and printed by William Caxton in 1473 in Bruges. Caxton was the first English printer, and in a concluding letter in the book, after a description of the laborious work on the translation, Caxton praises the new invention of print:

> And for as much as in the writing of the same my pen is worn, my hand weary and not steadfast, my eyes dimmed with overmuch looking on the white paper [...] and also because I have promised to diverse gentlemen and to my friends to address to them as hastily as I might the said book, therefore I have practiced and earned at my great charge and dispense to ordain this said book in print after the manner and form as you may here see, and is not written with pen and ink as other books been, to the end that every man may have them at once.[1]

William Caxton learned the print trade during stays in Cologne and Bruges. In London, he set up a print shop in Westminster, and his first major enterprise was to produce Geoffrey Chaucer's *The Canterbury Tales*, which was printed in 1476 (Caxton ca. 1476).

In the late Middle Ages, Latin was the language used by the clergy and scholars throughout Europe and, accordingly, most printed books (which were still luxury items) were in Latin, sold on a European market. Buyers of printed books in English were unlikely to be found outside the domestic establishment of nobilities, clergymen, and rich merchants. The expression "every man" in the above citation from 1473, reinterpreted as the totality of English-reading book buyers, would not have comprised very many people. Nevertheless, Caxton found a market for books printed in the vernacular, and the shrewd choice of *The Canterbury Tales* as his first book printed in England was probably based on carefully calculated sale assessments: the many surviving medieval manuscripts suggest that Chaucer's tales, written in the 1390s, were already established as popular classic readings at the time of Caxton. As soon as in 1482, Caxton printed a second edition of the tales, this time with woodcut illustrations. In a preface to this edition, Caxton tells how he had received complaints about the accuracy of the text in the first printed edition. According to Caxton, the first edition was printed from a manuscript containing a corrupt version of Chaucer's text, but corrections had been made in the second edition based on a borrowed manuscript containing a text that was truer to Chaucer's own writings. Being the first book trader to transfer manuscript versions of Chaucer to print, and in the process correcting and editing the text, arguably Caxton was the first critical editor of *The Canterbury Tales*; at least he was the first to remediate the text to a new technological platform. The original manuscripts Caxton refers to are both lost, but his printed editions have survived, and today every page of the two editions can be seen and read in image reproductions at the British Library website, along with historical and biographical information on Caxton and Chaucer. In addition to photographs, *The Canterbury Tales* are made accessible by critically edited transcripts of the text. Thus, the presentations on British Library's website represent yet another remediation—this time from early print to screen—in a seemingly endless succession of Chaucer presentations.

Geoffrey Chaucer lived most of his life in London, but he traveled abroad and knew the ideas evolving on the Continent; Boccaccio's *The Decameron* was probably a model for Chaucer's writing of the (unfinished) collection of tales. Manuscript copies and early printed versions of *The Canterbury Tales* have stimulated enduring interest not only because of their literary qualities and colorful—and often bawdy—descriptions of life in Middle Age England, but also because the texts are considered to be important witnesses of historical developments of the English language. Over the centuries a multiplicity of editions have been printed, both in Middle English and in modernized versions. Despite this interest, Geoffrey Chaucer's own manuscript, the presumed archetype (if it indeed existed as more than gatherings of autographed quires), has never been found. Still, many early manuscripts and incunabula did survive, and in England an ambitious effort has been made to digitize all extant manuscripts and printed versions of *The Canterbury Tales* produced before AD 1500. The Canterbury Tales Project officially started in 1993 under the leadership of Norman Blake and later under the supervision and leadership of Peter Robinson. The project's aim has been not merely to document the manuscripts and books but, in addition, to digitally transcribe and analyze the entire collection of early texts. The transcripts of Caxton's editions currently presented on the British Library website are done so in collaboration with the Canterbury Tales Project.

The British Library's publication of Caxton's editions of *The Canterbury Tales* online definitely represents the beginning of a new chapter in the long history of Chaucer and exemplifies a new phase in the history of written text. Since the medieval days of Chaucer and Caxton, the number of English-reading people has grown remarkably, and even if Middle English texts are slightly unfamiliar to most readers, with the proliferation of computers and diffusion of the Internet, more people than ever before, interested in reading or peeping at the original Caxton editions of *The Canterbury Tales*, can do so by accessing the digital reproductions at the British Library website.

This new phase in the history of text, however, is not exclusively attributed to the potential scale of text dissemination. The long-term consequences of the convergence of computer and network technologies into a new text medium are not at all obvious, but they are far-reaching and penetrating in more than geographical terms and degrees of diffusion. The writing system itself, meaning the characters and numbers, is as yet not dissimilar from the systems used in manuscripts and print publications. However, there are significant differences in how digital texts are created and stored and how they are distributed and presented to the reader, and as Roger Chartier (1995) points out, new text features will inevitably change our conception of text, intellectual habits, and ways of reading, thus creating an entirely new framework for digital text editions. For critical philology, these changes pose particularly significant challenges. To interpret and explain text from one cultural paradigm—the world of written and printed text—by exploring, analyzing, and presenting it within a rather different cultural paradigm—the world of digital text—raises seemingly insoluble questions, and editors must ask how it can be done without doing "violence to the texts by separating them from the original physical forms in which they appeared and which helped to constitute their historical significance" (Chartier 1995, 22). The first step in trying to solve the challenge would be to examine what biases a digital remediated text will insert on our understanding of the original written or printed text.

Remediation Reveals Differences

When analyzed, remediation reveals differences between the new medium and its predecessor, shedding light on both and in a subtle way deepening our understanding of the precursor. Thus, digital technology has clarified certain aspects of writing. For instance, in handwriting and printing, as in all traditional text technologies, storing and representation of text are done by the same means in a combined process. In books and manuscripts, patterns applied to the surface of parchment or paper both record the text and make it legible in an enduring and fixed physical form (Hillesund 2005). The Ellesmere and Hengwrt manuscripts have preserved versions of *The Canterbury Tales* for more than half a millennium, as have the Caxton printed editions. In a digital environment, by contrast, storing and representation of texts are done in separate operations; in the internal computer system, texts are stored electronically (or externally in magnetically or optical forms) as encoded binary digits independently of any visual representation of the texts. From computer storage systems the encoded text can be fetched and represented onscreen in word processors, web editors, or desktop publishing programs, in which they can be edited, altered, and recomposed. Digital texts are thus malleable and flexible, globally distributable, and easily accessible: from one computer the text can instantly be sent to another computer by way of e-mail, or it can be put online and globally accessed (Hillesund 2005).

On the web, texts are readable in browsers that are characterized by highly interactive interfaces, window presentation, hyperlinks, and the use of multiple media and multimodal presentation (text combined with graphics, photos, videos, or sound). In the new medium of connected computers, lots of new text genres and written communication forms have evolved: e-mail, news groups, chat features, blogs, online newspapers and magazines, electronic books, search engines, digital learning materials, corporate websites, web stores, digital libraries, and social networking sites. On the British Library website exhibiting Caxton's printed books, all pages of both books are presented. The photographic reproductions can be enlarged, and the text, typography, and illustrations can be studied in detail; the two editions can be compared in parallel windows; the texts can be searched; and there are links to transcripts, which pop up in additional windows.

When utilized in this way, texts are incorporated and represented in a new medium; the texts are transformed and put into new uses in a remediation process in which features and possibilities of digital technology and network connectivity are explored (Bolter and Grusin 2000; Bolter 2001; Bolter and Gromala 2003), inevitably resulting in new ways of reading and interpreting text (Chartier 1995). However, for text such remediation is not a new phenomenon. Ever since the Sumerians started to press a stylus into clay, forming their cuneiform characters in the first written languages, numerous technologies and physical means—or media—have been used in the production and dissemination of text, and a diversity of written communication forms have evolved, flourished, and diminished in a succession of remediation processes. At one time papyrus and parchment made written communication more portable, and, interestingly, the oldest-dated printed book yet found is a papyrus roll printed in China in AD 868 by the use of wooden blocks. A copy of this roll, the *Diamond Sutra*, is preserved at the British Library and presented on their website.

Among great media shifts in the history of written communication, prominent scholars have pointed to the importance of the transition from papyrus and parchment scrolls to codices (books in the form of bound pages) in the second and third centuries AD (Chartier 1995). Gradually replacing the scroll, which required both hands in reading, codices, with easily accessible pages, provided new and effective ways of organizing and navigating text. However, the early reading of densely written parchment pages with many abbreviations and no word spacing required the use of the voice, because the text had to be read aloud in order to be comprehensible. Then, during the Middle Ages, the introduction of smaller books and new text features, such as word spacing, punctuation, and paragraphs, gradually made books more portable and reading less demanding physically. According to Chartier (1995), these medieval developments in text materiality led to a consequential shift from oral reading, which had been indispensable for comprehension, to a process of reading that could be visual, silent, and fast—the modern way of fluent reading.

Nevertheless, it is the much later fifteenth-century transition from bound manuscripts to printed books in Europe that has attracted the widest interest, and most commentators call the invention of the printing press a revolution. However, without arguing its historical importance, one can reasonably question whether the invention of printing actually does inaugurate an entirely new and different medium. After all, printed books and manuscripts share some very basic similarities, most clearly manifested in the early stages of print. When Johan Gutenberg produced his famous Bible in 1455, he tried to imitate the beauty of contemporary handwritten and illuminated books and succeeded in doing so. During production, Gutenberg changed the printing method (from forty to forty-two lines) and the spelling of many words, and after the printing was done, initials, rubrics, decorations, and illustrations were written and painted by hand, making all the copies of the printed Bibles slightly different but still strikingly similar to preceding medieval manuscripts.

After Gutenberg the next generations of printers improved the printing techniques of text and illustrations and introduced both manuscript-like and new features to the overall printed text, gradually changing appearances of books. Over the centuries, new formats were developed, and the mechanization of print production made books, magazines, and newspaper the first mass media. Developments have continued, and new digital tools and printing technologies have made the physical appearances of books and magazines increasingly more sophisticated. Nevertheless, all printed publications still store and represent verbal text in a combined process, using ink on paper, creating a physical form in which texts of books, magazines, and newspapers are preserved, distributed, and read.

Compared to printed publications, the networked computer is a very different text medium. After almost twelve hundred years, the physical object conveying the *Diamond Sutra* text can still occasionally be seen by the public in the Sir John Ritblat Gallery at the British Library. The text is clearly legible and intelligible for readers of Chinese. Easily readable as well is the interactive version of the *Diamond Sutra* at the British Library's website. Whereas the exhibited physical paper roll displays a tiny section of this Buddhist text, the interactive virtual version lets the user scroll through the whole text of the roll using a mouse. However, although web browsers clearly present the text of the sutra, having lost its status as a physical object, it is hard to establish where the actual text is located. A machine-readable and humanly illegible binary representation is obviously stored at the British Library's web server or in a database, yet articulations of the text result from end users browsing the web. In order for the text to be visually presented, a lot of highly technical operations have to be initiated and performed. Commands must be processed by a computer; signals sent back and forth over the Internet; and digital representations and files fetched, packed, sent, unpacked, processed, and visually presented onscreen in such a complicated process that few people, if any, fully understand what is actually happening. In the *Diamond Sutra* case the text is visible and humanly readable only as long as the computer is online and every bit of software and hardware is functioning and the power is on. The readable text disappears the moment a user turns to another web page or turns off the computer. So where is the text? And more important, where will this particular text witness be in three or four decades, when computers and storage systems have changed and up-to-date operating systems run new applications over presently unknown network systems representing text on displays not yet invented? The original *Diamond Sutra* text, the one on the paper roll, will probably still be on display in the exhibition room at the British Library—at least on occasions.

Crisis and New Questions

The written and printed book has an extraordinary staying power, as Robert Darnton (1990) underscores, lasting for seventeen or eighteen centuries. The physical book is still dominant in many important areas of publishing and undeniably in the research field of critical editions. However, in the long history of writing, digital technologies have made a huge difference in a very short time. Whether Émile Baudot's development of a five-bit code system for the French telegraph service in 1874 is reckoned as the beginning of digital text (this code system later developed into ASCII and the current Unicode Standard), or the start of digital text is set to the 1960s and the utilizing of coded text in computers (first as an input/output method) can be a matter of taste. It is a fact that computers developed into a full-fledged media for text communication during the 1980s and beginning of the 1990s, with the spread of the Internet and introduction of the World Wide Web (Bolter 2001). In a very short time, historically speaking, the digitization and communication of text has played a crucial role in the development of the computer and Internet, and vice versa: the development of connected computers has profoundly changed text creation and dissemination. When these changes of text are analyzed using a model of a communication circuit (Darnton 1990) or a text cycle (Hillesund 2005), it becomes clear that all stages or phases of the circuit or cycle are changed. Digital texts are written and composed using computers in word processors and editing software; they are magnetically, electronically, or optically stored; they are transmitted (or rather accessed) over networks; they are represented in browsers (and other reading software); and they are eventually read on computer screens, either of stationary or handheld devices. The entire text cycle has been digitized, and the social, economic, and legal apparatus surrounding text circulation is correspondingly affected. Even the seemingly immutable Western writing system is changing, or at least the use of it, which is clearly seen in the communication forms of e-mail, chat, and text messages; in these a lot of new and creative ways of combining and using characters are established, especially among the young.

It is no exaggeration to state that, for traditional text cultures, digitization represents a crisis because it involves abrupt cultural changes, new rules of production and diffusion, a challenge to inherited expertise that is threatened to fall into obsolescence, and possibly a paradigm shift, which the second part of this chapter considers, as defined by Thomas Kuhn (1962). According to Jay David Bolter, "Digital technology is turning out to be one of the more traumatic remediations in the history of Western writing" (2001, 24). One reason, Bolter says, is that digital technology changes the physical "look and feel" of writing and reading, and he quotes Roger Chartier, who argues that the current shift from print to digital technology entails a change greater than the one from manuscript to print:

> Our current revolution is obviously more extensive then Gutenberg's. It modifies not only the technology for reproduction of the text, but even the materiality of the object that communicates the text to the readers. Until now, the printed book has been heir to the manuscript in its organization of leaves and pages [. . .] and its aids to reading (concordances, indices, tables). The substitution of screen for codex is a far more radical transformation because it changes methods of organization, structure, consultation, even the appearance of the written word. (Chartier 1995, 15).

By using the term "remediation," Bolter is primarily preoccupied with the changes in form and function of texts when adopted in the medium of connected computers, characterized, as they are, by interactivity, multimedia, hypertext, and immaterial and highly dynamic (or fluctuating) ways of representing content. Chartier emphasizes the constraints that new media forms impose on the interpretation of text and the construction of meaning. For Chartier, the "same" text apprehended through very different mechanisms of representation is no longer the same. In his analysis Chartier examines how forms of transmission influence the styles of reading and how they define and construct new readership.

Digitization thus reformulates all questions regarding text. For scholars working with digital critical text editions, therefore, an awareness of transformation and remediation processes is of particular importance. Usually the objects of study in critical editions are written or printed text from earlier periods (such as the Chaucer manuscripts and Caxton's printed editions). These are transformed into digital formats for documentation, preservation, study, and research. Further research is conducted on the basis of remediated versions of texts, and questions inevitably arise regarding the status of the digitized texts and their relations to the original texts. Are the researchers studying the same texts? How does digitization affect the comprehension of the concept "text"? How does it affect habits of reading? In a new digital paradigm, researchers will have to reflect on how the transformation process—the digital encoding and transcription of text—entails methodological and theoretical considerations and contentions. Researchers are further required to ask if the remediation of text—its visual representation in new media—promotes new styles of reading and thus imposes constraints upon our understanding of texts of the past.

A digital critical text edition is itself a significant witness of the long remediation history of important texts, such as *The Canterbury Tales*. As a result of the work in the Canterbury Tales Project, six editions so far have been published on CD-ROM, comprising photographic reproductions and transcripts of every early text witness, commentaries, and software for manipulation of text data. The ambition of such digital scholarly editions is to bring the past into the future. Unfortunately, many CD-ROM editions and Internet editions have already left the future behind. The storage media of CD-ROMs, along with software and equipment used to present their content, is doomed to be obsolete relatively soon. If the materials and programs of these systems—contrary to expectations—stand prolonged erosion, future researchers studying initial phases of digitization will probably have to endure rigid library application procedures to be allowed to use the delicate equipment needed to get a touch and feel of how early pioneers presented their attempts in the area of digital critical text editions. The situation is paralleled in other domains, such as music and film, in which content that has been stored as vinyl records and rolls of film necessarily has to be converted and remediated in order to be presented anew. In this respect, obviously, the advantages of manuscripts and printed books are evident: as long as the object is preserved and it doesn't severely deteriorate, the recorded content is represented in its original form. For libraries, preservation of digital content is a major issue, and for digital scholarly editions, this is a circumstance that researchers have to contemplate.

But "outdatedness" is not only a matter of obsolescent storage format. It may also be the result of obsolescent modes of production and control of these texts.

Digital Photographic Text

In the Canterbury Tales Project the philologists have wisely made sure that their transcripts and documentations at a prepublication level are recorded in formats that are capable of uncomplicated conversions and continued remediations in future digital media, presumably taking advantage of network distribution. The editions so far published in the project are composed of three main elements: digital images or facsimiles showing the text of the original manuscripts or books, digital transcripts of the texts, and collation and phylogenetic software. Generally, digital photography has more or less superseded traditional film-based photography, and digital remediation of photography is in itself a very interesting process. Digital images are extremely manipulable and versatile, and digital photos are brought to new uses in print and in digital environments—that is, on the web and in multimedia presentations. Digital images are displayed on all kind of devices, from small mobile phones and computers to wide-screen televisions, posters, and cinema screens. In scholarly editions, digital photos of pages and objects are very useful, and some editions of *The Canterbury Tales* set a new standard for manuscript photography. Indeed, photographic shooting of delicate book materials is a skilled craft, and experts from Keiō University in Japan photographed the Caxton editions in British Library.

As with all remediation, digital photography introduces biases. No photos can ever reproduce the smell, look, and feel of real books, and digital photography cannot replace the meticulous examination of paper, ink, and binding—the materiality—of manuscripts. However, digital images accurately represent the text, along with the layout and illustrations in codices and printed books, and for studies of details and character patterns, digital photos represent an enhancement; they allow for great enlargements and use of pattern collation software. For some digital text collections, optical character recognition (OCR) can even be a viable alternative as part of the transcription process. Further, as limitations on Internet bandwidth are no longer an issue, digital image formats render possible a wide distribution of pictorial text representations to researchers and students with no direct access to the fragile and rigorously protected original artifacts, which are often kept in the most sacred parts of libraries.

In the editions published from the Canterbury Tales Project, the photos used are of varied qualities. In *Geoffrey Chaucer: "The General Prologue" on CD-ROM* (Solopova 2000), the images are digitized versions of microfilm pictures. These images are rude black-and-white representations of characters and illuminations that are difficult to read or decipher, giving very little sense of the original manuscript. Totally different, then, are the manuscript photos in *The Hengwrt Chaucer Digital Facsimile* (Stubbs 2000; see fig. 4-1). In this edition the images

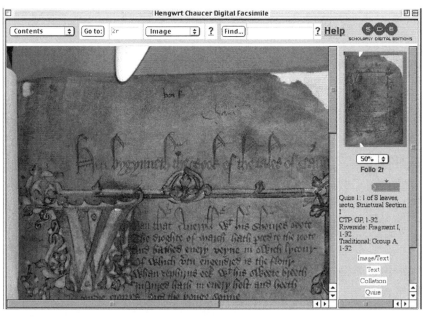

Figure 4-1: Screen dump of the Hengwrt Chaucer Digital facsimile (http://www .sd-editions.com/AnaServer?HengwrtEx+0+start.anv).

are high-quality color photos allowing detailed scrutiny of the manuscripts and illuminations. They also provide a touch of the visual beauty of medieval manuscripts (even if all the Chaucer manuscripts are rather straightforward compared to carefully made medieval manuscripts, many of which are beautifully illuminated and illustrated). Of similar high quality are the images in *Caxton's Canterbury Tales: The British Libraries Copies* (Bordalejo 2003), whereas other editions (such as those of *The Miller's Tale* and *The Nun's Priest's Tale*) have a combination of black-and-white, gray-scale, and color pictures. Digitally remediated onscreen, there is no doubt that high-quality photos add substantial value to critical editions of manuscripts, not least in that readers and researchers can control, question, and even rectify the accompanying transcripts.

Coping Digitally with the Protean Status of Texts

In scholarly projects, in addition to serving as documentation and illustration, onscreen image reproductions are the virtual starting point of another comprehensive process: the transcription of the manuscript's text, which, of course, is done digitally. On the website of the Clerk's Tale Project at New York University, one of the collaborative partners in the Canterbury Tales Project, four stages of this editorial work are described. As the first step, each manuscript is transcribed and encoded. Transcription uses a character set designed to accommodate late-medieval English manuscripts, and encoding conforms to the guidelines of the TEI (Text Encoding Initiative, discussed elsewhere in this book), which is a widely accepted standard for markup of electronic texts in the humanities. In the next steps, the different transcriptions are compared using a collation software program, and the body of variants is analyzed using phylogenetic methods and software developed in evolutionary biology. Finally each tale is published on CD-ROM in a format allowing users to access images of every page of every manuscript and full-text electronic transcriptions of the tale, as well as making collocations and analyses based on stemmatic models, or so-called split-tree models. All elements of an edition are presented in an e-book reader, a software application in which multiple windows allow users to work in parallel modes, compare different versions of a tale, and simultaneously carry out collocations and analyses. Since the first CD-ROM from the project was published, both interface and software have improved, showing that digital remediation of text is a continuous process. In the latest editions, the e-book reader is loaded and integrated into the default web browser of actual users.

As with all digital remediations of text, the digital way of storing, representing, and manipulating text in scholarly editions challenges many deep-rooted representations of text. A text is usually regarded as a collection or weave of words of a certain length or extension. In linguistics the term "text" is used for both written and spoken texts, but sometimes it refers to written text only. In semiotics the concept of text is extended to all kinds of representations: writing, speech, pictures, music, videos, and computer games, and any combination of these. Scholarly digital editions deal mostly with texts produced and represented in written forms, sometimes including illustrations and certainly comprising analysis of the form and materiality of the texts: most editions of *The Canterbury Tales* include witness descriptions in which the styles of the scribes or composers are described along with accounts of ink, parchment, or paper and the binding of the manuscripts and incunabula. A text is thus traditionally regarded to be a product rather than a process; the text is the product of a process of text production. In this sense, the text, as an artifact, has a physical existence of its own, independent of its sender and receiver. In addition to this concrete meaning, the word "text" is frequently used in an abstract sense, signifying the verbal structure, or wordings, or the narrative structure underlying the physical representations of the text. Taken in this abstract sense, the same text can be given different presentations, as when the text of an ancient manuscript is reproduced in modern print, on the web, or as an e-book. Though different in form, all articulations can be said to represent the same text. This two-sided concept of text is inherent in much research on the subject: in editorial philology, as in the case of *The Canterbury Tales*, when the original physical version of a text is missing, scholars carry out thorough stemmatic and genealogical analysis of the extant text copies in order to reconstruct the closest possible approximation to the original text, which exists only in an abstract and theoretical form. The double meaning of the concept of text is also present in bibliographical theory, and the dual meaning clearly underpins the FRBR (Functional Requirements for Bibliographic Records) model, published by the International Federation of Library Associations and Institutions in 1998. Conceptually, the model identifies entities on different levels representing different aspects of user interests in the products of intellectual endeavor and their bibliographic records (and it is not restricted to books) (see fig. 4-2).

The entity "work," as defined in the model, is a distinct intellectual creation and can usually be ascribed to one or more creator(s), as *The Canterbury Tales* is ascribed to Geoffrey Chaucer. "Work" is a completely abstract entity, and a work exists only in the commonality of content between and among the various expressions of the work. The entity "expression" is the realization of a work and encompasses, for example, the specific words and sentences of a text (in the abstract meaning of the term). When a work is realized, the resulting expression of the work may be physically embodied in a medium such as parchment, paper, or compact discs. That embodiment constitutes a "manifestation" of the work (such as in the form of a text in the physical sense). In some instances, only a single exemplar is produced of the manifestation of a work, such as an author's

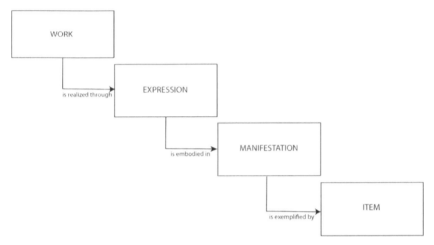

Figure 4-2: The FRBR (Functional Requirements for Bibliographic Records) model, published by the International Federation of Library Associations and Institutions in 1998 (freely drawn from the International Federation of Library Associations' [IFLA] *FRBR Report*, p. 13).

manuscript or medieval scribes' slightly differing copies making up disparate manifestations of the work, as in the example of Chaucer's *Tales*. In other cases, multiple copies of a manifestation are produced in order to facilitate public dissemination, as in Caxton's printings. When the production process involves modifications, additions, or deletions affecting the intellectual or artistic content, such as a new edition of a book, the result is a new manifestation embodying a new expression of the work. An "item," in the model, is a concrete entity defined as a single exemplar of a manifestation in the form of one or more physical objects, such as a manuscript, a printed book, or a two-volume monograph. In the FRBR model, the entities defined as "work" and "expression" reflect intellectual content, whereas "manifestation" and "item" reflect physical form.

The dual concept of text and the FRBR model may very well be suited to define and characterize text and to identify specific texts in a world of written and printed publications. However, both concept and model prove inadequate when applied to text in a digital environment, an intricacy the FRBR report seems to recognize when it recommends further analysis of the dynamic nature of entities recorded in digital formats.

Digital texts do not exist as distinct physical objects, and the unfeasible task of unambiguously locating such a text clearly illustrates the absence of easily identifiable and limitable items representing text in a digital environment. In the case of Caxton's texts on the British Library's website, the web pages are certainly pointed to by URLs (Universal Resource Locators) or links, but when realized onscreen, the texts are compound bits of illustrations and text apportioned around servers at the British Library and Montfort University. For text encapsulated in a single document (as an e-book) or physically stored on a CD-ROM, the articulation of the text is dependent on highly sophisticated processes, including text representations on many levels, from the basic level of storage to the final—yet temporal—presentation onscreen. When realized onscreen, even encapsulated texts point to external text recourses, sometimes directly through created links and always indirectly by links from words and phrases to dictionaries and search engines or, for that matter, to automatic translation software or artificial reading applications. In online environments, which form a vast semantic web, it is almost impossible to clearly delimit a text the same way as in manuscripts and printed books. In these, of course, the covers of the book define the boundaries of the text. The flexibility of digital texts, such as in digital scholarly editions, also allows users to constantly rearrange text, use multiple windows and multiple media, bring in external resources, and manipulate the appearances of the text, such as the layout and font properties. In the FRBR model, these are changes that define new manifestations of the text, implying that digital users continuously create new momentary expressions of the original work.

As the above discussion indicates, neither the FRBR model nor the traditional definitions of "text" are very well suited to categorize or describe digital texts, a fact clearly illustrating that as far as important basic features are concerned, digital texts are very different from texts conveyed by physical items, such as manuscripts and printed books. Digital humanist researchers, for whom a digital version is said to represent the text of a physical source document, have to be extremely conscious of these differences, because the asserted representation is by no means built on a one-to-one relation. In this respect, the status of the transcription documents in TEI format, which is based on XML (Extensible Markup Language), is of particular interest for scholarly text editors. Being an important part of the editing process (see fig. 4-3), the TEI transcription documents are packed with information on the source documents, such as typography (titles, paragraphs, capital and small characters, punctuation, underscores), wording, spelling, abbreviations, and corrections. However, these TEI transcripts are merely intermediate documents. Before publication the TEI documents are converted by using special conversion tools, such as XSLT (Extensible Stylesheet Language Transformation), in order to attain a readable form. Such conversions are necessary in order to give proper presentations of the information that is marked up and encoded in TEI. Further, TEI documents are often so rich in information that several presentations have to be given—for instance, one facsimiled, one diplomatic, and one normalized transcript, all pointing to commentaries and descriptions. On the one hand, each of these versions simply presents parts of the information in the TEI document. On the

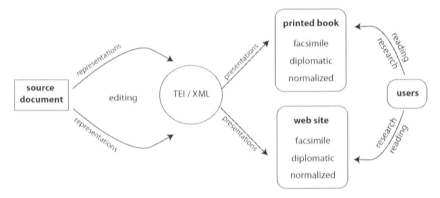

Figure 4-3: The digital text editing and publication process. The digital editing process, with intermediate TEI documents, produces several text versions, all representing the source document(s) in different ways.

other hand, these readable versions are provided with presentational information that makes them more applicable representations of the source documents than the TEI version. This clearly illustrates the ambiguous status of XML/TEI documents: in some respect, they contain the most thorough representation of the original documents, yet they depend on external style sheets and transformations in order for this information to be presented in legible form.

Challenging Opportunities for the Future of Editorial Philology

However, having pondered on digital text features and the ambiguity of XML and TEI, it is important to recognize that the intermediate nature of TEI and the separation of verbal information from presentation bring huge advantages. From TEI documents, diplomatic and normalized transcripts of the source documents can be presented in several media, such as in printed books, on the web, on CD-ROMs, or in e-books. Whether the primary publication from a project is planned to be in print or on CD-ROM or DVD-ROM, new editions may be made from the XML files at later stages as web and e-book technologies mature. In any case, the XML format ensures future compatibility. Further, in digital editions the quantity of published matters may also be vast and much greater than in any printed edition. Digital editions may even be complete, including all the editorial material as well as the intermediate XML files. Free publication of the XML files is the ambition of the "open transcription policy," which is based on principles in the Open Source software movement and initiated by participants of the Canterbury Tales Project (2006). Advocates of the open transcription policy argue that all digital transcripts (XML or not) should be published and made freely available to all researchers. This would encourage continued research and accumulation of knowledge, not least by allowing competing researchers to provide new perspectives and methods in the study of the transcribed historical texts.

In research the logical structure of XML and the editorial markup and encoding of all kinds of variants make the huge task of collation possible through the use of specialized software, a task that would be more or less impossible without properly encoded transcriptions and the processing powers of computers. In the Canterbury Tales Project, every word and every line of the many edited manuscripts are collated and the records made available for users of the editions. Peter Robinson and his colleagues also use phylogenetic software, adapted from evolutionary biology, to achieve comprehensive stemmatic analyses of the extant manuscripts. To a large degree these analyses confirm earlier researchers' gathering of the manuscripts in related ancestral groups, but the analyses also shed new light on the textual history of the tales, especially the process of early scribal compilation and copying. In the published editions of the tales, users can place variants of spellings and words in split-tree models generated by the phylogenetic tools. At least in the Chaucer studies, it seems that the digital transformation of the editing and publication process so far has reinforced and enhanced traditional methods of editorial philology, especially in the use of collation and stemmatic analysis tracing the process of copying in search for the original version of the text.

Thus, insofar as editorial philology is concerned, even if new analytics have been deployed, research aims and methods have not changed substantially as a result of the digitization and remediation of text, which, of course is notable because the digital transformation has created a new text paradigm with altered text characteristics and new text concepts. In the future, additional tools will be developed, gradually changing the focus and methods of textual research. When a phenomenon is studied using new tools, new and fruitful research questions may arise and a new scientific paradigm may evolve, often generating new insights and better understanding of the phenomenon in question. For the digital humanities, however, the current changes bring about a particular challenge. In textual editing the original texts are given new characteristics as a result of the remediation: when studied in a digital environment, the texts are no longer the objects they used to be. As we have seen, the separation of storage and representation in digital text makes it transformable, highly malleable and flexible, easily distributable, searchable, and globally accessible. Critically edited texts are stored in intermediary formats, and their onscreen presentation is technologically dependent. Presentation of a text is usually in a multimodal environment and as a node in a hypertext structure in which the text is evanescent and physically intangible. Thus, digital text does not have the object status of written and printed text, it is not easily located, it lacks the unity of books, and it is very difficult to determine as an entity—digital text even allows for instant creation of new and temporary expressions of the original work. When historical texts are remediated and studied within this new text paradigm, researchers necessarily have to ask, with Roger Chartier, if the text they are studying is still the same.

As Odd Einar Haugen and Daniel Apollon explain in chapter 1, the emerging digital textual scholarship may be understood from the perspectives of textual editors looking backward, outward, or inward. "Looking backward" means to search for the origin of a text and to trace its development. In a classical setting it means to track the process of copying from the very original and then from one exemplar to the next, and in a post-Gutenberg setting, to trace the development from the first drafts made by the author until the printed end product. "Looking outward" means to view the text as a sociohistorically situated product, and "looking inward" implies reading and understanding the text as an individual expression of its own right, as a self-contained document. Evidently, many of the research questions related to these perspectives are intrinsically tied to basic characteristics of written or printed text, such as the physical materiality of the text, its object status, fixedness, durability, the authors' integrity, and the unity of the work. When the object of study—the text itself—changes as a result of remediation, taking on a range of new features, researchers also have to ask if the traditional research problems are still relevant. Contending that the research questions are still valid, as a minimum requirement, researchers have to clarify the relation between the object that is studied, the digital text, and the original historical text the study is supposed to illuminate. This is absolutely critical, because text is by no means a dead object but permeated with meaning and basically defined by its interpretation. Following the fact that texts are given new basic features, at a basic interpretative level, digital remediation of text encourages new ways of reading and new reading practices, inevitably raising questions of how these new practices influence the interpretation of historical texts when presented in digital environments.

Remediation or Revolution in Reading Practices?

The word "revolution" can sound a bit far-fetched for talking about reading, but it is a fact that in the last fifteen years many researchers, such as Sven Birkerts (1994), Roger Chartier and his *Le Livre en révolutions* (1997), George Landow (2006), or Maryanne Wolf (2008), have drawn attention to the important transformations affecting not only texts, written works, but more specifically the writing and reading mind. As Umberto Eco puts it, it is not a question of "*Ceci tuera cela*" (which refers to the book's capacity to kill the cathedral), as the quote from Victor Hugo's *Hunchback of Notre Dame* implies, for "in the history of culture it has never happened that something has simply killed something else. Something has profoundly changed something else" (1996, 304). Eco is referring here to successive inventions, such as photography or cinema, that have changed the process of artistic representation. These cultural changes do not happen overnight but take a long time to become pervasive and result in developments not necessarily foreseen or predicted. Because the effects of digital technology on reading have already become a hotly debated issue, it is not premature to consider if the new practices represent a real threat to humanistic values and the reading brain or if they herald a new era of novel thoughts, creative thinking, and a new democratic relation to reading and writing.

In the first part of this chapter, scholarly editions were revisited with a view of challenging the prophecy of newness that digital technology carries for the study of texts by reinterpreting as a process of remediation the changes duly experienced by editors in going from paper to digital technology. This has made evident that the contents of the new media are closely linked to their predecessors, as they pay tribute to the same intellectual, literary, and historical principles. It has also brought forth the fact that these contents were themselves often the result of earlier remediation from other media representation. Remediation can thus largely account for the value added to existing scholarly editions when they are transposed from one media to another, or also attributed to digitally native editions, which, although developed with digital tools, follow existing printed work requirements.

But it has also been shown that the original texts acquire new features because of remediation; it is not the same objects that the researchers interact with, nor the same tools, and this opens the domain to new and fruitful research questions and the possible emergence of a new scientific paradigm. In this second part of the chapter, reading practices are reviewed in the light of not only the remediation process but also of the new digital reading modalities and the new relationships to texts and knowledge that are dawning with the development of digital technologies. For as scholarly editions migrate to the digital world, it is important to appreciate whether scholarly reading practices can be remediated or if they will be radically transformed when dealing with digital texts on screens.

Alarms are being raised to avoid the death of the book; the end of reading; the dissolution of our beliefs, values, and cultural aspirations. It seems obvious that the ongoing changes in information technology are concomitant with cultural changes, and as the world becomes more and more digital, the enormity of the changes under way is raising concern, fears, and even rejection. It is important at this point to understand what changes are occurring, if the acquisitions of "literacy" will be enduring, or if it will give way to new innovative and powerful ways of being, thinking, and understanding.

What is happening to reading practices in a digital world? Are we also witnessing a remediation process—that is, a crossover from one media to another of reading habits and expectations—or are we confronted today with an authentic revolution in reading and in the modalities of relating to documents and texts? It is argued here that if, generally speaking, reading practices are still referred to as reading on paper, the changes already observed in reading with digital media can be understood as the beginnings of a profound cultural evolution that scholarly reading and editions will not be able to elude. Our argument here is based on confronting what constitutes the digital practices of reading today with the enduring representations of reading developed in reference to reading on paper and by looking at how digital critical editions can meet the expectations and demands of readers and their multiform, multitasking, multimedia reading in a digital world.

Science fiction author and media theory professor Paul Levinson (1998) has defined remediation as the "anthropotropic" ("anthropo-" for "human" and "tropic" for "toward") process by which new media technologies improve upon or remedy prior technologies in their rendering of human performance. As readers go from paper to digital, the challenge in transposing the remediation concept is to assess if digital reading does offer improved conditions for reading and how new media develop their cultural acceptance and significance. According to Bolter (2000), as referred to in the first part of this chapter, remediation more specifically characterizes the way in which new media refashion earlier media forms. The two main strategies of remediation are immediacy or transparency (trying to make the viewer forget the presence of the medium) and hypermediacy or opacity (trying to multiply mediation so as to create a feeling of fullness, a satiety of experience, an excess of media). When considering reading, can such strategies help to understand what is at stake? Immediacy would be what qualifies uninterrupted reading, an immersive experience of being involved in a narrative such that both decoding and page turning become transparent. The opposite of this, hypermediacy, applies quite aptly to the reading of scholarly works, where the critical apparatus, the variants, and the annotated text constantly converge to inform and convince the reader that he is accessing the complete and authentic meaning or interpretation of the text of document through an augmented version of the original document.

However, if applying the remediation strategies to reading is to shed sufficient light on the changes in reading, much deeper transformations must be taken into account. Experienced print readers are very sensitive to the changes in their physical and pleasurable experience of reading when screens replace paper, and most are convinced that their preference for paper is irrevocable. But the change from paper to screen is only the emerged tip of the iceberg. One needs to take into consideration the changes that the digital world brings to the social representations, the professional constraints, and the cultural criteria that organize one's reading experience. As reading practices become more complex and diversified, scholars need to ensure that the digitization of their texts, manuscripts, and diverse sources of contents are not only compatible with the new capabilities, expectations, research criteria, and competences of their intended readers but are also capable of bringing about authentic cultural experiences worthy of the works presented.

The End of Reading as an Experience of Interiority?

For centuries, reading has been the core cultural activity of Western culture, and the book has been seen as "modernity's quintessential technology—'a means of transportation through the space of experience, at the speed of a turning page,'" as the poet Joseph Brodsky puts it (Rosen 2008). For university professor Nathalie Piégay-Gros (2002), "Reading is an activity comparable to interpreting a musical score" (15; our translation). Well-known testimonies put reading as the source of interiority, intellectual awakening, self-construction, and pure enjoyment of life. Reading can be the lifeline of the solitary child, as described by Alberto Manguel (1996): "Sitting at my desk, elbows on the page, chin on my hands, abstracted for a moment from the changing light outside and the sounds that rise from the street, I am seeing, listening to, following (but these words don't do justice to what is taking place within me) a story, a description, an argument. Nothing moves except my eyes and my hand occasionally turning a page, and yet something not exactly defined by the word "text" unfurls, progresses, grows and takes root as I read" (28). These lines stand in echo of Proust's (1971) well-known "praise of reading," in a text beginning with "There are perhaps no days of our childhood we lived so fully as those we believe we left without having lived them, those we spent with a favorite book." Describing his experiences of reading during his personal childhood, Proust has strong metaphors as he presents reading as both a "fiery and sedate bliss" (2000, 73), "this contract with other minds" (61), "this pure and calm friendship" (56), or "this divine pleasure" (7; our translations).

This dominant reference to printed books in the reading experience comes with a preferred reading object: literature. Reading fictional or poetic texts has long been the prototypical reading experience, as least in the Western world. Based on attention and concentration, intense and intentional reading, especially in the case of literary texts, is still largely the dominant representation of what reading is. Literature is credited with feeding concentrated and refined emotions, desires, and knowledge that are aroused in a reading experience:

> For literature remains the unexcelled means of interior exploration and connection-making. The whole art—fiction, poetry, and drama—is fundamentally pledged to coherence, not just in terms of contents, but in forms as well. (Birkerts 1994, 197)

> Literature in particular, in all its forms (myths and legends, fairy tales, poems, novels, theatre, personal journals, comics, albums, essays—as long as it's "written"), offers a remarkable medium to awaken interiority, put thought in movement, stimulate symbolic activity, meaning construction, and foster seminal sharings. (Petit 2008, 224)

Hence there is an importance that is attributed to investing in texts, developing reading as a pleasurable experience and as an emotional and aesthetic encounter.

This vision of reading has recently been brought into perspective by ethnologists who underline that this understanding of reading, as an individual activity focused on an experience of interiority, is basically a Western approach within a specific historical time span. Brian Stock pleads for opening up the concept of reading: "The only way to move beyond the limits of our present understanding is to expand the archive of known reading practices; and this knowledge is perhaps the best guarantee that contemporary practices will not be made the standard for evaluating the different roles that reading plays elsewhere" (1993, 271). For, according to this ethnologist, "It is likewise recognized by historians and anthropologists that the notion of literature, as a type of discourse accessible through reading written texts for their nonvisible, allegorical, or spiritual significance, is largely a Western invention. The implied connection between writings and inner realities since Plato is one of the successful fictions that antiquity and the Middle Ages perpetrated on the modern world" (272).

A historian of intellectual practices such as Christian Jacob also relativizes the importance of individual reading: "Silent and solitary reading is only one modality amongst others, that has developed because of the emergence of intimate spaces and a personal relation to books and literature, and of the acknowledgement of individual subjectivity and sensitivity, fashioned by the evolution of society, customs and education" (2003, 18–19; our translation).

These historical perspectives are introduced here because they provide a distance that is necessary in order to understand the ongoing changes in reading practices with the development of digital means. For in our culture, reading is so deeply fashioned by the paper book that it is difficult to think otherwise of reading, or at least to think in terms of legitimate and worthy modalities that do not rest on the use of paper and whose implicit model is not literary reading.

Reading as an Acquired Competence

Reading appears to be such a "natural experience" that we are easily led to forget that being capable of reading fluently is the result of three to five years of intensive study and practice, as schoolteachers and children will easily acknowledge. Well-read books by neuroscientists, such as Maryanne Wolf's *Proust and the Squid* (2008) or Stanislas Dehaene's *Les Neurones de la lecture* (2007), both on the "reading brain," have popularized the recently acknowledged discovery that "the act of reading" is not natural but instead results from adaptations in the circuitry of the human brain. Wolf begins by reminding us of this shaping of the brain's ability by our cultural experience: "We were never born to read" (3). Basically, from a neurologist's point of view, learning to read consists of connecting two cerebral systems that exist in every young child, even at an early age: the visual system, which is capable of recognizing forms, and the language system. In order to connect the two, or adapt itself to reading requirements, the brain exploits and expands "two of the most important features of the human brain—our capacity for specialization and our capacity for making new connections among association areas" (M. Wolf 2008, 29). For Dehaene, "At the interface between nature and culture, our reading capacity results from a fortunate combination of circumstances in which good teaching plays as fundamental a role as the presence of visual and phonological neuronal processors correctly interconnected" (2007, 319–20).

As historians have shown, our reading ability has undergone many important evolutions, often triggered by new technologies, but also spurred by cultural and intellectual changes in society (see Cavallo and Chartier 1997; Eisenstein 2005; Manguel 1996; Olson 1994; Vandendorpe 1999). These changes—because they usually involved faster reading and thinking rhythms, questioning of authorities, and less reverence coupled with more rationality in dealing with texts and documents—have repeatedly produced fear of losing the cultural gains achieved in earlier existing practices.

Reading: A Practice Shaped by Technologies

Reading is a technology-based activity. Technology refers here to artifacts understood within an instrumental approach. As Pierre Rabardel sums it up, "The notion of artifact designates in anthropology anything having been transformed, even minimally, by a human being" and has "the advantage of not restraining the meaning to material things (of the physical world) as it easily comprises symbolic systems that can also be instruments" (1995, 59). Artifacts, which can be cognitive, social, or material, are produced by humans and incorporated into their activities and thus become instruments or tools. Technology refers to those material artifacts whose integration in human activities improves the procedural or methodological efficacy of the activities. Volumens and codices yesterday, paper books today, as well as all digital reading devices, are part of the cultural technologies that help us relate to information, knowledge, and, more generally, to texts and documents.

What the advent of digital technology has brought about is not only a differentiation between texts and their material support but also a strong awareness of the collusion between print, text, and thinking processes. Because printing and books are technologies, and because "technology constitutes a crucial cultural force" (Landow 2006, 46), it is necessary to consider the development of digital technology not as an alien product intruding in a natural setting but as a continuing evolution and expansion of information technology. George Landow explains how each technology has a tendency to consistently affect its inner principles, which allow for a limited number of tendencies, even though it is not possible to determine the exact directions that this influence will take.

Transposing written texts from paper to digital forms has led to the awareness that many characteristics attributed to knowledge were in fact primarily characteristics of print, such as stable spelling; rigorous punctuation; and accurate, permanent, and structured texts. When one thinks of reading, it is usually an in-depth, solitary experience of interacting with text on paper. That's because the dominant representation of reading is intertwined with the representation of printed texts in books and most of our reading experiences have been with printed books.

Another awareness that the transfer brings about is the importance of form in grasping the meaning of texts. Don McKenzie (1991), Oxford bibliographer and text sociologist, conceived that the role of the bibliographer is to "show that the forms have an impact on meaning" (30). Christian Jacob, a historian of intellectual practices, addresses a similar issue when he writes: "The materiality of books and the constraints in their handling affect the modalities of text appropriation, the process of meaning construction, and this applies to all books, be they manuscripts, printed or displayed on a computer screen" (1996, 56). In other words, the reception of a text is conditioned by the form that has been given to it, because the material support, the graphical presentation, and the means of access will all affect the interpretative process, from connoting in certain ways the author, the text, the authority of the text, the importance of the text, the way of reading the text, and so on. The importance of the form for a text also stems from the strong emotional investments that most readers place in books as personal and valuable objects.

As historians have shown, because technology affects meaning construction, characteristics of texts came to be identified with the printed book. Not only did page layouts and composition reach a summit of readability with print settings, but also the perpetuity and authority of texts came to be identified with printed books. Paper printing gradually imposed a stabilized text, a page setup facilitating eye movements across the text, silent reading, and editorial references that legitimized documents. The use of specific presentation features, such as chunking text into paragraphs, highlighting titles and subtitles, using italics and page display, and providing blanks and margins, affects content composition, which in turn induces cognitive processes.

Scholarly Reading: A Case on Its Own?

Reading old texts and critical editions of heritage works corresponds to a particular modality of reading called scholarly or erudite reading. This reading mode comprises a certain number of features that correspond to ways of interacting with such texts and to the fact that this type of reading is usually associated with working on texts. Until recently, scholarly editions have been produced basically as printed books, and most of the researchers using digital tools for their work still produce paper editions as their final output. Consequently, scholarly or erudite reading refers to reading paper works. Is the reading of these works threatened, and will the heralded changes in reading practices apply to scholarly reading?

Jacob has pertinently analyzed this scholarly reading mode, distinguishing it clearly from ordinary reading: "Reading refers today to a kind of well-regulated solitary and silent relationship to writing, the dynamic encounter between two subjectivities, between two intentionalities, through the mediation of a written text that would have the identification and projection power of a mirror. This model is only one step in a long evolution, during which not only the nature and status of books, but also their uses and their handling have considerably varied" (Jacob 2003, 18). Unlike this reading mode, scholarly reading is defined as "the activity of those who handle books as deposits, knowledge, wisdom and meaning objects or instruments. This knowledge, this wisdom and this meaning itself, presumed inscribed within the text, are actualized as results of reading, as the fruits of work, as the production of watchful eyes, of attention and of intelligence" (20). Not only is scholarly reading closely associated with paper books, but it also favors a reading mode made possible through the existence of this type of books. "Reflexivity seems to us to be an essential dimension of this activity: the scholarly reader controls and modulates his practice, he orients and focuses his look, he exploits the text and his very reading" (21).

For scholarly reading is above all "slow and methodical, aiming at an in-depth understanding of the document itself" (Jacob 1987, 89). Often linked to writing and working on the texts, "learned reading is defined by specific protocols: the reader interposes between the text and himself grids or filters, in order to select data and impose a specific point of view on the text" (Jacob 2003, 21–22). The researcher works with note sheets on which he records "key words, cardinal passages," "recurrences and articulations" (Jacob 1987, 90). Jacob foresees already what computer tools could bring to this type of reading: "Reading then is simulating possible texts. And one can imagine the contribution that computer processing would bring with visualizing of recurrences, underlying semantic networks, all that marks the text" (90; our translation). Finally, scholarly reading involves an implicit epistemology of the reader's community: "Scholarly reading presupposes a conception of texts as deposits and vectors of wisdom and knowledge, capable of being reactivated with the proper intellectual techniques" (93; our translation).

The scholarly reading mode organizes a permanent questioning of each text, of the way the text works and of what it signifies. Very demanding for the reader, scholarly reading has been developed with critical editions on paper, even though it is obvious that this paper presentation most often shows little concern for the reader's activity. In the same line of thinking, Roger Laufer, reflecting upon his scholarly edition of *Le Diable boiteux* (a text of 1707), wrote about his own difficulties in trying to read it: "Coming back to it a few years after having finished it, I found that it was unreadable even for myself. Why? Because such an edition is only the materialization of a patient work of jotting down extracts and notes made with strained eyes, and not a system for reading. I am convinced that no one has ever read critically more than one or two pages in a row, perhaps three at the most" (Laufer 1988, 118). Questioning the pertinence of computer solutions, such as multi-windowing, he sees there a real taking into account of the reader: "Thanks to it [electronic interaction] the reader can really take over the work of comparing raw data that had been previously recorded and memorized; that is, organize them according to one's own objectives" (118). Laufer is aware of "the scope of necessary intellectual changes and the stakes of possibilities that open up" for researchers as well as for readers. Still, as Nina Catach words it, will "the crucial contradiction between the scientific requirement of exhaustiveness and the no less imperative one of readability be better resolved?" (1988b, 25). Questioning the readability of critical editions, John Lavagnino (1995) distinguishes between presentations to facilitate the research work and presentations to facilitate the reading activity. He observed again that critical editions on paper are not made for reading: "The book has become transparent for most of us, but scholarly editions with their critical apparatus do not offer a transparent presentation of the different versions and variants, because one has to resort to the apparatus and the apparatus is opaque for most of us." Lavagnino therefore pleads for editions that will allow the reader to be able to read without being interrupted, and for reading of works as a truly immersive experience and not just a collection of data: "The complaints about editions that do not expand ampersands and abbreviations, and the exaggerated responses of many people to errors in spelling and punctuation, testify to this desire for immediacy: these things do not render texts impossible to decode, but they trip us up, they make us work too much at the mere labour of routine decoding and so interrupt our experience." It follows from these comments that critical editions, as presented on paper, are far from enabling the activity of readers even if they allow researchers to work on the texts. Even if there is an awareness of the facilitating possibilities of digital means for readers, it appears that the digital editions are still conceived as very similar to literary reading on paper.

The Paper Paradigm Still Largely Organizes the Reading Experience

Until recently, hardly anybody outside the concerned Western scholars was aware of how important printing and paper had become for reading and conception of text. By the "paper paradigm" of reading we are referring to the set of assumptions, representations, and practices that have coalesced with the development of printing on paper. Therefore, the term "paradigm" is to be understood within the perspective brought by Thomas Kuhn as "the entire constellation of beliefs, values, techniques, and so on shared by the members of a given community" (1962, 175). With this concept, Kuhn introduced a rupture in the history of sciences, in conceiving it not as an accumulation of knowledge but as a series of revolutionary breaks, as a "succession of tradition-bound periods punctuated by non-cumulative breaks" (208). What the paper paradigm emphasizes is the quasi-irreversible connection between reading and paper books, which, because of their fixity, their recognized legitimacy, and their user friendliness, have become irreplaceable for sustaining the experience of comprehension, of concentration, of interiority, and of memorization that reading is believed to require. That is why, inasmuch as the paper page layout, the fractioning of texts, and their typography can be reproduced onscreen, the experience of digital reading can take place within a certain continuity and can be considered as a remediation of the practice and not a revolution.

Our dominant representation of reading is based on the printed book. When readers are asked what they want to read on, most will say they want it to be like paper. Sometimes readers do not even think they have read something unless they have read it on paper. When questioned after reading e-books, readers say that what they missed the most is "the feeling of paper." Not being able to feel and turn the pages deprived them of the feeling of progress in reading. Without page turning many people feel they no longer have a hold on their reading experience, because they don't have a sense of how far they've gone. High screen resolutions are appreciated inasmuch as they come close to the high quality of print norms. Readers are comforted in their thinking with the paper-like aspect of many web texts, the dominance of PDF format presentation geared to printing, and the efforts of the e-book industry to imitate paper book presentations, layouts, and structure. Even though digital technology has been around for more than half a century, people who share this paradigmatic understanding of reading still talk or write about books, or journalism, without feeling the need to specify "paper books" or "paper journalism," as if there were still only one kind of books around or still only paper journalism. When one reads as the title of a conference "The Death of the Book," the speaker is probably referring only to the death of the paper book. It is urgent to develop awareness of this paper paradigm in order to better understand the cultural changes that are taking place today.

Adolescents today have not left aside the paper experience, as evidenced by the sales figures of different novels geared to teenagers: 11 million copies of *Harry Potter and the Deadly Hallows*, by J. K. Rowling, had been sold in July 2007 within the first twenty-four hours of sale, and the number of books sold in the Harry Potter series was already at 325 million even before the seventh, and final, novel came out (BBC World News, July 23, 2007). The *Twilight* series of four best-selling novels (with a combined page count of over two thousand) by Stephanie Meyer also had record sales of 42 million copies four years after the first book went on sale. Whether this is a passing flurry or a real discovery for teenagers and the younger adults who compose the readership, their reading experience as an exploration of fantasy, witchcraft, and imaginary characters is now intensively being attended to by a large number of authors. What this mass popularity of printed books confirms is the need to closely examine whether reading is changing or whether reading practices are becoming more diversified, different, and distinctive.

Sven Birkerts, back in 1994, made a strong case for the printed text-based interiority experience, which he then considered as being specifically tied to the reading of printed books. He observed with dismay the new experience of digital reading as surface oriented, faster, and less engaging in opposition to this Western printed book experience. The conflict he described was reminiscent of similar fears that were voiced in the sixteenth and eighteenth centuries, when people started reading faster, because, among other reasons, print is read faster than manuscripts. But such fears have often been expressed throughout the history of reading as practices moved from the meditative, prayer-like reading of texts in the Middle Ages to the skimming and diagonal reading of twenty-first-century readers.

Although Birkerts has now moved into the digital workplace, he stresses the fact that there are "profound discontinuities in what we optimistically call the evolution of culture," and he stresses the need today "to orient ourselves to the new, its possibilities as well as its liabilities."

Change has not been overtly imposed so much as subtly and complexly distributed. Everything rearranges itself. What's more, much of the transfer has been in the direction of ease. To add exponentially increased processing power to a computer, new enabling software packages; to acquire a mobile phone or access to fifty new channels—these feel like expansions and augmentations, and we take them in our stride, one by one, mostly unaware that we embed ourselves ever more deeply in a mesh. And unaware, too, that at a certain point that embeddedness is comprehensive enough to mark a significant change in our way of living. It is necessary to grasp this fact of saturation if any headway is to be made in understanding the present situation. (Birkerts 2003)

In fact, the changes in reading practices are not so much a question of technology as a question of social practices. It is the users who decide if and when the new practices are preferable and if and for what reason the old ones should survive.

Changes in Reading as Symptoms

Changes happening with digital information technologies today are being discussed either to raise concern or to stimulate adoption. Non-biased facts are difficult to come across, and therefore the issues can be raised mainly in terms of questions asked. Different media are relaying a general alert concerning explicit changes in reading. Reading on screens is held responsible for shortening our attention spans and for reducing reading to just-in-time skimming, to scanning material very quickly (Marshall 2004), to processing smaller and smaller snippets of text. Is reading on screens putting an end to reading in depth (Levy 2001), dissolving disciplinary boundaries, weakening our ability to think things through for ourselves (Sanger 2008), radically changing public and private space, and destroying the isolation of distance? Of course, these questions do not stem specifically from digital scholarly practices, because the presentations of most digital scholarly editions are very similar to their paper ancestors. But it can be assumed that if these changes in reading habits are established, they will gradually concern all readers and, consequently, digital scholarly editors will need to be aware of the kind of readers their works will be addressing.

In a seminal article with the provocative title "Is Google Making Us Stupid?" which resonated all across the Western hemisphere in the summer of 2008, journalist Nicholas Carr formulated the problem with digital technology as being related to the shaping of the mind by the tools used, Google being the most terrifying. This shaping had previously been described as becoming incapable of dense, in-depth reading and capable only of surfing across the web with only short spans of reading. Carr goes further in providing arguments that point to noticeable changes not only in reading activities but also in the way of thinking, in evolving mental habits, perhaps signaling a reprogramming of the brain. What worries Carr is not so much the changes as such, but the fact that it is the Internet that is "reprogramming us" and the fact that "the Net's intellectual ethic remains obscure." Google's declared mission, "to organize the world's information and make it universally accessible and useful," as stated on their website, coupled with their interest in artificial intelligence, does not really reassure him.

Carr also refers to Maryanne Wolf's book on reading as a reorganization of neuronal circuits, in order to understand the ongoing changes in the brain due to digital activity. For Wolf there is cause for alarm: "We must be vigilant not to lose the profound generativity of the reading brain as we add new dimensions to our intellectual repertoire" (M. Wolf 2008, 23). The "partial attention" culture that is typical of Internet browsing and multitasking could foster information illiteracy.

Even though most people are aware of differences in their use of the Internet and of paper books, they are often unable to identify or explain these differences and often have a feeling that digital technology does not provide for reading activities that are as engaging and in-depth as reading paper books. Therefore, they are genuinely questioning whether digital uses are developing new cultural grounds, attitudes, and perspectives and doing away with strongly established and precious values.

What this brings home is that culture in a digital world is not primarily based on or referring to books. We are probably in the midst of a shockwave equivalent to the one the printing press initiated in the sixteenth century, as documented by historians such as Guglielmo Cavallo and Roger Chartier (1997) or Elisabeth Eisenstein (1983). For in addition to providing a new support for text, printing changed the hierarchy of information production and the communication circuits in fundamental ways. The sixteenth century saw not only the development of print but also the rise of the Renaissance, of the Reform, and of humanism. "Within decades, a new intellectual community was fashioning and feeding the Renaissance, that sudden and dynamic expansion of Western culture that dared to transgress the margins of medievalism" (Fischer 2003, 206). "Printing's emancipation of the written word defined that essential dynamic of our modern world, the accelerated accessing of information" (207). And as the French historian Henri-Jean Martin has reminded us, "The gradual shift from the world of orality to the society of writing . . . led, in the final analysis, to something quite new—the unleashing of mechanisms that prompted a new view of self and a spirit of abstraction . . . It encouraged a logic of the act as well as a logic of the word, and also an ability to reach reasoned decisions and a higher measure of self-control" (Martin 1996, 321, as quoted by Fischer 2004, 207). Are we facing an evolution that is similar in momentum to the one that was initiated during the sixteenth century in Europe, a diversification in intellectual approaches and in relating to knowledge through digital reading? The changes developing in the digital environment could have such deep consequences as the rejection of ancestral knowledge deposits in favor of quests for updated information deemed more pertinent along with a receding of authority figures and mediating institutions. Even if the creativity of a new generation of writers producing on the web and their new interactive and multimedia presentation schemas take a long time in finding their readers, there is a building up of changes in reading modes that progressively compel recognition by all.

Scholarly editing is particularly concerned with the results of this evolution in reading practices. Because of commanding changes in the technological, organizational, and economic editing processes, scholarly editions will have to adapt more and more to constraints in decisions concerning contents that are edited and presented, the public that is being addressed, scientific exhaustiveness, and legibility policies. Will such evolutions be sufficient to ensure a privileged niche for these works in a developing digital world? Or will researchers who work with digital tools be called upon to completely rethink their aims and methods in order to face the digital challenges?

Emergence of the Digital Paradigm in Reading

With the paper paradigm in reading being dominant, it can easily be described and delimited with varied examples. The digital paradigm, however, is only just emerging in new reading practices, and one cannot rely on representations and existing practices for an obvious recognition of these practices. "Digital paradigm" refers here to the set of beliefs, values, and practices shared by those for whom digital tools cannot be ignored, as much in their daily life as in the evolution of society. Our focus in this section is on the specific changes that digital reading tools bring about in our relationship to content and knowledge, for the ongoing changes in reading are not independent of a much wider digital environment.

The digital paradigm appears with computer technology, but it is rooted in the profound changes that media practices have brought about throughout the twentieth century. As the different media—photography, film, radio, comic strips, press, and television—have developed in the last century, cultural practices have experienced important changes and reading on paper has become seriously challenged as the main enriching pastime. While some sociologists keep stressing the general stupefying effect of media on masses, most users have not simply passively adapted to the different media but have learned to read ingenious magazine layouts; to zap commercials and uninteresting TV programs; and to find their own personal preferences and gems in the profusion of games, shows, and activities that media have made available.

What characterizes the digital reading paradigm can be drawn from the behaviors already considered as typical of a digital world. The digital world is one of evolving powerful technology where all activities are mediated by technological interactive tools. These tools can be personalized and are geared mainly to communication. The user is not a viewer or a listener but an actor, intervening in the flow of data that relates him to the world through a digital device. Whether it's through a game, a commercial transaction, or a search for information, the Internet user is constantly picking up information, making decisions, and intervening in the unfolding of the action. This also applies to reading on screens, as computers were not designed for continuous reading but for reading and writing. This basically active approach is coupled with an unreserved and open approach to documents and information, with an authentic belief that mediators and intermediaries are superfluous. A good example of this belief is the use of encyclopedias like Wikipedia, where users are confident that they can understand the explanations and presentations, whatever the topic, which is not the case with the authoritative encyclopedias such as *Britannica* or *Universalis*. This is coupled with a renewed faith in democracy and sharing, as exemplified by the social networks that have been set up and the extreme confidence with which people share their lives, their aspirations, their feelings, and their daily activities with their friends, usually, but also with total strangers.

Digital tools allow readers to explore new reading modalities: fine textual investigation with analytical tools, and instant hypothesis testing with tools for translating, researching, clustering, classifying, synthesizing. These are important challenges for trailblazers. There is a need to deconstruct the reading concept and construct new reception schemas. Second-generation e-book users easily expressed in a survey (Bélisle et al. 2004a) their new requirements as they became familiar with the possibilities of the e-book devices they were using for reading. They wanted new features, such as more contextual information, dictionaries, and Internet access. Thus, because they were working with a digital tool that offered potentially numerous possibilities, they were modifying their reading habits, even for reading novels. It is obvious to foresee that evolving reading practices will rapidly impose new interfaces and new content concepts, such as "collections," which could have an important role in organizing access, while the distribution in book units seems less pertinent in a digital context. Those who are leading the way in reading technology will find stimulating challenges in mastering these tools.

The first generation of e-books, the handheld reading devices, which almost made it to popularity at the end of the twentieth century, gained their appeal through their printed-book-like presentation of text, answering readers' expectations of legibility in bringing printing norms into the digital world. Long texts with just a scroll button remain unacceptable. E-books brought to the screen the page format, the division of texts into pages, providing a reading rhythm one does not have when scrolling. But this first generation of e-books did not survive, because it had too many drawbacks (weight, autonomy, availability of books, etc.). Having overcome the main initial obstacles, a new generation of e-books is trying to attract a reading public with a presentation that reproduces the paper book layout. This renewed offer in e-books has brought digital reading to a new level with the use of E Ink (a type of electronic paper) as well as different formats and digital stores where users can buy and upload books and other texts no matter what device they want to read on: PC, Mac, mobile phone, dedicated reading device with electronic paper display (E Ink) or tablets with LED-backlit IPS (in-plane switching) display. Most devices now have virtual keyboards, multi-touch screens, and Wi-Fi connections.

Other innovative technologies are already in use with dedicated readers (devices) that are being experimented with, mainly by the online daily newspapers. These viewers allow page turning, zooming in on any element, which a mouse click seamlessly presents in a high-definition window, or navigating by thumbnail images of each page presented in a column on the left. This allows the reader to have a rapid view of the newspaper content and to focus on specific articles. Other tools include saving text in a personalized folder, printing, or tagging, and, of course, connecting to the newspaper's main portal or simply navigating the web to obtain further information, check the contents with other sources, or use publishing tools to spread the information. Even if the text presentation, in the case of e-books, is still very dependent on the achievements of the paper page layout, it is easy to understand that using these new reading devices allows one to imagine other ways of reading and brings up the wish to experiment with them.

What these tools are implementing is a full use of new reading techniques, mixing skimming and focusing modalities, integrating comparing and classifying with discovering, and allowing concomitant multilevel presentations. If one also takes into consideration the new aggregators and portals that give access to a large selection of similar websites (for example, news or cultural videos), it is obvious that a new standard in reading technologies is emerging progressively. In some ways these technologies are converging with scholarly editing practices already established in philological work. It would be highly beneficial for digital critical editions not only to become available through these tools but also to have an influence on their development by making known the requirements of scholars who want to access the different text modalities of critical editions.

New Practices and Approaches to the Text: Digital Natives

There is a significant gap between people over thirty and most young readers who have grown up with digital technology and have no firsthand experience of a world not organized by digital devices, computers, and networks. These "digital natives" (Prensky 2001), as they have been labeled, are truly at ease with digital technology, even if their skills are often limited and superficial. But they do not hesitate to venture into the unknown, using "implicit trial-and-error" strategies and usually succeed in surfing easily on the web. For them, "knowing how" is more important than "knowing what," and knowing how comes with practice and with participation in a community of practice as well as sharing its ways of seeing, understanding, interpreting, and acting.

As Marc Prensky has stressed for the last decade, "Today's students think and process information fundamentally differently from their predecessors" as a result of their immersion in a digital technology environment and the "sheer volume of their interaction" (2001) within it. Surveys, for example, at the European University of Bretagne (Henriet, Malingre, and Serres 2008) or at the British Library (Williams and Rowlands 2007), show that there is a general low level of competence in working with documents. At the same time, the researchers were baffled by the gap between what they were expecting as far as routines and attitudes in coherence with the students' university training, and the actual behaviors of the users. For example, the "Google generation" (Google was created in 1998) prefers rapid information, already summarized, and is not interested in format nor in the original support that would have allowed users to contextualize the information found.

It is not that the "digital natives" are more or less competent in searching for information than previous students (this is what interests teachers); it is that they are not looking with the same criteria and not appreciating what they find with the same values. There is still very little information on this difference in processing information, but it does appear that digital natives have a more detached and functional relation to texts and meaning. Texts and documents are means to interact with the world and are not immediately the basic witnesses of civilization, to be revered and preserved. Among the different characteristics that are developing in the way one relates to knowledge, there is the personalized access to information, a growing individualization of requests and demands, and the development of services and dynamic editing. Finding one's way in the new semantic spaces is becoming more important than the in-depth construction of meaning.

As can be expected, "Any medium will facilitate, emphasize, amplify and enhance some kinds of use or experience whilst inhibiting, restricting or reducing other kinds" (Chandler 1995). The reading practices today take place while an important change is developing in the way society is relating to texts and documents. Can this be as important a shift as the one brought about in reading habits by the humanists, which was to open the way for modern thought? "'Humanism' turned reading private, questioned received wisdom and creatively sought new alternatives" (Fischer 2003, 214). How can the work on critical editions take into account these evolutions in order to ensure that these publications are present in a world of digital knowledge?

More Information and Less Structure

Two basic changes in the way readers relate to information are brought about by digital technology: (1) the access to vast quantities of information, which has led to the involvement of intermediary software in reading, and (2) the emergence of new and evolving information structures. The first change involves the well-known and researched explosive increase and facilitation in accessing information and the resulting information overload for the user. Digital devices such as computers (portable or desktop), cellular phones, or digital offers such as online libraries or websites provide more and more information and access to different types of resources: not only texts and images but also newspapers, journals, radio and television podcasts, raw data coming in from existing databases, or online recordings of remote sensors in real time (for example, those used by the European space station or the National Aeronautics and Space Administration). These offers also include access to rare and fragile materials—for example, medieval manuscripts—but also multilingual information software (e.g., translation of a Japanese text for Western readers—not the same as if you were really reading Japanese, but still something that breaks the barrier). Accessing digital resources also means changes in the way people learn; as can be observed over the last ten years, the thrust is not so much in memorizing sciences such as physics, history, or geography but in providing students with opportunities to engage in scientific inquiry, in comparative understanding, or in documented presentations. This situation has given rise to a new category of tools: search engines, now well known through the problematic success of Google. Searches are performed in an ocean of information, with results that can be staggering; millions of links may be signaled, but usually the first dozen references are sufficiently pertinent to satisfy the user.

The second basic change in how readers relate to technology is the dimension of information structuring. This fundamental change is much less spectacular but probably entails more crucial consequences for reading processes and practices. The disciplinary structured information is decreasing proportionately as more and more diversely structured information becomes accessible online, whether because of the formats such as databases or because of the content such as multimedia, multilingual, and multicultural documents and files.

Thus online reading gives access not only to large quantities of texts but also to texts that are generally not organized in a disciplinary approach. Disciplinary categories are usually situated within a culture and specific to that culture. They can transcend linguistic frontiers and be common to a sociocultural entity. While information research on paper sources is usually carried out within a disciplinary approach of knowledge, the use of digital support favors a more contextualized, thematic, and personalized approach based on dynamic searching, editing, and publishing. This unmoderated, adisciplinary information introduces a specific new challenge for readers: they must simultaneously understand what they are reading while trying to identify the kind of information they are interacting with. This implies an ongoing meta-cognitive attention to identifying information while the basic interaction between knowledge and construction is happening. Attending thus to categorizing activities while reading is not usually required in paper reading, because the different formats provide us with visual cues that reveal what kind of information one can expect to find.

This new way of reading could represent a real opportunity for scholarly editing with works that usually interact with several disciplinary fields. The real challenge, besides getting interesting, interactive, and authoritative material online, is for editors to be able to reach out to their intended public, taking into account the changes that will inevitably affect their relation to reading and to knowledge. In this sea of information, how will scholarly editions find their reading public? Will specific reading tools be proposed to facilitate and accelerate access to the works: textual and visual synthesis tools, semantic indexation tools, and different navigation tools such as dynamic menus, icons, semantic maps, and personalized paths? Which are the most adequate tools for scholarly reading, as digital editions would require?

As the evolving, dynamic, updated text becomes the norm, digital tools are becoming increasingly intuitive and interactive. What will this imply in terms of allowing access to heritage works without damaging the integrity of the legacy? With digital technology, readers' annotations can be seamlessly incorporated into the original text, thus producing a new text with each annotated reading. Special care must be taken if one wants to distinguish between the original texts and the annotations—and make the distinction visible to all. What must scholars deploy and include in their production so as to alert users to the heritage value of what they have worked so hard on? How can they reconcile the values of authority, authenticity, and scientificity with the changing reading environments? These are problems that will have to be solved by researchers if scholarly editions are to be present and visible in the digital world.

Meta-Reading: The Future of Reading Critical Editions

The gulf between the digital literacy of humanities scholars and the skills and competence necessary for handling digital editing and publishing software in their present state will need to be greatly reduced by time and training. Furthermore, there are two major flaws that hinder the reader's interaction with digital editions. The first one is the multiplicity of "isolated and incompatible platform-dependent" (Shillingsburg 2006) systems, each providing "at least one unique capability not found in the others" (90) and each requiring from the user a significant investment to master the intricacies of its tools. The second drawback is the lack of assured conversion tools; as technological systems are constantly developing and being updated, it is not acceptable that a critical edition produced in year n will no longer be accessible with the technology of year n+1 or n+2. Therefore two obvious demands must be met for scholars, other than a few pioneers, to embrace digital critical editions: (1) an interface (or a browser) that provides integrated or built-in access to the main tools necessary to attend to the needs of the different script acts that scholars choose to engage in, and (2) a file format that ensures easy conversion and updating, compatible with user-friendly reading and writing tools.

If these serious technological deterrents can be overcome, can digital editions replace paper editions? Up to now readers' opinions did not have much weight in decisions concerning editing of scholarly works. By implicit consensus these editions could be produced—and can still be produced—without any consideration for readers and can even end up without having any actual readers. The goal of these editions is to arrive at a recognized and established text, with the double aim of conservation and authenticity. As librarians have observed, readers who are not scholars but are nevertheless interested in ancient manuscripts, books, or texts generally ask to have access to documents they can understand, and this might mean not necessarily the originals but versions in modern fonts and spelling. These two aims, scholarly and amateur, do not necessarily converge.

Readers of historic texts do not discredit the different academic disputes over what constitutes textuality, but it is most often of no use to these readers to enter into such nuances, because they do not usually have the background to have a critical understanding of the issues addressed. Unless it is decided that critical editions are aimed only at the small population of students and researchers cognizant of the works edited, it is necessary to rethink the editorial objectives of critical editions in the light of reader expectations and needs. Furthermore, the digital representation of texts is bringing about new reading and critical analysis strategies. As digital representation alters the conditions of textuality, making it possible for readers to pursue new and diversified goals, editors must provide readers with alternative approaches and paths.

With universal accessibility, what has changed are the readers' goals, with a whole new range of possibilities for interacting with texts and documents. Most readers today do not go to historical texts to participate in obscure quarrels about alphabetical and punctuation signs. They do not ignore the cumulative nature of scholarship, nor do they necessarily dismiss the proofs of scientificity that the critical apparatus provides. But very few will seek a "definitive" text. Their questions do not address claims of truth and authority, or reliability, or completeness of an edited work. Readers are interested in knowing clearly and rapidly what are the contents of a work; they also want navigation tools that allow freedom of movement, browsing, and examination, tools that facilitate critical and associative reading by the user through the use of hyperlinks.

Editors present the text for reflexive and critical readers as if these readers want to read the entire text or work in depth. However, because of the evolving way of researching information, readers will increasingly want to be able to choose, to read only parts, and to pursue a text only if they find interest in what is being read. There may be a basic dissymmetry between reader and producer of digital editions: producers want to present the final complete version, whereas readers want to access segments of a text, depending on the objectives of their search. It is interesting to observe that a library such as the New York Municipal Library has undertaken to completely overhaul its online catalog in order to attend to the developing digital experience of those users who want to access only chapters, extracts, or parts of works.

Taking into account the increased differentiation between reading practices, which can already be observed, the main issue is what new possibilities digital technology brings for discovering, understanding, and interpreting scholarly editions of literary works. Two main characteristics are gradually changing the cultural background and expectations of digital readers: (1) the cultural and linguistic diversity inherent to digital resources; and (2) increasingly multimodal processes of learning and understanding. Written, linguistic modes are now accompanied much more by visual, audio, and spatial patterns of meaning. Different meaning conventions address different cognitive skills.

What advantages over paper editions do digital scholarly editions offer to readers?

- Access to more inclusive and richer versions of texts, through archives, multiple editions, eventually access to all related materials, with the capacity to represent the complexity of literary works
- Development of new methods for critical studies and analysis, allowing flexibility and taking into account the cumulative nature of scholarly work
- Open navigation, richer experiences, and parallel readings

- Ability to add comments, links, and annotations
- Opportunities for collective productions of new editions blurring the boundaries between "editor" and "user"

Umberto Eco, in *The Future of the Book* (1996), explained that students could read at such high speeds that even university teachers could not attain them: "The new generation is trained to read at an incredible speed. An old-fashioned university professor is today incapable of reading a computer screen at the same speed as a teenager" (297). This is usually seen as a problem because professors typically refer to only one representation of reading: intensive, repetitious reading—ultimately the religious practice of holy texts meditation. It is a constant observation in the history of reading that each important change in reading modalities, reading publics, and reading sources has seen acceleration in the reading rhythm.

The Unresolved Ambitions of Digital Critical Editions

In order to develop beyond a small circle of erudite professors and students, digital scholarly editions have to address a public wider than disciples, those who abide by the discipline, who appreciate conforming to academic norms. With the renewed interest in heritage, multiculturalism, and in humanities generally, there is probably a very large potential public for scholarly editions, but before this public is attended to or reached, critical editors must rethink how to present what they have to offer.

The main issue is what new possibilities for discovering, understanding, and interpreting scholarly editions of literary works that digital technology can bring. Editors need to reconcile themselves with the fact that users will be looking at their productions in significantly different ways than those provided until now. Users access texts to find information with very different objectives, from participating in a media contest to writing one's thesis. Documents in critical editions can be consulted only partially, sometimes very rapidly, and often with processing tools such as search engines, translators, annotators, metadata harvesters, and so on. It is up to critical editors to develop access to their material if they want their production to be part of the continuing cultural heritage and therefore accessible by most digital tools used for interacting with this heritage today.

Ambitious prospects for critical editions are not new. As early as 1991, Jay Bolter was already explaining how the electronic (one would now say digital) space held unsuspected promises that could be attained by moving humanistic study to the computer. Referring to the Divine Comedy Project, of putting "into the computer the text of the *Divine Comedy* together with all its Renaissance commentaries," Bolter sees the computer as the ideal writing space for such an ongoing project, "both because it handles change so easily and because it grants equal status to all the elements in the evolving structure" (2001, 203). Hailing the electronic library as a "new republic of letters," he saw the computer as making "the seductive promise to break down the barrier between thought and writing, to join the mind and writing surface into a seamless whole" (206).

These promising outlooks for critical digital editions have been tested to some degree over the years. Today a much more complex understanding of the digital possibilities prevails. Important changes are under way in the world of scholarly edition. As Peter Shillingsburg summarizes it:

> Textual critics [. . .] discovered that texts were more than simply correct or erroneous. Textual shape was in flux, affected by authorial revision and by the acts of editors meeting new needs: new target audiences, censorship, and the tastes of new times. Tracing the history of these textual changes and their various cultural implications became an activity parallel to that of literary critics pursuing new ways to (mis)read texts. Taking into account these important evolutions in the discipline, researchers are gradually acknowledging that constructing a scholarly edition has now gone beyond the capacities of print technology, making it more and more inescapable that scholarly editions should be constructed and published electronically. (2006, 81)

In fact, there are good reasons that explain why scholars have not been persuaded of the advances that digital editions can embody. A number of drawbacks have severely hampered the digital turnover. As has been shown in other digital areas, users will adopt only technology that is user-friendly, that does not require an investment considered outrageous in the light of the gains achieved, that does not entail an important deviation from one's course of action, and that provides greater satisfaction through peer recognition or social status enhancement. This is still not the case with digital critical editions. The work undertaken by different scholars has produced an array of tools, most of them requiring their own system, installment, and work method. This results in tools that are not easily mastered, even for prospective digital native readers, and for scholars it signals a real challenge still to be met of putting scholarly editions at the level of readers' expectations.

Digital space does seem particularly challenging for scholarly editing. It constitutes a medium that is capable of meeting readers' expectations through representing different versions of a work and the complex relationships between them through hyperlinking and multiple window and multitasking interfaces. However, how exactly these interactive navigational expectations can be met is still highly unspecified. Digital editions can also answer readers' new requirements in text access and reading by providing an array of tools that allow word and thematic searches, creation of links, extractions, annotations, and comparisons, with the possibility of keeping track of all these activities. Yet if there is a general trend toward interactive involvement in digital space, there are very few identified and confirmed uses beyond e-mail, games, commercial transactions, and social networks. Visualization tools, which could present visually complex levels of meanings, of relations, and of historical evolution, are growing in number and capacity, but they have yet to be integrated significantly in scholarly editions.

Diverse modalities of reading are embedded within representation systems. The new reading practices have yet to prove that they are not simply remediated practices from within the paper paradigm but that they effectively represent a breakthrough in cognitive processing of data, information, and knowledge. Whether surfing, skimming, or navigating within multitasking is a decline in reading or the premises of new cognitive processes, and whether the systematic use of summaries, highlights, keywords, hyperlinks, and the resulting new types of reading paths will lead to greater enlightenment are issues still debated. Understanding what is at stake and maintaining belief in the value of these practices are fundamental to setting up critical editions that will correspond to today's dynamic reading. Digital surroundings are developing much faster than we can imagine. Digital critical editions need to find their place in these new surroundings, and this involves mainly focusing on how they will be able to bring about "compelling new cultural experiences" through dynamic reading of the enduring works of authors, heritage writers, and poets.

Note

1. Quoted from Lefèvre (n.d.).

PART II

Text Technologies

5. Markup Technology and Textual Scholarship

CLAUS HUITFELDT

This chapter gives a brief overview of the background and development of markup systems—that is, formal languages for the representation of electronic documents.[1] The chapter focuses on aspects of markup technology that are particularly relevant to textual scholarship. It gives an introduction to some of the key concepts of the Extensible Markup Language (XML) and the Text Encoding Initiative (TEI) and considers some of their limitations, possibilities, and future potential.

Introduction

About This Chapter

This chapter is intended as an introduction to markup for textual scholars who are new to the subject. In order to assess the relevance or utility of markup to activities within textual scholarship, there is no need to be conversant with all aspects and details of the technology. What is required, however, is a grasp of its basic presuppositions, possibilities and limitations, and the investments and risks involved. Therefore, most of what is covered here is of a quite general nature, though focusing on issues assumed to be of particular relevance for textual scholarship. Much that would be appropriate for a wider or different audience has been left out, and little will be of interest for readers of this chapter who are already familiar with the basics of markup.

Why Textual Scholars Should Care about Markup

According to one usage of the word "markup," all documents are marked up. In this view both punctuation, page layout, and typography are examples of markup. Consequently, the reason why textual scholars should care about markup is simply that it is present in all documents, whether in the form of electronic or printed documents, manuscripts, or other written documents.[2]

In a more specific usage of the word, "markup" refers to the use of special markers in electronic document files in order to signal certain properties of the document. However, even according to this more restricted usage of the word "markup," it may firmly be maintained that virtually all electronic documents are marked up. And since textual scholarship increasingly has to relate to electronic documents in some way or another, the argument can again be made that markup is essential to its concerns.

In this chapter I focus on markup in a yet more specific sense of the word, so-called generalized markup. Before proceeding to explain more precisely what is meant by the term in this more specific sense, however, it may be instructive for readers who are unacquainted with generalized markup to note that it is an essential part of a number of high-quality document processing and publication systems. It is also an important part of the technology underlying the World Wide Web (henceforth referred to as "the web").

Today the production of any scholarly edition inevitably relies on the use of computer-based publication methods, and thus also markup, whether those responsible for the edition are aware of it or not. The most popular text-processing systems in use today, off-the-shelf word processors and web or print publication systems, do not make use of generalized markup. Moreover, they take care of the markup "in the background" and allow the user to interact directly with documents displayed in the intended (or at least the resulting) visual layout (so-called WYSIWYG, or "what you see is what you get").

The kind of use of generalized markup discussed here, however, exposes the markup to the user and forces him at least sometimes to work with documents in an intermediate form that is visually much less close to the finished, printed, or displayed result. The path from the initial work at the keyboard to the finished product may seem—and indeed mostly is—more cumbersome and time consuming than it may be by using off-the-shelf software. If the sole aim of preparing an electronic document is the production of the visual result on screen or paper, adoption of generalized markup certainly does not save intellectual effort, work, time, or money.

However, if the aim of preparing the edition is extended to include making it available for use with modern tools for search and retrieval, computer-assisted concordancing, collation, word-frequency counts, collocation analysis, linguistic or stylistic analysis, and so forth, then in practice there is no alternative to employing standards for generalized markup. Thus, even in cases where the editors or the primary target audience themselves have no intentions to employ methods of search or analysis, the documents will be readily available for such use by the increasing number of readers who do have such intentions.

Perhaps equally or more important, documents prepared adhering to standards for generalized markup have better chances of long survival in a world of ever-changing computer systems, software, and formats. Many are those who have suffered the experience of discovering that documents that have been excellently prepared with easy-to-use off-the-shelf software become increasingly difficult to access—and finally, in practice, completely unusable—as the technology supporting the format they were prepared in becomes obsolete. The digital world, in which software and storage formats continuously change, is in many ways an ephemeral world. Preparing documents using standard generalized markup is the best way of ensuring usability and maximizing the chances that documents prepared today can still be read and used in a more distant future. Thus, one of the main reasons for recommending generalized markup is longevity.

On the other hand, the use of markup is always associated with underlying assumptions about the nature of texts and of textual editing. All too often such assumptions are made only silently, without explicit reflection, and uninformed by the specific nature of textual scholarship. It is only when these underlying assumptions about the nature of the object and task at hand are made explicit and the markup system adapted to the basic theoretical presuppositions and practical requirements of textual scholarship that markup can be put to its best use for the purposes of such scholarship.

Different editorial approaches vary not only in the methods of establishing the text but even in their basic assumptions about what they are trying to represent—that is, the object of their study. While *genetic editing* aims to record the sequence of scribal acts of which the manuscript is the tangible result, the *copy text* tradition aims at establishing a text that is as close to the author's intentions as possible. Whereas the *diplomatic edition* aims to accurately represent a manuscript down to grapheme and even allograph level, the *normalized edition* contents itself with a morphologically correct and "normalized" representation where spelling errors and slips of the pen have been silently corrected. While the *best text* approach usually contents itself with representing one witness and records variants in an apparatus, so-called *eclectic editions* establish a main text that is a selection from several or all of its witnesses.

There is no markup system that supports the requirements of all these editorial methods equally well. The strength of generalized markup is that the markup system can be adapted to suit the needs of each individual editorial effort in the best way possible. Of course that does not mean that generalized markup provides the answer to all editorial problems. But it does force each editorial endeavor to make its methods and its requirements explicit, and, to the extent that this is possible, to make them explicit in a way that lends itself to rigorous formal treatment. This incentive to explication of editorial methods may in itself be a good thing. Even so, large parts, and perhaps the essential parts, of editorial scholarship do not lend themselves to rigorous formal treatment. What markup systems can help with is to make it easier for the textual scholar to concentrate on those parts rather than the more trivial aspects of the work.

All of this is to say that markup technology is a useful tool for textual scholarship. However, the opposite argument may also be made: textual scholars probably know more than anyone else about the richness of the various technologies that have supported transmission of texts down through history, in and between different literate cultures. Maybe this is why textual scholars and other representatives of the arts and humanities have already been able to contribute a great deal to markup theory and to the development of markup systems. So an additional reason for textual scholars to engage in work on markup is altruistic: through their participation, the shaping of future text technology may benefit from their knowledge rather than being left entirely to computer and information scientists, software developers, industry, and commerce.

Some Remarks on Terminology

Before we proceed further, three remarks on terminology are probably in order. First, as already mentioned, this chapter focuses on matters that are assumed to be of particular interest to textual scholars. The term "textual scholarship" is sometimes understood in a rather narrow sense: textual scholars are assumed primarily to be concerned with scholarly, critical, or documentary editing of monuments of the literary canon. Sometimes, however, textual scholarship is taken to also include various other sorts of scholarly or scientific study of almost any kind of text, ranging from ancient and modern literary studies to, for example, quantitative analyses of nonliterary texts. For the purpose of this chapter, the emphasis is on the former, more conservative understanding, although I have tried to also take into account the wider audience indicated by the latter understanding.

Second, the terms "text" and "document" are often used interchangeably and without difference in meaning in the literature on markup, and so are compounds like "document markup" and "text markup." For most text scholars, who are used to distinguishing carefully between a document and its text, or between a text and its states or witnesses, this fact alone may be enough to give rise to some skepticism. Although admittedly this terminological conflation is sometimes the result of unawareness of the importance of the distinction, most markup theorists are acutely aware of the problem.

But the distinction, which has traditionally been honored by textual scholars, has turned out to be difficult to adapt to electronic documents in general and to the use of generalized markup in particular. For example, an electronic document is not a physical object on par with books, sheets of paper, or clay tablets, and it has no weight and no colors; rather, it consists of a certain constellation of electromagnetic or other kinds of traces or marks on some carrier. And when one talks about an electronic document, it is usually not even this physical substrate that is referred to, but rather the pattern itself on some more abstract level, such as a bit sequence, a character sequence, or the like. (Ironically, the term "text file" has become the standard term for computer files of a specific format.) This is not the place for an in-depth discussion of such issues, however. Instead, I have used the term "document" indiscriminately throughout the rest of this chapter, except where it has seemed important to signal that "text" in some more abstract sense is what is discussed.

Finally, what the English term "markup" refers to in this chapter is in other contexts sometimes called "encoding," "coding," "tagging," or "annotation" (corresponding terms in German are *Auszeichnung* or *Kodierung*; in French, *balisage*). The term "markup" itself was originally used to refer to marks or remarks made on the physical copy of a document to communicate instructions about modifications to be performed in the form of corrections, intended typography, and other details of concern to authors, editors, and printers, and thus carries associations to conventional editing and printing. The terms "encoding" or "coding," however, may carry associations to the practice frequent in social sciences and psychology of mapping instances of more finely differentiated data onto a limited set of values. The term "annotation" is typically used in linguistics, where linguistic data are frequently enriched with information about their linguistic properties, such as part of speech category, lexical forms, case, gender, and so on.

In the following section I implicitly try to introduce a more systematic terminology, but no attempt is made to relate this to the unfortunately rather confusing multitude of variant terminologies found in the literature on the subject.

Markup and Markup Standards

What Markup Is

A digital document may be seen as a linear sequence of discrete characters. Each character is associated with a letter or other sign from a given writing system, but each is also assigned a numeric value. Thus, characters (letters) and character strings (words) may easily be identified, counted, sorted, and manipulated by computer programs.

However, documents are not just linear sequences of characters. Scholarly editions, for example, generally have a complex, nonlinear structure, including cross-references, one or more apparatuses with variant readings, and so on; and the manuscripts from which they are made may contain inter- and intralinear insertions, marginalia, deletions, substitutions, and so on. This may be one end of a spectrum ranging from very simple to extremely complex documents, but few documents are entirely linear. For example, modern business documents and technical manuals also contain nonlinear features such as tables, cross-references, footnotes, endnotes, and marginalia. In general, typography, letter size, color, and other kinds of visual layout are important aspects of all kinds of manuscripts as well as printed documents (and, indeed, also of electronic documents presented on the computer screen).

None of this easily lends itself to representation in the form of linear sequences of characters. For this reason it soon became usual practice to insert reserved character strings into electronic document files in order to represent features of the documents that could not readily be represented as letters, punctuation marks, and other visual features. In analogy with editors' and proofreaders' marks on manuscripts in preparation for traditional print, these reserved character strings came to be called markup.

For example, the sentence "J. S. Bach was a great composer" could be marked up like this:

```
.bold J. S. Bach
.endbold was a
.italics great
.enditalics composer.
```

Or like this:

```
$b\J. S. Bach\ was a $i\great\ composer.
```

Or in any other way that allows a computer program to assign to it the desired layout and typography.[3]

We may thus define markup as the use of reserved character strings inserted into the sequence of characters of electronic document files in order to denote or signal features of the document that cannot readily be conveyed by characters directly representing its verbal content.

In general, a *markup language* consists of an explicitly defined markup *syntax* and a controlled markup *vocabulary*. As such, a markup language is an essential part of any *markup system*, which in addition to the markup language also contains methods, tools, and associated practices for exploiting the markup.

The Need for Standards

Standards can sometimes and for some uses be helpful, but at other times and for other uses they may be harmful. Generalized markup is one of the areas where standardization at a certain basic level has proved beneficial for quite general purposes, though when enforced at a somewhat higher level it is detrimental, at least to purposes of relevance for textual scholarship.

In the early days of computer-based document processing there was no generally accepted standard for markup. Most markup systems were directed toward capturing and controlling the visual appearance of documents rather than taking advantage of new opportunities provided by digital media. Documents with this kind of *procedural* or *presentational* markup were well suited for computer-assisted printing, but less well suited for retrieval, linguistic analysis, and other uses that are peculiar to digital documents.[4]

Software producers used their own mutually more or less incompatible markup systems in the form of proprietary file formats. The functionality of the markup was tightly dependent on the specific software, which kept the markup invisible to the user. For a long time the software houses seemed to regard their markup systems as strategic means for holding on to their customers. The multitude of incompatible systems and the lack of publicly available documentation made the exchange and reuse of electronic documents as well as document-processing software difficult, time-consuming, and expensive.

The result was considerable expense and inconvenience for users in general, but quite possibly it created an even greater problem for textual scholarship than it did elsewhere. In other contexts, documents may function primarily as a medium for the transmission of information about some subject matter that is external to the document. In textual scholarship, however, the object of study frequently is the document itself. In other contexts, documents may be of interest for only limited periods of time, yet textual scholars often work with documents containing texts that are transmitted over hundreds or even thousands of years. For humanities research in general and for textual scholarship in particular, it is therefore important not only to facilitate the exchange and reuse of electronic documents for the purposes of those documents' authors and intended users but also to ensure that the documents are preserved in a form that will make them accessible to present and future research and scholarship.

In addition, textual scholarship often relies on software that is specially developed for its own specific purposes, such as manuscript transcription and collation, critical editing, production of thesauri, and grammatical and lexical analyses. The difficulty and expense of developing such software was increased by the costs of maintaining it and ensuring that it could be used on documents stored in various and ever-changing proprietary formats. Textual scholars and the institutions responsible for preserving the sources and results of their work, such as archives and libraries, were among the first to encourage standardization of markup languages.

Therefore, considerable effort came to be (and still is) invested in the development of common standards for document markup. Not only public institutions and some of the major players in the computer industry but also scholarly organizations from the humanities threw their support behind these developments, the principal aim of which can be described as improved efficiency in the production and distribution of electronic documents and the associated software.

Standard Generalized Markup Language (SGML)

What follows in this and the next section is a brief introduction to two markup systems, SGML and HTML, the first of which only a subset is still widely in use, and the second not at all recommended for use as a primary representational format in textual scholarship. They are introduced here, however, because they are both precursors of XML (which will be introduced later), and because I believe in the helpfulness of historical background to the proper understanding of the present, also in a context like this.

One important outcome of the standardization efforts described above was the adoption of SGML as an ISO (International Organization for Standardization) standard in 1986.[5] Strictly speaking, SGML is not itself a markup system or even a markup language, but a markup syntax specification—that is, a set of syntactic rules for how to construct markup languages.

Documents complying with markup languages that are constructed according to this syntax consist of various elements, each of which may be associated with document features such as layout (e.g., pages, columns, lines, font type and size), composition (e.g., chapters, sections, paragraphs; acts, scenes; cantos, stanzas, lines), linguistic structure (e.g., sentences, parts of speech), or thematic content-related information (e.g., names of persons, places, or organizations, bibliographical references).

Here is an example of how our simple sentence "J. S. Bach was a great composer" could be marked up in SGML:

```
<s><name>J. S. Bach</name> was a <emp>great</emp> composer.</s>
```

Whereas most earlier markup systems had been designed for presentational or procedural markup, SGML encouraged so-called *descriptive* or *declarative* markup. In this example, the markup indicates that the entire string is a sentence ("s"), that one part of the string is a name, and another part of it is emphasized ("emp"). In other words, the markup indicates what kinds of objects these objects are rather than indicating their intended or actual typographic features.

The SGML syntax as such, however, does not dictate which features of a document should be marked up. This is decided partly by the author or other person responsible for the actual markup of any specific document and partly by the person who has designed the specific SGML markup language in question. In SGML terms this amounts to defining a document type definition (DTD). A document type definition specifies a markup vocabulary as well as rules for the ordering and containment relations between elements.

The introduction of SGML had a number of advantages compared to the earlier situation described above. One advantage was that any SGML-compliant document could be processed with software written for SGML. Since SGML was public and well documented, users were free to design their own markup languages and were not restricted to use software from any particular vendor. Another advantage was that not only did SGML provide a means for specifying quite precise rules for document structure adapted to the needs of individual users, but with SGML-aware software it was also possible to check automatically whether any given document complied with the rules specified.

However, the adoption of SGML progressed only slowly. The most important reason was likely its complexity. SGML included a number of optional features that turned out to be not widely used or requested. Partly because of this, and partly because of other design features, writing software for SGML was quite demanding.

HyperText Markup Language (HTML)

Since 1993 the propagation of SGML received a boost from the explosive growth of the web. The document standard used on the web, HTML (HyperText Markup Language), is based on SGML.[6] Therefore, it might be claimed that the popularity of the web also represents a success for SGML.

Even so, HTML had a number of drawbacks in the form of peculiar characteristics that conflict with many of the fundamental ideas underlying SGML. First, during the first ten years or so, web browsers were not designed for reading any form of SGML documents other than HTML. In effect, this meant that readers as well as authors were confined to this particular markup language and unable to make use of the flexibility to define markup for individual purposes, which had been central to the whole idea of SGML.

Second, the producers of web browsers started to compete by adding new "features" to HTML. In other words, HTML itself started to change, or to coexist in several different versions. The result was that even today web documents may be accompanied by remarks such as "Best read with [Browser X (version *n* or later)]."

Third, the opportunities for automatic checking were only rarely exploited. The result was that a large number of the documents on the web were not valid—they did not actually comply with the rules defined by HTML and SGML.

Fourth, HTML was entirely directed toward a (rather simplistic) visual presentation of documents and contained no or only very limited means for the representation of aspects such as their compositional, grammatical, dramatic, poetic, thematic, or editorial structure.

Later HTML has been modified to emphasize the representation of compositional structure of documents and extended with means for much more sophisticated layout and typography. Although HTML is still entirely unsatisfactory for the purposes of textual scholarship, it now offers a viable format for the visual presentation of such scholarly editions in electronic form.

These drawbacks motivated a search for alternative ways to transfer SGML documents via the web. It was against this background that work was begun on XML (Extensible Markup Language). The aim was to combine the simplicity of HTML with the expressive power and flexibility of SGML.

Extensible Markup Language (XML)

The World Wide Web Consortium (W3C) published XML as a W3C Recommendation in 1998.[7] Roughly, XML is a simplified subset of SGML. XML has gained considerable popularity, and it is probably fair to say that today it is favored by most practitioners of markup. This section gives a very brief introduction to the basics of XML.

THE BASIC ELEMENTS   Let us once again take the simple sentence "J. S. Bach was a great composer" as our starting point. Here is an example of one way this sentence could be marked up in XML:

```
<s><name>J. S. Bach</name> was a <emp>great</emp> composer.</s>
```

In XML the angle bracket characters "<" and ">" are *delimiters* marking the beginning and end of a tag. A tag may be either a *start tag*, like "<s>", or an *end tag*, like "</s>". The strings inside the tags ("s", "name", and "emp") are called *generic identifiers*. The character string delimited by a start tag and the corresponding end tag is called an *element*, and the character string between these start and end tags is called *element content*.

Thus, the element "<name>J. S. Bach</name>" has the start tag "<name>", the element content "J. S. Bach", and the end tag "</name>". Because the generic identifier of the element is "name," the element is said to be of type *name*.

What XML defines is the delimiters and the way we are supposed to use them to compose tags and elements and so on. However, there is nothing in XML as such that dictates we must mark up the sentence in this particular way or that we must apply the generic identifiers used here. If we want to, we may just as well mark up the sentence as follows:

```
<line><bold>J. S. Bach</bold> was a <italics>great</italics>
   composer.</line>
```

In the first example, the identifiers are mnemonic shorthands for sentences, names, and emphasized strings, whereas in the second example, they stand for lines, bold print, and italic print. It is considered good practice to use generic identifiers that give some indication to the human reader or user of the document as to what they stand for. Anyone using the first kind of markup is probably marking up the semantic structure of the document, whereas someone using the second kind is probably more concerned with its visual appearance.[8]

XML offers a mechanism that may allow one to combine both views in a case like this. For example, we could choose to mark the sentence up as follows:

```
<s rend="line"><name rend="bold">J. S. Bach</name> was a <emp
   rend="italics">great</emp> composer.</s>
```

In this example, each start tag has been enriched with an *attribute* ("rend," for rendition) that has been given different values in each case ("line," "bold," and "italics").

Attributes are useful for many purposes. We might also want to add information to the "name" element about what kind of name it is (personal name, place name, etc.) and what the full normalized form of the name is. This may be achieved, for example, by adding attributes to the name element as follows:

```
<name rend="bold" type="person" full="Bach, Johan Sebastian">J. S.
   Bach</name>
```

In addition to elements, there is one more markup construct that any user of XML needs to know: *character entities*. As many users will have experienced, it is sometimes difficult to ensure correct transfer of non-Latin characters between different computer systems, or even between applications on the same computer.

The "special" Norwegian letters "æ," "ø" and "å," for example, often come out wrong. XML offers the possibility of representing them by character entities, such as "æ", "ø", and "å" instead. Thus, the name "Pål Færøy" may look like this in XML:

```
"P&aring;l F&aelig;r&oslash;y"
```

Admittedly, this encoding makes the XML form of the name considerably less readable to the human eye. But it has the important advantage that the letters can be transferred and displayed correctly by any XML-aware program. And, as is sometimes said, XML documents are not primarily meant for a human to read but for computer programs to process into readable form.[9]

XML entities can be used for other purposes as well, and XML contains mechanisms that have not been mentioned here. Even so, what has been outlined above should be enough for anyone to understand the basics of an XML document when they see one.

DOCUMENTS   Consider the following facsimile of the bottom of a page and the top of the following page of a hypothetical reprint of the 1896 edition of Thomas Hardy's *The Woodlanders* (see fig. 5-1).[10]

What would a transcription of this fragment in XML look like? Again, XML as such does not dictate exactly how this should be done. However, here is one example of how we could go about it:

```
<?xml version="1.0" encoding="UTF-8"?>
<!DOCTYPE doc SYSTEM "file:/D/Book/2009/Aurora/hardy01.dtd">
<doc>
<front>
        <author>Thomas Hardy</author>
        <title>The Woodlanders</title>
        <edition>Hardy,Thomas: The Woodlanders, Osgoood,
            McIlvaine, London 1896.</edition>
</front>
<body>
<!-- Beginning of excerpt from pages 365-366 ... -->
```

> She started back suddenly from his long embrace and kiss, influenced by a sort of inspiration. 'O, I suppose,' she stammered, 'that I am really free?'— that this is right? Is there *really* a new law? Father cannot have been too sanguine in saying—'
>
> He did not answer, and a moment afterwards Grace

> burst into tears in spite of herself. 'O, why does not my father come home and explain!' she sobbed upon his breast, 'and let me know clearly what I am! It is too trying, this, to ask me to—and then to leave me so long in so vague a state that I do not know what to do, and perhaps do wrong!'

Figure 5-1: Fragment from the facsimile of the bottom of page and the top of page of a hypothetical reprint of the 1896 edition of Thomas Hardy's *The Woodlanders*.

```
<tab><para>She started back suddenly from his long embrace<lb/>and
    kiss, influenced by a sort of inspiration. <ds>O, I<lb/> suppose,
    </ds> she stammered, <ds>that I am really free?&mdash;<lb/> that
    this is right? Is there <emp>really</emp> a new law? Father<lb/>
    cannot have been too sanguine in saying&mdash;</ds><lb/></para>
<tab><para>He did not answer, and a moment afterwards Grace<lb/><pb
    no="366"/></para> burst into tears in spite of herself. <ds>O, why
    does</lb> not my father come home and explain!</ds> she sobbed
    </lb> upon his breast, <ds>and let me know clearly what I<lb/> am!
    It is too trying, this to ask me to&mdash;and then<lb/> to leave me
    so long in so vague a state that I do<lb/> not know what to do, and
    perhaps do wrong!</ds><lb/></para>
        <!-- ... end of excerpt. -->
</body>
</doc>
```

The first line is an XML declaration, indicating which version of XML and which character set has been used. The second line is a document type declaration, which will be explained in the next section.

The document proper (or, in XML terms, the *document instance*) starts with the start tag "<doc>" and ends with the end tag "</doc>"—meaning the document is an XML element of type doc. As in all XML documents, elements are linearly ordered and hierarchically nested inside each other. The doc element contains two further elements: front and body. The front element, in turn, consists of an author, a title, and an edition element, while body consists of two para (paragraph) elements. The para elements contain ds (direct speech), emp (emphasis), lb (line break), and pb (page break) elements.

The example contains two mechanisms not discussed earlier. First, the line starting with "<!--" and ending with "-->". These markers indicate that the enclosed character string is an XML comment. Comments are simply supposed to be disregarded by XML-compliant software. Second, instead of marking lines and pages of the original document as "line" and "page" elements, we have marked line endings by lb (line break) elements and the start of a new page by a pb (page break) element. Note that their delimiters "<" and "/>" indicate that the lb and pb tags are neither start tags nor end tags. They are empty elements, marking points rather than spans of the document.

Empty elements are often used in order to mark parts of the document that do not fit into the general hierarchical organization required by XML. (If we had decided to mark lines as elements with content in the example above, for example, we would have faced the problem that some of the ds (direct speech) elements start inside one line and end inside another, thus causing line elements and ds elements to overlap.) Empty elements are also used for recording phenomena such as images or hypertext anchors, which occur at specific points rather than spanning any part of a document.

The fact that XML documents must be element hierarchies—that is, that elements cannot overlap—has been the subject of much discussion. It does not mean that overlapping phenomena cannot be represented in XML. But the mechanisms for doing so are often cumbersome, and it is not easy to make XML software recognize such mechanisms.[11]

Well-Formedness

An XML document is organized in the form of a hierarchy of elements. The document element (in this case the doc element), which is commonly referred to as the *root element*, contains further elements, which in turn may contain yet further elements, and so on, until we finally reach a "bottom" level of elements containing no further elements, either in the form of empty elements or in the form of PCDATA—that is, character strings (often informally referred to as document content or even as "the text itself.")

Roughly, any document that adheres to these very basic syntactic rules is said to be *well formed*. It is a simple but also very important requirement that all XML documents should be well formed in this sense. If they are, any XML-compliant software will be able to parse the document—in other words, it can recognize its element structure and other mechanisms. If documents are not well formed, there is no guarantee that they behave as expected when processed by XML-based software.

Validity

For some purposes, tighter control over the structure of documents is required. This is the point at which we may return to the second line of our example from the previous section—its document type declaration—which reads:

```
<!DOCTYPE doc SYSTEM "file:/D:/Fag/2009/Aurora/hardy01.dtd">
```

This line declares that the root element of the document is of type doc, and it also informs us that a *document type definition* (DTD) for this element type can be found on the system resource referred to as "file:/D:/Fag/2009/Aurora/hardy01.dtd".

As mentioned earlier, a document type definition specifies a markup vocabulary—that is, a set of generic identifiers—and rules for the ordering and containment relations between elements of different types. In our example, the DTD might look like this:

```
<!ELEMENT doc(front,body)>
<!ELEMENT front(author,title,edition)>
<!ELEMENT author(#PCDATA)>
```

```
<!ELEMENT title(#PCDATA)>
<!ELEMENT edition(#PCDATA)>
<!ELEMENT body(para)+>
<!ELEMENT para(#PCDATA | ds | lb | pb | emp)*>
<!ELEMENT ds(#PCDATA | ds | lb | pb | emp)*>
<!ELEMENT emp(#PCDATA | ds | lb | pb)*>
<!ELEMENT lb EMPTY>
<!ELEMENT pb EMPTY>
<!ATTLIST pb no CDATA #IMPLIED>
<!ENTITY mdash '—'>
```

The lines starting with "<!ELEMENT" can be read as follows: "<!" signals the beginning of a declaration, and the key word "ELEMENT" tells us that indeed what is declared is an element. The key word is immediately followed by the generic identifier of the element, doc. The parentheses contain the element's *document model*. In this case, the document model—(front, body)—states that the doc element must contain one front element followed by one body element.

The content models of the various other element declarations tell us, for example, that author may contain PCDATA but no further elements, that body must contain one or more para elements, and so on. The last two lines declare the attribute no of the pb element and the character entity mdash.

As can be seen, the rules formulated in the DTD are considerably tighter and more precise than what is required for well-formedness alone. Any document conforming to the rules declared in this DTD is said to be valid according to the DTD.

It is sometimes said that DTDs are not required in XML. This is true in the sense that any well-formed XML document can be correctly parsed by XML software without access to its DTD. It is also true in the sense that alternative formalisms for document validation exist. The general term for DTDs and other formalisms for specifying constraints on XML documents is *schema languages*. Schema languages are extremely useful for a number of purposes, especially for document creation, editing, and quality assurance.

Data Structure

The elements directly contained by an element are called its *children*. Taken together, the children and any other elements contained by them are called the *descendants* of the element. Conversely, the element directly containing an element is called its *parent*. Taken together, the parent and any other element containing the parent are called the *ancestors* of the element. Two elements directly contained by the same element are called *siblings*.

In our example, the doc and body elements are ancestors of the first para element, while its ds, emp, lb, and pb elements are among its descendants. The body element is its parent, while the next para element is its sibling. This terminology points us in the direction of another feature of XML documents that is considered extremely useful by many: the fact that any XML document can be represented as a specific kind of directed acyclic graph, a so-called *document tree*. The XML tree for our sample document is illustrated in figure 5-2.[12] The XML document tree illustrates a way of thinking about documents that is useful for at least two reasons: (1) because it is a visual representation of an abstract model of the various parts of a document and their relationships, a model that may be helpful in reasoning about document structures; and (2) because this kind of abstract model also underlies a data structure used for the internal representation of documents by XML-aware software applications.

In conversation with XML systems or application developers one will often hear references to document trees and their elements; the ancestors, descendants, siblings of these elements; and so on. Textual scholars who rely on XML applications or on developers of such applications are therefore well advised to acquire a basic grasp of this way of thinking about documents.

Transformations

At this point readers may understandably have become impatient. What is the use, after all, of representing documents in the form exemplified by the XML example above? It is verbose, it is hard to read, it is ugly, and it does not seem to provide any information that could not have been presented in a more readable form by conventional means of print typography and layout.

This is all true. The reasons for preferring an XML representation have been given above, and further reasons will be given later; in essence they have to do

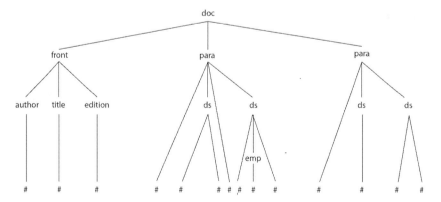

Figure 5-2: The XML tree of a sample document.

with increased usability, flexibility, and longevity. I have mentioned that XML documents lend themselves to automatic retrieval, concordancing, indexing, linguistic and stylistic analysis, and so on. None of this would be worth the effort, however, unless we could also produce conventional visual presentations of our documents, employing conventional means of visual presentation. Therefore, and because space does not allow for discussion of retrieval, analysis, and so forth, we now proceed to look at how XML documents can be transformed to presentational forms by the means of *style sheets*.

XML's style sheet language is called XSL (Extensible Stylesheet Language). XSL style sheets are typically designed for presentation of documents in different layouts and with varying degree of detail. The output can be formatted as PDF or PostScript for high-quality print or HTML for presentation on the web.

Here is an example of the most relevant parts of a very simple style sheet for our sample document fragment:

```
<xsl:template match="para">
        <xsl:element name="p">
           <xsl:apply-templates/>
        </xsl:element>
</xsl:template>
<xsl:template match="emp">
        <xsl:element name="i">
           <xsl:apply-templates/>
        </xsl:element>
</xsl:template>
<xsl:template match="ds">
        <xsl:text>"</xsl:text>
        <xsl:apply-templates/>
        <xsl:text>"</xsl:text>
</xsl:template>
```

It is not necessary here to go into any details of how style sheets work. Let it just be mentioned that of the three sections displayed above, the first one indicates roughly that para elements should be separated by blank lines, the second that emp elements should be printed or displayed in italics, and the third that ds elements should be printed with a double-quote open before and a double-quote close after. If we give our sample document and this style sheet to an XSL processor, it produces the output found in figure 5-3.

Alternatively, we might apply a different style sheet and have the sample printed in a different font, mark the original's page breaks, and retain its line breaks and its use of single quotation marks, as illustrated in figure 5-4.

This illustrates one of the advantages of preparing a document in XML: that it may subsequently be presented in a variety of different formats and styles without requiring interference with the XML source file in any way, thus both saving work and ensuring data integrity.

Figure 5-3: Sample document using the XML code after being processed by the XSL processor using the XSL style sheet.

She started back suddenly from his long embrace and kiss, influenced by a sort of inspiration. 'O, I suppose,' she stammered, "that I am really free?—that this is right? Is there *really* a new law? Father cannot have been too sanguine in saying—"

He did not answer, and a moment afterwards Grace burst into tears in spite of herself. "O, why does not my father come home and explain!" she sobbed upon his breast, "and let me know clearly what I am! It is too trying, this, to ask me to—and then to leave me so long in so vague a state that I do not know what to do, and perhaps do wrong!"

Figure 5-4: Sample document using the XML code after being processed by the XSL processor using another XSL style sheet.

She started back suddenly from his long embrace and kiss, influenced by a sort of inspiration. 'O, I suppose,' she stammered, 'that I am really free?'—that this is right? Is there really a new law? Father cannot have been too sanguine in saying—'
He did not answer, and a moment afterwards Grace
— Page 366 —
burst into tears in spite of herself. 'O, why does not my father come home and explain!' she sobbed upon his breast, 'and let me know clearly what I am! It is too trying, this, to ask me to—and then to leave me so long in so vague a state that I do not know what to do, and perhaps do wrong!'

The Text Encoding Initiative

XML provides a standardized syntax for how documents can be marked up, but it does not say a word about which features of a document should be marked. Supplying a semantics to the syntax—in other words, defining a vocabulary of tags used for marking elements and specifying what they mean and how they can be combined—is a task left to the users. While this certainly seems to allow for the kind of freedom and flexibility required in textual scholarship, where "[e]very textual situation is unique,"[13] it also seems to put a large burden of preparation on new users. And although nobody in their right mind would insist that every editorial project should be expected to use the same schema, record the same features, and adapt to the same basic document structure, there are enough similar phenomena to be recorded to make it seem a waste to have every project do roughly similar things in radically different ways.

One response to these dilemmas is provided by the Text Encoding Initiative. There certainly are editorial projects that choose to build their own encoding scheme from scratch, and there certainly is no lack of document schemas, but few of them answer the needs of textual scholarship. So even if the Text Encoding Initiative does not provide the answer to every question, it has gained enough recognition and is broadly enough used in order to deserve attention from anyone planning to embark on an editorial project.

Work on the Text Encoding Initiative began in 1987, just one year after SGML had been approved as an ISO standard. The *TEI Guidelines for Electronic Text Encoding and Interchange*, the result of a collaborative effort by researchers from a variety of humanities backgrounds, was first published in 1994 and has subsequently appeared in a number of revised and extended editions.[14]

The *TEI Guidelines* describe a markup system that consists of a series of DTD modules, or *tag sets*, which can be combined and adapted to special needs. A core tag set defines elements for features that are assumed to occur in practically any type of document. On top of the core tag set, users select one base tag set. There are four base tag sets to choose from: one for prose, verse, and drama; one for transcriptions of speech; one for print dictionaries; and one for terminological databases. In addition to the core and base tag sets, one can choose freely from a range of additional tag sets that serve various needs such as manuscript description, representation of primary sources, critical apparatus, linguistic analysis, and the like.

For many phenomena the TEI offers not just one but a variety of suggestions for how they may be represented. The *TEI Guidelines* discuss the pros and cons of these various approaches and encourage users to assess for themselves which alternative is best in each respective case.

The *TEI Guidelines* deal with almost every conceivable type of document, from papyri and palimpsests to modern office documentation and hypertext. Even so, it is stressed time and time again that the system should not be regarded as complete and that the need for further elaboration and modification should always be kept in mind. Indeed, the system includes provisions that allow it to be extended and modified by individual users.

What the *TEI Guidelines* offer is therefore an extensive yet liberal system that caters to a very broad range of document types and a large variety of textual phenomena. The system has a modular structure and permits modification. It has been widely applied in the humanities and is also used outside of academic circles. Since the conclusion of the developmental project in 1994, the number of people actively using the TEI system has grown into a considerable community. Their interests are now formally represented by the TEI Consortium, established in 2000, and further development of the system is an ongoing concern.

The fundamental features of the TEI's system—modularity, modifiability, numerous alternative means of handling analogous phenomena—can make it seem too complex in cases where the requirements are simple and the difficulties few. Therefore, the TEI has also developed a "light" version of its system, called TEILite.

Pros, Cons, and Perspectives

XML has become pervasive in nearly all kinds of document processing, ranging from publication on the web to high-quality print production. It has also found applications in a number of other areas of potential interest to textual scholarship, such as representation and processing of musical, mathematical, and chemical notation as well as graphics and multimedia documents. The many available tools for retrieval, collation, annotation, and analysis are also of obvious relevance for textual scholars.

The number and diversity of available systems, tools, and applications for XML-based markup is of course one of its strengths. At the same time, it may be a source of confusion and bewilderment among prospective users. The jungle of technicalities, standards, software packages, and acronyms may seem forbidding to someone new to the technology. It is a comforting fact, however, that the average user of XML does not need to enter this jungle.

Even so, if the immediate or even the ultimate aim of a project is a high-quality print edition, why not prepare documents with WYSIWYG editors for page-description languages like PDF or some other widespread proprietary format? After all, these tools are simple to use and at least as ubiquitous as XML. At least the following three reasons may be given: First of all, WYSIWYG tools are indeed available also for XML editing. The time is past when XML users had to work directly with "angle bracket notation." Second, converting a document from a proprietary format to XML may be difficult, unreliable, and sometimes impossible in practice, while conversion from XML to other formats is comparatively easy, as it is part of the whole idea behind XML. Third, proprietary formats are generally not publicly documented, because they bind users to commercial or proprietary software, and there is considerable risk that documents prepared in such formats will sooner or later become obsolete.

One complaint often made about XML is that there are certain document structures that are difficult to represent in XML. And this is indeed true: XML's insistence on hierarchical nesting of document elements does make it difficult to represent overlapping hierarchies, discontinuous or interrupted elements, and alternate orderings of document elements. On the other hand, there are well-known techniques for handling these problems in XML. The *TEI Guidelines*, for example, provide a number of such methods.

None of the known alternatives to XML combine a viable solution to these problems with the strengths of XML, such as the tight integration of notation, constraint language, and data structure; a host of general-purpose as well as specialized application software; and, most important, none of them are international standards that may be assumed to exist and be supported in the future.

There is no reason to believe that XML is the ultimate answer to all problems of document representation and processing or that it will last forever. There are good reasons to believe, however, that XML will stay with us for a long while. With the large investments already made in XML technology, there are also good reasons to believe that whatever the next generation of document technology might look like, it will have little chance of acceptance unless easy and lossless conversion from XML is made possible. Thus, adoption of XML in textual scholarship may also be in the interest of preservation.

Notes

1. I wish to thank Daniel Apollon, Alois Pichler, Tone Merete Bruvik, and Odd Einar Haugen for their useful comments and advice on earlier drafts of this chapter, the shortcomings of which they are of course in no way responsible.

2. This view is expressed in one of the earliest seminal papers on markup theory; see Coombs et al. 1987.

3. The examples are fictional. The first example uses full stops at the start of lines to signal markup and thus exploits the fact that full stops rarely occur at the beginning of a line in normal documents. The second example uses reserved characters "$" and "\" to separate the markup from the rest of the document. The observant reader will already have noticed that the markup in the examples does not allow a program to distinguish personal names from other items that may have been marked as "bold," or to distinguish emphasized words from other items that may have been marked as "italics."

4. This use of the term "presentational" is not strictly in accordance with the terminology as originally introduced in Coombs et al., where the visual layout itself is what is considered "presentational markup." It has become customary, however, to use "presentational markup" to refer to markup that records visual layout.

5. SGML: Information Processing—Text and Office Systems—Standard Generalized Markup Language (SGML), ISO 88791986, International Organization for Standardization, Geneva 1986.

6. This is a slight simplification of historical facts. HTML was not strictly defined as an SGML standard until sometime after its initial use on the web.

7. The World Wide Web Consortium's website can be found at http://www.w3.org/XML.

8. It is true that most practitioners of XML will recommend the first kind of markup rather than the second, and for good reasons. However, this is a fact about common usage of XML: there is nothing in XML as such that prevents the second kind of markup.

9. For a long time the number of characters on any given computer system was severely limited, and hardware and software suppliers used different conventions for the representation of identical character sets. The computer world is currently moving toward generally accepted standards that include the majority of characters of major past and present writing systems. Problems remain in this field concerning some writing systems that are clearly of interest to textual scholarship, but the issue will not be further pursued here.

10. We have made this facsimile for demonstration purposes.

11. See, for example, DeRose 2004 and Witt et al. 2005.

12. For the sake of simplicity, empty elements have been left out from this illustration.

13. Gaskell 1978, 6.

14. Sperberg-McQueen and Burnard 2002.

6. Digital Critical Editing

Separating Encoding from Presentation

ALOIS PICHLER AND TONE MERETE BRUVIK

The Principle

What happens to "critical editing" in the digital context?[1] What tells us that digital tools and media facilitate critical editing? Do digital media make critical editions more accessible and therefore more democratic? Does the quality of critical editions increase when they are produced with digital tools? These are some of the questions asked by the editors in the introduction to this volume, to which this chapter responds. It does so by invoking and describing a principle of editorial philology that for many will seem trivial, or, at least standard, while others may disagree with it. The principle we are talking about is the principle of separating transcription from presentation issues when engaging in activities of scholarly editing. Though this principle is defended here in the context of scholarly digital editing, we believe it applies to scholarly editing in general. It is, however, only through the digital turn and with the rise of digital publishing that this principle has made its strong entrance and has become practicable on a large scale, overcoming the material limitations of publishing on paper only. In this chapter we also describe specific methods and tools that we consider adequate for practicing this principle in a digital context, especially in the context of preparing digital scholarly editions. In order to illustrate and give substance to our points, we draw on our specific experiences with editing Ludwig Wittgenstein's manuscripts in the Wittgenstein Archives at the University of Bergen (WAB) and Henrik Ibsen's complete works in the Henrik Ibsen's Writings (Henrik Ibsens Skrifter [HIS]) projects. From 1990 to 1999 WAB prepared a machine-readable version of Wittgenstein's *Nachlass* with source transcriptions from which different outputs and editions can be derived and which is developed and enriched further today. The most important output so far has been the Bergen Electronic Edition of Wittgenstein's *Nachlass* (BEE) in the year 2000. Similarly, during the period from 1998 to 2009, the HIS project prepared a machine-readable version of *Henrik Ibsen's Writings* (HIS), from which a book edition (published by Aschehoug 2005–2010) and an open online text archive are derived. In both projects, WAB and HIS, constant attention is being paid to separating transcription from presentation issues. WAB has transcribed and now maintains the twenty thousand pages of the Wittgenstein *Nachlass* in a machine-readable version consisting of marked-up source transcriptions, which, since 2000, have used an XML markup following the guidelines of the Text Encoding Initiative (TEI). Outputs from this encoded machine-readable version are then produced through filters and conversion for the purpose of presentation. The same principle applies for the HIS project: a text base using a comparable XML markup takes care of the transcription, and from this base the entire book edition (presentation) is produced.[2]

Three clarifications will be helpful at this point: First, when speaking of primary sources, we center on text materials that are relatively complex and extensive rather than straightforward and small. Thus, the principle of separating transcription from presentation issues is imperative when one wants to prepare for the publication of texts that have a considerable degree of complexity and extent, such as the twenty thousand heavily revised pages of the Wittgenstein *Nachlass*. Second, we talk only about scholarly editions—that is, editions that are prepared in response to certain social, academic, and economic interests that one describes as "scholarly." Third, we focus on situations where publication is not restricted to a certain format, and we leave a range of options open rather than settle on specific formats only (e.g., on book or web or CD-ROM edition). This is not to say that the principle of separating transcription from presentation does not apply to situations where these conditions are not present, but that there may be good reasons not to follow it if these conditions are not present. Still, while we do not claim that it is adequate or necessary in all cases of editing to make a wide range of options possible, we nevertheless consider it an advantage when publication is not restricted to a certain format. In general, it is our view that editorial projects and textual scholarship benefit from a conscious attitude and reflection as to the relevance of distinguishing between transcription and presentation issues as proposed here.

We distinguish between the *source material* to be edited, the *transcription* of its data, and their *presentation*. The particular format and form in which the source material is transmitted to the user is a matter of presentation rather than of transcription. In short, the principle of separating transcription from presentation issues implies that the editor needs to keep two kinds of procedure strictly apart from each other: One is the set of procedures aiming to record and document the physical, structural, and semantic data that the editor understands the source material to contain or require (*transcription*). The other is the set of acts to determine and instruct how the registered data of the source material are to be processed with regard to selection, display, and format (*presentation*). This distinction was generally blurred in traditional book publishing, mainly for economic reasons. But in scholarly digital editing, too, where economic reasons are less relevant, it often happens that the first set of procedures, transcription, is biased by the second, presentation. This we consider a mistake. What the separation of the two amounts to in philosophical, methodological, and technical terms shall become clear in more detail in the following pages. One methodological consequence is a recommendation for the use of *text encoding* for the purpose of scholarly edition text preparation. It is indeed a claim of this chapter that scholarly editing in an electronic context properly works only on the principle we describe and thus should involve text encoding or *markup*. These views and positions are presented in the sections below: section 2 covers theoretical issues, while sections 3 and 4 address practical issues.

In section 2, "Scholarly Editing in the Digital Age," we describe the role of our guiding principle in the context of editorial philology's recent developments from paper-based editing toward digital editing. Here the distinction between transcription and presentation is related to traditional scholarly editing on the one hand and to scholarly editing in the e-context on the other. Though the separation of transcription and presentation may always, at least partly, have been present as an ideal in editorial philology, it is only now possible, through the digital medium and the discipline of text encoding, to put it into practice. Special attention is drawn to an element of digital scholarly editing that is possible only in a digital context: *interactive dynamic editing*, which is distinguished into interactive dynamic presentation and interactive dynamic transcription.

Section 3, "Text Encoding: Distinctions," and section 4, "Text Encoding: Tools and Methods," derive from the principle best practices involving diverse tools and methods in digital editorial philology. In section 3 we describe how markup *syntaxes* and *nomenclatures* can be combined into markup *languages*. It is the combination of a markup syntax with a markup nomenclature that forms a markup language, rather than the markup syntax alone, as mainstream use of "markup language" amounts to, for example, when speaking of XML as a markup language. Thus, this contribution contains a proposal for a revision of the way we talk about text encoding or markup. This could seem a minor point to the general reader, who may not be particularly interested in the technicalities of text encoding and talk about text encoding. However, it is crucial to stick to a clear and distinct terminology where one introduces and describes different markup solutions that are relevant to the field of editorial philology. In our view, it is only a special type of text encoding or markup that is apt for giving life to our principle—namely, *descriptive markup* as distinct from *procedural* markup. However, both kinds of markup are discussed and examples given. Recommendations are offered for how to use, for the purpose of the transcription of primary sources, the descriptive and hierarchical markup language XML TEI(P5). We also present briefly a nonhierarchical markup language, MECS WIT.

In section 4, text editors and tools for the production of transcriptions in the XML TEI(P5) markup language are presented. This section also covers tools that enable validation of the markup of such transcriptions and other tools useful for the conversion of these transcriptions to outputs in different formats. In this section we also briefly describe techniques and methods for linking digital facsimiles with their text editions.[3]

Scholarly Editing in the Digital Age

In traditional paper-based scholarly editions, transcription and presentation of the source text converge, at least from the user perspective. This has advantages and disadvantages. Advantages include that the traditional edition is a stable entity that allows for easily established reference and usage. Disadvantages include opaqueness and lack of verifiability of the edition, since the distinction between transcription of the data and presentation of the data is not carried through. Instead, because of material limitations, the textual situation is generally under-documented.[4] In contrast to this, scholarly editing today, adequately exploiting its digital environment, implements a separation between the two. It follows from this separation that the constitution of the text, including selection and editorial intervention, becomes best visible at the presentation level, whereas it is already prepared and best documented and can be verified and revised at the transcription level. Though the separation may always have been an ideal for many scholarly editors, it has had to remain underdeveloped and unevenly practiced in traditional editorial philology, mainly because of material limitations. It is only now, with the digital medium, that we are technologically enabled to fully comply with this principle. Consequently, scholarly editing will remain in the conceptual grip of print technology where this principle is not respected.

The separation brings advantages and possibilities with it. These include that the editor explicates and documents the scholarly interests that guide his work, and that the user is empowered to distinguish transcription from presentation matters, and is in a position to produce alternative presentations according to her own edition needs and interests. Opened to users' verification and also steered by the user, digital editing empowers these users with possibilities that are unparalleled in traditional editing.[5] In traditional editing it is the editor or publisher who decides the presentation of the source, while the user generally remains in a passive role, receiving what the expert has prepared and without the possibility to play an active role and participate in the editing, or at least to verify it adequately. This situation has changed considerably with the digital context. Here, the user can take on attributes and functions of an editor himself. With digital editorial philology's possibility of user-steered editing, users are able to create texts that respond to the specific needs of their research situation or alternative usage. They need no longer be bound to accept decisions made by the editor on the basis of good faith but are asked to control the editor's decisions and improve on it or provide alternatives themselves. This kind of editorial activity, which is only possible on digital grounds, we call interactive dynamic editing.[6] Interactive dynamic editing marks a new approach to and understanding of scholarly editing, which has to be seen together with Web 2.0 developments encouraging interaction and user-created content. While in traditional editions—and even in dynamic digital editions such as BEE, which offers a range of alternative presentations of the source, including diplomatic and normalized versions (importantly, all with a basis in the same source *transcription*)—it is still the expert editor alone who provides the presentation(s) to work with, with interactive dynamic editing, reader/user participation enters the editing scene. Here the reader is asked—on the basis of the very transcription that was prepared by the editor—to engage in filtering and presentation of the source transcription and metadata according to his own specific research needs, and thus to take on features of the editor. Thus, with interactive dynamic editing, both the editorial process and the editorial product are conceived as dynamic rather than static. Interactions between the expert editor and her transcription and between the same expert editor and the reader/user become fundamental ingredients of scholarly editing.

Interactive dynamic editing as described in the previous paragraph can be called *interactive dynamic presentation* since it involves user participation on the levels of filtering and presentation of source data and metadata. From this we can distinguish *interactive dynamic editing* in the sense of interactive dynamic transcription that involves user participation that is also on the level of the transcription of source data and metadata. Thus, with interactive dynamic transcription, a community of users is enabled to jointly engage in the transcription endeavor while the entire editorial collaboration can still be coordinated by an editor.[7] If digital scholarly editing is to be more than just transposing traditional methods and techniques into the electronic environment, then a situation providing for interactive dynamic editing (in both senses) should increasingly become standard. From this perspective, publishing PDF files of scholarly book editions, for example, should not count as digital scholarly editing, though of course it is digital publishing of scholarly editions. It is not publication in the digital medium as such—with its search functions and extended carrier and transport capacity—that makes scholarly editing digital scholarly editing. Rather, what matters in our view is the digital environment's inherent possibilities to separate transcription from presentation matters and to subsequently exploit the benefits from such distinction.

Having now explicated our basic "philosophy," in the following sections we address current methodological and technological approaches with regard to what is thought to best serve our principle and to contribute in this way to empower the user. We describe the methodology that offers the best procedures for keeping the transcription processes apart from the presentation processes. This methodology thus serves to organize editions as outputs that are reproducible and revisable by users and based on underlying platform-independent resources that belong to the level prior to presentation. As already stated earlier, it is the discipline of text encoding or markup and the technologies connected with it that allow scholarly editing to respond to the new situation in adequate ways and to put the ideal into practice. It is thanks to encoded or marked-up source transcriptions and to filtering software that the editor is able to document and satisfactorily communicate his editorial construction. It is also thanks to the same transcription principles and filtering software that in interactive dynamic editing the user becomes empowered to verify the editor's editorial construction and to modify or add to it in complementary or competing ways through interactive interfaces. But not all markup is equally apt for fleshing out the separation of transcription and presentation and, consequently, also apt to guarantee the adequate transparency and flexibility of the editorial process and edition we promote. In the following section, we present and discuss markup in greater detail. But first we must address a possible misunderstanding of the relation between transcription and interpretation.

An often misrepresented issue is the role that interpretation plays in transcription acts. It is usually granted that interpretation plays a key role in the presentation of source text materials—in particular, autograph materials—although many people think that interpretation has no part in transcription, or that it should have no part in transcription procedures: the acts of transcription are seen to be "objective," or to aim for objectivity in a sense of "interpretation-free" objectivity. However, interpretation-independent transcription is neither possible nor needed. Sometimes editions and editorial projects seem to be guided by an illusory ideal of objective text representation—illusory not because objective text representation would not be achievable in principle, but because objective text representation is not something that exists and needs to exist independently of our interpretational acts. Both presentation and transcription are fundamentally involved with selection, construction, and interpretation. While in this chapter there is not space to elaborate further on this issue, it needs to be said that the view that textual scholarship intimately involves interpretational activities has nothing to do with an acceptance of an "anything goes" approach to matters of editorial philology,[8] and that we believe the dichotomy between transcription and interpretation has no bearing on the principal distinction between presentation and transcription procedures.

Text Encoding: Some Important Distinctions to Make

Markup Syntax vs. Markup Nomenclature

As has already become clear, we defend the view that digital scholarly text editing should implement and practice the principle of separating transcription from presentation issues and should therefore involve tools and methods of text encoding or markup in comprehensive and consistent ways. It is only through the disciplines and technologies of markup that one can carry out this separation on all levels. But at the same time it is also within markup that the distinction between transcription and presentation becomes most relevant and visible. For not all markup solutions are capable of handling such distinction, but only a specific type of markup, known as descriptive markup. But before diving into more details, we need to explain the vocabulary we are using to describe markup. We distinguish between *markup syntaxes* or *grammars,* on the one hand, and *markup nomenclatures* or *vocabularies,* on the other hand, and refer to their combinations as *markup languages.* While this terminology, and the distinction it carries, is not common usage, it is proposed here in order to provide a more consistent and functional way of talking. For it allows one to see and to describe more clearly, for instance, how markup syntaxes and nomenclatures can be combined in other ways than those that are used in standard combinations, of which XML TEI(P5) is an example.

XML is a markup syntax, while TEI(P5)—the current version of the TEI Guidelines—contains a nomenclature and rules for its application, though it is essentially coupled with XML. Figure 6-1 shows markup syntaxes, vocabularies (nomenclatures), and languages when organized through this terminology. Thus, SGML (Standard Generalized Markup Language, ISO 8879–1986), XML, and MECS (Multi-Element Code System[9]) all offer us a syntax.[10] If a markup syntax is combined with a markup nomenclature, we get a markup language—for example, MECS WIT (MECS applied to Wittgenstein, or "WIT") was the language of WAB's machine-readable version of Wittgenstein's *Nachlass* in the years 1990–2000 and combines MECS with WIT.[11] Another example of a markup language is XML TEI(P4), the language in which *Henrik Ibsen's Writings* were marked-up in the HIS project. But one has to keep in mind that in addition to these existing markup languages other ones could be formed, and not unreasonably. For example, MECS TEI or XML WIT—that is, WAB's MECS instead of WIT—could have taken on a version of TEI's guidelines as its nomenclature, while one could also pair XML syntax with WAB's WIT instead of with, for example, TEI(P5). (See figures 6-1 and 6-2 for a visual representation of the history of markup.)

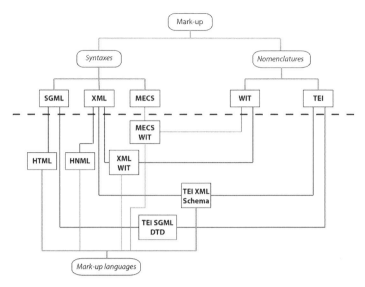

Figure 6-1: Taxonomy of markup syntaxes, nomenclatures, and languages.

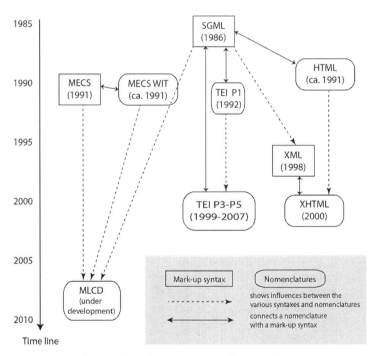

Figure 6-2: Evolution of markup syntaxes and nomenclatures.

Descriptive vs. Procedural Markup

This discussion of XML TEI and MECS WIT gives us the opportunity for an important distinction in markup: Markup can either be descriptive or presentational (Goldfarb 1993). XML TEI and MECS WIT are descriptive markup languages, while HTML usually is regarded to be presentational or prescriptive or procedural markup. With regard to this distinction, HTML and XML TEI, although both subsets of SGML, are thus fundamentally different.

In a descriptive markup language the markup tags do little more than categorize, document, and describe aspects of the source. For example, the markup tag <para> simply identifies a portion of a document and registers that it is a paragraph. By contrast, procedural markup defines what processing is to be carried out at particular points in a document: "call procedure PARA with parameters 1, b, and x here" or "move the left margin 2 quads left, move the right margin 2 quads right, skip down one line, and go to the new left margin," and so on. In XML environments the instructions needed to process the transcription of a document for some particular purpose (for example, to format it) are sharply distinguished from the descriptive markup for it. The former are collected outside the transcription in separate procedures or programs and are usually expressed in a distinct document called a *style sheet*. This use of the term "style sheet" must be understood correctly, since style sheets of this kind do much more than simply define the rendition or visual appearance of a document; they are in fact responsible for any aspect of filtering and presentation of the source or the registered data. Consequently, with the help of a style sheet, a descriptively marked-up transcription can readily be processed in many different ways, using only those parts of it that are considered relevant. For example, on the basis of an XML transcription, a content analysis program might entirely disregard the footnotes embedded in an annotated text, while a formatting program might extract and collect them all together for printing at the end of each chapter.

With XML being an international recommendation for markup syntax and TEI(P5) or TEI(P4) being international guidelines for markup nomenclature, XML TEI makes and keeps document contents accessible and usable for a range of purposes and for a larger community of researchers, scholars, and other users than would be possible with a procedural markup language. Since XML allows for great versatility, one of its important advantages lies in the fact that the XML-encoded text can function as a basis for multiple research and publishing purposes. It is possible to produce from the same marked-up XML version of a work of literature editions suited for primary schools and editions of the kind that fit the needs of teaching and research at universities, including different search and retrieval procedures. In addition, XML secures the longevity of information because it is an open and well-documented recommendation.

Even as computers and programs evolve, the information once created in XML will last, since it will always be possible to easily transport it into formats and standards that will eventually replace XML. With relation to the principle of separation between transcription and presentation, we can summarize that it is the XML TEI(P5) source transcription that takes care of the transcription aspects, while it is the separate and subsequent process of converting these source transcriptions to different outputs, and in different formats, that takes care of the presentational aspects.

Hierarchical vs. Nonhierarchical Markup

There is, however, one issue that for a number of text-encoding theorists and practitioners casts a shadow on XML (and in fact on all subsets of SGML, including HTML): XML demands a strictly hierarchical way of markup. According to these people, this hierarchical organization is not adequate for the transcription of manuscript sources, since texts are not hierarchical and linear entities but rather nonhierarchical structures with many nonlinear and overlapping elements. However, although there can be many good reasons for developing and using markup languages that allow overlapping and nonhierarchical structuring,[12] it does not seem correct to defend this idea with reference to "nonhierarchical textual reality." In our view, texts cannot be said to be either hierarchical or nonhierarchical, and such aspects belong to the spheres of text reception and text transcription rather than the level of the text itself.[13] Thus it does not seem adequate to challenge the application of XML on text-ontological grounds.

The basic concept of SGML and XML is to add markup in the form of tags to the text like this:

```
<page>
<title>My page</title>
<text>
<headline>There are several markup syntaxes:</headline>
<textline>MECS (Multi-Element Code System)</textline>
<textline>XML
(eXtensible Markup Language)</textline>
<textline>SGML (Standard Generalized Markup Language)</textline>
</text>
</page>
```

A substantial part of a markup language is made up by its *elements*. An element usually has a start tag and an end tag. In this XML example, <page> is the start tag for the page element, while its end tag has the same identifier but with a "/" added to it, thus </page>. Everything between the start tag and the end tag is called the *content* of the element. The content may include text as well as additional markup. But elements may also have no content. For instance, a page break may be encoded as `<pagebreak/>`, where the start and the end tags are merged together into what is called a *milestone tag*. Elements may also have *attributes* that add information to them; such attributes have *attribute values* and are included in the start tag, as in the following example, where a song text is encoded and the element `<poem>` is specified through an attribute type with the value *song*:

```
<poem type="song"><title>I've been high</title> by <author>Bucks,
    Mills, Stipe, R.E.M.</author>
<stanza n="1">
<line n="1">have you seen?</line>
<line n="2">have not, will travel.</line>
<line n="3">have I missed the big reveal?</line>
</stanza>
<stanza n="2">
<line n="1">do my eyes</line>
<line n="2">do my eyes seem empty?</line>
<line n="3">I've forgotten how this feels.</line>
</stanza>
</poem>
```

We see from these examples that the structure of XML markup is strictly hierarchical. The elements nest like boxes inside each other. This is different from markup that allows overlapping structures like the following:

```
The <underline>trees <italic>are green</underline> with white</
    italic> flowers.
```

In this example, the content of the `<italic>`-element is not fully embedded in technical language: not nesting in the content of the `<underline>`-element, but rather overlapping with it. Such markup can be used in order to represent text structures such as the following:

The <u>trees *are green*</u> with *white* flowers.

Note, however, that the same sample could also be transcribed in the following way:

```
The <underline>trees <italic>are green</italic></underline>
    <italic>with white</italic> flowers.14
```

As we said above, the view that the overlap in this sample is "objectively existing" overlap in the source, rather than an aspect of our mapping of the source, seems at least debatable. Independent of the answer to this question, many scholars have seen good reasons for allowing overlap and for this purpose have created markup syntaxes that deviate from SGML. One such alternative syntax is MECS. In the following section we briefly discuss the markup language MECS WIT, which allows overlapping and nonhierarchical structuring. This can shed further light on the nature and possibilities of markup. MECS WIT originates from the combination of the markup syntax MECS with the markup nomenclature WIT. In MECS WIT, the above example can be transcribed in the following way:

```
The <us1/trees <i/are green/us1> with white/i> flowers.
```

MECS was created exactly on the grounds that, in contrast to SGML and its successors, it should permit overlap. However, as a result of this very same feature, MECS also has disadvantages, because the requirement of well-formedness of a MECS WIT transcription—namely, its conformity with syntax rules—is not as strong as it is for an XML transcription. This implies that the check of the well-formedness and the validation of a MECS WIT transcription—that is, its conformity with well-formedness and nomenclature rules—cannot be as rigorous and complete as for an XML transcription. Nevertheless, it must not be forgotten that MECS WIT has been one of the most successful markup languages. It has demonstrated its efficiency not only to encode the general structures and the fine details of the Wittgenstein *Nachlass* documents but also to bring it to publication on CD-ROM edition (Wittgenstein 2000) and other media.

Text Encoding: Tools and Methods

Markup syntaxes propose a set of rules for the syntax of a markup language. For example, it is a question of markup syntax, rather than of markup nomenclature, whether elements use the structure <...> for their start tags and the structure </...> for their end tags (as in XML) or, alternatively, <.../ for start tags and /...> for end tags (as in MECS). In contrast, it is entirely a question of nomenclature whether one uses del (as in TEI P5) or d (as in WIT) in order to register spans of text that are deleted, as deleted. The same string ~~deleted text~~ can thus be registered in a range of different ways, depending on which syntax and nomenclature one chooses. Combining XML and WIT, one encodes it as <d>deleted text</d>; combining XML and TEI(P5) (which nowadays would be most standard), one encodes it as <del>deleted text</del>; combining MECS with WIT, one encodes it as <d/deleted text/d>; and combining MECS with TEI(P5), one encodes it as <del/deleted text/del>. For all of these four different ways of encoding there is software support to process the encoded transcriptions, and while one may want to use MECS for reasons of admitting overlap, one may at the same time still want to stick in one's naming of the tags to the widely shared TEI(P5) nomenclature.

WIT and TEI(P5) are just two examples of markup nomenclatures; in order to pay tribute to the existing range of available markup nomenclatures, we also want to mention two others: HNML (HyperNietzsche Markup Language) and MathML.[15] HNML was developed in the HyperNietzsche Project for the transcription of the Nietzsche *Nachlass* and has its strength in genetic markup—that is, transcription of structures of text genesis and text layers. MathML was developed for the markup of mathematical sources and allows transcription and analysis within a framework oriented toward mathematics. It is possible (and sometimes advisable) to combine nomenclatures; thus, one may choose TEI(P5) as one's set for the overall transcription of an item while using MathML for the transcription of mathematical parts within that item. A new nomenclature is often developed for transcription in a specific project, of a specific author's archive, or even of an individual text, or, alternatively, of texts that are distributed among many different authors and projects but all belonging to the same type. The *TEI Guidelines*, with their proposals from P1 (1990) up to the most recent P5 (2007), belong to the latter and represent the most general set of guidelines available for the transcription of texts.

The remaining discussion in this chapter is focused on XML and TEI(P5), since they enjoy the most popularity and software support among text-encoding projects. We present a small transcription sample in full XML TEI(P5) dress and use it as our touchstone for discussing concepts such as *schema* and *Document Type Definition*. Rendering the above song in minimum-required XML TEI(P5) yields the following:

```
<?xml version="1.0" encoding="UTF-8"?>
<!DOCTYPE TEI SYSTEM "teilite.dtd">
  <TEI>
  <teiHeader>
  <fileDesc>
  <titleStmt>
  <title></title>
  <author></author>
  </titleStmt>
  <publicationStmt><p></p></publicationStmt>
  <sourceDesc><p></p></sourceDesc>
  </fileDesc>
  </teiHeader>
  <text>
  <body>
  <div type="song">
  <head>I've been high</head>
  <p>by Bucks, Mills, Stipe, R.E.M.</p>
  <lg n="1">
  <l n="1">have you seen?</l>
  <l n="2">have not, will travel.</l>
  <l n="3">have I missed the big reveal?</l>
  </lg>
  <lg n="2">
  <l n="1">do my eyes</l>
<l n="2">do my eyes seem empty?</l>
```

```
<l n="3">I've forgotten how this feels.</l>
</lg>
</div>
</body>
</text>
</TEI>
```

This transcription consists of a root element, `<TEI>`; a header, `<teiHeader>`; and a `<text>` element. Each XML TEI(P5) transcription has to contain these three elements. Further, for each element there are additional requirements with regard to which other elements it can or must occur in and which other elements can or must occur in it. In order to make sure these requirements are actually fulfilled, one uses software that parses the transcription and checks whether its markup corresponds to the rules laid down in the XML schema. This is called *validation*. A check that parses the transcription alone with regard to whether it obeys the syntax rules of its declared markup syntax is called a *well-formedness check*.

An XML schema comes in two main variants. The first, and the only one that is actually part of the XML language recommendation, is called Document Type Definition (DTD). Alternatively, nowadays one uses predominantly the term "schema" to refer to a new group of non-DTD schemas. While all non-DTD schemas are written in XML, the DTD schema is actually not written in XML syntax (though it follows an XML recommendation). There are several benefits from using non-DTD schemas. There can be aspects of a transcription that are important to validate but that cannot be validated by using a DTD. For instance, it may be important to restrict date values to conform to specific calendars so that, for example, dates like "February 29" will be discovered as invalid for years that are not leap years. Such restrictions can be specified in schema languages such as Relax NG and W3C Schema. This functionality is particularly important where XML is used for markup in transactions like those in the bank sector. But the same functionality also applies to markup of texts and other cultural artifacts and is used by TEI, for example, to define its proposal P5 in Relax NG. WAB currently utilizes a schema in Relax NG to completely define the required and possible values for its elements for transcription of the Wittgenstein *Nachlass*.

Reference to a DTD—usually an external file—is included right at the beginning of the XML document, immediately following the XML declaration that starts every XML document. The top of an XML document with DTD reference, then, looks like this (the DTD reference is in the second line):

```
<?xml version="1.0" encoding="UTF-8"?>
<!DOCTYPE TEI SYSTEM"teilite.dtd">
```

Alternatively, reference to non-DTD schemas looks much the same, though the XML recommendation does not prescribe a specific place for it. In the following sample, a Relax NG schema is related to an XML document in the Oxygen XML editor:[16]

```
<?xml version="1.0" encoding="UTF-8"?>
<?oxygen RNGSchema="tei_xinclude.rng" type="xml"?>
<TEI xmlns="http://www.tei-c.org/ns/1.0">
```

Analogous to our point above that markup nomenclatures can be created for specific authors or specific projects, schemas may also be written on an individual basis, or they may be chosen from a set of preexisting generic schemas such as DocBook or the TEI.[17] It is always recommendable to first investigate to what extent it is possible to use an already existing and common schema before considering developing a new one from scratch. Adherence to already existing schemas and standards does not mean that adaptations to individual needs are not possible or accepted. The *TEI Guidelines* allow for such adaptation; however, it is best done with the tools and methods that the TEI itself offers for such adaptation. Doing so not only guarantees compatibility and coherence with the overarching set of rules, but it also produces thorough documentation of the changes and additions introduced, which can be valuable for a number of reasons, including other projects that may benefit from the same changes and as feedback on the *TEI Guidelines* themselves. Since the *TEI Guidelines* are intended to apply to a wide range of texts, they offer, in the form of schemas, a set of modules rather than one single schema. This set of modules can be customized, through a software-supported selection and combination procedure, to yield exactly the schema that is needed and that at the same time is as strict as possible.[18]

Whether one produces the first layer of a transcription through use of OCR software or simply by typing it in using an ordinary word processor, it is recommended that a specialized XML editor, such as XMLSpy from Altova or Oxygen from SyncRO Soft Ltd., be used for the markup. Such editors have built-in tools for validation and well-formedness checks, and they usually offer validation as one proceeds with the transcription (comparable to the continuous spell-check function in Microsoft Word). They even implement schema definitions so that one's assignment of attributes and attribute values can be guided by information on attributes and attribute values foreseen by the schema for the element in question.

Up to now we have spoken about markup making use of element tags that relate to spans of text (elements in the narrow sense) or points in the text (milestones). There is an additional level of transcription that we yet have to address: *character sets* and, connected with it, *entities*. It is important that the character set of the transcription is understandable and transportable across different platforms and programs. For this purpose, it is best to utilize reference to Unicode, be it on the character set level or on the entity level. Unicode UTF-8 is a good character set candidate for texts using the Latin, Cyrillic, or Hebrew scripts, where all ASCII characters (ISO-8859-1) use one byte, and characters above ASCII use more than one byte. UTF-16, on the other hand, is more suited for texts that are dominated by characters in the sixteen-bit range (two bytes). In order to specify in an XML document that a specific character set is used, like UTF-8 in the following example, the XML declaration in the first line of the document should look like this:

```
<?xml version="1.0" encoding="UTF-8"?>
```

Most often, one wants to produce marked-up transcriptions in order to subsequently analyze or view or publish them—in short, present them—whether it is just on a local computer screen, on the web, or on paper. For such presentation the markup is transformed in accordance with the specific purpose one may have with the presentation. If one targets an edition on paper, one will want to transform the markup—for instance, transforming a tag for emphasis into a conventional representation of emphasis, such as italics, on paper. If one's presentational interest is to study handwritten revisions in the manuscript described, one will already have marked all such revisions through special transcription and will now present them in a focused way for research. There is no default way for presentation of an XML transcription. This does not mean there wouldn't exist pre-created templates to transform our XML transcriptions; such templates do exist (especially in the TEI domain), and if one's transcription follows the same standard for which the template was produced, the transformation template can effectively be run on one's own transcription. But there may be so many different purposes connected with transcriptions that the need for either modifying such templates or creating new ones from scratch may always arise.

These templates, which are called *XML style sheets*, are usually referred to as XSLT (Extensible Stylesheet Language Transformation).[19] The expression "style sheet" in the digital context is most commonly used for HTML CSS (Cascading Style Sheets),[20] which can be used in combination with XSLTs. XSLTs are written in XML and give a series of instructions on how the transcription markup should be transformed for the single purposes. Thus for each single XML tag, an XSLT may contain a series of different and alternative instructions, dependent on the desired output. For example, one and the same element in the transcription of a primary source may be converted to different renderings in normalized and diplomatic presentations of this source, respectively. XSLTs can also be utilized in a great number of other ways, including the introduction of global changes into a transcription file—for example, when shifting adherence from one schema/nomenclature to another. The conversion of WAB's machine-readable version from MECS WIT to XML TEI(P5) markup was largely carried out through the

use of specially designed XSLT style sheets. In turn, the conversion of the resulting XML TEI(P5) transcriptions to reader-friendly presentation outputs—most
typically in HTML or PDF format—is equally carried out through XSLT style
sheets. It is on this level of processing the transcription for presentation purposes to outputs that the transcription's entities are converted to their respective
renderings, as previously defined with reference to Unicode in an explicit list
of correlations. A great number of XSLT style sheets are freely available from
the web, but most projects will need specific adaptation for which professional
assistance may be needed.

One should make special mention of including facsimiles as an integral part
of one's scholarly edition of primary sources. The same principle of separating transcription from presentation that we have been discussing all along
applies here. While the correlation of source transcription and facsimile is a
matter of transcription for which we propose a standard XML TEI(P5) encoding, the question of how this correlation is subsequently realized is a matter
of presentation. A standard way of putting it to work in digital editions is,
naturally, to hyperlink a page break with a digital facsimile file of the page
this page break introduces. In an XML TEI(P5) transcription, reference to the
facsimiles can be implemented in a number of ways. For our purpose here
we choose a method that prepares for the possibility of hyperlinking text and
facsimile in the resulting edition on page levels and for having each, including the facsimile edition, on their own. This may be required, since for the
text edition one will often want to render the source in text sequence, while
for the facsimile edition, one may want to stick to the physical sequence of
the pages, and the two often do not coincide. The following sample is taken
from WAB's XML TEI(P5) transcription of Wittgenstein *Nachlass* item Ms-
139a, where text and page sequence diverge, and therefore the transcription
needs to make adequate and specific records of both the physical and the text
sequence. This can then be exploited for presentations that follow either the
first or the second sequence.

```
<facsimile>
<surface lrx="2048" lry="3072" n="24" xml:id="Ms-139a_1r">
<graphic url="http://wab.aksis.uib.no/cost-a32_fax/139a/Ms-139a,1r.
   jpg"/>
</surface>
<surface lrx="2048" lry="3072" n="24" xml:id="Ms-139a_1v">
<graphic url="http://wab.aksis.uib.no/cost-a32_fax/139a/Ms-139a,1v.
   jpg"/>
</surface>
<surface lrx="2048" lry="3072" n="24" xml:id="Ms-139a_2r">
<graphic url="http://wab.aksis.uib.no/cost-a32_fax/139a/Ms-139a,2r.
   jpg"/></surface>
<surface lrx="2048" lry="3072" n="24" xml:id="Ms-139a_2v">
```

```
<graphic url="http://wab.aksis.uib.no/cost-a32_fax/139a/Ms-139a,2v.
  jpg"/>
</surface>
...
</facsimile>
```

Conclusions

At this point we wish to briefly respond to a potential challenge—that is, the view that because of the fast progress of information technology, much of what has been said in this chapter, in particular about technical tools and formats, may soon be outdated. Our general view is that if the reader agrees that the distinction between transcription and presentation is adequate, he or she will also agree that text encoding today has a crucial function for practicing this distinction and that even though technical tools and formats may change, text encoding will not become outdated, inasmuch as it embeds and carries this distinction. If the reader does not agree with the first statement, then he or she may still find other good reasons for applying text encoding. To conclude, we now summarize our answers to the editors' questions quoted in the beginning of this contribution. Naturally, these answers are informed by our view of the role and character of descriptive text encoding or markup as paradigm implementation of the principle of separating transcription from presentation issues and procedures.

Does technology call into question traditional practices? Yes. Digital editing, as it is proposed here, should be seen to call into question traditional editorial philology, and we should consider carefully which traditional practices we shall continue to adhere to and which we shall abandon since they are affiliated with traditional technologies rather than substantiated methodological truths.

What happens to "critical editing"? The concept of "critical editing" will continue to play an important role and may even become a clearer and more concise concept than it is now. Against the background of interactive dynamic editing, "critical editing" could start to denote the editing activities by the expert editors as compared to the editing of less-expert users. Editing may increasingly develop toward building digital research platforms that offer text archives for user-steered interactive dynamic editing. But this will make the expert editor even more necessary rather than superfluous.

What proof is there that using digital tools and media facilitates critical editing? Text encoding as it has been presented here is a tool to explicate, document, and communicate one's editorial decisions and practices. By making these decisions and practices transparent, text encoding or markup also makes them controllable. In that sense we can hope for discussions of an edition's value that make reference to the editor's encoding and transformation schemes. Such discussions will serve as evidence that using digital tools and media facilitates critical editing.

Do digital media make critical editions more accessible and therefore more democratic? Yes. By using international recommendations like XML and TEI(P5) for preparing and sharing digital editions, these editions will in principle become more accessible, and editing will therefore become a more democratic enterprise. While digital editing, including interactive dynamic editing, in the way proposed here resembles the situation in a republic ruled according to principles that are not beyond the possibility of community control and revision and participation through individual community members, traditional editing resembles the situation under an enlightened monarch in eighteenth-century Europe.

Does the quality of critical editions increase when they are produced with digital tools? Yes. Although the quality of editions naturally does not depend on the tools with which they are produced alone, digital tools such as text encoding not only immensely improve the quality of an edition by improving the entire production process, but they also improve the quality and scope of controlling and revising the edition. This may be their most novel and unprecedented achievement.

Notes

1. We thank Deirdre Smith for help with the English and the editors, especially Daniel Apollon, for their valuable comments. We also thank Philipp Steinkrüger and Patrick Sahle for discussions on the concept of interactive dynamic editing and Špela Vidmar for responses and suggestions from a novice's point of view. Our contribution overlaps in parts with Huitfeldt's contribution to this volume, but we recommend that the reader reads both chapters in their entirety, since where they treat the same subject, including markup systems and XML, they present it from different perspectives or with different levels of detail.

2. XML is a recommendation by the World Wide Web Consortium (1998; see http://www.w3.org/XML). TEI is an international effort started in 1987 to develop an independent, portable, and open file format for texts in the humanities for long-term storage, analysis, and interchange of texts. Results from this work include the *TEI Guidelines: Guidelines for Electronic Text Encoding and Interchange* and a set of DTD modules that define markup languages for texts. The first draft version TEI(P1) was available in 1990. The DTD modules were in the P4 version (2001), available in both SGML and XML, and in the TEI(P5) version as DTD, Relax NG, and W3C Schema (on this see below). On TEI, see http://www.tei-c.org; the P5 version is found at http://www.tei-c.org/release/doc/tei-p5–doc/html. On XML and TEI, see also Huitfeldt's contribution to this volume.

3. In this chapter we have used the term "transcription" instead of the word "registration" to designate the activity of recording primary source data and metadata. The word "registration" is used in exactly this sense by a number of projects, including WAB, which

with MECS WIT in the 1990s developed a "registration standard" for the transcription of the Wittgenstein *Nachlass*. (On MECS WIT, see below).

4. In traditional paper-based editing an attempt to also provide the user with the possibility of verifying the editor's decisions has been to supplement the text with a facsimile edition. But this is the exception rather than the rule.

5. This is not to say that the user falls out of the traditional editing scheme entirely; also there we find types of editions that are related to target users. This is well documented and described in Modalsli 2005.

6. For an example of earlier use and discussion of "dynamic editing," see Rehbein 1998.

7. The concept of interactive dynamic editing has been applied at WAB and HIS since 2000, foremost with reference to interactive dynamic presentation (for a pilot site, see http://wab.aksis.uib.no/transform/wab.php). For models of how interactive dynamic transcription can work in practice, see, for example, COST Action "Interedition" (http://interedition.huygensinstituut.nl; Robinson 2009) and the HyperNietzsche Project (http://www.hypernietzsche.org/base.html; D'Iorio 2002b). Interactive dynamic transcription typically involves *standoff markup*, a branch of markup we do not have the space to discuss in this chapter.

8. If in this context we want to reserve a level where understanding and interpretation have not yet entered, a level of "physical being" without mental and social "contamination," we can call it the level of the "scripts." This is the level of the marks on the paper, of the signs, without and before any mental processing, and involving neither semantic or syntactic understanding—in other words, without reading with some sort of understanding. But as soon as we convert the signs to function and meaning, they are symbolized, and understanding comes in (see Pichler 2004, 22ff). However, this is not to deny that transcription can involve fundamentally *different* types of understanding and interpretation and that one can explicate and document them. An attempt to do this for the editorial work of WAB was made in Pichler 1995. Our use of the term "data" is indifferent to the issue whether it includes the interpretational (symbol) element or just refers to the pure physical level, the script. However, we are aware of the debate, which centers on the use of this concept with regard to the question of interpretation (see, for example, Floridi 2005).

9. Claus Huitfeldt developed MECS in the 1990s; it is related to SGML, but the syntax is different because it allows overlaps.

10. To be accurate, SGML also offers a nomenclature for encoding and thus for documenting the content and structure of a text.

11. Since 2001, WAB has developed methods and tools for migrating the machine-readable version from MECS WIT to XML TEI, now XML TEI(P5).

12. For contributions to this discussion, see, on the one side, DeRose et al. 1990, who defend a hierarchic view of text, as well as Huitfeldt 1994 and Buzzetti 2002, who challenge the hierarchic view of text with reference to handwritten texts' multidimensionality, nonlinearity, and overlapping structures.

13. Allan Renear has coined the term "antirealist" view for this position (Biggs and Huitfeldt 1997, 353). For an outline of the "antirealist" position, see Pichler 1995 and

Pichler 2004, 22ff. It is an overarching aim of textual antirealism to reconstruct text ontological claims, be they from the hierarchical or the nonhierarchical camp, as claims and demands to text practices rather than metaphysical claims of text ontology.

14. This method is called *fragmentation*, but other well-known techniques can be used. See *TEI P5 Guidelines,* ch. 20, "Non-hierarchical Structures," for an overview of methods.

15. On HNML, see full reference in bibliography (Zapf n.d.). For MathML, see http://www.w3.org/Math.

16. See http://www.oxygenxml.com.

17. See http://www.docbook.org.

18. The tool ROMA helps in this process; it is available from http://www.tei-c.org/Roma. Here one can make one's own customizations as well as choose among predefined sets from "TEI Absolutely Bare" to "TEI with maximal setup, plus external additions."

19. XSLT is a W3C Recommendation; see http://www.w3.org/Style/XSL.

20. CSS is a W3C Recommendation; see http://www.w3.org/Style/CSS.

PART III

New Practices, New Contents,
New Policies

7. The Making of an Edition

Three Crucial Dimensions

ODD EINAR HAUGEN

The Gutenberg Watershed

This chapter gives a brief overview of the historical development of textual editing. While the practice of editing has a long history, it is commonly accepted that the foundation of editing as a scholarly or even scientific activity was created in the first half of the nineteenth century. From this time, strict and to a certain extent formal methods were being introduced in textual editing—notably, the use of shared errors. Yet, generally, textual editing remained a qualitative enterprise. From the beginning of the twentieth century, there has been a search for more objective methods, and a number of mathematical techniques have been put to the test. This chapter discusses how various qualitative and quantitative methods have been used in modern editions and proposes a typology of editions based on three dimensions: the reproduction of the source, the rendering of the process lying behind the text, and the selection of sources for the actual edition. In conclusion, a brief discussion is given of how these dimensions can be combined in an edition.

The editing of texts is often thought of as an activity belonging to the modern, post-Gutenberg period, the period when handwritten manuscripts finally could be turned into a printed and stable form. However, the post-Gutenberg period is only the most recent part of the history of editing. In Western culture the practice of editing goes a long way back, at least to the time of Alexandrian philology, when the Homeric texts, several hundred years old and already in a state of textual flux, called for establishing a "correct" version of the text. In the third century BC, the Jewish Hellenistic community undertook to produce an authoritative Greek text of the Hebrew Bible, combining critical selection of handwritten sources, editorial processing, and translation from Hebrew and

Aramaic. The resulting *Septuagint* was not only a translation but also should be regarded as an edition. These characteristics also apply to the *Vulgata* of Hiero-nymus, who mastered a Latin edition of the Bible based on translations from various Hebrew, Greek, and Aramaic sources (while the older *Vetus Latina* was based exclusively on Greek texts). The *Hexapla* of Origenes, in which several versions of the Bible were brought together, was a full-blown synoptic edition that displayed the various versions in parallel columns. Later, when Charlemagne ordered the copying of classical literature around 800 AD, this enterprise could also be seen as a major editorial project. Many classical texts have been preserved to this day only because of the work being done in the Carolingian period.

The vernacular literature is no exception. In writing the history of the Nor-wegian kings, the Icelandic historian Snorri Sturluson (1179–1241) based his text on earlier sources, and he described his work as that of *setja saman* ("put together," the equivalent to Latin *componere)*. It was an authorial as well as an editorial piece of work. In the manuscript culture, texts were copied by hand, and in many traditions the copyists would substantially alter the text. Should they be seen as co-authors or as editors? This may be a question of definition, but there are many examples of medieval books that should also be regarded as editions from a modern point of view. When the Eddic poems were collected in the humble manuscript Reykjavík, Gamle Kongelige Samling (GKS), 2365 4° (ca. 1270), this was an edition of a genre that had lived for many hundred years but by the 13th century was on the wane.

The Eddic poems are ordered according to subject matter, with a first listing of eleven poems of gods, beginning with the apocalyptic *Vǫluspá*, then twelve poems of heroes, and, in several places, with added pieces of explanatory prose. The manuscript has no title page (medieval manuscripts do not carry title pages) nor does it contain an introduction. Yet, for all intents and purposes it is the work of an editor who brought together and ordered the twenty-three poems that make up this manuscript (see fig. 7-1). The manuscript often referred to as *Hauksbók*, by the Icelander Haukr Erlendsson (d. 1334 in Bergen), is a col-lection of texts from a broad number of sources.[1] It contains historical and semi-historical works, mathematical treatises, and philosophical or theological dialogues; some of the historical works were originally written in Old Norse, while the rest was translated from Latin.[2] In a sense it is a private library in a single volume, but it is also an edition. It was collected by Haukr, who wrote much of it in his own hand and had other parts written by scribes in his service. What more can be claimed of an edition?

The introduction of printing by movable types added two new roles. The scribe was replaced by the typesetter and printer, and the dissemination of texts by the medieval scriptorium, or copying room, was replaced by publishers and booksellers. Some, like William Caxton (1415/1422–1492), did it all—typesetting,

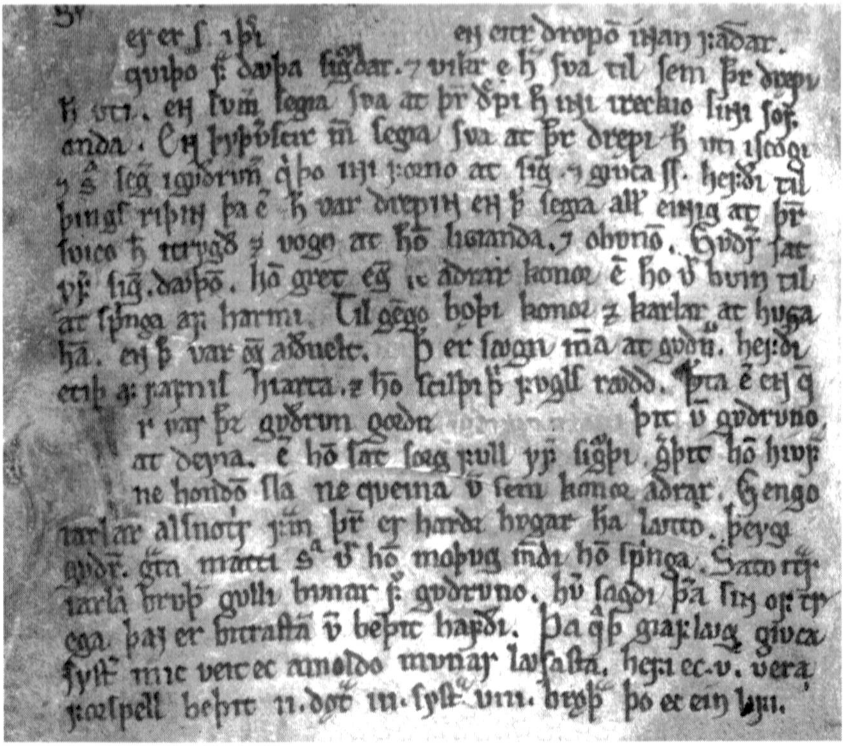

Figure 7-1: The main manuscript of the Eddic poems, Reykjavík, Gamle Kongelige Samling (GKS), 2365 4° (ca. 1270). The page shown here is fol. 33v, which contains the concluding stanzas of an incomplete lay on Sigurd the Dragon Slayer, *Sigurðarkviða*, and the beginning of the lay of Gudrun, *Guðrúnarkviða*. In between these poems, the editor of the manuscript adds a short passage in which he reflects on the sources for Sigurd's death—"en sumir segja svá at þeir dræpi hann inni í rekkju sinni sofanda, en þýðverskir menn segja svá at þeir dræpi hann úti í skógi" (some say that they killed him inside while he slept in his bed, while German men say that they killed him out in the woods). (Photograph used by permission of the Árni Magnússon Institute, Reykjavík. From: GKS 2365 4°, fol. 33v. Photographer: Jóhanna Ólafsdóttir).

printing, and publishing; others introduced a division of labor. Aldus Manutius (1449/1450–1515), for example, published no less than thirty-three first editions of Greek works, but he had the type cut by Francesco Griffo (1450–1518), and a large number of Greek scholars gathered around him in Venice and helped him in his grand editorial enterprise.

A great number of early printed books are essentially editions of earlier medieval works, even if the name on the title page may be that of a printer or a publisher. Henri Estienne (1528–1598), the famous Parisian printer, published among many other works the dialogues of Plato in 1578, and he collated himself the manuscripts behind the edition. He referred to himself as Typographus Parisiensis, but he was also a collator and an editor. From his workshop came a large number of books in Greek as well as Latin, of which nineteen were the first edition, *editio princeps*, of the work. The pagination of Henri Estienne's Plato edition (1578) is in fact still used in citations, referred to as the Stephanus pagination.[3]

Throughout this history, the act of editing stands out as the conscious effort, anonymous or non-anonymous, of making existing texts available in a new form—since the time of Gutenberg, typically in print. The early editors-cum-publishers may not have thought of themselves as anything more than humble mediators, but over the years the editor emerges as a role in its own right. Until the recent advent of digital texts, the shape of editions has hardly changed. In the edition of the *Greek New Testament* by Erasmus of Rotterdam (1466/1469–1536), published in Basel in 1516, the display of the text and the apparatus is basically the same as in any modern edition. What this means is that the interface of an edition has been so well established that the editor can expect it to be understood by all users—the introduction, the text with its apparatus, the indices, and the commentary. It should be added, though, that some editions are so highly structured that they do need a companion; *Der Text des Neuen Testaments* by Kurt and Barbara Aland (German edition 1982, English translation 1987), was written as an explanation of how modern editions of the *Greek New Testament* should be read and used.

While the printed editions of the Old and New Testaments may be complex and multilayered, many editions are straightforward and should not be construed as more difficult than they actually are. The edition of a single document, such as a medieval charter, may not entail more than performing a faithful transcription of the document, word by word and line by line. In this sense the editor is essentially a copyist, and, like the great majority of medieval copyists, one might think he should remain anonymous. Is there any reason to add one's name to a text that has been conceived and written down by someone else? Yet any editor will add something to the text; no editor will produce an edition that is identical to the source, however faithful the transcription is. In general, editing requires skill and knowledge. The document may be difficult to read, the linguistic idiom opaque, and the context partly lost. Even for the simplest of documents, codicological, paleographical, and historical knowledge will be called for. For these reasons the editor should be recognized as a participant in the mediating of a text, even in cases where the edition is based on a single document and no analysis of the textual tradition has been necessary.

Until recent decades, editing has fallen into two main categories: the editing of texts from the manuscript era and the editing of printed texts, making Gutenberg the turning point. The former is sometimes referred to as "old" philology and the latter as "new," but since the term "new philology" lately has been coined for a specific material approach to medieval manuscripts, I will avoid these terms and refer to manuscript and print culture instead. This is, of course, a simplification, because the transition from manuscript to print culture has indeed been a surprisingly long changeover. For example, manuscripts were copied by hand in Iceland by some farmers until the end of the nineteenth century, even if Iceland got its first printing press as early as around 1540. During the Second World War, illegal texts were sometimes copied by hand, and that also happened in the *samizdat* literature in the former Eastern Europe during the Communist Era.[4]

In spite of these modifications, there is no question that the invention of the printing press changed the way texts were disseminated. Rather than being copied one by one in unique manuscripts, texts could be printed in large runs, creating a number of identical copies. It is true that some medieval scriptoria turned out large numbers of texts, especially after the rise of universities in the thirteenth century, but even so, each manuscript of some length would contain some textual variation. Conversely, printers often set books several times during fairly short periods, because they needed the lead type for other books. Thus, textual variation crept into a production, which in principle should be able to remove variation. Only in very recent times, after the introduction of digital texts, can we talk about completely loss-free reproduction of texts. So if the printing press represents a major divide for the history of textual scholarship, one may well ask whether the digital age, with its loss-free reproduction of texts, represents a new divide.

This chapter, however, discusses scholarly editing of pre-digital texts and does not attempt to chart what is going to happen with the editing of truly digital texts. It does not discuss the editing of texts on hard disk drives, Short Message Service (SMS) texts on cellular telephones, e-mail correspondence, or blogs. It does discuss digital editions to some extent, but these are editions of pre-digital texts, using the computer in order to reproduce and display them in a manner that basically belongs within the Gutenberg paradigm. In these editions the screen serves as a replica of the printed page. The displays of digital text editions look like printed editions in the same manner as early printed books looked like medieval manuscripts. The two-dimensional page with its margin and its text in ordered columns also remains the carrier of texts in digital editions. Even the use of windows allowing access to several files at the same time is really nothing more than having several printed sources lying on the table. The desktop of a modern computer relies on an organization of the data that is based on the physical desktop, and most applications have printer-friendly versions that answer to the same physical and visual limitations as traditional printed material.

The chapter also restricts itself to editions of texts in the Latin alphabet, although with a brief discussion of epigraphical editions in runes and ogham. In a European context, this leaves out the literature written in alphabets such as Cyrillic and Greek. Apart from the question of how to render texts with different directions of writing from the Latin alphabet (such as most ogham inscriptions and many runic ones), editing is not script-dependent, and it is unlikely that the chapter would have looked much different if the texts discussed had been in another alphabet.

Searching for the Origins

The editing of manuscript texts has often taken the form of a reconstructive enterprise in which the editor tries to trace the text back to its original, removing errors and innovations in the manuscript transmission as he or she slowly sifts through the preserved material. Since the original in almost all classical and medieval texts has been irrevocably lost, the reconstruction can be no more than an approximation of the original.[5] The approximated text cannot claim to be the original, but it can claim to be the optimal text, in so far as the point of the editorial exercise is to trace the history of the text as far back as possible. This program is what Karl Lachmann (1793–1851) succinctly formulated in a review published in 1817, which was also quoted in chapter 1: "On the basis of a sufficient number of good manuscripts, we should and we must build a text which reflects all of these, a text which either would be the original text or a text which would come very close to the original."[6]

The approximation to the original has later been termed the *archetype* (e.g., in Maas 1960, 6). Since the generation of Karl Lachmann, the process of copying a text has been modeled as a tree turned upside down, a *stemma codicum*. The *stemma* has the original on top, the archetype right below, and the preserved manuscripts on the branches below that (fig. 7-2).

The copying of a text inevitably introduces errors, and while Lachmann and his generation of scholars shared the traditional belief that errors should be removed, their new and distinct method was to use errors as pointers to what had happened during the filiation of the text. If an error was introduced in a manuscript, it was likely to remain in all copies of this manuscript (unless it was such an obvious error that a later scribe might correct it without having access to the original). The error would thus identify a particular branch of the filiation. The analysis of shared errors became the basic of a new, formal method of analyzing the manuscripts: the *genealogical method*. The critic became a skeptic; he was looking for errors, and since late manuscripts were often full of errors, they were usually regarded as being of little value for the approximation to the original text. More specifically, if a manuscript could be proven to be a copy of

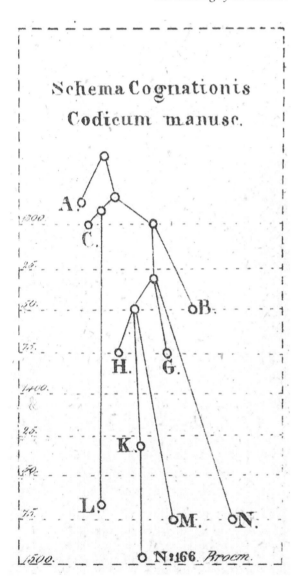

Schema Cognationis
Codicum manusc.

Figure 7-2: The stemma for the manuscripts of *Vestgötalagen* published by the Swedish scholars Carl Johan Schlyter and Hans Samuel Collin in 1827. This is probably the first stemma ever published, but it remained isolated. It was classical scholars like the German Friedrich Ritschl and the Dane Johan Ludvig Madvig who, in the tradition of Karl Lachmann, published the first stemmata in the 1830s. Lachmann himself never published a stemma, but he founded the genealogical method for which the stemma is the prime model.

another, known manuscript, it would be of no critical value. At best it would have exactly the same readings as the *exemplar* (the manuscript from which it was copied) and would not add anything to the tradition. More likely, it would add some new errors to the text and should therefore be disregarded. The process of removing such manuscripts was later termed *eliminatio codicum descriptorum* (see, e.g., Maas 1960, 5) and meant that the editor pruned the lower branches in the stemma with the aim of leaving only the best manuscripts—that is, those that were closest to the original. The editorial process was essentially a process of reconstruction and simplification.

The editing of texts created in the print culture is also reconstructive, but the direction of this view is rather the opposite of the Lachmannian approach. In a well-known analogy, the German Hölderlin editor Friedrich Beißner has compared the two approaches to traveling along a river (Beißner 1964, 74–76). While the editor of texts from the manuscript era travels upstream toward the spring of the river, looking for the lost original, the editor of texts from the print era travels downstream toward the sea, looking for the final version of the work and its dissemination. What unites the two approaches is the diachronic aspect, the search for and analysis of the development of the text. For a classical or medieval work transmitted in manuscripts, the editor has to move backward in time, because younger manuscripts in general are better preserved and less fragmentary than older ones. In fact, the originals of classical and most medieval works are irrevocably lost. As explained above, the editor can hope for no more than an approximation of the original work. For editions of printed texts, the *editio princeps* is usually in existence, as well as all later editions. The process of editorial reconstruction can thus begin much closer to the origin than what is the case for works preserved in manuscripts, and it can safely move forward in time.

Unlike the study of classical and medieval texts, which in many cases were anonymous and in almost all cases were copied by anonymous scribes, modern (in the sense of post-medieval) texts are predominantly non-anonymous. The editor may have access to drafts by the author and often several printed editions. It is usually not his aim to trace the earliest, unfinished draft from the hand of the author, but instead to chart what happened through the dissemination of the printed editions. To what extent was the text revised, and by whom? In some cases the author was responsible for the revision; in other cases it may have been the publisher or composer, or even later editors. Some editors believe that the first version from the hand of the author is the preferred text, leading to an *Ausgabe erster Hand*, while other editors prefer the last state of the text in the author's lifetime, the *Ausgabe letzter Hand*. The choice between the two is not obvious and may depend on the particular author. The editors of the works by the Danish theologian and philosopher Søren Kierkegaard (1813–1855) have chosen the first printed edition (*førstetrykket*) as their base text, for example, while the editors of the collected works of the Swedish author August Strindberg (1849–1912) have chosen to establish the versions they believe are in best accordance with the author's intentions, which typically lead to an *Ausgabe letzter Hand*.[7]

Many authors, not only Strindberg, have revised their work extensively from the first print and presumably intended that their last version should be preferred. The playwright Henrik Ibsen (1828–1906) made two versions of his *Brand*:

an unfinished epic version (1864–1865) and the revised, dramatic poem, which he wrote while in Italy, *Brand: Et dramatisk Digt i 5 Akter* (1866). For a long time, the draft to the epic *Brand* was thought to be destroyed by Ibsen himself, leaving only the dramatic *Brand*.[8] After his death it was discovered and published for the first time in 1907. It now helps us to see how Ibsen developed his moral ideas in *Brand*. The composer Edvard Grieg (1843–1907) wrote "maa aldrig opføres" (must never be performed) on the score of his "forbidden" Symphony in C minor, which had its first performance in 1864. It was not played until 1980, when it was performed in Moscow based on a photocopy of the original score, and the following year in Bergen. It is still debated whether Grieg's wish should be heeded. The editors of Ludwig Wittgenstein's manuscripts were faced with a similar problem in cases where Wittgenstein himself had written "this is of absolutely no value" at the end of a whole manuscript.[9] Should the manuscript be published anyway? These are ethical, not methodological, questions, and they can be answered only in the context of a full assessment of the creator's work. Unless the work is of a very private or intimate nature, with possible repercussions for other people, the tendency seems to be that editors believe in "the right to know"—in other words, the creator of the work may not be the best judge as to the quality of the work. In the case of Ibsen and Grieg, the publications are probably not so controversial, but for a *roman à clef*, it may be another matter, especially when it comes to the question of identifying people in an introduction or commentary to the work. The passing of time and the status of the persons described may alter this judgment. Victor Hugo's play *Le roi s'amuse* (1832), based on the life of Francis I of France (1494–1597), was banned after one performance because the censors believed it referred negatively to the incumbent King Louis-Philippe (1773–1850). The ban was upheld for fifty years, but Hugo made a successful case for the freedom of speech, and the ban was eventually lifted.

Even if the direction of the textual reconstruction is different for editors on either side of the Gutenberg watershed, they share, as mentioned above, a diachronic approach to the text. Editing a text thus means to chart the development of the text, whether by anonymous manuscript copying or by authorial revisions, and to constitute the edition on the basis of this diachronic understanding. In my view the major editorial divide is not between editors of manuscript texts and printed texts but between editors who approach the text from a diachronic perspective and those who approach it from a purely synchronic point of view. Some of the proponents of the new philology of the 1990s seem to do exactly this (see, e.g., Nichols 1990a for a statement of the new, or material, philology). In the view of the new philology, the text should no longer be restrained by the creator but should be allowed to lead its own life, attain new meanings, and enter into new contexts. It should be allowed to be appreciated as an individual expression, valid and representative for its time and setting. The new philology could also be seen as a late reflection of the New Criticism of the mid-twentieth century and its belief in the autonomy of the work.[10]

At this stage I think it may be helpful to draw an analogy between editing and linguistics. Since Ferdinand de Saussure's work, it has been commonly accepted that linguistic studies fall into one of two categories: synchronic and diachronic. The synchronic investigation of a linguistic state contains no references to what has gone before or comes after this particular state, while the diachronic investigation links one linguistic state to other states along a timeline. In Saussure's model one may claim that the synchronic study has logical primacy, for the reason that a linguistic development can be described only as a succession of states. Synchrony is thus a prerequisite for diachrony.

By analogy, the new philology may be said to have logical primacy over the old philology, because any recension of manuscripts must begin with the description of each individual manuscript, in the same way that each linguistic stage must be described before the process of linguistic development can be understood. However, if the new philology restricts itself to the description and edition of a single manuscript and nothing more, this is at best a very limited view of what an editor can, and should, do.

The view taken in this chapter is that an editor should take upon himself (or herself) to try to chart the textual tradition, to put each stage of the text into its historical context. Even if the editor chooses to focus on a single manuscript, and there may be many good reasons for doing so, it should be done in the context of its historical setting. As argued also in chapter 1 in this book (see "Looking Inward" in that chapter), the opposition between the "old," reconstructive way of editing and the "new," synchronic approach may turn out to be smaller than often claimed. In fact, the "old" way of editing has always begun with the description and analysis of the individual manuscripts. However, it does not restrict itself to this stage.

Organizing the Data

The first step for any editor is to survey and organize the data. An edition is an edition of one or more texts, unified or diverse. If the edition is going to be based on a single source, the survey is quickly done, but in most cases there will be several states of the text to consider. In classical and medieval literature, each manuscript will typically contain a textual state, sometimes close to the state found in other manuscripts, sometimes far removed. The word "manuscript" is used here in a generic sense for any handwritten document, whether it is a single leaf, such as in a charter; or bound in a book, a codex; or a fragment of a larger whole. For the editing of classical and medieval texts, several manuscripts means (in all but a few cases) several scribes and several interpretations of the work. Organizing the manuscripts thus means to try to chart their history, their internal relations, and to try to decide what has been added and what has been deleted in the process. For the editing of printed texts there may also be manuscripts to consider, but usually of a single author and typically leading up to a printed version of the text. Otherwise, the work to be done and the questions to be raised are the same for editors of printed texts as for editors of manuscript texts. How many witnesses to the text are there? It may be manuscripts, printed texts, or both categories, but the vehicles—the documents as such—are of less interest than the text they carry.

At this point a few words on the notion of text are needed. In textual scholarship "text" is a broad term covering several aspects of a literary work. Many critics refer to a tripartite distinction between the *work* (as an abstract conception), the *version* (which is a manifestation of the work), and the *document* (which is the physical carrier of the text). Recently, FRBR (Functional Requirements for Bibliographic Records) has introduced a four-tier model, as discussed in chapter 4 in this book (by Hillesund and Bélisle). Here the *work* is the intellectual or artistic creation, the *expression* is the realization of a work, the *manifestation* is the physical embodiment of an expression, and the *item* is a single exemplar of an expression.

In general, the FRBR model is well suited for modern printed publications, but it is less suited for works preserved and transmitted in manuscripts. Most importantly, individual manuscripts are items of a work in the same sense as individual copies of a book are items of a work. Manuscripts, however, display much more textual variation than printed books, even early printed books. For a librarian it is usually irrelevant which item (i.e., copy) of a book she puts on the shelf; for a textual critic the choice of which manuscript to follow is an extremely important question. One might even argue that each manuscript is a manifestation of its own, thus making the bottom level of the model, the items, redundant for works preserved in manuscripts. That would also apply to large scriptoria, where many manuscripts were produced at the same time, and to the *pecia* system of manuscript copying in the medieval universities.[11] Even here, textual variation crept into the individual manuscripts, the more so the humbler the circumstances. While large scriptoria would strive toward uniformity of their texts, the students copying pecia texts would not be equally thorough. For these reasons the FRBR model may be less suited in a general discussion of textual editing. For the purposes of the discussion in this chapter, however, it seems that the tripartite distinction of *work*, *version*, and *document* is sufficient.

It is worth noticing that in neither model—the four-tier FRBR model or the three-tier model recommended here—does the concept of *text* appear. Why is that? The text can be accessed at every level. The text is not restricted to the carrier, such as the item, nor to its abstract state of the work. When referring to the text of an author, one may in some cases refer to the work, in other cases to a version, and in even other cases to the actual document that is carrying the text. Thus, the concept of text is simply too ambiguous to be used for a specific tier of the model. In fact, the FRBR model can be understood as a text model and should therefore avoid referring to the concept of a text in the definition itself.[12] When "text" is used in this chapter, it is as a general term in contexts where it is not deemed necessary to make further distinctions.

In classical and medieval editing, the process of surveying the manuscripts of a work is traditionally called the *recension*, from Latin *recensio*, literally an enumeration or assessment; in several European languages the word is now being used for book reviews, which often tend to go through the book in question from beginning to end. Apart from actually listing and describing the manuscripts (in modern editing often referred to as *descriptive bibliography*), the aim of the recension is to explain their transmission: which are copies and which are exemplars? The prime method for the recension is the genealogical method, which charts the distribution of errors in the text or, to put it more neutrally, of secondary readings in the text. If two manuscripts, *a* and *b*, have shared errors against a third manuscript, *c*, the two manuscripts are most likely copies of a common exemplar (German: *Vorlage*; French: *modèle*), as shown in figure 7-3.

In some textual traditions the genealogical method works fine and is as yet unsurpassed. The only requirement is that the manuscripts have been copied without interference from other manuscripts, because if more than one exemplar has been used by a copyist, errors may travel from one branch of the transmission to another and can no longer be used as indications of common descent. In other words, the transmission has to be uncontaminated, or as Giorgio Pasquali (1885–1952) put it, the transmission has to be vertical (cf. West 1973, 14). If it is also horizontal (i.e., adding readings from other branches of the text), the genealogical method may break down, depending on the amount of contamination. Paul Maas (1880–1964) dejectedly concluded that there was no remedy against contamination (1960, 30). While this conclusion is generally accepted, many textual critics believe that some amount of contamination can be dealt with even within the framework of the genealogical method.[13]

The genealogical method is a qualitative method in the sense that is based on the evaluation of which readings are correct (or primary) and which readings are incorrect (or secondary). Even if there are obvious cases among variant readings, there will always be an amount of subjective judgment on the part of the critic. Since the method cannot handle contaminated traditions, or only a limited amount of contamination, a number of quantitative methods have been developed over the last century, partly in order to avoid the subjectivity of the

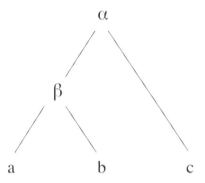

Figure 7-3: A stemma of the three manuscripts *a, b,* and *c*. Since *a* and *b* have common errors, it is unlikely that these errors have been introduced in *a* and *b* independently of each other, but rather that they were introduced in an exemplar for both manuscripts, beta. This branch of the transmission thus differs from that of *c*, which does not have the said errors and therefore most likely is a copy of an ancestor, α, also lacking these errors. The lost manuscript β is thus the manuscript that introduced the errors into the tradition, and as long as there is no horizontal interference between *a, b,* and *c,* the genealogical method is able to explain the filiation of the manuscripts based on the distribution of errors in them. It should be added that the method only works with significant errors—i.e., errors that would not have been likely to be corrected by later copyists, or errors that may be termed "resistant."

shared error analysis, and partly in order to get to grips with contaminated transmission.[14] According to Henri Quentin (1872–1935), the critic should no longer work with "good" or "bad" readings, but solely with variants (1926, 37). Even if Quentin's edition of the early books of the Old Testament has not been deemed successful, his program has appealed to many critics. In this tradition can be found scholars like Walter Wilson Greg (1875–1959) and Dom Jacques Froger, and, to a certain extent, Bernard Cerquiglini in his above-mentioned *Éloge de la variante* (1989).

As mentioned in chapter 1, already in 1963, dealing with the rich inventory of New Testament manuscripts, Ernest Colwell and Ernest Tune advocated carrying out a statistical comparison of each manuscript to all other available manuscripts witnessing a given text. In the late 1960s John Griffith took this program further, using taxonomic methods for exploring the manuscripts of Juvenal (1968) and subsequently some of the Gospel manuscripts (1969). Dietmar Najock (1973) broadened this approach to include multivariate statistics. In retrospect, this was a period of great optimism for what may be termed "quantitative manuscript recension"—that is, textual criticism based on mathematical models. The Centre National de la Recherche Scientifique (CNRS) published in 1979 the conference report *La pratique des ordinateurs dans la critique des textes*, a report that demonstrates the versatility of methods being tested at the time. The CNRS survey has been complemented by two more recent collections, *Studies in Stemmatology I* (1996) and *Studies in Stemmatology II* (2004), both edited by Pieter van Reenen and Margot van Mulken, and a broad conference report, *The Evolution of Texts* (2006), edited by Caroline Macé and colleagues. After a somewhat quiet period in the 1980s, the last couple of decades have seen a continued exploration of the field, bringing in new methods and approaches.

Multivariate methods do not make any assumption about the diachronic axis of the transmission, but simply state their synchronic relationship. In the words of Jacques Froger, they can establish a network but cannot orient it.[15] This is also true of another type of multivariate technique, correspondence analysis, nowadays well known from the works of the sociologist Pierre Bourdieu, but used conjointly with partial least squares analysis (PLS) on binary data in New Testament criticism in a pioneering study by Daniel Apollon (1985). It is striking that few of the authors who have contributed in this field are recurring, and to the best of my knowledge there has not evolved a consensus on which multivariate technique is best suited for analyzing textual data. One explanation may be the fact that such methods require a degree of mathematical training that is seldom found among textual scholars; another (and more depressing) explanation is that they simply do not yield sufficiently good results. In my own study in this field, inspired by Apollon's work, I analyzed the filiation of the thirteenth-century Old Norse version of the Gospel of Nicodemus, *Niðrstigningar saga* (Haugen 1992). I found that correspondence analysis produced much better results than cluster analysis, but that it could not be used to build a traditional stemma. I concluded that a multivariate analysis can point toward the *focal text*, understood as the text shared by most manuscripts, but it cannot decide the *archetypical text*—that is, the text that may be closest to the origin of the textual filiation. Nevertheless, for any tradition, perhaps especially for large traditions, multivariate techniques can be of great help for the textual critic, but it is not the endpoint in the analysis of the filiation.

From the early 1990s, phylogenetic methods have been borrowed from the life sciences in order to map the diachronic aspect of textual transmissions. These methods are used to analyze the development of natural species and use concepts that come close to the notion of errors in manuscript transmission. For example, a *synapomorphy* is a shared, derived character between two or more species, such as the hardened front wings that are characteristic of beetles. This is an enticing parallel to the notion of a common error in the genealogical method; just as the presence of hardened front wings sets beetles apart from other insects, a particular shared, derivative reading can identify a subgroup of manuscripts of a literary work. The stemma in figure 7-3 is thus a model that equally well could describe the filiation of three species, in which *a* and *b* form a family against *c*. Early contributions in this field came from Henry M. Hoeningswald, who began using quantitative techniques in linguistic classification (Hoeningswald 1960) and has also explored the use of phylogenetic analysis in textual criticism (Hoeningswald and Wiener 1987). Lately, Peter Robinson and his colleagues have tried phylogenetic analysis in the Canterbury Tales Project, inspired by the promising outcome of his Textual Criticism Challenge in 1991.[16] In Robinson's view a phylogenetic analysis of the manuscript filiation of *The Wife of Bath's Prologue* in the *Canterbury Tales* comes close to what he believes is the original text, which probably was not a fair copy from Chaucer's hand but a working draft with the author's own comments (Barbrook, Blake, Howe, and Robinson 1998). Additional work in this field has been reported in the *Studies in Stemmatology* report (2004), by among others Ben J. P. Salesman, as well as in a number of articles within the field of what has been called New Stemmatics.[17]

In 2007 a new challenge was launched by a group of three Finnish researchers, Teemu Roos, Tuomas Heikkilä, and Petri Myllymäki, called "The Computer-Assisted Stemmatology Challenge." The results were published in an article in *Literary and Linguistic Computing* (Roos and Heikkilä 2009). Three textual cases were presented, and the competitors tried out thirteen different methods on these cases. The results showed that some methods had a strikingly different success rate on the three data sets, while other methods had much more even results. All had a success rate of at least 50 percent, but only one method reached a rate of 87 percent, and only in a single case. The two best methods were phylogenetic analysis using the PAUP (Phylogenetic Analysis Using Parsimony) software, which was the winner of the 1991 challenge, and a method termed RHM, proposed by the Roos team.[18] Of the two, they found that RHM produced slightly better results, with an average of 78 percent, while PAUP got an average of 76 percent. Roos and Heikkilä claim that while the automated methods are not able to root a tree (as Froger had underlined in his 1968 study), this may not be much of a stumbling block in many cases: "The directing of a network is not always a problem: in most cases it is relatively easy to find the root of a network manually, knowing the textual contents of the witnesses" (Roos and Heikkilä 2009, 13, 17).[19] See figure 7-4 for an example.

In these early days of quantitative criticism, there are probably many textual traditions that are too dynamic or too fragmented for any method to give reliable answers. It is the nature of textual critics to try to trace a text until the blade of the spade metaphorically turns. What this means is that several types of editions are called from, ranging from editions of a single manuscript to editions that reconstruct a whole work.

A Typology of Editions

In *Textual Scholarship* David C. Greetham identifies nine different types of scholarly editions, all of which are exemplified with extracts and brief comments. They range from what he calls "single-document transcriptions to multiple-witness eclectic and genetic texts" (1994, 383). To Greetham's corpus could be added several types of biblical, classical, and medieval editions. This makes for a complex and diverse corpus, reflecting very different textual traditions and editorial ambitions. I believe, though, it can be helpful to reduce the variance of this corpus to three underlying dimensions. The first dimension concerns how the text should be reproduced; the second, to what extent the edition should reflect the growth of the text; and the third, which versions (or states) of the text should be selected for the edition.[20] I address each dimension at some length here, discussing the various editorial solutions for each of them.

First Dimension: Reproduction

The question of how the text should be reproduced may be more pressing for the editing of classical and medieval manuscripts, in which modern type can reflect only some of the aspects of the script, than it is in the case of modern texts. There is a span ranging from the most faithful reproduction, using tailor-made type, to the fully normalized one, in which orthography and punctuation have been regularized. To a lesser extent this also applies to the editing of modern texts (once again with the reminder that texts belonging to the print culture are labeled as "modern" in this chapter), but also here the text reproduction is a matter of discussion. Some editors would also like to keep to the source as close as possible in what is called the *accidentals*—that is, minor orthographical traits—while others are willing to do some amount of normalization, such as editing early modern authors in "new" spelling.

FACSIMILE EDITIONS   The facsimile is the most faithful reproduction possible of an original. Early facsimiles were drawn by hand, often in the form of etchings, and are thus true to the etymology of the word, *fac simile*, meaning "make similar" (see figs. 7-5a and 7-5b). From the middle of the nineteenth century, new photographic techniques made it easier and much faster to produce facsimiles, and in the early twentieth century a number of large facsimile series were initiated in many countries.[21] Since manuscripts are typically reproduced in one-to-one format, they are in many cases large, heavy—and expensive. Eventually facsimiles in color photography made their way into the field, and lately digital facsimiles have appeared that can be made accessible via the Internet. The majority of manuscript libraries and archives have now started a program

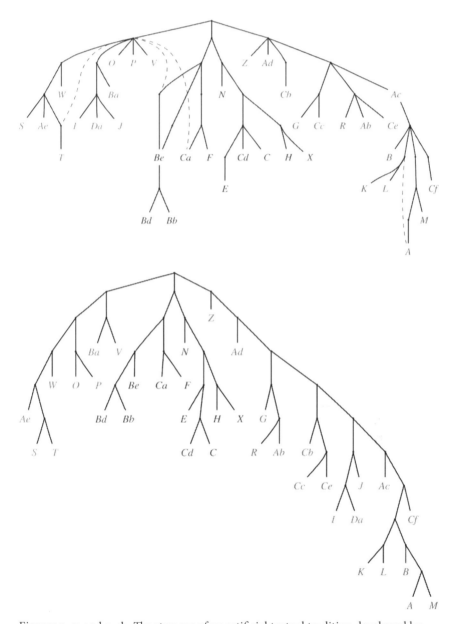

Figures 7-4a and 7-4b: The stemma of an artificial textual tradition developed by the Finnish researchers Roos, Heikkilä, and Myllymäki, the Heinrichi text. The first is the true stemma of the textual tradition made by the researchers and, as such, is rooted in the original version of the text. The second is an unrooted tree from the RHM analysis. From Roos and Heikkilä (2009, figs. 3 and 4); reproduced with the permission of the authors.

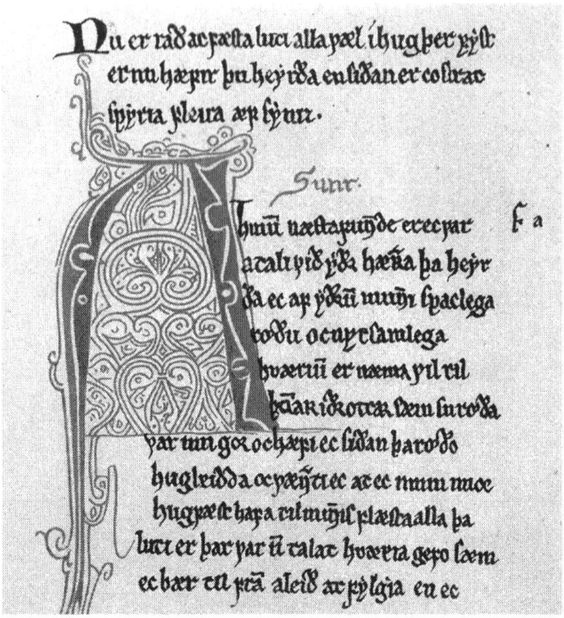

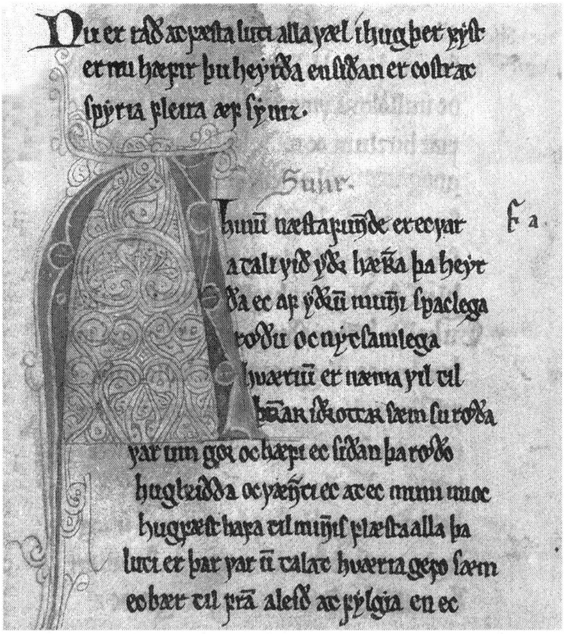

Figures 7-5a and 7-5b: Two facsimiles of an Old Norwegian manuscript. The first was drawn by Peter Andreas Munch and published as a specimen in the edition of *Konungs skuggsjá* (1848), while the other is a photographic facsimile taken at the Arnamagnæan Collection in Copenhagen, where the manuscript, AM 243 b α fol, is kept (Photograph © Arnamagnæan Institute, Copenhagen, used by permission).

of digital photography, and it is likely that the major part of the earliest manuscripts will be made available in the coming decades. This is a field that has seen a rapid development, and because many manuscripts contain illuminations, they also appeal to art historians as well as to people who simply like to view the manuscripts as aesthetic artifacts. Some libraries have begun the program of digital photography with their finest examples, typically illuminated manuscripts (sometimes photographing only the illuminated pages), before moving on to more humble specimens.

Out-of-print books are also being photographed and digitized rapidly. With the advent of Google Books, this has taken on an unprecedented growth. It seems likely that in a few decades the majority of books in libraries will be available over the Internet. The digitization of classical and medieval manuscripts may take more time, because they sometimes are quite fragile and some of them may be of limited interest.

Some manuscripts are so easily readable that one might be excused for asking why an edition is really called for other than a facsimile edition. Most manuscripts, however, have their peculiarities and need an interpretation by a skilled editor. Classical and early medieval manuscripts often lack word division, being written in *scriptio continua*, and in some manuscripts—for instance, the famous *Book of Kells* or the *Lindisfarne Gospels*—the writing is so integrated with the artistic design of the page that it can be difficult to draw the line between text and artwork. Moreover, in many medieval manuscripts there are a large number of abbreviations, often polyvalent, which must be expanded. All too often the state of the manuscript is deplorable.

In some cases, as with the diary kept by Samuel Pepys (1633–1703), the text is written in shorthand and has to be deciphered. Pepys used the system prescribed in 1626 by Thomas Shelton (d.? 1650), with some minor modifications; it is not supposed to be difficult to learn, but it is far from immediately readable.[22] Some authors have gone even further and written their text in code. Ludwig Wittgenstein (1889–1951), for example, wrote some of his manuscripts in a *Geheimschrift*, a secret code. It is a reversal of the alphabet, so that *a* is rendered with *z*, *b* with *y*, *c* with *x*, and so forth. A few, highly experienced readers are able to do the deciphering on the fly, but the overwhelming majority would prefer to have "rxs yrn," for example, normalized to "ich bin."[23] Wittgenstein himself must have been able to encode his writing in *Geheimschrift* as he wrote.

In many digital editions the facsimile has become a natural companion to the transcribed text. Thanks to the decreasing price of storage, facsimiles can be made at a very high resolution and colorimetric quality with little additional cost, and thanks to computer technology they can be made accessible to anyone with an acceptable Internet connection. Apart from democratizing the access to archives and libraries, it also saves the primary sources from wear and tear.

In surprisingly many cases, a facsimile can be easier to read than the original because of good photographic work and, until recently, the photography of difficult passages in ultraviolet light.

One might ask whether a facsimile edition is truly an edition. It is not an edition in the sense that it is based on a transcription of the manuscript in question. For many purposes, such as text searches, a facsimile edition is of limited value. The facsimile is an image of a text, not itself a text. However, a manuscript may be photographed and cropped in different ways so that one facsimile will not be identical to another. Modern scanning equipment in fact makes it possible to reproduce various physical levels of the manuscript page, such as highlighting the underlying text in a palimpsest. In other words, the facsimile edition shares one fundamental aspect with other, transcription-based editions: it is one of several possible renderings of the manuscript, the result of a process of editorial selection. For this reason, the facsimile has been recognized as an edition in the present typology.

RECORD TYPE EDITIONS   When Abraham Farley (?1712–1791) published the *Domesday Book* in 1783, he chose to reproduce the manuscript pages as faithfully as possible. This meant that the two columns of the manuscript were displayed with exactly the same number of lines in the edition as in the manuscript. Furthermore, all abbreviations in the text were reproduced in the shape they had in the manuscript—for example, the abbreviation sign "7" for "and" (originally a Tironian nota), and the horizontal stroke for the nasals *n* or *m*, or in more general usage as a marker of contraction (cf. fig. 7-6). This kind of typesetting is usually referred to as record type, and it found some favor in the edition of English and other European charters in the early nineteenth century. The type had been developed and cut ten years earlier by Farley's co-editor, John Nichols (1745–1826).

It should be added that the motivations behind the choice of record type in the edition of the *Domesday Book* were not purely typographical but were also based on the fact that the exact position of text on the page might have bearings on the legal interpretation of the text. The *Domesday Book* was the first recording of land ownership in England and was thus studied in great detail. Farley edited this text in facsimile form before photographic facsimiles made it possible to reproduce whole books in full detail.

The idea of using record type was later taken up for some Old Norse editions, notably the one of the early kings' saga *Ágrip* by Verner Dahlerup (1880). After the introduction of photographic facsimiles in the late nineteenth century, no more editions of this type were seen. However, it has been revitalized in recent years thanks to the democratizing of font technology. While Farley, Dahlerup, and other editors had to order—and pay for—tailor-made lead types, today

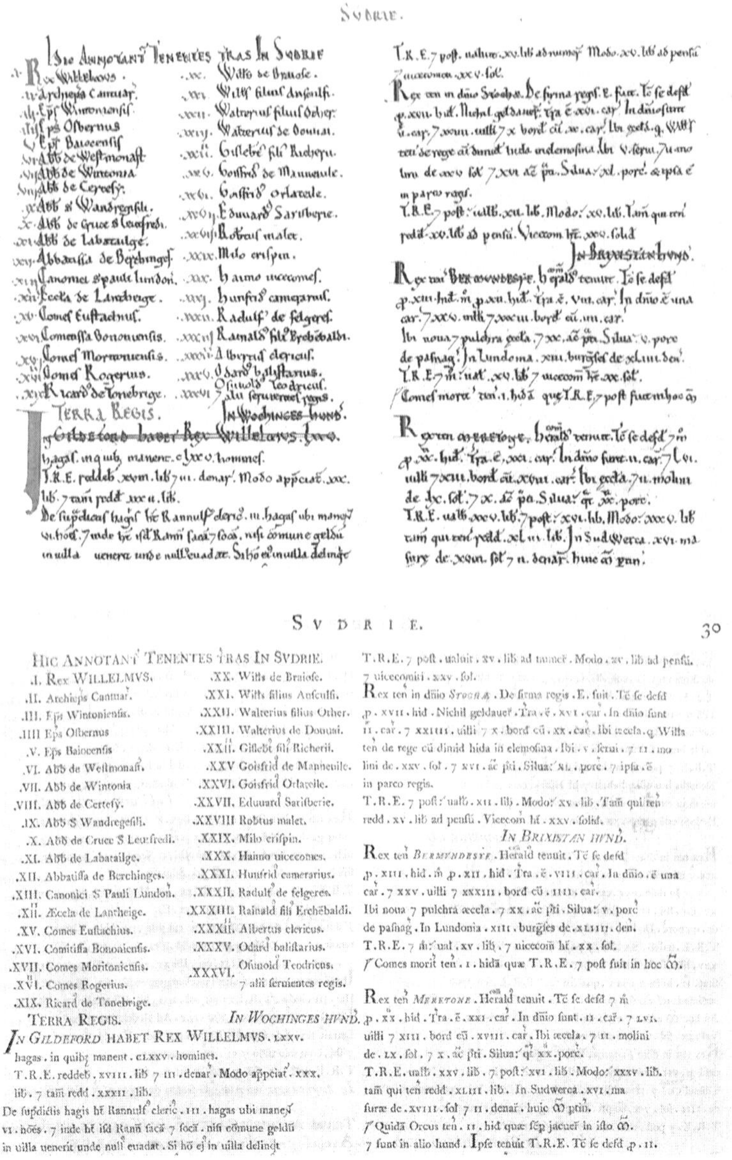
SVDRIE. 30

HIC ANNOTANT TENENTES TRAS IN SVDRIE.

.I. Rex WILLELMVS.
.II. Archieps Cantuar.
.III. Eps Wintoniensis.
.IIII Eps Osbernus
.V. Eps Baiocensis
.VI. Abb de Westmonast.
.VII. Abb de Wintonia
.VIII. Abb de Certesy.
.IX. Abb S Wandregesili.
.X. Abb de Cruce S Leutfredi.
.XI. Abb de Labatailge.
.XII. Abbatissa de Berchinges.
.XIII. Canonici S Pauli Lundon.
.XIIII. Æccla de Lantheige.
.XV. Comes Eustachius.
.XVI. Comitissa Bononiensis.
.XVII. Comes Moritoniensis.
.XVIII. Comes Rogerius.
.XIX. Ricard de Tonebrige.
.XX. Wills de Braiose.
.XXI. Wills filius Ansculfi.
.XXII. Walterius filius Other.
.XXIII. Walterius de Douuai.
.XXIIII. Gislebt fili Richerii.
.XXV Goisfrid de Manneuile.
.XXVI. Goisfrid Orlateile.
.XXVII. Eduuard Sarisberie.
.XXVIII Robtus malet.
.XXIX. Milo crispin.
.XXX. Hanno uicecomes.
.XXXI. Hunfrid camerarius.
.XXXII. Radulf de felgeres.
.XXXIII. Rainald fili Erchëbaldi.
.XXXIIII. Albertus clericus.
.XXXV. Odard balistarius.
.XXXVI. Osuuold Teodricus. 7 alii seruientes regis.

TERRA REGIS.

IN WOCHINGES HVND.

IN GILDEFORD HABET REX WILLELMVS . LXXV. hagas . in quib; manent . CLXXV . homines. T.R.E. reddeb . XVIII . lib 7 III . denar . Modo appciat . XXX. lib . 7 tam redd . XXXII . lib. De supdictis hagis ht Rannulf cleric . III . hagas ubi manen VI . hoes . 7 inde ht isd Rann saca 7 soca . nisi comune geldu in uilla uenerit unde null euadat . Si ho ej in uilla delinqt

T.R.E. 7 post . ualuit . XV . lib ad numer . Modo . XV . lib ad pensu. 7 uicecomiti . XXV . sol.

Rex ten in dnio STOCHAE . De firma regis . E . fuit . Tc se defd p . XVII . hid . Nichil geldauer . Tra . e . XVI . car . In dnio sunt II . car . 7 XXIIII . uilli 7 X . bord cu . XX . car . Ibi æccla . q Wills ten de rege cu dimid hida in elemosina . Ibi . V . serui . 7 II . molini de . XXV . sol . 7 XVI . ac pti . Silua . XL . porc . 7 ipsa . e in parco regis. T.R.E. 7 post . ualb . XII . lib . Modo . XV . lib . Tam qui ten redd . XV . lib ad pensu . Vicecom ht . XXV . solid.

IN BRIXISTAN HVND.

Rex ten BERMVNDESYE . Herald com tenuit . Tc se defd p . XIII . hid . m p . XII . hid . Tra . e . VIII . car . In dnio . e una car . 7 XXV . uilli 7 XXXIII . bord cu . IIII . car. Ibi noua 7 pulchra æccla . 7 XX . ac pti . Silua . V . porc de pasnag . In Lundonia . XIII . burgses de . XLIIII . den. T.R.E. 7 m . ual . XV . lib . 7 uicecom ht . XX . sol. Comes morit ten . I . hida quæ T.R.E. 7 post fuit in hoc co.

Rex ten MERETONE . Herald com tenuit . Tc se defd 7 m p . XX . hid . Tra . e . XXI . car . In dnio sunt . II . car . 7 LVI . uilli 7 XIII . bord cu . XVIII . car . Ibi æccla . 7 II . molini de . LX . sol . 7 X . ac pti . Silua . qt XX . porc. T.R.E. ualb . XXV . lib . 7 post . XVI . lib . Modo . XXXV . lib. tam qui ten redd . XLIII . lib . In Sudwerca . XVI . ma furæ de . XVIII . sol 7 II . denar . huic co ptin. Quida Orcus ten . II . hid quæ sep jacuer in isto co. 7 sunt in alio hund . Ipse tenuit T.R.E. Tc se defd p . II.

Figure 7-6a and 7-6b: Extract from Abraham Farley's edition of the *Domesday Book* (1783). The first part is from the hand-drawn facsimile on fol. 2v of vol. 2; the second part is from the corresponding edition on fol. 30r of the same volume, using record types to represent the letter forms and layout of the manuscript.

record type can be designed by anyone with a font-creation application. The edition of the fourteenth-century Icelandic manuscript *Möðruvallabók* by Andrea van Arkel-de Leeuw van Weenen (1987) is a recent example. This edition comes close to the photographic facsimile and can be quite helpful for the first reading of the manuscript itself, in which characters and abbreviation marks must be identified before they can be interpreted. It is not an edition for reading the text witnessed by the manuscript, though.

DIPLOMATIC EDITIONS   The diplomatic edition has been the preferred edition of historical documents such as charters, letters, and the like. In his *Editing Historical Records*, P. D. A. Harvey (2001) has given a fine and pragmatic introduction to this type of editing, and although he does not use the term "diplomatic," the type of edition he discusses is what is otherwise called diplomatic.[24]

Harvey has a refreshingly simple summary of what the editor should do: (1) be accurate, (2) say what you are going to do and do it, and (3) give full reference of the document and describe it. It has also been the preferred edition for vernacular texts to be studied from a linguistic point of view. In *The Menota Handbook* (Haugen 2008, ch. 3) the diplomatic edition is recognized as a major type of edition, alongside editions on the facsimile and the normalized level. As a rule, the text is rendered with a minimal amount of interpretation in a diplomatic edition. It does not use record type but will usually interpret the abbreviations and expand them, silently or by using italics or parentheses. Since the diplomatic edition thus adds a certain amount of interpretation to the source text, it has been termed "interpretative diplomatic edition" (e.g., by Foulet and Speer 1979, 44). For an example of a diplomatic edition, see figure 7-7.

The diplomatic edition, as defined here, is really a cluster of editions ranging from those that keep very close to the source text to those that introduce a certain level of normalization. In a more detailed classification, one should probably make a distinction between, say, strict diplomatic editions, middle-of-the-road diplomatic editions, and lightly normalized diplomatic editions.[25]

Most diplomatic editions will record only graphemic variation that is believed to have phonological value. For example, the distinction between the Insular and Carolingian *f* types in medieval Nordic texts is usually disregarded, since both reflect the same phoneme /f/, while the distinction between the long "ſ" and the small capital "s" is heeded, since the latter may be used for the geminate sound, /s:/, as opposed to the tall *s* that is used only for the short /s/. Thus, the number of phonological oppositions in the underlying linguistic structure will decide the number of graphemic oppositions—in other words, there should be no distinctions between characters that are not reflections of phonological distinctions. This distinction is parallel to the one drawn between the *etic* and *emic* level in linguistics—that is, between graphetics and phonetics on the one hand and graphemics and phonemics on the other (see, e.g., Pike 1967, ch. 2). There may, of course, be border cases, and the editor would then usually record a possible distinction rather than overlooking it.

Moreover, punctuation may be slightly normalized and capitalization may be introduced in names and the first word of a sentence so that these elements are more recognizable. If the source lacks word division, that may also be introduced by the editor. In spite of these elements of normalization, diplomatic editions are intended to reflect their source faithfully and to be true to them from a linguistic point of view. In the Bergen Electronic Edition of Wittgenstein's *Nachlass* (2000), the diplomatic level is the basic level, and it is aligned with the digital facsimiles of the source. In many cases a diplomatic edition comes close to a transcription, a rendering that does not add more than strictly necessary to the source.

In the context of modern editions, diplomatic editions are usually characterized by rendering the accidentals of the text, such as idiosyncrasies of spelling and punctuation. If the author uses different spellings for the same word in his manuscript, the diplomatic edition will record this without any attempt at correction. It is, in a sense, a strictly positivist type of edition—nothing added, nothing deleted. With reference to Walter Wilson Greg's distinction between substantives and accidentals in a text, one can say that the diplomatic edition would typically keep accidentals as well as substantives.[26]

NORMALIZED EDITIONS   The normalized edition is a further step away from the source. In this type of edition, spelling and punctuation is normalized according to either an internal norm (the manuscript itself) or an external norm (similar manuscripts or a standard orthography). The latter is the most common form of normalization. In many European countries, early modern texts are frequently edited with modern spelling, especially for use in schools. Pupils in Norwegian schools usually read Henrik Ibsen's plays in editions with modern spelling, using *å* rather than *aa*, leaving out capitalization in nouns, and so on. The same applies to many Old Norse editions, which are normalized according to the mid-thirteenth-century orthography established in modern times and now found in all grammars and dictionaries of Old Norse (i.e., Old Norwegian and Old Icelandic). Figure 7-8 shows an example of a text rendered on three levels, with the normalized level as the final one. Normalized editions are the preferred type for studies that focus on the contents rather than the form. The series *Íslenzk fornrit* of Old Norse texts has normalized orthography and is the one usually referred to in literary and historical studies.

Normalized editions are also found in introductions and elementary texts for didactic purposes. The Bergen Electronic Edition of Wittgenstein's *Nachlass* adds a normalized level to the diplomatic one. Here the text is regularized in several respects, and the *Geheimschrift* is interpreted.[27]

gran dereit a de trist andar.ca sellela non
quer prestar al do mundo non lla mest[1].
mais que mester lle pod auer. o que
5   lle non pod toller.tal cuita como
sigo ten.
E se estom aq̃ dn̄ quer.
p algũa mētira dar.
dela ben.log acuidar.
10   deu esto se scient[1] óuuer.
ca ỹnda o a de pder.
e creo q̃ deu[2] amorrer.
se o cuidar cõ pesar en.
E tod ome q̃ se poder.
15   p algũa guisa gr̄dar.
de nunca mollr̄ muit amar
fara bõ sẽ seó fezer
q̃ en os dias q̃ uíuer.
q̃ pesar pode ia p[i]nder.
20   eno mũdo p outra ren
Mais q̃n sen bẽ gr̄dar q[i]ser
guarde se ben de ir a logar
u ueia o bon semellar.
da mia señor selle de9[3] der.
25   q̃ atal fez end ó poder
ca se o uir logọ a dauer.
mui gran cuita se neum ben.

VI

(81, 2)   Como uos sodes.mia sennor muí
quit e de me ben fazer assi mar quiteu
de querer.al ben[4] en quanteu uíuo for
se non uos.7 sei uã ren se me uos non
5   fazedes ben. nen eu non uos fazo prazer.
E per bõa fe mia señor
por quite me tenneu dauer.
uosso ben en quãteu uíuer
nen al en q̃ aia sabor.
10   mais uos en preíto sodes en

---

[1] *scient*   *n* partially smudged.
[2] *deu*   erasure of a final *ę* after *u*.
[3] *de9*   symbol *9* is superposed over *e*.
[4] Superposed *o* high between *al* and *ben*.

Figure 7-7: A diplomatic edition of *Cancioneiro da Ajuda*, a collection of
Portuguese poems from the late thirteenth century, based on the *Ajuda
Codex*, which is kept in the library of the Palácio Nacional da Ajuda in
Lisbon. This edition by Henry H. Carter (1941) supplements the critical
edition by Carolina Michaëlis de Vasconcellos (1904). The extract here
is from page 4 and shows that the transcription is strictly diplomatic,
preserving abbreviated letter forms, and that the comments in the apparatus
refer to only the actual readings of the manuscript.

> ## Vǫluspá
>
> Hlıoðſ bıð ec allar kındır meırı ⁊ mını maugo
> heımðalar uılðo at ec ualɸaþ uel ɸyr telıa ɸoʒn
> ſpıoll ɸíra þav é ɸremſt ū man. Ec mán ıotna
>
> | ## Vǫluspá | ## Vǫluspá |
> |---|---|
> | Hlioðs bið ec allar | Hljóðs bið ek allar |
> | kindir | kindir |
> | meiri *oc* mıni | meiri ok minni |
> | maugo heimdalar | mǫgu Heimdalar |
> | uilðo at ec ualɸaþr | vildu at ek Valfǫðr |
> | uel fyr telia | vel fyr telja |
> | forn spioll fíra | forn spjǫll fira |
> | þav *er* fremst u*m* man | þau er fremst um man. |

Figure 7-8: A stanza from the Eddic poem *Vǫluspá* in three versions.
The first version renders the text line by line as it is preserved
in the manuscript Reykjavík, Gamle Kongelige Samling (GKS),
2365 4° (ca. 1270). The second version is a diplomatic one, and the
third is fully normalized. For the encoding of this stanza, see *The
Menota Handbook*, ch. 1 (Photograph © Odd Einar Haugen, used by
permission).

Second Dimension: Process

While some texts have been preserved over the years or even centuries with
little textual variation, other texts have seen many changes. Medieval texts have
often been handed down to us in many versions and with little respect, it seems,
to whatever original there may have been. In his *Essai de poétique médiévale*,
Paul Zumthor (1972) observed that while texts of known late-medieval French
authors seemed to be copied faithfully, many anonymous texts underwent great
changes, sometimes so great that it became a case of rewriting rather than
copying. He named this process *mouvance*, and it soon caught up with other
scholars witnessing the same processes in their own fields of literature.[28] Even
if the concept of mouvance was born of medieval studies, it seems to be equally
relevant to classical literature, and it also finds resonance in the development
of many texts belonging to the print culture.

Any editor will agree that a work known in more than one form is the result of some kind of process (whether that is the vagaries of the typesetter, authorial revisions, or the corruption in medieval scriptoria), but it is not evident how this process should be treated. Some editors would like to document every stage of a text, from its conception to its final form (if there ever was one); others would like to focus on the major stages; while yet other editors believe that a uniform, clear-type text should be the aim of an edition. For those editors who would like to document the textual development, it is a challenge to do that in a manner that does not attract too much attention to itself. To the extent that each stage can be identified or reconstructed, they can be displayed sequentially in full. If the changes between each stage are considerable, that may prove to be the only practical solution, but it may then become difficult for readers to get an overview of the development. They then need to do their own collation. If the process should be displayed in a uniform text, within the limitations of the two-dimensional pages of a printed book, some sort of symbolism is needed other than the symbolism known from the critical apparatus of traditional editions. The readers could then relate to several stages of the text while reading the same page. This will obviously be at the cost of clarity. The more complex the textual development, the more complex its display will be.

RESULTATIVE EDITIONS   What I have chosen to call resultative editions are editions where the growth of the text is not displayed in any way, either because the edition is based on a single witness or because the editor has constituted the text on the basis of several versions without wanting to attest to this. While the latter may seem a rather outdated or even pre-theoretical type of edition, many popular editions and "school editions" are of this type; it is assumed that the readers will not be interested in the textual variation and that they should be allowed to focus on the text itself. A standard translated Bible is of this type, for example; it does not inform the readers of any underlying textual variation, only of corresponding readings in other parts of the book. Indeed, for several hundred years the thought of textual instability in the Bible was anathema, something for which early editors were prosecuted. As late as in 1730, the Swiss theologian Johann Jakob Wettstein (1693–1754) had to leave his post as curate in Basel because of rumors about heretical readings in his new edition of the Greek New Testament; he subsequently moved to Amsterdam, where his edition was finally published in 1751. While textual variation has been accepted in the transmission of the Bible for the last couple of centuries, the authoritative text of the present Qur'an (Koran) is still regarded as the original text, unchanged since it was authored or dictated by the prophet Muhammad in the seventh century. For this reason translations of the Qur'an are generally held to be interpretations rather than representations of the holy Arabic text itself.

Editions based on a single witness are by definition resultative. In these cases there is simply no process to inspect, no variation to report. Nevertheless, the editor still has work to do, as the source may be difficult to read, the contents may need clarification, or the context may require comment. However, the text as such does not bear witness to any process, nor can the edition do so.

APPARATUS-STYLE EDITIONS   The critical apparatus of an edition documents the textual variation and may also contain paleographical or codicological observations, emendations of the text, parallel readings, and so on. The criteria for selecting variants differ: in some editions the selection of variants is based on a recension of the manuscripts; in other editions it is a selection of what the editor believes are the substantial variants. In Greek New Testament editions, variants are usually listed in order of importance, beginning with the Greek manuscript evidence then moving on to ancient versions and concluding with the church fathers.

In some editions the apparatus may fill only a line or two, but there are also editions in which the apparatus threatens to overtake the text completely. While the critical apparatus usually sits at the bottom of the page, there are some editions that put it at the end. Fredson Bowers has been credited with establishing this tradition in the editing of American writers. It has the advantage of making the text uncluttered, but it is impractical for those who want to consult the apparatus frequently. It presents a clear-type text, as does the resultative edition, but it remains an apparatus-style edition.

In the great majority of editions, the critical apparatus contains only a selection of the variant readings. The only exceptions are the *variorum* editions, containing all variants of a given text. For good reasons, there are few variorum editions of works with a high degree of textual variation. There are, as one would expect, variorum editions of such important texts as the Bible and the plays of Shakespeare, but apart from these, variorum editions are few.

A critical apparatus can show the growth of the text only indirectly, even if it is a variorum edition; it is not possible for a reader to reconstruct the various stages of the text from a standard critical apparatus. That also applies to a variorum edition, even if the reader here will be presented with the total textual variation. Variants may be listed according to importance, as they are in many New Testament editions, but the actual development of the text cannot be directly inferred from this order. The advantage apparatus-style editions have over resultative editions lies in the fact that they reflect the textual variation to at least some extent, but the users of the edition will not be able to reproduce the textual transmission on the basis of the apparatus alone.

GENETIC EDITIONS   A genetic edition is an edition that tries to display the growth of a text, typically in a single conflated display. For this end it uses various graphical devices such as special signs, layout, or fonts, or a combination of these. A successful genetic edition is able to display the variation in the edited text itself without resorting to an apparatus. In the German tradition a genetic edition is usually referred to as a *Handschriftenedition*, while the somewhat younger French tradition uses the term *édition génétique*. Although it is possible to draw a distinction between the two traditions, I believe they share so many traits of similarity that both types of editions can be taken together and described as being genetic.[29]

Friedrich Beißner, who is regarded as the initiator of genetic editing with his Hölderlin edition (8 vols., 1943–1985), wanted to show how a text grew through several stages. Hölderlin's poem "Hymne an die Göttin der Harmonie" will be taken as an example, a poem that like so many of his other poems was extensively revised. In the following lines of the hymn, the textual stage (3) supersedes (2), which supersedes (1), and the stage (*b*) supersedes (*a*). Finally, the stage in II supersedes the one in I:

I Von der Meere   (1) Riesenarm
                      (2) raschem
                      (3) wildem Arm umfangen
   Bebt das Land in niegefülter Lust,
   (1) Wie
   (2) Schön und stoltz, wie   (*a*) Riesenkinder,
                                  (*b*) Göttersöhne, hangen
   Felsen an der   (1) treuen   (*a*) Mutterst
                                      (*b*) Mutterbrust.
                      (2) mütterlichen Brust.
II *Durch die vorgefügten Nummern (2) und (1) werden die beiden*
   Verspaare umgestellt.

The final reading of Hölderlin's text is thus the one given here:

Schön und stolz wie Göttersöhne hangen
Felsen an der mütterlichen Brust,Von der Meere wildem Arm umfangen,
Bebt das Land in niegefühlter Lust.

For example, the line, "Von der Meere wildem Arm umfangen" began as "Von der Meere Risenarm," was changed to "Von der Meere raschem," and then to "Von der Meere wildem Arm umfangen," and, finally, switched place with the verse pair below.

While arguably there is an aesthetic appeal in this kind of editing and it is fairly simple for readers to understand, the editor soon runs into difficulties in the analysis of the textual development as well as in the representation of it. Poems, with their short lines and typically self-contained stanzas, may be a border case for which the method may work. For prose texts it becomes quite space-consuming, and while a poem can be read line by line, prose texts should preferably be rendered in a more continuous flow. It seems that Beißner himself also realized the limitation of this type of edition and of the editorial analysis lying behind it. "The actual process, in all its phases, cannot be reconstructed," he concluded some years later (1964, 81).[30]

The "terraced" apparatus of Beißner requires a lot of space in an edition. For this reason, many genetic editors have been looking for simpler ways of representing the textual variation. In their edition of Ralph Waldo Emerson's *Journals*, William Gilman and his colleagues (1960–1982) use brackets and arrows to indicate how certain words or phrases have been supplanted by others (see Greetham 1994, 408f). This edition displays both readings in the edited text and also indicates which reading is older and which is newer. Since brackets are used to indicate the older text and arrows the newer, one [can] →could← easily use this method [to] →in order to← display simple cases of variance. However, the system breaks down if there are overlapping structures, transpositions, or larger pieces of text that have been revised and changed.

In his edition of the poems of Conrad Ferdinand Meyer, Hans Zeller underlined the need to lay bare the whole process of the textual development, not just what the editor thought was the final product. In this sense he was far more descriptive than Beißner. An editor will often be faced with ambiguity in the development of a text: what came first and what came second may be a matter of discussion. In a hypothetical example, Zeller discussed the original reading "im tiefen Tal," in which "tiefen" has been crossed out and "düstern" put above, and, separately, "Tal" has been crossed out and "Wald" put above (1958, 368–70). Assuming that "düstern" superseded "tiefen" and that "Wald" superseded "Tal," the process could be represented in this way, following the example of Beißner:

im	(1) tiefen	
	(2) düstern	(a) Tal
		(b) Wald

This would mean that "düstern" first replaced "tiefen," and "Wald" then replaced "Tal." However, the genesis may have been the other way around—that is, the deletion of "Tal" may have occurred before the deletion of "tiefen." That ambiguity cannot be represented in Beißner's system. Zeller proposed a kind of switch to allow the reader to appreciate this ambiguity. Here, the deleted words have been put in square brackets, and the "×" sign indicates the non-ordered sequence of deletions:

Im	(a) [tiefen]		(c) [Tal]
	(b) düstern	×	(d) Wald

While this way of representing the textual development does not presuppose a specific textual development, it can hardly be said to be simple to grasp, nor is it particularly space-saving. Furthermore, it is all too easy to find examples of more complex and overlapping examples of textual variation in which the system breaks down.

In a more complex case, Hans Walter Gabler has investigated how the text of Virginia Woolf's *To the Lighthouse* can be represented in a genetic edition (Gabler 2007, 74–79). For this case study, he uses six editorial signs:

< . . . >	deleted text
}+< . . . > . . . +{	deleted and supplied text
|m| . . . |m|	text in the margin
|i| . . . |i|	text between the lines
=:|	discontinued text
[?]	unreadable text

Additionally, he uses bold type to indicate a continuous reading of the text, intended as a help for the reader rather than as the final text arrived at by the editor. The opening of the middle part of *To the Lighthouse*, "Time passes," goes like this in his edition:

> **It grew darker. Clouds covered the moon, & in the early**
> **hours of the morning** <the> **a light rain drummed on the**
> **roof, & starlight moon light, or the lights at sea seemed**
> **put out.**
> }+<What> **Nothing** +{   1/ 5
> **could withstand the flood**
> **the profusion, the downpouring of this immense darkness,**
> **which** <like a> <flood> **let** \|i\|**crept**\|i\| **in at keyholes &**
> <crv> **crevices & stealing round the window blinds, came**
> <trickling> **in at the bedrooms & the sitting rooms, &**   1/10
> <doors of=:\|>
> **swallowed up here the** <glint> **white of china & there the**
> **flower, the sharp edged furniture. When everything**
> **was confused & confounded, there was scarcely any identity**
> **left, either of bodies or of thoughts** }+,+{ <& only=:\|>   1/15

The symbols used here might have been simplified. Following the example of Gilman and his colleagues (1960), "}+<What> **Nothing** +{ **could withstand the flood**" could have been represented as "<What> ↑Nothing↓ could withstand the flood" and following the guidelines of the Text Encoding Initiative it might have been encoded as "<corr sic="What">Nothing</corr> could withstand the flood".[31] These alternative ways of representing the text underline the lack of common guidelines for genetic editions, or, in general, for any in-line representation of textual variation. Genetic editions are still at an experimental stage, but, more importantly, they may represent the limitation of what a printed edition can offer. It seems that Gabler has come to a similar conclusion as Beißner did before him: "Perhaps we are faced with a more radical impasse. It may be that the dynamism of the manuscripts simply cannot be represented, translated or displayed on the page of a book" (2007, 65).

As Gabler also points out, the process lying behind a text may be seen as a third dimension in the document, in addition to the two spatial dimensions (63). In the finished manuscript, the third, procedural dimension has been, as it were, conflated. Additions to the text, whether in the margin or between the lines, are easy to identify as such, but it is not always obvious whether they have been made by a younger hand, a contemporaneous hand, or indeed by the scribe or author himself.

Third Dimension: Selection

If the text appears in only one document, the editor can move straight to the task. The main question will then be on which level the text should be reproduced. There is not a single, correct answer to this question. If the aim is to render the source as faithfully as possible, the reproduction should lean toward the diplomatic end of the scale. If the aim with the edition is to make it easily accessible, a normalized rendering is preferable. The editor may also choose to render the source on more than one level. For example, the standard edition of the Old Norse skaldic poems has the poems in two versions, one diplomatic and one normalized (Jónsson 1912–1915). For a printed edition this solution means that the edition will be twice the size; in the case of Finnur Jónsson's edition, the skaldic poems were published in four rather than two volumes. For economic reasons, this way of editing is restricted to major texts. A digital edition, however, may easily contain several levels of text reproduction because the cost for data storage has become so low that it is no longer an important factor. The Bergen Electronic Edition of Wittgenstein's *Nachlass* fits on a single CD-ROM, and that includes the complete diplomatic and normalized text. However, the production of an edition carries approximately the same costs, whether it is for printed or for digital distribution. This fact should not be forgotten in the joy over low-cost storage and distribution for digital editions. In most editorial projects, the printing costs are a very modest part of the total costs.

DOCUMENTARY EDITIONS   The documentary edition, as the term is used here, is an edition of a single source and for this reason will not contain variants from other documents. Even if the diplomatic level of text reproduction is the preferred level, editors may choose to normalize the text to some extent. All documentary editions will make a note of folio or page breaks in the document, and most will also indicate line breaks. If there are accompanying facsimiles, this is very useful. The diplomatic edition is usually also a documentary edition (see fig. 7-7).

Epigraphic editions are a particular type of documentary editions. They are editions of inscriptions typically on hard surfaces like stone, bone, or metal, or sometimes, especially for runic inscriptions, on soft surfaces like wood and leather. Inscriptions are by nature unique documents, frequently short, and often of a commemorative nature. Since many of them have been preserved on objects that have been subject to wear over the years, they may be difficult to read and in many cases fragmentary. These circumstances lead to documentary editions that keep very close to the source, always with a photographic facsimile (or a drawing or a cast), a transcription, and a translation. If the inscription is in runes, ogham, or another non-Latin script, it is usually transliterated into the Latin alphabet (as shown in fig. 7-9).

Some inscriptions have other directions of writing than the left-to-right writing of the Latin alphabet. Runes are sometimes written from left to right, from right to left, or in a combination of both, *boustrophedon* (literally, "as the ox ploughs"). Ogham inscriptions often follow the border of stones and go from the bottom and upward. In the edition of both, the transcription follows the left-to-right direction of the Latin alphabet. The photographic facsimile (or the drawing) will show the actual direction of writing.

BEST-MANUSCRIPT EDITIONS   Even if a work has been preserved in several manuscripts, the editor may choose to base his edition on a single manuscript, preferably the best one, the *codex optimus*. There may be several reasons for picking a single manuscript. In some cases the manuscript tradition is so dynamic that it is very difficult to establish a single, unified text. In other cases the manuscripts are so fragmented that the only viable solution is to pick the most complete and preferably the earliest among the complete ones. In addition, the best manuscript may be chosen because it is of particular value, such as from a linguistic point of view.

Best-manuscript editions have been frequent in Old French philology (see Foulet and Speer 1979, 4–7). The rationale for this type of edition goes back to the Renaissance but was overturned by the new Lachmannian method of editing in the middle of the nineteenth century. However, it was revitalized by Joseph Bédier (1864–1938) in his revolt against the Lachmannian style of editing

ᛁᛩ : ᛒᛁᚦ : ᚠᛁᚱᛁ : ᚠᚢᚦᚱᛁ : ᛌᛆᛩᛆᚱ : ᚼᚦᚱ : ᛚᛆᚱᚦᛂ : ᛘᛂᚾᚾ : ᛁᚱ
ᚾᛆᚱᛈᚢᚨᛁᛏᛂ : ᛌᛏᛂᚦ : ᚦᛆᚾᚾᛂ : ᛆᛩ : ᛆᚵᚵᛂ : ᚦᛂ : ᛁᚱ : ᚱᛆᚦᛂ : ᚠᚢᚾᚾᚢ
ᛒᚧᚾ : ᛘᛁᚾᛂ : ᛘᛁᚾᚾᛁᛌᛈ : ᛌᛆᛏᛂ : ᛘᛁᚾᚾᛆᚱ : ᛁᚼᛆᛚᚵᚢᛘ : ᛒᚧᚾᛆᛘ : ᛁᛂ
ᛁᛩ : ᛂᛏ : ᚠᚢᚾᚾᛆᚱ : ᛆᛩ : ᛩᛆᚱᚦᛁ : ᛁᛩ : ᚼᚢᛌ : ᚦᛂᛏᛏᛂ ᚢᛆᛚᛂᛏᛂ

ek biþ firi guþrs sakar yþr lærþa men͡n er / uarþuæita staþ þæn͡na ok
al͡la þa er raþa kun͡nu / bøn mina min͡nizk sal͡o min͡nar ihælgum bønom
en / ek et gun͡nar ok gærþi ek hus þætta ual͡ete

Ek bið fyrir Guðs sakar yðr lárða menn, er varðveita stað þenna, ok alla þá er ráða
kunnu bøn mína: minnizk sálu minnar í helgum bønum. En ek hét Gunnarr, ok
gerða ek hús þetta. Valete!

'Ich bitte um Gottes Willen die gelehrten Männer, die dieser [heiligen] Stätte
vorstehen, und all jene, die meine Bitte verstehen können: Erinnert euch
meiner Seele in heiligen Gebeten. Und ich heiße Gunnarr und ich machte die-
ses Haus. Lebt wohl!'

Figure 7-9: An edition of a runic inscription. It contains (a) a photographic facsimile
of the inscription, (b) a transcription in the runic alphabet, (c) a transliteration into
the Latin alphabet, and (d) a translation to a modern language (Seim 2007, 204).
Runes were mostly used for writing in the Germanic vernaculars, but there are also
some inscriptions in Latin of a religious nature. (Photograph © Odd Einar Haugen,
used by permission).

adapted and advocated by the towering figure of Gaston Paris (1839–1903). As
mentioned in chapter 1, Bédier himself had edited the medieval text *Le Lai de*
l'Ombre in a true Lachmannian fashion in 1890. Over the years, Bédier grew
uneasy with this edition and with the single stemma he had established for the
manuscripts, and in a groundbreaking article in *Romania* (1928) he showed that
there were no fewer than eleven possible stemmata for the manuscripts of *Le*

Lai de l'Ombre. Moreover, he had observed that the vast majority of stemmata published by Romance scholars had two, and only two, main branches. Bédier suspected that behind this massive bifidity lay the force of dichotomy—in other words, that the stemma construction reflected a methodological skewness and did not tell the true story of the manuscript filiation. Bédier's conclusion was to return to the ways of the old humanists, to rely on the critic's own judgment, *le goût*, and pick out a *codex optimus*.

Many medieval Nordic texts have been published in best-manuscript editions. The major exceptions are the Old Icelandic texts, which usually are preserved in a number of fairly complete manuscripts and for which interest often has focused on the work rather than the textual carrier. Old Norwegian, Swedish, and Danish texts are to a much greater extent preserved in fewer manuscripts, and many of them have met with little literary interest. Since they are important sources for language history, they have by and large been published in best-manuscript editions on the diplomatic level. The Old Norwegian *Konungs skuggsjá* (The Royal Mirror) is but one example. The recent edition by Ludvig Holm-Olsen (1945, rev. 1983) is a typical best-manuscript edition of the codex optimus, the Norwegian manuscript Copenhagen, The Arnamagnæan Collection (AM), 243 b α fol (ca. 1275). It is rendered on a strictly diplomatic level and is thus a faithful source to the Norwegian language at the time.

There seems to have been little or no influence from Romance philology on Old Norse philology, in spite of the mediating role played by Paul Rubow (1896–1972) in his *Den kritiske kunst* (1938). In this book, which was aimed at the general public as well as the academic public, the French debate was discussed at some length, including not only the Bédier controversy but also contemporary work by Henri Quentin and others.

SYNOPTIC EDITIONS   The alternative to editing a single manuscript, even if it is by all accounts the best manuscript, is to edit the text of several manuscripts and arrange the edition so that they can be read on the same page or spread of pages. This is the synoptic edition, which had its forerunners in Bible editions like Origenes's *Hexapla* and the Spanish multilingual *Complutense* (begun in 1502 and finished in 1517). Since the first synoptic edition of the Gospels was published in 1774 by Johann Jakob Griesbach (1745–1812), it has been a favored type of edition in New Testament philology. It has also proven popular in other editorial branches. For example, the edition of the Old French text *Le lai de Lanval* by Jean Rychner (1958) presents the four major manuscripts page by page, each in its own orthography. The synoptic edition thus fits well with the diplomatic level of textual reproduction; since each selected manuscript is given in full, there is no need to normalize the orthography. A similar solution will be made in the forthcoming edition of Wolfram von Eschenbach's *Parzival* by Michael Stolz and his colleagues in Bern.[32]

Synoptic editions are also frequent for modern texts. In his *Textual Scholarship*, David Greetham gives two examples, both termed "parallel text editions," one being an edition of William Wordsworth's *The Prelude* (1799), in which the 1805 and the 1850 texts are compared on facing pages, and the other an edition of Shakespeare's *Sonnets*, in which a facsimile of the quarto text is compared with a modern-spelling version (1994, 402f and 404f). A true synoptic edition is limited to the page or the page spread, and it is also best for manuscripts in which the texts are fairly parallel. Missing pieces of texts or transpositions (text in different order) are difficult to handle within the confines of the printed page. The gospels of Matthew, Mark, and Luke are so close that they easily can be published synoptically, and that was what Griesbach did in his first edition (1774). The gospel of John is more deviant, so when Griesbach added this in a later edition (1797), it meant the pages had to be rearranged and that some white space was unavoidable. For this reason, some editors choose to publish the textual versions consecutively, one after another. This can hardly be called a synoptic edition, although it is a close cousin. The Old Norse translation of the Gospel of Nicodemus, titled *Niðrstigningar saga* (the saga of the descent), has so much textual variation, in addition to being rather fragmented, that Carl Richard Unger chose to publish the four manuscripts consecutively and on the diplomatic level (1877).

ECLECTIC EDITIONS   An eclectic edition is an edition that is based on more than one document and selects readings from several documents. The critical edition of modern classical philology is the time-honored example of an eclectic edition, but eclectic editions have also played a major part in the editing of printed texts. Especially in the United States, there has been a lively debate on the virtues and failings of eclectic editing of American authors. In Germany the historical-critical edition, also an eclectic type of edition, has been the standard way of editing the grand authors, often in large multivolume projects.

In the editing of classical works, the critical edition, at least in its classical shape, is an edition that is based on a full manuscript recension and on this foundation establishes the text as an approximation to the archetype. Karl Lachmann's edition of *De rerum natura* by Lucretius (1850) was hailed as a masterpiece of critical editing in its time and is still highly regarded. In this edition Lachmann made a recension of all known manuscripts and demonstrated that they had to descend from a single archetype. This archetype, he claimed, had 302 pages, with 26 lines on each page. On the basis of this reconstruction, Lachmann was able to restore some passages that had been transposed during the transmission of the text.

The English poet and textual critic Alfred Edward Housman (1859–1936) had nothing but scorn for those editors who did not try to establish the best text possible on the basis of the preserved manuscripts. Of editions based on a single best manuscript, he observed that the only merit of these editions was that they saved lazy editors from working and stupid ones from thinking (1962, 36). Equally convinced, though more sotto voce, was Alphonse Dain (1896–1964); if the preserved text seems corrupt, he claimed, it is the duty of the editor to try to emend it (1975, 173).

The majority of biblical editions are eclectic. It is unusual for an edition to be based on a single manuscript, whatever its merits. For texts of such great importance, the search for the original wording is essential. In the case of the Greek New Testament, approximately 95 percent of the readings are well supported in the great majority of manuscripts. This leaves 5 percent of the readings to be considered, and in some editions the possible certainty of the variant readings have been assessed on a scale from A to D, in which A means "virtually certain"; B, "less certain"; C, "doubtful"; and D, "highly doubtful."[33] Since in all probability it is impossible to establish the textual transmission of the approximately five thousand manuscripts of the Greek New Testament, readings have to be evaluated on internal as well as external criteria. As a result, most editions of the Greek New Testament are basically eclectic.[34] The important United Bible Society edition has been prepared by a committee of scholars and is thus a highly eclectic text.[35] Translations of the New Testament and other biblical books rely on these editions and thus carry the eclectic text further.

Eclectic editions have also played a major role in medieval studies. The edition of *Le lai de Lanval* by Jean Rychner (1958), which already has been mentioned, is an eclectic edition. It is also a synoptic edition, because in addition to an eclectic text it contains a diplomatic transcription of the four manuscripts that have preserved the work. It thus falls into the same category as the edition of James Joyce's *Ulysses* by Hans Walter Gabler and his colleagues (1984), as exemplified by Greetham (1994, 411–15). As for Old Norse editions, eclectic editions have been few in the last hundred years or so, but there are many examples from the nineteenth century. *Konungs skuggsjá*, mentioned above, was published in an eclectic edition by Peter Andreas Munch, Rudolf Keyser, and Carl Richard Unger in 1848. In this edition the work is convincingly reconstructed, even if there is not a single manuscript that contains the whole text, and the orthography is regularized according to the prevailing Old Norse norm of the mid-thirteenth century.[36]

A great number of American editions of modern texts have been eclectic, following a single copy text but emending it where necessary. The concept of the copy text was introduced by Ronald B. McKerrow in his edition of *Thomas Nashe* (1904). McKerrow believed that the stemmatic method would not work for this edition and decided to base his edition on a specific copy of the text, which he would emend only when he believed it to be obviously wrong. This approach is thus close to the best-manuscript edition discussed above, and McKerrow's conclusion may be said to antedate the one drawn by Joseph Bédier a couple of decades later. However, it was Walter Wilson Greg who made the concept famous, as it were, in his widely influential article "The Rationale of the Copy Text" (1950–1951). In this, Greg draws a distinction between two types of variation: "A distinction between the significant, or as I shall call them 'substantive,' readings of the text, those namely that affect the author's meaning or the essence of his expression, and others, such in general as spelling, punctuation, word-division, and the like, affecting mainly its formal presentation, which may be regarded as the accidents, or as I shall call them 'accidentals,' of the text" (21). Greg observed that typesetters were likely to respect the text in the substantive readings but might be less careful with the accidentals of the text. Thus, for accidentals it is permissible to follow a single copy text, but for the substantives one should look toward the general principles of textual criticism and not feel restricted by a single copy text. As a consequence, editions following this theory will be eclectic in the sense that they typically use a single source as the authority for the accidentals of the text, but that the substantive readings are selected by the editor in each case, not relying on a single source.

Greg did not live to see what his rationale would lead to, but his principles were adopted by Fredson Bowers (1964) and later by G. Thomas Tanselle (1976 and 1991), so much so that one often talks about the Greg-Bowers-Tanselle method of editing. Greg had used English renaissance drama texts as examples for his copy-text editing, but Bowers claimed that the principles were valid for all texts of the print era, from Shakespeare to modern authors. An eclectic edition produced along these lines will also turn out to be an *Ausgabe letzer Hand*, or, as Bowers put it, will serve to "represent the nearest approximation in every respect of the author's final intentions." (1964, 227).

While the Greg-Bowers-Tanselle method of editing continues to have a powerful influence, especially in American editing, many scholars are skeptical, and claim that an eclectic text is not the text that once was, but a text that never was. Although Bowers argued for moving the critical apparatus to an appendix in the edition, thus leaving the main text uncluttered, British editors tended to leave the apparatus at the bottom of the page. As Peter Shillingsburg has observed, that may show a greater modesty than what has been the case in American editing (1989, 56).

The historical-critical edition so highly regarded in Germany is also an eclectic type of edition. It is historical in the sense that it is based on a full recension of the witnesses that are relevant for the development of the text, such as manuscripts, typescripts, and printed versions. It will use a specific version, *Fassung,* as its base, but will collate this with other versions and report deviations in the critical apparatus. It is critical in the sense that the editor will evaluate variant readings and, where necessary, emend the text. While an eclectic edition of a classical or a medieval work commonly is referred to as a critical edition, *kritische Ausgabe* in German parlance, and an edition of a modern work as a historical-critical edition, *historisch-kritisch Ausgabe*, both types share the same approach to the text: recension, then emendation. The towering figure of Karl Lachmann seems to be looming in the background. Lachmann himself had a tremendous influence on German editing and was active in all major fields: in biblical studies with his new edition of the Greek New Testament (1831), in classical studies with his above-mentioned edition of Lucretius's *De rerum natura* (1850), and in medieval studies with his edition of *Nibelungen Lied* (1826) and of *Parzival* (1833).

The Art of Combination

The typology given above contains typical solutions to the three dimensions of reproduction, process, and selection. The values of these dimensions can be combined in various ways in any one edition. However, not all values can be combined, and some can be combined only in marginal cases. For example, an edition of a single source may be reproduced in a diplomatic or a normalized fashion, but since it is based on a single source, it cannot be the object for an eclectic edition (which as a minimum requires two sources). Conversely, an eclectic edition will typically select a normalized orthography rather than rendering each source in its own orthography. The latter solution leads to a text that vacillates between several orthographies. This problem is especially acute in vernacular medieval texts, where hardly one manuscript has the same orthography as another.

The combinations of the three dimensions discussed here can be displayed in a matrix (see fig. 7-10). In this matrix, resultative editions can be found over the whole specter, apart from among the synoptic editions, because a synoptic perspective on the text would be essentially against the single text version established in the resultative edition. The majority of resultative editions belong to the documentary and best-manuscript type of editions. Apparatus-style editions are typical of eclectic editions, in which the apparatus is a necessary tool for displaying the variation lying behind the established text. They can also be found in best-manuscript editions, in which the editor wants to document other sources, especially in the case where they exhibit readings that must be regarded as better than those in the chosen best manuscript. Finally, genetic editions are typically synoptic editions, although these can also be of a conflated type, as illustrated in the *Ulysses* text above, and as such should probably be classified as

		Selection			
		Documentary	Best-manuscript	Synoptical	Eclectic
Reproduction	Facsimile	R	R		
	Record	R	R	G	
	Diplomatic	R	R A	G	(R) (A) (G)
	Normalised	R	R A	G	R A G

Process: R = resultative editions   A = apparatus-style editions   G = genetic editions

Figure 7-10: The three dimensions of editions. In this matrix the dimension of reproduction is displayed along the vertical axis and the dimension of selection along the horizontal axis. The dimension of process is displayed with its values in each cell of the matrix.

eclectic. In general, eclectic editions have a normalized orthography, although it is possible (if not often seen) to make a diplomatic version of an eclectic edition. In this type of edition the orthography changes throughout the text, depending on which source has been selected.

The traditional printed edition typically had to choose one way, or at best a few ways, to present the text. The need to focus was of economic nature: lack of space and cost of printing. The digital edition, as so often observed, is no longer limited by economy in the same sense as a printed edition. Full facsimiles may be presented alongside diplomatic and normalized transcriptions of the text, as in the Wittgenstein edition, or in three levels of transcription, as in the Menota-style editions (for an example, see fig. 7-8). All manuscripts may be transcribed (with photographic facsimiles), as in the edition of the *Wife of Bath's Prologue* in the *Canterbury Tales* (Robinson 1996), and they may even be supplemented by a full critical text, as in the edition of the *General Prologue* to the *Canterbury Tales* (Solopova 2000). Until recently, the synoptic edition was a cornucopia in the history of editing, an extravaganza, but it has now been superseded by the complete collection of texts made possible by digital editions.

The digital age has in many ways redefined textual scholarship and will have profound effects on editorial practice. However, this redefinition has in no way, or at least not so far, led to any revolution in our understanding of texts. What it has revolutionized is our way of working with texts, because it has given us new and extremely versatile tools in organizing and analyzing texts and their history. Moreover, digital editions have become dynamic and interactive. In many cases they have moved the focus from the editor to the users, from the editor as a controller of the text to users as re-creators of texts. In short, digital editions have the potential of being truly dynamic in a sense that a printed, paper-based edition never can be. Yet any revolution does not lie in the tools as such but in the extent that these tools are being used in ways that lead to a new understanding of texts, to new questions being raised. Whether that is the case is as yet an open question.

Notes

1. Hauksbók was a single codex by the time of Árni Magnússon (1663–1730), but was later broken up into three parts, AM 371 4° (in the Arnamagnæan Collection, Reykjavík) and AM 544 4° and 675 4° (in the Arnamagnæan Collection, Copenhagen). The book originally contained at least 210 leaves; of these, 141 leaves have been preserved.

2. Among these works were *Landnámabók*, *Kristni saga*, *Trójumanna saga*, *Breta Sǫgur*, *Merlínusspá*, *Fóstbrøðra saga*, *Eiríks saga rauða*, *Heiðreks saga*, *Skálda saga*, three shorter stories (*þættir*), *Algorismus*, *Prognostica temporum*, and a couple of dialogues.

3. This was not in fact the first edition of Plato's dialogues; the honor of delivering the *editio princeps* goes to Aldus Manutius in Venice in 1513, but the Stephanus edition became the *textus receptus* for several centuries.

4. *Samizdat* is a Russian word ("self-publication") for self-published dissident litterature that was censored in the former Soviet Union and distributed clandestinely from reader to reader. This procedure is also known from other political regimes in recent times, often brought together under the term *samizdat publishing*.

5. Paul Maas states this in the very first paragraph of his *Textkritik* (1960, 1): "Eigenhändige Niederschriften (Autographa) der griechischen und lateinischen Klassiker besitzen wir nicht, auch keine Abschriften, die mit dem Original verglichen sind, sondern nur solche Abschriften, die durch Vermittlung einer unbekannten Zahl von Zwischenhandschriften aus dem Original abgeleitet, also von fragwürdiger Zuverlässigkeit sind" ("We have no autographed manuscripts of the Greek and Roman classical writers and no copies which have been collated with the originals; the manuscripts we possess derive from the originals through an unknown number of intermediate copies, and are consequentially of questionable trustworthiness." [Translation by Barbara Flowers 1958.])

6. "Wir sollen und wollen aus einer hinreichenden Menge von guten Handschriften einen allen diesen zum Grunde liegenden Text darstellen, der entweder der ursprüngliche selbst seyn, oder ihm doch sehr nahe kommen muss" (Müllenhoff and Vahlen 1876, 82).

7. For a description of the critical guidelines of the Kierkegaard editorial project (Søren Kierkegaards Skrifter), see http://sks.dk/red/retningslinier_ts.pdf. The guidelines of the national edition of August Strindberg's complete work can be assessed at http://www.strind.su.se/preskomp.htm. It should be noted that Strindberg proofread and actively corrected his own books and that some of his works are preserved in more than one version. In these cases the editors have established the version that Strindberg himself regarded as the final one.

8. This is the case in Ibsen's *Samlede Værker,* vol. 3 (1898). See the introduction by Jens B. Halvorsen, p. ii.

9. Discussed in Pichler and Haugen (2005, 203).

10. There is a considerable amount of literature on the distinctions between the old versus the new philology; in addition to Stephen G. Nichols (1990), see also Eckehardt Simon (1990), Nichols (1994 and 1997b), Karl Stackmann (1994), Rüdiger Schnell (1997), and Jürgen Wolf (2002). Bernard Cerquiglini's *Éloge de la variante* (1983) can also be seen as an apology for the new philology. For a couple of recent discussions within Old Norse philology, see the contributions by Odd Einar Haugen, Karl G. Johansson, and Matthew J. Driscoll in *Creating the Medieval Saga,* edited by Judy Quinn and Emily Lethbridge (2010).

11. In the *pecia* system, developed at Italian and French universities in the thirteenth century, manuscripts containing teaching material were given to students for a limited time so that they could make their own copies. A pecia was a section of a manuscript, usually four folios long, and students thus copied a manuscript section by section without having to borrow the whole manuscript for a longer period of time.

12. It should be noted, however, that the FRBR model also applies to other types of artistic creations, such as musical compositions, that are not always referred to and understood as texts.

13. Martin West discusses contamination ("open recension") at some length in his introduction (1973, 37–47), and Sten Eklund, among others, tries to deal with it, making a distinction between manifest and latent variation (1977).

14. Text critical methods were briefly discussed in chapter 1 in this book (Haugen and Apollon), but are described in greater detail here.

15. See Froger 1968. This restriction in fact applies to a number of diagrams, including the phylogenetic trees used in cladistic analysis.

16. For a summary of this challenge, see Robinson and O'Hara (2003).

17. New Stemmatics is briefly discussed by Barbara Bordalejo on the Textual Scholarship website, http://www.textualscholarship.org.

18. The acronym RHM comes from the initials of the three surnames of the researchers, Roos, Heikkilä, and Myllymäki.

19. The Finnish researchers have initiated an international research project, *Studia Stemmatologica,* which at the time of this writing gathers many of the people working in this field and seems likely to reflect the state of the art; see Heikkilä et al. 2010–2011.

20. In the following, I am to a large extent basing myself on an earlier publication on the editing of medieval Nordic texts (Haugen 2004), in which I used the two dimensions of reproduction and selection as a basis for a typology of editions. Since I have been taking editions of printed texts into account in this chapter, I believe that a procedural dimension should be added, reflecting the growth of a text and how it should be displayed in the edition.

21. They often carry series titles like *Corpus Codicum,* such as *Corpus Codicum Norvegicorum Medii Aevi* or, somewhat surprisingly, *Corpus Codicum Americanorum Medii Aevi.* The Danish publisher Einar Munksgaard was an important contributor in this field,

also in an international context, with his grand series *Corpus Codicum Islandicorum Medii Aevi* (first volume published in 1930).

22. See Pepys's *Short Writing* and *Tachygraphy* discussed in Carlton (1940, 29–46).

23. For an example of his *Geheimschrift*, with facsimile and transcription, see Pichler and Haugen (2005, 200).

24. The term "diplomatic" goes back to Jean Mabillon's *De re diplomatica* (1681), in which diplomas refer to documents in general and charters (letters) in particular. A diplomatic edition is an edition that renders the document as faithfully as possible so that it can be used for historical, linguistic, and other studies. In recent times, François Masai (1950) has given a useful summary of the conventions of diplomatic editing.

25. In the context of Old Norse editing, Guðvarður Már Gunnlaugsson (2003) has identified several subtypes of diplomatic editions. For the purposes of a survey, however, it should not be necessary to go into this degree of detail.

26. The accidentals of a text are such things as spelling, punctuation, word division, and the like, while the substantives are those aspects that carry and can alter the meaning of the text. While the distinction not always is clear-cut, it is important, and most editors are forced to draw a line between the two types unless the textual variation is very limited. The terms were introduced in Walter Wilson Greg's influential essay "The Rationale of Copy-Text" (1950–1951), but the distinction as such is much older.

27. The normalization includes such things as correction of syntactical errors, unification of the orthography, expansion of unusual abbreviations, and regularization of the punctuation. See Pichler and Haugen (2005, 188).

28. For a more recent observation, see Cerquiglini (1989a, 57): "L'œuvre littéraire, au Moyen Age, est une variable . . . Qu'une main fut première, parfois, sans doute, importe moins que cette incessante récriture d'une œuvre qui appartient à celui qui, de nouveau, la dispose et lui donne forme." (The literary work, in the Middle Ages, is a variable . . . The fact that one hand was the first is sometimes, undoubtedly, less significant than this constant rewriting of a work which belongs to whoever recasts it and gives it a new form.)

29. Gabler (2007, 62) argues that while the German *Handschriftenedition* typically focuses on the result of the textual development, the French *critique génétique* is geared toward the totality of the textual web, on the various ways a text can be read and understood.

30. After the *Große Stuttgarter Ausgabe* of Friedrich Beißner, Dietrich E. Sattler has launched a major and ambitious edition of Hölderlin's poems, usually referred to as the *Frankfurter Hölderlin-Ausgabe* (Sattler 1975ff.). In this experimental edition, the growth of the text is traced in a number of stages, beginning with a photographic facsimile and a corresponding typographical transcription, moving on to a linear representation, and finally presenting a constituted text. The example given here can be found in vol. 2, *Lieder und Hymnen* (1978, 66–67, 77, and 79), as the *Hymne an die Wahrheit II*. For a survey of Hölderlin editions, see Janns 2005.

31. *Guidelines for Electronic Text Encoding and Interchange* (TEI P5), ch. 11, "Representation of primary sources" (http://www.tei-c.org/release/doc/tei-p5-doc/en/html/PH.html).

32. See the presentation of the Parzival Project at http://www.parzival.unibe.ch/home .html.

33. This scale is used in the United Bible Society (UBS) editions, of which the first edition, *The Greek New Testament,* appeared in 1966 and the fourth edition in 1983, with later reprints.

34. One exception is Junack, *Das Neue Testament auf Papyrus* (1986–), in which the UBS edition is printed alongside the extant papyri. The aim is to document how much of the testament is preserved in the oldest witnesses, and the UBS text has simply been added as a way of organizing this material.

35. The latest edition of *The Greek New Testament* is the 4th revised edition, 4th printing (2000), which was compiled by Barbara Aland, Kurt Aland, Johannes Karavidopoulos, Carlo M. Martini, and Bruce M. Metzger.

36. See Haugen (2009) for a discussion of the various editions of *Konungs skuggsjá* and their principles for the text reproduction.

8. From Books to Collections

Critical Editions of Heterogeneous Documents

SARAH MOMBERT

The French writer François Bon recently described online the attitude of literary circles (writers, critics, publishers) when confronted with the changes brought about in editing and publishing with digital technology: "We are lost, we are afraid. The editing world is like a brick building that is being shaken and that trembles. [. . .] Internet is to blame: partly, if the possibility of choice and of finding points of reference bypasses mediation as it still existed ten years ago" (Bon 2006).[1] Indeed, in the last few years numerous European intellectuals have had the opportunity to voice their preoccupation concerning the growth of the digital edition phenomenon and the aggressiveness with which some actors in the internet economy attack books. They usually analyze this phenomenon as an exit from what Marshall McLuhan (1962) not long ago called the "Gutenberg Galaxy," and this analysis is probably right. But opinions may legitimately diverge as to the consequences that this change of era entails for the humanists: does digital edition represent a danger for humanities, whose fate would be intrinsically linked to that of the printed book, or on the contrary, is it offering new horizons to extend the science of texts that has been accumulated for centuries? From the viewpoint of non-canonical texts (e.g., documents that until now had been deemed not worthy of reeditions with a critical apparatus and were kept out of the traditional circuit of learned books), there is now a rather clearly profiled response: for these books, digital technology represents not only the opportunity of being salvaged from the ravages of time but also the end of a marginal editorial status.

Only a very small number of the documents published since the advent of mass printing in the nineteenth century have been honored with a critical edition, while the greater number of them lie dormant in library storage rooms and, sometimes, like all printed material of the middle of the nineteenth century, are eroding away under the effect of self-destructing paper acidity. With their drastic measures for conserving and limiting their communication, librarians, conscious of the necessity of saving these documents, paradoxically accentuate their oblivion by severing all contact with the public. After microfilming, which represented an initial solution to the preservation problem but has not solved the one of insufficient circulation, digital editing could very well become a salvation solution for this ocean of documents, be they depreciated (press texts), unclassifiable texts (writers' papers), or left for private collectors (posters and illustrated editions).

But beyond the heritage concern there is another reason for digital editions' interest in documents excluded from the academic pantheon. Several of the new human science approaches (cultural history and cultural sociology, compared artistic studies, mediology, history of science, etc.) clearly show the utility of searching for critical editions of documents of varied nature that come under distinct editorial protocols, such as texts and images. The new research incentive in human sciences, more interdisciplinary and more contextual, needs extended corpuses that are easily available, analyzable by different methods (traditional or computer-based), and accessible to researchers working often in multisite networks, on an international scale. If one takes the study of nineteenth-century press, for example, one sees clearly that the new links that are being set up among historians, literary researchers, sociologists, communication and media specialists, and others deeply affect the relation that each of these disciplines used to have with press documents. Researchers for whom press texts had only a testimonial value, as proof of the existence of a historical fact (a war, the publication of a novel, etc.), now want to study newspapers in their multiple interactions with the world: as testimonial documents but also as discourse, as socially elaborated objects, even as aesthetic objects. Along the same lines, a writer's documentation is now of interest—and not only as the draft text of a canonical literary work—for all those who are trying to analyze the place of writing in the cultural and scientific configuration of the era when the artist lived. In going far beyond the usual recognition assigned to texts, digital editions are being disconnected from the institutional value of books, and in offering a possible answer to some of the new practical and theoretical needs of human science research, they seem to want to enter the collection era.

From Books to Collections

This movement, which is apparently taking on momentum, represents a genuine editorial regime change because it supposes going from the book regime, within which fall the inherited editorial practices, to the digital collection regime, which presently does not benefit from the reassuring framework of century-old values for grounding editorial actors' expertise.

One of the most crucial points of the regime change deals with the relation between texts and images, apprehended as two fundamentally heterogeneous objects.[2] In the paper critical edition regime, the relation between texts and images is fixed by implicit or explicit values that are specific to the editorial regime in which they occur. Thus, in the critical edition of a literary work, images serve the texts. This means there is an illustrative dependence relation between texts; the main object of the editorial work; and facsimiles, photographs, or engravings, considered as secondary documents, and often reproduced in inserts, their very place testifying to this ancillary position. On the contrary, in an exhibition catalog, texts (notes, captions, etc.), scholarly as they may be, are peripheral and contingent as compared to images. In both cases, text and image heterogeneity, considered as a difference of nature and of value, brings about a fixed hierarchical relationship between the two.

In the electronic regime, even if a difference of nature persists between text files and image files, the hypertextual structure of the edition makes it possible to avoid a fixed hierarchical relationship and an illustrative dependence. It becomes possible to produce critical editions of mixed collections, with an interplay between texts and images instead of a competition. Defining the rules of this game will be the new task of scholarly editors. For this, links will need to be established between scholarly edition protocols that advise on what must be edited and how, with prescriptions based on a scholarly expertise resulting from centuries of editions along with the new rules of digital edition in progress. In the digital data (especially text) representation, the liberties and constraints linked to encoding seem to invite collection editors to "remediatization." Besides problems that are specific to electronic documents, such as access or rapid format obsolescence, one of the main issues of the digital turning point for critical editions is likely to be the way digital collection editors will succeed in reconciling the new opportunities offered by the digital medium and the quality guaranteed by scholarly expertise.

The Notion of Collection

The digital "collection" notion has not yet been theorized, and within the vocabulary of digital edition practitioners, it is often in competition with related notions, such as "corpus" or "archive." The term "corpus," very trendy in the humanities, is usually used in corpus linguistics, a discipline that stands out within computational linguistics by its empirical approach consisting in a posteriori formalization of recurrent linguistic phenomena (lexical uses, collocations, phraseology, etc.) analyzed within a set of utterances (a "corpus" conceived as an empirical base of linguistic data) using automatic processing methods such as concordances, statistics, or annotations. Even though a collection edited on a digital support can be analyzed with corpus linguistic methods, this is not what it was initially set up for, specifically because, unlike a linguistic corpus, it constitutes an evolutionary set of heterogeneous documents that can hardly be subjected to an analysis according to invariable protocols.

The Anglo-Saxon term "archive" refers to editorial practices that are very close to those of collections, but the French language is reluctant to adopt it because of the risk of confusion between meanings that pertain to archival storage practices and those that refer to editorial ones. For example, in archive science the notion of archive is based on that of holdings or on the computer backup files, for which an archive is the previous version of a software or a computer file. The Anglo-Saxon use is not exempt from ambiguity either, and using the term "archive" in a digital editorial context often calls for a definition. The William Blake Archive project editors propose the following wording in a page titled "What Do We Mean by an Archive?": "Though 'archive' is the term we have fallen back on, in fact we envision a unique resource unlike any other currently available for the study of Blake—a hybrid all-in-one edition, catalogue, database, and set of scholarly tools capable of taking full advantage of the opportunities offered by new information technology."[3]

The term "collection" has the advantage of being historically linked to the domains concerned with critical edition: culture and science. In the cultural domain it evokes more specifically the book or periodical collections of libraries and the collections of art (drawing, painting) constituted by informed amateurs or by museums. In the science history vocabulary it brings the values of openness and humanism linked to curio cabinets (*cabinet de curiosités*), which for quite a while were a privileged means of scientific knowledge dissemination, as is the web today. In the digital edition domain, where the use of the term "collection" is still not fixed, I would propose this minimal definition: a potentially evolutionary set of interlinked digital objects, with the intention of producing some meaning. This chapter attempts to cast new light on the possible implications of this definition that can already be derived from existing or forthcoming digital edition projects.

Unlike the digital edition of a unique literary work (or a writer's complete works), which often brings together homogeneous documents from the start, a collection can be composed of strongly heterogeneous documents or, if one wants to elude the derogatory connotations of this qualifier, documents of various nature and origin. Of course the limits can be very fuzzy between a collection and certain complex editorial projects, such as editing several manuscripts belonging to the same medieval Romanesque "matter" (e.g., the eight manuscripts of the the Princeton Charrette Project[4]). The most definite statement that can be made to establish the limits between the two is to say that a collection editor does not try to minimize or reduce the heterogeneity of the documents he assembles, whatever the pertinence of bringing them together.

Depending on the different cases, this heterogeneity applies to several possible levels of the collection. The first case can be represented by documents of diverse origins—for example, manuscripts stored in different libraries or press clippings coming from different newspapers. The second case could involve documents of diverse nature within the same field of cultural production; for a writer, for instance, the manuscripts of a writer's drafts, the edited copies, the corrected proofs, the pre-original press publications, the different printed editions of the text, and so forth. Some collections can comprise documents that come under different arts—for example, the paintings and poems of Dante Gabriel Rossetti, which function on a "double work" mode. The scholarly editor Jerome J. McGann presents this concept through an example:

> In the fall of 1848, while Rossetti was working on his first major painting, *The Girlhood of Mary Virgin*, he wrote a sonnet to accompany the picture. He finished the painting in time to exhibit it at the Hyde Park Corner Free Exhibition in March 1849 and at that time wrote a second sonnet for the painting. When the painting was exhibited, the pair of sonnets was attached to the picture frame on a piece of gold-leaf paper as an accompanying textual component. So using the title *The Girlhood of Mary Virgin* may designate simultaneously the sonnets he wrote in 1847–1848, the painting he completed in the same period, and the composite set of all the textual and visual materials that bear upon the visionary project of that name. This composite set of textual and pictorial materials on the subject of "Mary's Girlhood" (which was the title he gave to the first sonnet) defines what has come to be known as Rossetti's "double work of art."[5]

The media heterogeneity of "double works" does not prevent the assembled documents from belonging to a single artistic project. On the other hand, the Rossetti Archive (short name for "The Complete Writings and Pictures of Dante Gabriel Rossetti: A Hypermedia Archive") example illustrates another type of possible heterogeneity in a digital collection, because the Rossetti collection comprises all the textual and iconic documents that the editors have judged useful for the contextual understanding of the works: from inspirational material (paintings or books), letters testifying to the composition work, up to external testimonies such as recollections of persons having worked alongside of him. The subcollection of *The Blessed Damozel* brings together 105 documents.[6] As can be seen, heterogeneity among documents is intimately linked to that of gathering and of their selection.

By definition, a collection does not have natural boundaries but must be composed. Therefore, a scholarly editor's first role is to establish the collection, and in this domain the requirements of critical editing apply fully, obliging the editor to justify the pertinence and the coherence of his choices on the two complementary aspects: the gathering and the selection of the objects constituting the collection. Gathering and selecting are the first two editorial gestures that generate the meaning of the collection; they engage the editor's expertise and are motivated by a preliminary interpretation of the edited whole.

Unlike heritage digitizing such as practiced by librarians—for example, when they digitize a preexisting archival collection for conservation purposes—a digital collection editor can bring together documents coming from different documentary collections. The physical area where documents can be collected is therefore greater for a collection than for conservation. This is one of the most obvious interests in document dematerialization in a digital environment, where one can be free of the constraints of the physical conservation place; from (almost) anywhere in the world, a reader can consult documents whose physical copies are stored in a library, in a museum, or in a private collection very far from his location. Thus, the electronic edition of *Les Journaux d'Alexandre Dumas* brings together the periodical newspapers directed by Alexandre Dumas between 1848 and 1869, about ten titles coming from different libraries and private collections.[7] The missing issues of a newspaper in a library can be found elsewhere and added, thus making it possible to reconstitute a complete collection. A collection constituted by the initial editorial gesture of gathering documents creates a corpus that exists nowhere else in a physical location, with the aim of bringing out an aspect of Alexandre Dumas's career that the constraints of document conservation and editorial habits have always minimized: his career as a press professional.

But to build up a collection, gathering documents cannot be done without selection. In fact, marking out the collection is at least as important as assembling the objects that will constitute it. One can easily imagine that an infinitely increasing collection would have no relevance for a reader; the multiplicity of links between individual documents would dilute the design that had organized the gathering, and the pursuit of exhaustiveness would override the readability requirement. If it is to be edited according to scholarly standards—taking into account both the volume of initially selected documents, an eventual contribution of new documents, as well as the exponential increase of hyperlinks that render the increasingly refined structuring of the collection—a digital collection can therefore only very rarely aim at exhaustiveness. The pitfall of infinite growth can be easily avoided, in as much as it coincides with the limitations specific to editorial work: an editing project must be completed in a limited time frame, by a necessarily specific team, and within a budget that is usually also limited. The adequacy of the technological, budgetary, and human means to the project objectives is an important criterion for evaluating a digital edition project that needs funding.

Some collections avoid the pitfall of infinite expansion by delimiting the extension of the collection to be published ahead of time. Such is the case with the electronic edition of the *Dossiers de Bouvard et Pécuchet* by Gustave Flaubert.[8]

The object of this project is the edition of documentary files left by the writer in the state they were found at his death by his niece and stored as such by the Bibliothèque Municipale of Rouen. The contribution of a digital collection to a basic digitization of heritage archives is in the links that will be established, within the files, between the documents assembled by Flaubert and, external to the files, between the notes that he wrote while reading, and the "library" or even the scientific universe in which he wrote this encyclopedic novel.

Organizing a Collection

Theoretically a collection lacks the linearity (real or imagined) of a single text and therefore must necessarily be organized to be available for consultation. For collections comprising a large number of documents—for example, the dozens of thousands of pages of the Dumas newspapers—the question of structuring the documents stored in the database is crucial. The files of the documents and the information concerning the documents are registered in three bases: the newspaper base, that of the issues, and that of the authors. With the three bases being relational, meaning they are interlinked, it is possible to draw new bases from them—for example, the base of articles. The deep structure of the database does not correspond exactly to the apparent structure of the edited collection, as it can be accessed by an Internet surfer and it presents three types of information: textual (e.g., a newspaper article), para-textual (e.g., the name of the article author, the title of the column in which it was published), and contextual (e.g., explanation of a pseudonym, author's biography). But this data organization is only the computer representation of the collection structure such as the editors have chosen to describe it, according to editorial criteria they deem useful for the reading of modern press texts.

More generally there can be two scenarios with regard to the organization of the documents that make up the collection: it can be either intrinsic or extrinsic. The organization is intrinsic when the relations between the documents preexist their gathering and are therefore compelling for the editor, who has only to create an analogical computer representation of these links in the database and in the interface to be used for its consultation. For example, in an edition of periodical newspapers, at least two intrinsic principles preside over the collection organization: the chronology of the journal publication and the pagination of the copies. Thus, the digital edition of *L'Écho de la Fabrique*, a newspaper of the silk workers (*canuts*) in Lyon between 1831 and 1834, follows these two principles of chronology and pagination both for the organization of the digital data and for consultation. The organization mode can even be voluntarily underlined by the editors; such is the editorial choice made by the team that edits *L'Écho de la Fabrique* online, who have adopted, more than a century and a half later, the same weekly publication rhythm as that of the original newspaper editors. Each week, the digital collection presents the newspaper issue that was printed the same week 170 years earlier, thus recreating (at least symbolically) the link between the journal publication and the concomitant news environment that the critical apparatus of the edition attempts to reconstitute for the reader of today. In this case the digital editor has chosen to present a digital collection structured by a strict analogy principle with the printed documents he or she is editing.

Other collections come completely under an extrinsic organization; in this case the interpretative structure imposed on the content by the editors prevails largely over the collection's deep structure. When the assembled documents do not have preexisting explicit links, the editor chooses the organization mode for the collection and, if he does his work with conscientiousness, justifies his choices. This is the way, for example, that the part of the Rossetti Archive dedicated to related documents (Rossetti Archive Related Pictures) functions;[9] when no obvious citation link exists between the Rossetti work and the probable inspirational material—such as the popular colored image plates representing theatrical costumes[10]—the editors must objectify the links their knowledge allows them to establish between these works and those of Rossetti. Based on the pictorial analysis protocol and art history tools, a commentary presents the reader with the hypothesis of an influence that justifies the inclusion of the painting in the collection.

Of course, most digital collections simultaneously come under the two types of organization, and the editor adds to an intrinsic organization the one that his knowledge and his editorial project suggest. The *Dossiers de Bouvard et Pécuchet*, for example, are organized for a linear consultation that abides by the heritage organization of the documents—that is, the folders as they were found when Flaubert died—but they are also chronologically classified by the editors, depending on the presumed date they were written. The second organization criterion, by its extrinsic and often conjectural nature, requires that the editor be much more cautious than the more readily unbiased first.

Linking Documents

To go back to the minimal definition of a digital collection presented above, it appears that one of the most important elements of this definition is the linking of documents; that is where the hypertextuality of the collection acquires its full meaning. Computers allow the establishment of complex links between documents composing a collection by combining several types of relationships. For the clarity of this presentation, it is possible to distinguish three levels in these relationships that are superimposed or combined by the editorial activity.

The first level, which could be qualified as descriptive, corresponds more or less to the material bibliography of the document. It defines the links established by the editor between a document and its origin—for example, the authentication, which aims at establishing if the document is autograph or allograph (copyist manuscript or apocryphal version); its location (place of origin); and all the information for characterization (paper type, format, possible restorations, etc.). This first kind of link thus puts a single document in relation with information elements that are external to the collection, such as information on the physical environment of the material document (place and mode of conservation, etc.), and does not necessarily correspond to interlinking several documents of the base. An exception would be if some of the information is common to several documents, as in the case of several manuscripts written by the same copyist or of printings coming from the same engraving shop.

The second level represents the case where the editor highlights an organic relation between one or several documents from the database and an object external to the base. For instance, an organic relation exists when there is a quotation or a representation. When a text explicitly quotes another, the editor can translate this organic link between the text quoted and the text quoting by using a hypertextual link. However, the organic relation can be implicit, as in the case of an engraving or a drawing representing a real place, yet not identified in the document itself. In this case the editor can try to establish a relation between the document and the object represented by drawing from knowledge that is external to the collection in order to create an objective link. Another type of organic relation that is very important in critical edition accounts for the philologist's work in establishing the text. This internal organic relation signals the gaps in the text, its variants, its conjectural readings, its pagination, and so forth. It is rendered by a hypertextual link between the document and its critical apparatus or a series of other documents—for example, a series of text witnesses in the philological meaning of the word. The organic level, as I propose it to be understood here, brings together all the elements of an empirical description of the documents, but I think it would be naïve to pretend believing this description does not already involve an interpretation on the part of the editor. For example, the work of establishing a text, although it does not necessarily constitute a commentary of that text, is largely dependent on an interpretation of the text's history (composition, editorial history, dissemination, etc.) and, to a variable extent, of its meaning.

To illustrate the organic level of the hyperlinks, let's take the example of the *Dossiers de Bouvard et Pécuchet* edition, one of the objectives being to transcribe in hypertextual form the numerous and rich organic relations interconnecting the documents of the collection. For his unfinished encyclopedic novel,[11] Flaubert read more than fifteen hundred books, taking notes for most of them; he then used these notes to build and develop his fiction. The edition will bring to light the links of internal quotations that join the reading notes, with specific note taking for each work read, and the pages where Flaubert partially copies out these notes by regrouping them in themes (rococo style, hate of outstanding men, common stupidity, etc.) Among the external organic relations from these manuscript reading files, links that must be mentioned are those that the editors will establish with the printed books annotated by Flaubert (available on the website itself or in digital libraries such as Gallica[12]), the writer's correspondence, the "definite" text of *Bouvard et Pécuchet*, and so on.

While the second level includes the organic relations accounted for between documents, the third level, contextual and hermeneutic, is one of documents having no organic links between themselves, but whose interconnection is judged as relevant by editors basing their judgment on external knowledge. This third level commits the editor to a historical or interpretative approach that goes far beyond updating organic relations within the collection, such as can be established by philology. A good example of this contextual level can be found in the relations that the editors of Woolf Online seek to establish between "Time Passes," the central section of Virginia Woolf's novel *To the Lighthouse*, and its personal and general production context.[13] The genetic edition of the draft will thus be linked to two series of secondary documents: (1) a series outlining the personal context, based on the entries in Virginia Woolf's personal diary between April 30 and May 25, 1926 (the period period during which "Time Passes" was composed), and on the letters she exchanged with her sister and her friends, as well as two essays she wrote during the same period; and (2) a series of documents on the greater context—in particular, on the restlessness in England with the general strike, as evidenced in the letters and press clippings of May 15, 1926.

Also found in this level are the relations established by the editors for hermeneutic purposes, especially for text or iconic document interpretation. Such is the case for the commentary of the *Vita Nuova* of Dante, which, as the editors of the Rossetti Archive show, was read by Rossetti as a strictly autobiographical text, striking a chord with significant episodes of his own life, and as one of his great inspirational sources, particularly for his major poetic work, *The House of Life*.[14]

These three theoretical levels are generally combined in editorial practice to account for the complex relations between the documents in the collection. Some editorial projects, making the most of the possibilities offered by this combination, go beyond the simple critical elaboration to aim at a genuine "literary archaeology." In fact, it is with these words, "literary archaeology," that the editors of Woolf Online describe the objectives of the editorial work, hoping that this combination of a genetic edition, an in-depth work on the text, and a collection of secondary documents, will serve as a model for a new way of tackling digital editing not only as a more efficient means than a paper edition to report text genesis but also as a possible recreating of the whole intellectual, cultural, and contemporary historical universe of its birth.[15]

The Different Text States

One of the most interesting practical contributions of digital medium to electronic edition is without doubt the possibility of confronting a text with what the critical genetic school calls its avant-textes (drafts, copies, proofs, etc.) without the problems inherent to a paper edition. All scholarly editors have been confronted with the constraints inherent to editions published as printed books: there must necessarily be the choice of one, and only one, state of the text to be published; there is a limited space for variants and notes, which obliges one to proceed to the deceiving choice of variants; the variants are printed in such a small size and with so many abbreviations that there is the risk that no one, outside of the editor, is capable of reading them, and so on. On the contrary, in electronic editing it is possible, if one wishes, to be completely free of the very notions of reference text or variant. All the different text strata can be confronted: preparatory notes; reading notes; successive drafts; autograph and allograph copies; and prepublication in periodical, successive editions, and a final edition.

Through a spatial representation of the relations between documents, the synoptic layout proposes to the reader a way to try to grasp the system within which the work was produced. Here, for example, is a description of documents that will be presented in the digital edition of the *Pensées* of Montesquieu and the analysis perspectives outlined in the project Montédite: "The three volumes of the *Pensées*, kept at the Municipal Library of Bordeaux, are notebooks with comments, notions, pieces, and off cuts of printed or sketched works. Their content reflects Montesquieu's interests, knowledge, and culture in all their diversity, the very characteristic transit from reading with a pen in hand to writing, from documentary writing to creating. Their examination allows progressive insight in the chronology of the readings, of the work projects, and of the author's intellectual and aesthetic preoccupations."[16]

The richness of these working possibilities can be appreciated by consulting editions such as the *Edición Variorum Electrónica del Quijote* of the Cervantes Project,[17] which, with the Multi-Variant Contents Editor (MVED), allows confrontation of all the collected variants of the editions of *Quixote*.[18] Other promising tools are being developed, such as the software MEDITE—within the framework of the project EDITE (Étude Diachronique du Travail de l'Écrivain) by two research groups, ITEM and LIP6—to study the writer's work with integration of the temporal dimension. The authors define it as a tool that is capable of helping comparison of two text states, especially of two manuscripts (previously transcribed): "MEDITE mimes the operations done by hand by the philologist in comparing texts. In other works, he automatically recreates the temporal sequence of corrections, additions, and deletions done by the author in his manuscript by comparing two states of the same manuscript."[19]

Encoding the author's different operations reveals the philologist's work and offers the reader the possibility of distinguishing the text from the editor's contribution and even, if he wishes, of canceling it out. This type of analysis is not limited to textual documents and can perfectly be applied, as shown by the Rossetti Archive, to images and to text-image couples. One can imagine the possibilities that open up with this type of editorial tools for varied cultural materials, whose confrontation would greatly enrich existing knowledge.

The Manuscripts in Collections

Among the different text states likely to interest digital collection editors, special attention must be given to manuscripts. Nevertheless, a manuscript probably does not have the same place nor the same role in a collection as it has in the critical edition of a singular work or of complete works such as it is understood in the philological tradition. In the moving configuration of a collection, where the editorial gesture aims less to establish the text of a major work than to compose a relevant set of documents capable of accounting for a state of culture, art, or science at a given moment, manuscripts are not meant to occupy the central place, and their role is not necessarily to justify the establishment of the text freed of the corruptions that the copyists and the successive editions may have introduced. The manuscript's place in a collection is not determined in advance and can vary as the collection broadens or is reorganized.

A manuscript can thus have connections with other manuscripts that it quotes or that it rewrites, or with printed works for which it is neither a draft nor a preliminary copy, as, for example, in the case of a writer's reading notes, with iconographic documents if he describes the process for creating a painting or writes down the inspirational sources, and so on. The digital edition must allow the broadest analysis possible without immediately limiting the approaches; in different configurations the same manuscript could be the object of a material analysis, of a diplomatic transcription, or of an aesthetic study of the layout of the scriptural elements in the page.

For it is precisely for manuscripts that the digital medium represents the greatest change with regard to traditional means of edition. As aptly recalled by Kevin Kiernan: "Print is an extremely inefficient and inadequate means for representing manuscript texts" (Kiernan n.d.). With the condition of meeting the criteria for a quality digitization (optimal graphic resolution, chromatic fidelity, respect of document proportions, etc.), in order to retain a maximum of original graphic information the digital medium offers numerous presentation tools for manuscripts that are extremely useful for researchers. It allows blowups, contrast adjustment, and parasite "noise" reduction, all of which are operations that represent precious help in deciphering and transcribing texts. But mainly the digital medium allows dissociation of the manuscript storage place from the workplace of researchers, who are sometimes large in number in collaborating to the edition. The electronic edition can thus capitalize on the transcription efforts of distant researchers, as was the case for the *Manuscrits de Madame Bovary* and as it will be for the *Dossiers de Bouvard et Pécuchet*.[20]

The link between manuscripts and transcription is also new, since it is now possible to propose to the reader what used to be reserved for a few: the confrontation of the manuscript and its transcriptions, ideally under the double diplomatic and linearized forms, as in the Bergen Electronic Edition of Wittgenstein's *Nachlass*.[21] All scholars have been confronted with these manuscript editions where the complexity of the transcription mechanism, adopted by the editor to ensure precision and exhaustiveness, renders the transcription deciphering even more difficult for the reader than it would be with consulting the manuscript itself. In digital editions with a face-to-face layout, the transcription choices of the scholarly editor are still important—all the more so when they allow the reader to see or discuss the coherence or the relevance of these choices—but the coexistence of the two presentations of the texts, images of the manuscript and transcription, does not have the manuscript disappear behind the conjectural text.

Several software solutions exist or are being developed to optimize the confrontation of different text states and their transcription. The prototype work station Philectre, designed between 1994 and 1997, or the specific software developed for medieval manuscripts by the BAMBI project were headed that way.[22] Great progress has been made in this domain, particularly for complex manuscripts, such as sometimes are the avant-textes of modern writers. Thus, the manuscript editor EMMA (Édition de Manuscrits Modernes Assistée), developed at the University of Rouen for the manuscript transcription of *Madame Bovary*, allows visualization in the same window of a manuscript folio (draft or copyist manuscript) and its diplomatic transcription in a horizontal or vertical confrontation.[23] For strongly heterogeneous collections, more flexible tools need to be designed in order to offer, as proposed by the editors of the *Dossiers de Bouvard et Pécuchet*, the possibility of articulating the transcription of manuscript images that are graphically partitioned in as many fragments as necessary, likely to have an autonomous meaning, and likely interlinked with the others in a nonsequential manner.

Facsimiles and Texts

Manuscripts are not the only type of documents for which a digital image presentation can be greatly beneficial. It is also the case with, for example, editions of periodicals that confirm the importance of retaining the text image. Some of the first editions of digital collections by French researchers have been based on this principle as well, including the twelve CD-ROM collection of the *Gazette d'Amsterdam* distributed by the Voltaire Foundation.[24] This collection presents, in the form of PDF images, seventy-eight thousand pages of newspapers of diplomatic Europe published between 1691 and 1796. These pioneer editorial undertakings can work at establishing with increasing complexity the relations within the collection. This is what the editorial team of the *Gazettes* is doing in trying to achieve an automatic recognition of the italics in the images of the newspaper in order to allow readers to consult the newspaper according to the places mentioned, the geographical names having been printed in italics in these newspapers.[25] The graphical identification of these relevant elements of information, similar to that of the initial readers, requires that the documents be presented in the image mode rather than a linear text (or, ideally, added to it) that, given alone, would result in a loss of the specificity of these periodical newspapers of the eighteenth century.

Several factors explain the crucial importance taken by the edition of text images in a collection of periodicals. On one hand, the large format of newspapers from the middle of the nineteenth century and the very important number of pages represented by a collection of daily newspapers, for example, practically forbid a complete paper edition. Dumas's newspapers represent a collection of about fifteen thousand pages, for the most part in folio format. In the book regime, scholarly editors generally choose to present anthologies that belong to the same kind of editorial gesture as that of the collection if the anthologies did not generally present a linear version of the articles published in the newspaper. Now, to extract journalistic texts from the page context of the newspaper is a questionable choice, because, as one knows, the layout of the page influences the writing. One only has to appreciate the importance of the recursive ending in the writing of serial novels punctuated by the famous formula "to be continued," or to observe the richness of the exchanges between the text at the bottom of the page and the top of the page dedicated to the news—for example, the reciprocal influence of the news in brief and the first detective novels[26]—in order to measure the loss of information that results from editing press texts in a text mode without maintaining the original page layout. Of course, in a digital edition that retains the images of the texts, the images are not necessarily in the center of the documentary configuration. For example, the editors of *L'Écho de la Fabrique* have decided to present by default the text version of the newspaper, the facsimiles in the Djvu format being accessible on the page of each issue.[27] This choice is justified by the relative linearity of the newspaper articles, often long and printed in only two columns, without a bottom page section.

For nonlinear documents the opposite choice can be justified. Thus, the presentation of the edition of *Les Journaux d'Alexandre Dumas* begins with a reduced image of the page,[28] because most newspapers have a tabular composition, similar to that of modern daily newspapers, with three columns under a heading with a very large title and a bottom page section that runs across the whole width of the page topped by a thin line. With the image viewer it is possible to zoom in on each zone of the image, each of which can be printed separately, and eventually to recompose a serial article by putting together the image zones. Thus, the reader has access to the typographical information, such as the choice of titling, the laying out of paragraphs in the page, and so on, while benefiting from an interconnection of the image zones, which would be impossible in a paper facsimile, which can have only illustrative or testimonial value. Thus conceived, it seems that in a digital collection facsimiles of manuscripts or printed works can acquire their distinctive value, which is probably quite different from the one that has been assigned by the editorial regime of paper books.

The distinctive interest of facsimiles in a digital collection does not exclude the editor's relating them to a text version obtained, when possible, by using optical character recognition (OCR). The question of whether to use OCR may be useless for manuscript material, due to the current deficiencies of software programs, but it is much more crucial for collections of heterogeneous printed documents or documents organized in a tabular fashion, such as the periodical press, than for linear texts, such as the complete works of a writer. The OCR treatment of the old press raises specific problems. The structuring of the pages in columns, frontispiece, and eventually a bottom page section, imposes the necessity of checking by hand the zoning done by the OCR software. The use of a large variety of character sets, some of which are rare and not easily recognized by OCR software; the wear of the lead types; the bad quality of the paper; and the problem of document conservation, such as spots or folding marks due to their being sent by post, are all practical problems for which editors of digital collections must find solutions on an ad hoc basis, and this explains the extreme difficulty of "OCRizing" old newspapers.

One of the solutions often adopted by the editors of this type of collection consists in not displaying the OCRized text, often of mediocre quality, in answer to a full text search, but instead displaying the image zone corresponding to the answer, as is done, for example, in the periodical base JSTOR and the British Library Online Newspaper Archive.[29] This solution, although not quite satisfying, nevertheless offers the benefit of implementing the latest versions of OCR applications as soon as they are available and, therefore, of augmenting the relevance of the answers to the requests formulated by readers as editorial technologies evolve.

This evolutional aspect of digital collection editions is one of their greatest assets, for it faithfully reflects the adaptation of scholarly editors' work for the evolution of knowledge and the uses of readers.

The Uses of the Collection

If editorial practices in the domain of digital collections are still largely yet to be invented, the same is even more so for reading practices. In fact, the reading model of printed critical editions is no longer useful in apprehending the use that the public can make of the proposed digital collections, except perhaps for CD-ROM or DVD-ROM editions, for which we can suppose they are aimed at a library public and a learned public in ways that are probably very similar to how paper critical editions are targeted. On the Internet, the mastery of uses is largely outside the reach of editors. They have only analytical tools to statistically measure visits on edition sites and thus lack a real understanding of how readers apprehend the material.

The very definition of the public that digital collection editions aim at is fuzzy. Often larger than that of digital editions of complete works, the public of an online collection brings together researchers in humanities and social sciences, or at least those among them who have integrated digital tools in their research practice, including students, who are often reputed to be more technophiles than their teachers, and a part of the general public of Internet surfers. Obviously, a better knowledge of this public in the coming years will be crucial for editors' work, as it will allow design of consultation tools, research tools, and more convivial and intuitive tools for consultation that are perhaps not as directly focused on the research needs of the editors themselves as are those that exist today.

If one focuses on some of the characteristics of the well-known uses of digital critical collections, what stands out is that collections work very well for hypertextual, nonlinear, and non-exhaustive consulting, even better than digital editions of complete works. This is probably why the collection format is particularly well suited for editing heterogeneous and tabular documents such as newspapers or documentation files (dossiers), because digital collections can be used for transversal reading (pecking, overview, or rapid walk-through) similar to an occasional consultation of paper documents.

Editors usually propose two document access modes that are now familiar to Internet surfers: browsing and searching. The consultation path can follow predefined itineraries, such as the visit that the William Blake Archive editors propose,[30] or it can be free, in which case the visitor uses the tools that reflect the collection organization, such as chronological alphabetical, typical, or other classifications. The guided tour is a reading mode that is well adapted for the general public, who are usually curious to discover a collection and likely to be won over by the documents presented. A personal path will be more convenient for sustained reading or for systematic consultation—for example, by a student or specialized researcher who needs to acquire an extensive knowledge of the documentary corpus and who, in this impregnation phase, will rely on the structuring modes proposed by the editors.

On the contrary, the serach mode tries to answer the specific, limited, and systematic need for finding information in or about the collection; it is only as in a second stage that genuine reading will occur, often focused on the document or documents provided by the answer. This approach, which supposes that the user makes the effort of using formularies and search engines, allows full text searches, such as in *L'Écho de la Fabrique*, or indexed ones, such as in *Les Journaux d'Alexandre Dumas*. In this last case the critical enrichment of the collection represents a real added value for the surfer, because it allows using more sophisticated research criteria than a simple lexical search. *Les Journaux d'Alexandre Dumas* can be searched by newspaper title, date, or issue number but also by article author, article title, columns, or key word, without necessarily having to go through the often discouraging Boolean search procedure.

Editorial projects that exploit encoding techniques, such as XML, offer even more attractive possibilities, given the reader is able to exploit them. Here, for example, is the type of search promised by the Montédite Project: "With an encoding system, one can extract certain types of data in order to produce syntheses that can cast a new light on the author's work, to study the referral system, to make key word searches, to identify thematic networks and encourage the ongoing interdisciplinary annotation work, as well as the setting up of indexes."[31] Among the types of searches presented here, some correspond to quite old information processes, such as key word searches, and others to new collaborative work tools that hold the promise of facilitating a self-documented search practice. Above all, encoding allows the inclusion of images in the search engine results, and this can be crucial for collections that propose manuscript facsimiles. Correctly encoded, a collection like the *Dossiers de Bouvard et Pécuchet* would allow retrieval of deletions, abbreviations, or additions and the possibility of studying in depth the different composition operations practiced by Flaubert.

Huge possibilities are offered by digital critical collections, it seems, but the present lack of knowledge of the uses favored by the public makes their systematic exploration rather risky. The best known needs are, as always, those of the researchers themselves, who thus choose their peers as the first addressees of their work. Nevertheless, putting at the disposal of the research community the documents with which they will be working in the coming years, designing the research tools to come, and stimulating a methodological renewal are not trivial objectives.

Furthermore, in a particularly crucial manner, critical editions of digital collections raise the question of the place of critical editions in the new digital environment for culture. Because their object is not as clearly defined as that of critical editions of texts, because they use a greater variety of technological tools, and because their public is larger but much more difficult to identify, their future is quite uncertain.

Are they meant to amplify the "heritagization" of culture, with the risk that their "critical" dimension may be nothing more than a guarantee of serious-ness for cultural promotion? If one adopts this pessimistic view of the future, the scholarly editors who are engaged in the digital revolution could turn out to be the objective allies of human science liquidators. In accepting to submit their know-how, inherited from a rich history of scholarship and teaching, to technological choices and policies of actors who have no particular commit-ment to texts, we can assume that they are taking the risk of transforming these texts into negotiable objects and as such will need to be saved (preserved, read, edited, translated, commented, etc.) only if they represent promotion tools that are exploitable by a region, a city, an industrial sector, or a software company.

Or on the contrary, will digital collections be capable of coping with the chal-lenges of the emergence of new objects, methods, and actors in human science research? Will editors be capable of combining the requirements of scientific rigor with the opportunities offered by the surfers' appetites for widely varied "contents"? At the core of the edition and research sector that is trying to find its way between inherited knowledge and new know-how, digital collections will surely be a privileged observatory of important changes in critical edition in the coming years.

Notes

1. "Nous sommes perdus, nous avons peur. Le monde de l'édition est comme un édifice de briques qu'on secoue et qui tremble. [. . .] Internet fautif : en partie, si la possibilité de choix, de repérage, court-circuite la médiation telle qu'elle s'exerçait encore il y a dix ans."

2. This chapter focuses mainly on collections based on texts and images, although digital editions can also produce sound or video file collections. In fact, some of the editorial projects already produced contain texts, images, and sound—for example, the Walt Whitman Archive, which publishes a recording of Whitman's voice. (See full reference in bibliography.)

3. William Blake Archive, http://www.blakearchive.org/blake/archive.html.

4. The Charette Project (http://www.princeton.edu/~lancelot/ss/index.shtml) is a

critical edition of several manuscripts of Chretien de Troyes's novel *Le Chevalier de la Charette* (ca. 1180). It displays images of the medieval manuscripts together with a transcription and several rhetorical and lexical databases.

5. The Complete Writings and Pictures of Dante Gabriel Rossetti: A Hypermedia Archive, http://www.rossettiarchive.org/racs/doubleworks.rac.html. See links to and description of the site in the bibliography.

6. Rossetti Archive, http://www.rossettiarchive.org/docs/1–1847.s244.raw.html.

7. Les Journaux d'Alexandre Dumas, http://alexandredumas.org.

8. *Édition numérique des "Dossiers de Bouvard et Pécuchet" de Flaubert,* http://lire .ish-lyon.cnrs.fr/spip.php?article130.

9. Rosetti Archive, http://www.rossettiarchive.org/racs/otherpics.rac.html.

10. Rossetti Archive, http://www.rossettiarchive.org/docs/0p93.rap.html.

11. The novelist died before having had time to write the second volume of the story.

12. Gallica, http://gallica.bnf.fr.

13. Woolf Online, http://www.woolfonline.com.

14. Rossetti Archive, http://www.rossettiarchive.org/docs/9d-1861.raw.html.

15. For "a new form of literary archaeology," see Woolf Online, http://www.woolfonline .com/?q=about.

16. "Les trois volumes des Pensées, conservés à la bibliothèque municipale de Bordeaux, sont des cahiers de réflexions, de notes, morceaux et 'chutes' d'ouvrages imprimés ou ébauchés. Leur contenu reflète les intérêts, les savoirs et la culture de Montesquieu dans toute leur diversité, le passage très caractéristique de la lecture la plume à la main à l'écriture, de l'écriture documentaire à la création. Leur examen permet de progresser dans la connaissance de la chronologie des lectures, des projets d'œuvres et des préoccupations intellectuelles et esthétiques de l'auteur." http://montesquieu.ens-lsh.fr/article .php3?id_article=20.

17. Electronic Variorum Edition of the *Quixote*, http://cervantes.tamu.edu/V2/CPI/ variorum/index.htm.

18. El Editor de Documentos de Multiples Variantes (MVED), Electronic *Variorum* Edition of the *Quixote,* http://cervantes.tamu.edu/V2/CPI/variorum/edicioncritica .htm#mved.

19. "MEDITE mime les opérations exécutées à la main par le philologue qui compare des textes. Autrement dit, il reconstitue automatiquement la séquence temporelle des corrections, adjonctions et ratures opérées par l'auteur sur son manuscrit à partir de la comparaison de deux états de ce même manuscrit" (Ganascia et al. 2004).

20. Les manuscrits de *Madame Bovary,* Edition intégrale sur le Web. See bibliography.

21. The Bergen Electronic Edition of Wittgenstein's *Nachlass* is on six CDs. Wittgenstein Archives at the University of Bergen and Oxford University Press, 2000. See bibliography.

22. See Calabretto et al. 1999.

23. See an example of visualization at Les manuscrits de *Madame Bovary,* http://www .bovary.fr/folio_visu.php?mode=sequence&folio=6623&org=3&zoom=50&seq=1&ppl=3.

24. See full reference to the edition on twelve CD-ROMs in the bibliography.

25. See "Les gazettes européennes du 18e siècle." For a description of the onine edition of the gazettes, see also http://www.ish-lyon.cnrs.fr/spip.php?article104.

26. See Kalifa 2005, especially chapter 6, "Faits divers et romans criminels au XIXe siècle," 131–56.

27. Djvu is a file format designed to display scanned images on the web, as an alternative to pdf format.

28. See, e.g., for the newspaper *Le Mousquetaire,* http://alexandredumas.org/el/journal/Le_Mousquetaire_hebdomadaire/1854-10-01/1.

29. See JSTOR (http://www.jstor.org) and the British Library, ActivePaper Archive (http://www.uk.olivesoftware.com).

30. "A Tour of the William Blake Archive" is accessible online at http://www.blakearchive.org/blake/public/about/tour/index.html.

31. "Grâce au système de balisage on peut par ailleurs extraire certains types de données pour en faire des synthèses éclairant le travail de l'auteur, pour étudier les systèmes de renvois, faire des recherches par mots-clefs, mettre au jour des réseaux thématiques et favoriser le travail d'annotation interdisciplinaire en cours, ainsi que la constitution d'index." Montesquieu, http://montesquieu.ens-lsh.fr/article.php3?id_article=20 (accessed 2011); also see reference at the end of the chapter to a new Montédite site, http://www.unicaen.fr/services/puc/sources/index.html.

9. Toward a New Political Economy of Critical Editions

Producing critical editions is a reputedly old and not particularly profitable scholarly activity that essentially amounts to establishing, annotating, and presenting a text. What benefit can be obtained, then, by scrutinizing it from the perspective of political economy—especially at a time when critical editions are at last entering the digital realm, whose immateriality seems to open up wide possibilities and advantages, free of charge, to all users?

On the contrary, we believe that textual scholarship would have much to gain from questioning itself in terms of political economy, which for ages was the main branch of economics but has now been superseded by mathematical modeling and forecasting. Political economy combines factual considerations, economic theory, and philosophical and legal reflection on national and international institutions that are vested with political authority and in principle commissioned by the nations and established by national states and various international bodies to enforce rules, procedures, and objectives.

Back to the Reality Principle

The early 2000s witnessed the massive adoption of the Internet. During these years, which are already receding into oblivion, a minority of thinkers regularly advocated the view that the digital medium offered a providential solution to the general crisis that affected publishing in the humanities and social sciences, a crisis acknowledged and bemoaned in all industrialized countries. Earlier pioneers of digitization had based their views on expectations about gains in productivity, decreases in production costs, and quasi-instantaneous distribution. And since scholars who were using word processing and desktop publishing (DTP) applications were learning how to carry out tasks that previously required multiple typographical skills, one assumed they were close to being able to publish works by themselves, alone and at no cost. A decade later, however, this vision has proven to be illusory. To date, except for the case of already digitized text volumes, the digital medium makes operations more complicated for critical editions; extends the duration of the projects; is difficult to harness; and spectacularly blows up the costs of production, diffusion, and IPR (intellectual propety rights) protection costs. Moreover, in the wake of the Internet revolution, the liberal-libertarian ideology appears to prohibit by principle any return on investment. How can such a contradiction be resolved?

As a reminder, the mechanism of supply and demand remains a fundamental law of economy, generating trade and creating a more or less free market within which institutions and procedures ultimately determine values. Can digital critical editions escape economy? To what extent can they or should they constitute an exception and, as such, benefit from exceptional measures?

The fact is that with the expansion of digital technology, we are entering a new phase characterized by the economization, if not commoditization, of culture in the age of and at the scale of an ongoing globalization. As can be witnessed, immaterial economy has turned into a very real and actually increasingly material economy. For instance, online bookstores, although operating without street-level physical outlets in our cities, tend to multiply transactions and to establish large warehouses in industrial zones. Computer server farms established all over the world by large digital companies now cover physical areas that are comparable to old industrial plants. The vast majority of middle-class and even working-class individuals in industrialized countries, now equipped with personal computers, are insistently solicited through numerous advertisements to acquire not only one but at least two new mobile terminals, such as smartphones, netbooks, or tablets, in order to comply with the standards of *homo informaticus.*

This chapter does not intend to resolve all of these large problems in one sweep, but begins by initiating a reflection about the positioning and the goals of critical editions, two challenges that appear to be grossly underrated within the present context.

The Process of Revaluing Texts

While critical editions serve the purpose of providing university scholars as well as educated readers and enthusiasts with reliable texts and tools that facilitate reading, it goes without saying that stakes are very different for publishers, who, from a legal and practical point of view, are commercial and industrial enterprises.

Although it cannot be denied that the desire and pleasure of the founders of these publishing houses is to contribute to cultural life, the driving force of publishing companies is primarily to draw profit. From the point of view of the publisher, what counts is the potential of a book to attract readers in sufficient numbers in order to achieve at least an acceptable profitability. A good publisher, the successful one, is the one who appreciates the intellectual or aesthetic quality of a manuscript that has been submitted as measured by the quantity of copies that can be commercialized in the short, middle, and long term. In other words, the use value of a text is of interest to the publisher only if he or she can convert it into an exchange value. This is why an outstanding publisher such as Michel Lévy, the founder of the Calmann-Lévy publishing house in Paris, knew how to innovate brilliantly.[1] His creativity is demonstrated in his edition of the complete writings of Balzac: Calmann-Lévy innovated by drawing on the expertise of Baron Spoelberch de Lovenjoul, a renowned collector of literary manuscripts, and by acquiring Balzac's correspondence with his wife, who by that time had become his widow. The publication of this correspondence, which was full of information about the genesis of the *Comédie humaine,* constituted the main sales argument of this edition. As the correspondence was added to the baron's study of the variants and the genesis of Balzac's works, it gave this edition a decisive advantage over Alexandre Houssiaux's and Bourdillat's first posthumous editions of Balzac's writing.[2] Following the success of this first edition, other publishers began to add Balzac to their catalog reusing the same recipe. Having to compete with Calmann-Lévy and other forerunners, each new challenger being submitted to the pressure of competition was forced to produce complete editions—increasingly complete, one could say, and increasingly critical. The current winner in this commercial game, when it comes to Balzac, happens to be Gallimard, with its prestigious Bibliothèque de la Pléiade series.

Thus, whether he likes it or not, a scholarly editor takes part in the ongoing and never-ending process of revaluating the text, a process that actually started with the first editions during the author's lifetime. However, through the person labeled "the author" in the wording of the contracts and derived legal rights/IPR, simultaneously, the commercial publisher acting as the editor of a restored text takes over as the text owner, or, to put it more precisely, as one among its many owner-operators. One should heed another economical phenomenon that accompanies the revaluation of editorial work: the takeover by a private operator and by its academic contractor. There is no revaluation without reappropriation.

This constant, routine process, unchallenged until the early 2000s, has taken on a very different dimension and direction after the major initiative launched by Google in December 2004. Google Print, later to become later Google Books, thanks to a very clever communication policy,[3] has been perceived by scholars all over the world as an incredible bargain. It is indeed an incredible bargain. How could one not call it a bargain—and even more, a marvel—to be able all over the world, from home, within seconds, as Aladdin summons the genie of his magic lamp, to identify a book kept somewhere and make it appear on a display and enshrine it on one's hard drive?

But as the declared goal of Google, since 1998, was limited (so to speak, when it applies to such an incredible ambition) to "organizing information at a global scale in order to make it accessible and useful for everyone,"[4] nobody had discovered outright the exact contours of the strategic implications of such an immense prospect for a universal library, collected at the price of huge long-term investments, surpassing by far the resources available to universities and national states, even the wealthiest ones, but absolutely free of charge to its users. By reinvesting their huge advertisement revenues in digitizing not all books published in the world but at least a significant number of collections obtained from major libraries in the Western world, Google undertook nothing else, apparently, than sharing content for free. However, this sharing consequently implied a massive, dramatic devaluation of an entire heritage occurring at an unprecedented pace. Until recently the value of this heritage was derived from its rarity, depending on whether the works were still commercially exploitable (e.g., through new editions) or had lost all their commercial potential, even though they still generated intellectual property rights (as is the case in the United States and Europe for works or editions younger than seventy years).[5]

Never mind the commercial trick or, to put it differently, the fool's bargain that underpins the whole operation. Under the guise of an incredible generosity dispensed toward libraries ("You will not need to pay anything; you need only to allow us to digitize your collections and bestow us the exclusive rights to index these for the Internet. In return, we will give you a copy of the files"), these institutions are invited to trade the existence and the digital representation of a literally priceless heritage, which took centuries to acquire, catalog, and preserve, with investments in buildings, purchases, salaries, and public or private subsidies. All of this comes in exchange for digital copies with no estimation having been made, for good reasons, of the total costs incurred in the past. In other words, one may witness in such contracts an unavowed dispossession and appropriation (albeit on a partial and temporary basis). This offer also comes under the guise of an incredible generosity dispensed toward individuals ("You will have free access to all the books in the world, being exposed to minimal advertisement"), who are encouraged, without noticing what is going on, to acknowledge that their needs, habits, tastes, and use statistics while accessing Google Books may be sold to invisible advertisers, who are thereby guaranteed to see their goods offered to the largest possible number of potential customers all over the world. This exchange, as a matter of fact, takes place without a contract.

Never mind if this kind of indirect revaluation (via advertisement revenues that are generated by means of advertisements or ad words) betrays a ruse of progress (in the sense that Hegel wrote about the ruse of history) or if, on the contrary, from its onset it has been a devilish scheme concealing another operational plan (e.g., an online publisher and bookseller exploiting an online library, Google Publications, under Google Books).

However, three hard facts with serious implications do matter a lot: (1) the tremendous acceleration that Google has given to the digitization of printed text, (2) the kind of global competition that results, and (3) the emerging revaluation of this dormant heritage. No matter how vast and compelling the macroeconomic framework is, the following anecdote about two personal misadventures highlights what is at stake from our perspective: the perspective of critical edition.

A year and four months before the founding of Google (September 4, 1998), I contacted Henri Le More, then director of the publishing company Libris Éditions, located on rue Vivienne in Paris, close to the French National Library (Bibliothèque Nationale de France, or BnF). Being an expert on the writing of the Saint-Simonians (a militant movement inspired by the emancipatory philosophy of Henri Saint-Simon [1760–1825], the first thinker of industrial society), I was very willing to provide access to the most central Saint-Simonian texts. The appointment was arranged through a chief librarian at a cultural evening organized at theBnF. Formerly a sociologist, and graduated from the prestigious business school Ecole des Hautes Etudes Commerciales (HEC), Le More, with a remarkable sense of anticipation, had invented and developed during the 1990s a republishing (remediation?) concept "at the crossing of three new major technologies": the first being "a scanning device dedicated to digitize hardbound, fragile, and valuable books"; the second being "electronic printing [. . .] [allowing] then the production in a small number of copies on demand"; and the third being "commercialization through [the] Internet."[6] In other words, he intended to remarket in the public domain works with very little potential for enjoying a second life in mainstream publishing but of prime interest to the very particular users of the BnF. With all proportions kept in mind, the terms of the agreement passed between the French National Library and Libris Éditions, to which were added the large municipal libraries of Troyes and Lyon, are not without similarities to the agreements passed between Google and the New York Library, along with the Harvard and Stanford University libraries, since Le More's former commercial enterprise stipulated that it had the "ownership of the digital files of reprinted works" and that it "committed itself to give BnF a copy for non-commercial use and, in particular, onscreen reading" (according to Blasselle 1997, 26). The system marketed as "Livre à la carte" (book à la carte), allowing library users to republish true copies of works, was offered as a paid subscription "service" available at the entrance of the reading halls of the BnF and of the library of the Orsay Museum.[7] However, this system lacked access to two major technologies that were not yet available: optical character recognition, which would allow the transformation of pictures into text, and indexing, which would allow automatized queries across catalogs and texts. This led me to sign a contract with Henri Le More Libris Éditions on June 15, 1997, to head a collection labeled "Bibliothèque saint-simonienne" with the objective to "republish, on demand, in small number, copies of works, documents, pamphlets, engravings, illustrations not any more available in bookshops such as essays, memoirs, stories, studies, novels, journals, biographies of persons related to the Saint-Simonian ideological movement." Due to a disagreement between two partners, however, I was told later that the project would not take place. Nonetheless, a "Bibliothèque du XIXe siècle" (library of nineteenth-century works) was founded at the Orsay Museum based on the same principles, and when in February 1999 Le More's company was revived by an increase of capital with the symbolic name Phénix Éditions, a libertarian and anarchist library ("Bibliothèque libertaire et anarchiste") was created to build on this model.[8]

In matter of conclusion to this unfinished story about commercial and industrial innovation, the notion of digital republishing on paper of older out-of-print books is exploited nowadays in France by an online bookshop called Chapitre .com, which also has a network of physical outlets.[9]

Another instructive misadventure of mine took place later, when e-books and other "livrels" (French neologism for e-book) emerged. How surprised I was in 1999 when as I was typing for fun on a search engine, I discovered the title of a collection of Saint-Simonian manuscripts of which I had been the first editor in 1992. I found that "my" text had been reshaped into an e-book by the publisher eBooksLib and was selling for US$5.40, a price much inferior to the paper edition! It goes without saying that neither I nor my publisher from Du Lérot Editeur, in the Charentes region, well known for his dedication to paper editions, had been approached by this online publisher from Ottawa and asked to give away our respective intellectual property rights. The sale of this work continues these days through specialized online sites like the French online bookshop Numilog, owned by the Hachette Book Group.[10]

Probably, one may object, the trade value of the corpus I have cared for is minimal. I readily agree and rejoice accordingly whenever it is sold, but it is precisely because of the low trade value of such works, according to the cultural and economic model governing the publication of books on paper, that texts in the public domain—known as "orphan works," texts with unexploited rights—are of great interest to digital publishers. Such texts open a channel for other texts with active and profitable exploitation of rights. Orphan works offer a cheap testing ground for copyrighted works. They function as efficient pilot products, and because of their mere volume of text they constitute an unparalleled information resource. Even leaving aside the advertisement profits, imagine how much revenue could be generated within a few decades by subscriptions to online combined libraries and bookstores (*librairies-bibliothèques*), in addition to licenses, access rights, and pay-by-session setups, even with very low fees paid by millions or even billions of readers!

In 1832, while the first industrial revolution was struggling to start in France, and while artistic and literary circles complained daily of their own misery, the utopian socialist Charles Fourier and his followers, taking stock of the success achieved by the most renowned Romantic writers, prophesized in his *Prospectus général du Phalanstère* the globalization of fine arts and literature. He included two corollary predictions—the first being the endowment of formidable grants to artistic creators who would be acclaimed by the public all over the world, and the second being a wonderful second life bestowed to old books, especially the most outdated ones, becoming miraculous objects of curiosity: "With the establishment of the societal state, the most notable philosophical works will be reprinted in several million copies: these writings, while being astray from a dogmatic point of view, will be credited doubly, first as literary classics, as handsome moments from the childhood of human spirit, social cacographies. Their general and specific contradictions will be taught to children and their fathers [. . .] . They will be reprinted with the addition of a counter-index or an analysis of absurdities, at least as comprehensive as the work itself" (Fourier 1832, 16). One can certainly consider this vision naïve, and indeed it is. Nevertheless, it encourages us to reflect on two themes: first, the present and universally felt need, it seems, to revisit old writings when the chance is offered, and second, the formidable trend toward "immaterial" republishing motivated by this need. This amounts to reflecting on the dynamic of supply and demand implied by the massive digitization of our heritage on paper.

This is the mission emerging for critical edition: to enrich the millions of minimally indexed copies of works on the Internet in such a way that they can be made accessible again. Digital access and intellectual access are two different things.

In Defense of Philologists:
Their Role in the New Division of Labor

Written largely in response to serious concerns that were raised about the Google initiative in literary and academic circles as well as in publishing circles, an essay was published in 2009 with the beautiful title "The Case for Books: Past, Present, and Future" (Darnton 2010). The French translation promoted by the elitist New York publisher Public Affairs was quite significantly carried out and published in a hurry at the beginning of 2011 by Gallimard in Paris with the financial support of the French National Book Centre (Centre national du livre). The author of the book, Robert Darnton, is a French-speaking Francophile American scholar who was recruited at the top of his career to head the Harvard University Library. A specialist of the history of the book and of the history of reading in the eighteenth century, Darnton is also the initiator of Electronic Enlightenment, a database containing the correspondence of Voltaire, Rousseau, Benjamin Franklin, and Thomas Jefferson, and is far from being a detractor of digital media or the Enlightenment. He also has the merit of being the mastermind behind the digital book repository Gutenberg-e, established by Columbia University Press.[11] He therefore does not reject the eventuality of a complete migration of the printed book to the digital medium, or even, in a long-term perspective, a mutation or extinction of the artifact known as a book. Darnton endeavors to defend the values of knowledge, as well as the institutions and initiatives building upon these values: libraries and publishing houses. The first institutions, he claims, "were never book warehouses." This is why they serve today as "centers of learning," as "ideally suited to mediate between the printed and the digital modes of communication." Regarding publishers, Darnton describes publishers in a mythological manner as "gatekeepers who control the flow of knowledge." The book professionals' function amounts to "provid[ing] all the services that will survive all technological changes": "by selecting texts, editing them, [and] designing them to the attention of their readers."[12]

With a few nuances, I happen to share Darnton's opinion. But what should one say about the role of universities and research institutions? And within these institutions, what about the role of text experts, those who were called, according to Greek etymology, the lovers, the zealous servants of texts—the philologists? Robert Darnton does not write a word about them. Even from the hand of a historian whose job consists more of studying ancient documents than of editing them, such an omission is surprising.

Philological Logic versus Industrial Logic:
Past versus Present versus Future

This omission is probably linked to the general evolution of large libraries toward economic and information management. To put it briefly, the activities of libraries during the twentieth century have shrunk to practical services and acquisition techniques, as well as cataloguing, preservation, and communication. The services have been promoted at the expense of research functions, despite the fact that judging from their background and status their most qualified staff, the library curators, with their academic training, are rather close to researchers. Correspondingly, researchers have shrunk into the role of passive users, pure readers, deprived of any operational responsibilities for thinking and organizing collections, and, of course, for preserving texts. There is no need, then, to insist more deeply on this, beside the fact that a long-term evolution is underlying this situation, due to the nature of the printing techniques: originals are reproduced, checked for accuracy, and enriched with commentaries in places and by specialists totally alienated from libraries. The real question that may be elicited from this state of things is this: can such a situation meet the requirement of the age of digital edition?

It was not the case at all at the Library of Alexandria, funded by Ptolemy, the Google of the Hellenistic era, with the purpose of "gathering all books on earth."[13] The major operation at that time, involving the translation into Greek of all manuscripts written in other languages, mobilized scholars on site. Following this model, libraries in late antiquity focused on "the sole objective [. . .] to collect, preserve and transmit knowledge, and as a consequence, texts which are their repositories," associating within their walls, or in their immediate vicinity, very different competences and functions. The scribes who were occupied with writing or restoring books were the ancestors not only of the medieval copyists but also of the contemporary text digitizers, encoders, and other taggers of the twenty-first century. They worked together with the ancestors of today's researchers—"the Fathers and great figures" employed by Emperor Constantius II, as was the case with the Vivarium in Calabria—to carry out all kinds of "critical exegetical" tasks; that is, collating texts, writing commentaries, as well as "other works of various literary genres" (Cavallo 2001, 264). As a result, a text production chain secures the preservation and reproduction of manuscript copies under the supervision of a circle of scholars endowed with various degrees of religious authority. Through the work of various historians one can discern the rough outlines of a genuine division of labor that did not wait for the modern industrial managerial theories of Frederick Winslow Taylor or Henry Ford. The most striking feature of this system is a strong unity of place, power, and ideology.

And now, in an era of intensive digitization of our textual heritage, what system of thought, what kind of organization, what type of hierarchy, what chain of professional skills would be the equivalent today?

Since October 2009 the municipal library of Lyon has begun implementing a contract made with Google with the aim of achieving the impossible industrial goal of digitizing two thousand books a month. In order to cope with these practical priorities, archivists and curators bound by this contract are most likely flanked by specialists who have been specifically subcontracted for this purpose. They barely have time to check the catalog entry of the books extracted in bulk from their old collections before the books are loaded onto trucks and brought to a secret "technical center," where they are digitized following a secret protocol and using a secret technology under the sole authority of the subcontractor. They are then repatriated by the same trucks, in principle undamaged, and put back on their shelves.[14] To date, no midterm evaluation of this process has been made public addressing the successes and difficulties that the project has met. Meanwhile, the BnF made a deal in 2007 with French companies that specialize in digitization, resulting in an increase from six thousand to one hundred thousand works digitalized each year.

However, while acknowledging the real progress that has been made, the experiences gained after several years of digitization of books and a report from the authorities allows one to exercise a critical look at this process and the control strategy that underlies it and to try to look beyond.

This commitment to the logic of "massive digitization," as noted by the general inspectors of the Ministry of Finance who authored the above-mentioned report, poses "serious internal organizational problems" to the BnF. The library "fails to keep the expected pace, even though a large number of personnel (more than sixty) are mobilized for this purpose." The "resulting dysfunctions" are so evident that the reporters suggest falling back on a "logic of qualitative selection" and reallocating credits to "a more restrictive number of better selected works that offer an increased value after being digitized." The institution, they argue, should focus on "the quality of the digital library, as well as the editorial support it could offer, as opposed to Google" (Azoulay et al. 2009). Such attitudes pave the road for a profoundly different, alternative approach.

It is actually the whole chain of production—from digitization to editorial support spanning from the preservation to the transmission of text—that is in question. If one accepts the view that the migration from one medium to another through the use of computer languages and digital encoding schemes is very similar to translating into a common language (a koine), the extrapolation made earlier from the origins of libraries to the present situation seems less irrelevant than one imagines after a first reading.

If the twenty-first-century guild of philologists were invited to take part in this endeavor as were their ancient ancestors in Alexandria or Vivarium, they would lack neither ideas nor work. Most probably these philologists would request that methods be as rigorous as those applied since eternities to originals on paper (stamping, cataloging, labeling, paginating, etc.). In the 1960s such methods, seen as modern and outstanding techniques, for preservation and reproduction continued to be applied to microfilms and microfiches. Librarians and curators, deprived of some of their former responsibilities and upset by intensive work pressures, have failed to request or have not been able to impose the following measures: first, that the service providers should add to the digital reproduction of a text's title page images that display the physical appearance of the volume (its cover or its spine, depending on the case); second, that one should take care to display, and even highlight, the physical location and catalog number of the digitized volume. Moving into this direction, the "permalink" adopted by Gallica for some years more naturally implements an electronic catalog numbering that is much shorter than the endless URL addresses introduced and institutionalized by Google.

This is not, as you may think, a secondary issue. The whole digital library philosophy is at stake here—or, rather, the lack of principles that these short-comings reveal. Let's take another example. When Gallica began and the collection managers were invited to provide the machines with a copy in order to produce the digital version that would represent each text on the BnF website, decisions were made for material reasons based on preservation requirements and short-term economy. It seemed natural to sacrifice a reprint, because it was in the public domain, because other libraries had a copy, or because it was in bad physical condition (binding worn out, brittle paper, etc.).[15] Other texts were deemed unsuitable for digitizing because the more or less invaluable binding of the rare copies of its one and only edition, even though also in the public domain, would have to be disassembled in order for the pages to be flattened for digital scanning. According to the BnF president, Bruno Racine, in the ongoing mass digitizing phase, nowadays it is "the poor physical state of a document or its non-standard format, and not its intrinsic value, which leads to excluding some documents from the quasi industrial process" (Racine 2007, 17). All BnF users now know that all bound books are excluded from manual photocopy-ing, and justly so. The odds are that such books will also be excluded from the industrial digitizing process.[16]

Have we really taken stock of the fact that this way of proceeding is an outrage to human intelligence? For financial and administrative reasons, and in order to counter Google's dominance, the BnF, an institution created by the French state to be in charge of its written heritage and commissioned to ensure that personal access is a near universal right for everybody, finds itself confined to the default policy of putting online first and foremost the cheapest editions, those whose text has not been verified nor eventually established and whose critical apparatus, when it exists, is based on outdated knowledge. For example, even today the web surfer browsing Gallica can see *Le Misanthrope* by Molière only in its nineteenth-century editions or, at best, those from the very end of the eighteenth century. Of course these editions are of interest, but they are largely posthumous and, consequently, inauthentic. Yet the BnF owns the *editio princeps* of 1667 and keeps it in its manuscript department, which for a printed work is quite an honor. This error is not an exception; it is the rule. The initial goal was never to open the holy grail to the public, nor even, to say it in neutral terms, to provide open access to the best documents. For well-known and fortunately obsolete reasons (a public debate on the ratio between the operating costs of the new "very large library" and the services offered), it must be acknowledged that the objective was to fill the site as quickly and as publicly as possible in order to please politicians and senior officials. In other words, the quality objective that should have been hierarchically on top was actually the last to be attended to chronologically and is still not fully recognized.

Notwithstanding controversies and important legal and economic differences, the pragmatic Google alliance solution chosen by the municipal library of Lyon and the French National Library solution using "a private grouping of competences" as service providers are in fact two variants of one and the same dominant and dominating digitization model: "mass digitization."[17] However this expression, probably flattering at a time when mass media dominate the scene, refers to a purely quantitative, and thus indistinctive, digitization conducted on an industrial scale with industrial methods, and, consequently, whether one likes it or not, according to also industrial criteria and objectives. However, quantity is not and will never be the same as exhaustiveness. Like selective digitization, an exhaustive digitization entails scrutiny, investigation, and research. This brings us back to the case of the *editio princeps* edition of *Le Misanthrope*, among the hundreds and thousands of original editions that deserve to be online, that have been overlooked or left behind, and that will probably not be given a second chance for quite a while. Finally, and not least important, because of the rights linked to the most recent critical editions, this model turns away from all the progress that textual criticism has made.

Lucidity obliges us to conclude with the complete and absolute antagonism of the industrial model with the philological ideal. A forgotten evidence must be strongly reaffirmed: this ideal is consistent only with a qualitative model, working at a small-scale level, and, consequently, a much smaller but more negotiated, more balanced, and more integrated model.

An Emerging Alternative

With the information it offers about itself, the already discussed Heinrich-Heine-Portal (see chapter 2) is probably the online critical edition that offers the best insight into the qualitative model of the future. This website or online database—functioning under the authority of a public cultural structure, an "institute" dedicated for quite some time to Heinrich Heine and housing the only museum dedicated to him—owns and maintains editions, manuscripts, correspondence, and portraits. Governed by the city of Düsseldorf, the poet's birthplace, the Heine Institute shares responsibility for the project with the Competence Center for communication and electronic publishing processes, a technical service within the Department of Human and Social Sciences of the University of Trier. Not too many clicks are needed to find detailed information about the people doing the work: the project leader, Bernd Füllner, an academic specialist of Heine and a member of this institute; eight other academics; three members of the Competence Center; three members of the Heine Institute; and a dozen occasional collaborators, including a member with a PhD in computer science from the University of Trier. This adds up to a total of twenty-seven people, almost evenly distributed between philologists and engineers or technicians. In a remarkably frank admission, however, the Heinrich-Heine-Portal reports that the 26,500 or so pages of text (corresponding to about 72 million characters) have been captured and tagged with double-keying data entry by a Chinese service provider. After this task was completed, the XML data conversion was performed in Trier and was followed by an ultimate control by philologists.[18]

Although smaller in size, because it is limited to a single work of Flaubert, the successful project of online publication of the manuscripts, pre-texts, and the text of *Madame Bovary* confirms some key observations that could have been inferred from another example, the electronic Norwegian edition of *Henrik Ibsen's Writings*:

- Control and administration is in the hands of a more or less para-academic local institution whose duty is to cultivate the memory of the author.
- Engineers, technicians, and computer operators have a considerable role.
- The project is managed by philologists.

In this particular case the contracting authority is the Rouen Municipal Library, in support of the Flaubert Center of Rouen University, and the project managers are an academic, Yvan Leclerc, director of this center, and a high school teacher, Danielle Girard, who is particularly active in the management and organization of a team of six other reviewers and a network of 130 unpaid volunteer transcribers. This network is itself the core of a set of 600 participants from seventeen different countries worldwide (including sixteen-year-old teenagers as part of their French classes). The Bovary site is less integrated than the Heine portal, because, hosted by a municipal server, it is the foundation of a construction with a scalable architecture (the work in progress involves numerous projects that should result, at an undetermined date, in the digital publication of all of Flaubert's works). A substantial part of the work and information on the collaborators and the scientific objectives can be found on the twin site of the Gustave Flaubert Center, itself the emanation of an academic team and, as such, installed on a Rouen University server.[19] The team of philologists coming from the two sites totals nine members. The computer team has five members, belonging to the LITIS,[20] a computer research unit under the supervision of three institutions in the same region of the Haute-Normandie: an engineering school, the Rouen Institut national des sciences (INSA, or National Institute of Applied Sciences), and the Universities of Rouen and Le Havre. However, the philologists seem to have had only a design and supervision role, as two freelance information technology professionals developed the search engine, created the interface, structured the teleworking collaborative environments, and produced the website. Otherwise two civil servants from the library of the

University of Rouen were employed for unspecified tasks, with the addition of a photographer, who produced the high-resolution images of the original documents, and two computer graphic artists—a profession ignored in the organization chart of the Heinrich-Heine-Portal—who are responsible for the functional and aesthetic setting display. The total of professionals involved amounts to twenty-one people, transcribers not included.[21]

Reflecting on the experience with a good sense of humor and a literary capacity for understatement, Yvan Leclerc presents a schematic account of the team operation, highlighting the disparity of goals and thus the internal tensions of the project:

> The curators preserve: when digitizing, they serve the double task of preserving and ensuring public access. Even if they are not insensitive to derived intellectual added value, they give a privileged attention for the heritage that has been entrusted to them. As a consequence, the Municipal Library has not considered as a priority publishing on their site the documentary notes of *Madame Bovary*, that are preserved at the Bodmer Foundation, in Geneva, inasmuch as they do not belong to their own collection. The researchers do research: what constitutes an arrival point for curators constitutes a starting point for them. The primary material must be processed and assembled intellectually in order to be usable for future work. They are interested in the entire genetic records of the work, wherever these are physically stored. The computer scientists compute without always understanding the specific research requirements, and sometimes at the expense of a content that computer engineers ought to learn to serve silently instead of using it as a foil. (Leclerc 2006, 237)

Yet, *Madame Bovary* and the Heinrich-Heine-Portal are not the only digital critical edition sites to operate in this way. There are three other remarkable examples in this regard:

- The hosting by the Maison de Balzac, in Paris, of the online *Comédie humaine* produced in collaboration by the Groupe international de recherches balzaciennes[22]
- The publication of the Stendhal manuscripts by the Grenoble municipal library, in Stendhal's native city, with the scientific collaboration between a Stendhal University French literature team and a linguistic team from the same university, very much focused on automatic language processing and on informatics in general[23]
- The commitment of the University of Oslo to the critical edition of Ibsen, with the participation of specialists of the work involved and the assistance of text technology experts from the former Norwegian Computing Center for the Humanities at the University of Bergen (now UniDigital, formerly Aksis Unifob)[24]

It seems that we are witnessing the birth of a tripartite cooperation model between (1) librarians or the curators of patrimonial institutions, each of them owning, so to speak, a piece of the authentic relic (manuscripts, original editions, homes, furniture, or other memorabilia); (2) philologists who are academically recognized as specialists of the author concerned; and (3) computer engineers who are specialized in digital documents.

No doubt such cooperation involves difficulties and requires adaptations. Yvan Leclerc's testimony quoted above is quite explicit: the three associates each have distinct and sometimes divergent work specifications as well as distinct institutional and corporate interests—not to mention the situation of the computer specialists, who are not always at ease with the "natural" logic of humanities. It is clear that it puts to the test the two oldest corporations, obliged to either renew themselves deeply or give up some of their ground. Thus an ongoing debate among the most qualified personnel, be they librarians or curators, is whether they should be integrating documentary competences in their professions and in their initial and permanent training as the computerization of their catalogs and the digitization of their contents have brought digital data collection, management, and exploitation to the heart of their missions. This is especially challenging in France, where these two professions, librarian and documentalist, have developed separately. For their part, those philologists who turn to digital critical editing, even if they intend to be only users of new technologies, will not be able to manage without some training, even elementary, not only in computer programming but also in basic principles and effects in digital media—in other words, communication sciences. Emboldened by their mastery of these new tools, these information and communication sciences are rapidly growing in higher education, have at least partly assimilated literary methods, and are close to challenging the literary monopoly on texts. Finally, specialists in corpus linguistics are among emerging partners for philologists. Without intervening on the contents as such, they offer to use information sciences to renew discourse analysis methods (see Adam and Viprey 2009).

Nevertheless, the role of philologist remains, more than ever, inherently essential and central as part of the chain of operations and even as part of the human networks springing up, within which new products are built and communicated. As explained in chapter 2, it is the philologist's scientific authority, practiced most often within a team, that has the upper hand not only on the establishment of the text and its enrichment by a critical apparatus but also on the additional editorial responsibilities: he or she has to determine which are the necessary original documents and select the best; certify the digital copies; and conceive a corpus, its intellectual architecture, its reading paths, its internal and external links, and other details.

The Problem of Economic Structures and Models

This is certainly not the place to discuss the future or the morality of triumphing capitalism, its creativity or its devastating effects, its intelligence or its blindness, its exclusive submission to profit or its capacity to serve philanthropic objectives. But it is not outside of our considerations to situate critical editions within the context of ongoing restructuring of the media economy. These more or less random yet massive changes do and will influence digital texts in the same way that texts were changed by the development of printing and by the expansion of bookshops and the growth of the periodic press.

Even if the broad outlines of this future are still far from being written, the agenda of the 2010s, so to say, seems to be both a tendency toward a growing influence of the private sector and a tendency for industrial enterprises toward agglomeration and concentration. Thus the main online bookstore, Amazon, did not stop at selling traditional paper books, but made headlines as early as 2007 with the success of its Kindle, one of the first reading machines to have really gone beyond the prototype stage to become a well-distributed commercial product. Thus Amazon can also sell digital books. For its part, the most innovative computer manufacturer, Apple, has become engaged in wireless telephony and with dazzling rapidity succeeded in imposing a new kind of smartphone through what has become its flagship product, the iPhone. Not satisfied in having established a dominant position in the online music market with its version of Sony's Walkman, the iPod, and its application store, iTunes, since 2010 Apple has clearly set up the goal of a similar success in multimedia, especially with e-books, by coupling its tactile tablet, the iPad, and its agreements with publishers who are interested in providing content, such as the Perseus Books Group, owner of Public Affairs (the publisher incidentally referred to above). On the contrary, Google Inc., whose power was initially built exclusively through the famous algorithm of its search engine, is moving more and more toward hardware. Not satisfied with having gained a foothold in mobile telephony (with its open source operating system, Android, bought in 2005 and developed since under the Google leadership, as well as a smartphone that Google has introduced, the Nexus tablet), Google is taking its share of the tablet sector through the adoption of its Android operating system by different manufacturers—the American Motorola, the Chinese Lenovo, the Korean Samsung, or the French Archos—but also through its own tablet, the above-mentioned Nexus. What has particularly caught our attention is its online "open" bookstore project—that is, a bookstore that can be accessed from any terminal connected to the Internet. This service would connect to different bookstores partnered with Google eBooks but would also include

Google's own online bookstore, Google eBookstore.[25] The strategy here is to bypass Amazon by leading the Internet surfer who is browsing with Google to purchase books directly through Google, and if Google does not have the book, connecting him directly with the network of independent bookstores in partnership with Google. In other words, he is routed away from Google's direct competitors, especially away from Amazon. So that no one gets the wrong idea about what the term "independent bookstores" implies, it is sufficient to state that in November 2010 the Hachette Book Group, third-largest worldwide publisher, signed a memorandum of understanding with Google Editions to digitize the books whose royalties are under the control of Hachette France. Given these circumstances, the anxiety of traditional publishers and their partners—that is, the bookstores—is perfectly understandable. Will they be able to set up in time online distribution platforms that are capable of competing with the platforms of the American companies? It is not surprising that in fighting back against the wall for their survival they are opposing a fierce resistance to the Google bookstore, which at the time of this writing, moreover, remains blocked at the border by different countries, including France and Norway.[26] A collateral consequence of this struggle for life is that in the concerns of the publishers closest to intellectual creation, digital critical editions are relegated to last place. In so doing these publishers align themselves, wrongly perhaps, not only with Amazon, Google, and Apple but also with large international publishing groups such as Hachette, Bertelsmann, Elsevier, or Springer, for whom critical editions constitute a negligible market share.

Presently, the publishers' confrontation with Google confines them to an e-book logic that is completely opposite to the emerging critical edition and text archive logic we have referred to above. In the United States as well as in Europe, as evidenced by the ongoing trials against Google's unauthorized digitizations, some of which have had significant successes, the issue of the book saturates the public debate.[27] One has only to look at the way Antoine Gallimard, president of the French National Publishing Association (Syndicat national de l'édition, or SNE) and director of the publishing house of the same name, incites the French government to regulate digital publications with measures similar to those existing for the printed books: a single selling price (international market included) and a reduced rate on the value-added tax (VAT). The two "basic principles" on which his argument rests leave no room for the assumption of any new form or structure of the digital book:

> The digital book is primarily a book. Basically an intellectual work, the nature of a book does not change because the media changes from paper to digital file. The nature of music also does not change when going from LP to cassette, then from CD to MP3.

> To publish is to make a work available to readers, wherever they are, in a book-
> store or in front of a screen. [. . .] It is the same exploitation that must be coordi-
> nated by a publisher whose job it is to harmonize the distribution of the work in
> different media and channels. (Gallimard 2011)

In alliance with authors and booksellers, the publishers' strategy is therefore
to replicate in digital form, as much as possible, the economic model that has
proven so successful in print. This can easily be confirmed by referring to the
standard contract and endorsements that a publisher of critical editions as important as *Les Classiques Garnier* obliges all of its authors, including its scholarly
editors, to sign. Under the unequivocal heading "Multimedia Contract," the
document cautiously includes in its scope "any computer processing technique,
current or future, open (Internet, WAP, etc.) or closed (Intranet, internal library
network, or company network, etc.) allowing access to contents by users through
servers or any magnetic, optical, digital or electronic, present or future recording
media." Extending to digital publishing the copyrights usually applied to printed
publishing, it stipulates that the "reproduction, representation, adaptation and
translation rights" include "the rights to digitize, store and reproduce all or part
of the 'work' and its adaptations and translations on all memories of all devices
for storing scanned data, such as a computer hard disk, an e-book (electronic
book), PDAs, smart phones, CD-ROM, DVD-ROM, DivX, etc."[28]

But that is not all. In anticipation of scholarly multimedia sites that could
constitute the highest standard for tomorrow's digital critical editions, this
same contract does not omit the "right to inclusion in a multimedia work or
adaptation in the form of a multimedia work," specifying that "multimedia"
here refers not to audiovisual productions but to the combination on the same
media, "generally digital," of "works of different nature, such as photographs,
reproduction of works of art, texts, musical sequences, services by artists and
performers, whose structure and access is controlled by software allowing interactivity and consultation." Finally, in order to take into account all the new
ownership forms to which the sociologists of modernity attach great importance,
and which can be fragmented and focused on the right of access or use, the same
contract includes among the publisher's rights "the right to collect and organize
the collection in all countries of the rights due lending or renting copies of the
'work,' its adaptations and translations on any media."

Will these legal walls be sufficient to curb the momentum of the "major
technological operators," to quote the euphemistic expression used by Antoine
Gallimard? Traditional publishers have tended to be slow in investing in digital
processes, especially multimedia. Will the pressure of competition be sufficient
to bring them to renew and impose their expertise in producing, distributing,
and promoting printed works? More is at stake here for critical editions than

for essays or contemporary fiction, as answering these questions is less a matter of rational forecasting than one of economic and technological hypotheses for the future.

The uncertainties relate primarily to the cost and the profitability and therefore, more generally, the economic model. We are not concerned here with the category of critical editions as e-books, whose economic model is within sight, despite what Antoine Gallimard is saying,[29] but mainly with the category of critical editions/database, the future of which is still uncertain.

While the level of return on investment of a film can be quite high, and the time necessary to attain and surpass its equilibrium point relatively short, as is the case for a successful book, the situation of critical editions is a quite different matter. It is much more difficult to play on the novelty aspect, and the work upgraded by the efforts of the philologist initially interests only a very limited public and must count on long-term appeal. Demonstrated by its survival, its attractiveness certainly offers long-term guarantees. But when observing the productions available today, one is forced to acknowledge that private publishers, with rare exceptions heavily subsidized by public resources and whose commercial success is not so spectacular, are reluctant to venture further into digital critical editing.[30] That is why the vast majority of the small number of productions is due to essentially public, and never recovered, financial arrangements, sometimes supplemented by public or private patronage.[31]

Production costs are rarely consolidated and thus are practically never published. To get an idea of these costs, *Henrik Ibsen's Writings*, a hybrid edition that promises to be a model of its kind, provides a valuable benchmark: NOK 70 million (nearly EUR 9 million) finally for the sixteen imposing bound twin volumes and originally NOK 5 million (approximately EUR 625,000) for the digital edition itself, excluding the fixed salaries of tenured philologists. This is the amount for eleven years of work (1999–2010), taking into account the fact that the first public funding includes several fairly heavy expenditure items that only a digital edition must necessarily assume initially (secretarial work, scanning, transcription, collation, XML markup). The total investment, amounting to grossly EUR 10 million, is to be partly compensated by the sale of books at a price lower than actual costs in order not to be prohibitive. This slow redemption—which is only partial, since the online edition will be accessible free of charge—can be compared to the original edition of a cinematographic production: the notable art-house film *La Princesse de Montpensier*, directed in 2009 by filmmaker Bertrand Tavernier and adapted from a short story by Mme de La Fayette, had a rather modest budget of EUR 13.5 million.[32] A second point of comparison, upstream this time, can be made with the acquisition of the material essential for a critical edition: the author's manuscripts. Here's an example that will add to the vertigo of philologists, who are used to counting in thousands of euros for their paper editions: at a public auction in 2009 by the municipal library of Grenoble, the preemption of the 335 manuscript pages of Stendhal required more than EUR 900,000.[33] Taking into account the fact that the library's Stendhal collection already contained 40,000 pages, its total current value at this rate would amount to over EUR 100 million. In terms of public service, these proportions more than adequately justify the curators' will to provide a maximum of accessibility to this municipal heritage and this *gratis pro Deo*. The cost of simple scanning, scientific description, and transcription of these pages, along with their critical enhancement, would never exceed some 10 to 15 percent of their market value, and would amount to much less (a few percentage points) without philological enrichment. But it is also obvious that if the entire chain of investments is taken into account, neither the capital of traditional publishing houses nor even the funds allocated for humanities research are at the level required for the task.

Even leaving aside profitability, the sole payback of these investments would require either that all material produced would be commercially published on a disk (as with the model used for the Bergen Electronic Edition of Wittgenstein's *Nachlass* [BEE]); or that renewable access rights would be established in more or less grouped subscriptions (as with library or museum access passes or with access through payment per article for online scholarly journals); or that an online bookstore–private library would be developed where one could download not files, but databases.

Conceding exploitation to private publishers is an alternative that could inspire greater numbers of cultural heritage institutions to undertake enhancement of their textual heritage. These publishers would probably try to produce less costly commercial versions, thus taking advantage of the encoding already performed and especially of the philological added value: books, e-books, or digital files intended for different uses or market segments (specialists, enlightened amateurs, schools, universities, etc.). This is the line followed by the French National Library when it asks for royalties for any commercial use of its files of documents downloadable on Gallica.[34] Is this not what publishing houses have learned through centuries of printing production when they exchange for modest counterparts the knowledge accumulated by scholarly research and the public library resources?

The Problem of Legal Philosophy: Property versus Commons? Toward a Conclusion

Besides the economy and the market, another great cloud of uncertainty that has already been foreseen in previous analyses deters one from establishing as clear an outlook as one would like when it comes to the future of digital critical editions. These doubts concern the invention of legal solutions to deal with the new questions that digital editing brings up. In this regard we need to have a general approach without losing sight of the specific problems. Among those problems, we must examine the very particular nature and the best achievements of critical editions that are already available digitally.

Some digital critical editions are—and in the future will still be—digital books; in other words, digital copies of existing paper editions or their representation on a screen of virtual paper editions. In fact, this scenario is the only one, to our knowledge, that is included in the major trials against Google that have already been arbitrated or are ongoing. The standard editing contract we referred to above foresees this and frames it quite well. There is no reason to dissociate this rather straightforward variety of digital critical editions from the common lot of essays, novels, practical books, beautiful books, and art books—books already existing or that will soon invade our tactile tablets or our portable computers to be flicked and possibly annotated. Digitization is now at the negotiating stage, where the balance of power will decide what formal arrangements need to be made—the most serious difficulty, but also the most promising horizon, being copyright on the one hand, and on the other, royalties and the single book price. However, one can bet that in fear of hackers already picking up those books online (they have already succeeded in moving them freely, as with music files and films, to peer-to-peer file-sharing networks[35]), Gallimard publishers have not yet decided to upload their precious Bibliothèque de la Pléiade series on Eden Livres (a digital distribution company), the platform they have shared since 2009 with publishing companies Flammarion and La Martinière.

However, the problem is quite different with digital critical editions set up as databases and where this feature—or, more exactly, logic—constitutes the most interesting element. There has not been much discussion on the decision taken in 2006 by the European Union to extend the copyright to multimedia databases in order to protect intellectual property.[36] Furthermore, this copyright applies to their structure as well as their content. This has resulted in a major and regrettable consequence: the great editorial endeavors described (Heine, Ibsen, Nietzsche, etc.), some of them discussed in this chapter, are closed systems, worlds that are mostly incapable of intercommunicating, in brief, monads. Now, it just so happens that this segregated system is not only contrary to the recognized ethical and technical principles of the digital revolution. It also contravenes to the meaning regimes of the textual and documentary contents of these editions, whose interactional and reticular nature have been revealed by intertextuality and intermediality theories. In the cases studied here the "author" status of the concerned philologists is never mentioned explicitly as such, as the Creative Commons licenses tend to replace the copyright. To this day there has been no confirmation of the lucrative stimulant effects of such extensions of the notion of copyright, as we have been told by some experts, that could justify its application to printed works.[37] We do not intend to discuss this immense topic further, but only to integrate it with the perspective we are establishing here.

Identification and free disposal of digital common goods, including conservation, transmission, and permanent reinterpretation of heritage texts, are topics that partake of the discussions strongly punctuated by the Open Source Initiative (launched in Palo Alto in 1998) and the Budapest Open Access Initiative (launched in 2001) and that the World Social Forum of Belem (2009) chose to mention in its manifesto "Reclaim the Commons."[38] The notions of open sources, open access, and commons are, needless to say, completely new with regard to the "cultural goods" notion made official in 1970 by UNESCO. It is this notion that about ten years before the Open Source Initiative led to the recognition by the same United Nations authority of the much more encompassing and convergent "immaterial cultural heritage."[39] Lawrence Lessig, a professor of law and the main initiator of the Creative Commons, enlightens us in exhorting us to consider the problem not as an ideological one, but as one to be taken very seriously, while it is still time, and at its proper level. The real issue, he says, is to decide on the limits to be established between the code layer and the content layer and, within this last one, between the open (free) contents and the protected (paying) contents. It is the drawing of such boundaries, according to Lessig, that conditions the accessibility of digital common goods. These boundaries must therefore be established in such a way so as to feed and stimulate Internet creativity rather than curb it.[40] More radically still, Roger Chartier, with the benefit of hindsight coming from his mastery of comparative book history dating back to the sixteenth century, dares to ask if copyright could turn out to be a parenthesis in history and if the twenty-first century is not entering into "a world of circulation of works that is radically different from all the esthetical and legal criteria that have governed the constitution of artistic and literary property." This leads the historian to wonder about the mutability of the works themselves, underlining how much "the electronic text is an open, malleable, polyphonic text."[41] Such afterthoughts are of prime interest for philologists, inasmuch as they have the responsibility of guaranteeing the works' authenticity, of ensuring their integrity, and even, perhaps, of accompanying their posthumous life.

Awareness that this issue transcends economy and requires intervention and rules tends to be, as is the case with common sense, according to Descartes, "the best shared thing in the world." This has been largely illustrated by the controversy and initiatives of the French state, followed by those of the European Union, triggered in 2005 by *Google and the Myth of Universal Knowledge: A View from Europe* (2007), the twice-reprinted and amply translated book by

Jean-Noël Jeanneney, media historian and then president of the French National Library. It is hoped, however, that the discussion goes beyond the new impetus that has come about with the mass digitization of the BnF and its only library, Gallica, beyond also the birth of Europeana, the multilingual library/archives/museum/music library/film library/etc., created in 2008 by the European Union. Should not all digital copies, including their encoding and their indexing on the Internet, be declared common goods and managed by national and international instances? And should this status and backing not be more or less equally given to the contents and structure of editions produced with a lot of public subventions as database websites? All of these suggestions, it must be made clear, essentially concern the shareable and less questionable part of this new edition type. What would remain optional are the inclusion in the common domain of the particular computer architectures, proposals for text revisions, inventive reading paths, and unpublished explanations or interpretations whose "authors" and, where appropriate, "editors" would like to retain moral copyright and intellectual mastery.

The tenacity with which some sponsors and partners of the Ibsen edition have been competing for gaining control over the digital version, up to the point of delaying for several years its publication online, clearly illustrates that plain market economy in these matters is in no way the mistress of the game. Obviously equal at stake here are institutional or political communication, power symbols, as well as principles and values (and not only money). The physical and symbolic link that has already been observed (territorial, biographical, virtually consubstantial) between a greater part of digital critical editions and the institutions that carry them is due not only to ownership of the originals or of premises. Just as this ownership is frequently motivated by a memory to preserve and present, digital editorial activity, apparently motivated by scientific and cultural purposes, is simultaneously and deeply driven by claims of belonging and identity. This explains why it is the tourist bureau of a small town in southern France, Pézenas (approximately nine thousand inhabitants), that has the responsibility of the multi-public (schoolchildren, amateurs, researchers) reference site dedicated to Molière's comedies. One can read the complete critically established and annotated versions. The reason for such a cult, as explained on the website, is the six-year stay in Pézenas of the playwright's drama company, which gave rise to the "Flame of Remembrance of Molière" that is loyally rekindled and maintained in the city since the nineteenth century.[42] The French National Library would certainly be very embarrassed if it would be charged with a mission, such as the Norwegian National Library has for Ibsen, to erect a critical monument to all the notables of the French national literary pantheon, or, in order to cope with the large number, to privilege some while rejecting the greater part in purgatory or in hell. On what criteria would their choices be based? And with the authors chosen, how can one escape the charge of wanting to impose a state culture, or even of wanting to institute something like a state ideology or religion? That is why in his counterattack against Google unleashed since 2005, Jean-Noël Jeanneney, the former president of the French National Library (2002–2007), has set forth arguments in favor of a public model for digitizing the country's textual heritage that have endeavored to reach the maximal level of consensus: in defense of the French language, of francophony, and of the French and European cultural autonomy against the Anglo-Saxon "domination."[43] His successor, Bruno Racine, is open to the idea of a conditional alliance with Google on more technical grounds, focusing on the survival of the book format as central to the survival of "intelligence." This has led him to the hypothesis that when massively digitizing French books preserved outside of France, Google could actually turn out to be the most efficient "propagator" of "our cultural heritage."[44] At the level of the Europeana initiative, this last argument is in line with the vision of preserving the linguistic and cultural diversity of the countries of the European Union. A variant of this sublimation of a national motive by the international motive of understanding between people through culture is that of bilateralism. It is Franco-American friendship, for instance, that motivates the collection of French writings of the seventeenth and eighteenth centuries about the French colonies of North America and the United States in *statu nascendi* (exploration voyages, narratives, and testimonies relating to the contribution of France to the foundation of the American Republic).[45] It is also Franco-German friendship that forms the background of the project of a "Franco-German corpus on the history of Protestantism."[46] Thus, at a macro level as well as a micro level, we are ultimately brought back not to economy and market arbitrations but to priceless values, to ethno-anthropology, and to considerations relating to the building of cultures and their interrelationships.

As determining as these general challenges may be for digital critical editions, however, a conclusion that addresses more concrete issues seems more appropriate. After having taken into account such an exciting and overwhelming context, have we succeeded in drawing the reader's attention to what appears to us to be the crucial issue: the necessity to anchor digital edition in digital critical textual scholarship? In our opinion, such a question is the quintessential question.

Every reader of this book should allow himself or herself to engage in a summary investigation of the websites, blogs, and articles that constitute a reference in digital textual studies: does the adjective "critical" appear, and if it does, how many times does it appear? It is a plain fact that in 2010 two specialists of digital edition, Marin Dacos and Pierre Mounier—whose theoretical approach relies on a widely acknowledged practice, as witnessed by the French web portal for scholarly journals Revue.org—managed to publish a tentative synthesis about digital edition (Dacos and Mounier 2010; see also Dacos 2010) with neither addressing nor mentioning this topic.

However, to repeat this issue with emphasis: in the digital sphere, critical edition adds to its traditional tasks new specific tasks that are of crucial importance for the textual heritage and for its commercial as well as its cultural revaluation:

- Facilitating the *memory* of text and their *certification*—in other words, securing their intellectual transmission; preserving their identity, their integrity, and their original qualities, and, if needed, their *restoration*; correcting all kinds of corruptions at all levels resulting from their industrial or amateur-like digitization and their wild dissemination (introducing word errors, lacunae, interpolations, etc.)
- Facilitating their *selection, organization,* and, to some extent, their *legitimation* and their *hierarchization* within identified and structured wholes, the aim being to provide or preserve a place for them in literature despite the large and universally pervading atomization of works—in other words, physical libraries generated by mass digitization
- Facilitating their *explanation and enrichment* by providing *commentaries* through means of a *critical apparatus,* without which, as time passes, these texts, disembedded from their original context, stripped of their history, and kept aside from the accumulated knowledge about them, will lose their readability and, in the worst or best case, will not gain any new readability

In spite of what seems to be the evolution of Google Books toward a Google eBookstore equipped with "bookshelves" that are classified according to very vague categories such as "Biographies & Memoirs," "Cooking, Food & Wines," "Textbooks," "Science Fiction & Fantasy," and so on, Google eBookstore is still struggling to fill its bookshelves with advertised selections of e-books.[47] It is obvious that this task is not the responsibility, nor the primary interest, nor part of the competence of this huge international private digital network operator that with neither control nor external norms has claimed the power to digitize, index, and distribute on the Internet "millions of books from all the world from libraries and publishers."

However, when libraries begin to care about creating digital libraries, and when publishers begin to publish digital books, both of which are indeed the case, we can foresee that in a medium- to long-term perspective they will turn toward philologists and ask for their assistance to conceive and build collections and digital critical editions.

Notes

1. Calmann-Lévy has now merged into the Hachette Book Group, which contributed so much to the promotion of literature in the nineteenth century.
2. See Mollier 1984, 340f and 378f.

3. And while pursuing a vision possibly driven by a residue of the academic ethics and philanthropic views that inspired the beginnings of Larry Page and Sergey Brin's search engine.

4. This famous formula can be found at the top of the main page of Google's website at http://www.google.com/intl/fr/corporate.

5. Here we touch only superficially on a discussion about the notions of "collection" and the "value of a collection." It is not because some old books have no commercial value and hardly any use value that a collection of these books, even if it is not sellable, does not possess an unquantifiable cultural value. In this case, as in many others, the whole is greater than the sum of its parts.

6. See http://droits.reproduction.free.fr/images/Librissimo.ppt.

7. An example is Alphonse Daudet's *Les femmes d'artistes* (1878).

8. Some texts of this library can be found at the Phénix site (see bibliography).

9. This paragraph in the main text was written in June 2011. As for what concerns texts belonging to the public domain, the BnF has since resumed producing digital reprints that are expected to become profitable thanks to the online bookstore. In October 2011, the BnF entered into a special partnership with two private French publishers, The-BookEdition (http://TheBookEdition.fr) and Edilivre (http://www.Edilivre.fr), both recently established and specialized in self-publishing. Selling reprints online at rates similar to those charged for new books of the same size, these two partners of the public institution now offer on-demand digital reprints of one hundred thousand ancient volumes cataloged by the Gallica digital library. The financial terms of the agreement with these two companies have not been made public. At the same time, the duplication department of the BnF continues to provide high-definition digital images to its readers and customers at the same rates that were charged before this agreement. So far the BnF has not raised the possibility of marketing these ancient texts as e-books online, probably because of the lack of competence and decision-making power of the contractors, who are facing a major editorial problem discussed in the conclusion to this chapter: should one be able to at least certify the quality of the text, and, most important, should one be able to transform and enrich textual data to make an edition worthy of being considered a digital critical edition? Such an endeavor necessarily involves the work of philologists—a slow and difficult craftsmanship practiced on a case-by-case basis, but one that alone can restore the intellectual and commercial value of a text. Copyrighted critical editions published in the twentieth century but no longer commercialized probably represent a category of books that are implicitly already part of a recent framework agreement between the BnF and Edilivre, waiting for a future reform of intellectual property laws in France, but already approved and ratified by the French Association of Publishers (SNE) and the French Association of Writers (SGDL). This framework agreement plans to digitize five hundred thousand books that fall into this definition within five years. The operation is to be carried out by a subsidiary of Edilivre, i-Kiosk (http://www. i-Kiosk.fr), and financed by government funds designated to promote the development of digital economy. Digital copies of these copyrighted books will be accessible through Gallica. Hence, these books can experience a new commercial life—this time not on paper, but online and in e-book format.

10. See http://www.numilog.com/Pages/Livres/Fiche.aspx?LIVRE_ID=58079.

11. See http://www.gutenberg-e.org.

12. The text is quoted from the digital Kindle version of Darnton's original 2010 text.

13. Quotations in this paragraph are borrowed from Sirinelli (2001, 46f), himself also receptive to the analogy between the current digital ambition and the ancient dream of "'Globalization' by the book" inspired in Ptolemy by the philosopher Demetrius Phalereus.

14. See particularly an article signed by Patrick Bazin, director of the municipal library of Lyon in the newspaper *Le Monde,* September 12, 2009 (Bazin 2009, 21). See also Bruno Icher's article in the newspaper *Libération* (Icher 2009, 4).

15. Sacrificing in this context implies first cutting up the book and then destroying it. Scanners and OCR programs produced acceptable results only with pages that were lying completely flat.

16. The BnF published a video on this matter online in July 2010. It is accessible on its website (see bibliography) or on YouTube and briefly covers the process and techniques but not the problems. One of these is that the so-called manual or semi-automatic digitization for works that need to be opened delicately is simply not feasible if the binding is in bad shape, or if the sides of the text are too close to the margin and the page cannot be laid flat but has a curvature that is too accentuated to allow retrieval of all the text. Different methods are available, ranging from recovery of the image through computer processing to a more radical manual solution that affects the authenticity of the document and is very expensive and difficult to implement. It involves undoing the original binding and, after having photographed the pages, rebinding them, trying to be as close to the original as possible. Laudably, the BnF has put online a file named "La Numérisation de masse à la BnF" (mass digitization at BnF) with all the details pertaining to the digitization process in an effort to be as transparent as possible on these issues. See bibliography.

17. The main members in this consortium of service providers are the two companies Jouve and SAFIG. (Jouve has since taken control of SAFIG.)

18. The quantitative coverage of workforce stops at the door of the Chinese company. Seldom disclosed but well known, the use of subcontracting a large French-speaking workforce at low cost, in particular Malagasies, is also part of French digital operators' practices. The use of manual labor for data capture is required because research and development of automatic OCR of old printed texts (before the twentieth century) has not yet provided solutions with an acceptable error rate. It is difficult to know if the technology developed by Google on this issue has reduced the percentage of manual interventions. Users nevertheless note that it is effective but remains far short of the philological norm of 100 percent accuracy, particularly for old printed texts. All of this information can be found on the Heinrich-Heine-Portal site (see Groß 2005).

19. Centre d'Études et de Recherche Éditer/Interpréter (CÉRÉdI, EA 3229). The URL address is http://www.bovary.fr.

20. Laboratoire d'Informatique, de Traitement de l'Information et des Systèmes, EA 4108.

21. All of this information can be found on the above-mentioned site.

22. See bibliography.

23. See full reference to the site Les Manuscrits de Stendhal in the bibliography.

24. See detailed reference to the upcoming electronic edition of *Henrik Ibsen's Writings* in the bibliography.

25. Accessible online at http://books.google.com/ebooks.

26. With regard to the digitization of now unavailable but still copyrighted works (i.e., as digital reprints on demand), Hachette Livre, the largest French publisher and second-largest world publisher, signed a final agreement with Google in July 2011. The publisher selects works to be digitized and shares part of benefits from sales not only with authors but also with public institutions such as BnF (see Hertzberg 2011). However, the majority of French publishers with no presence in the U.S. market are still in legal litigation with Google and appear to have opted to develop their own online platform. This is especially true of those publishers with catalogs boasting of a whole spectrum of critical editions that contribute greatly to their reputation, such as Gallimard, Garnier, Flammarion, or Presses Universitaires de France (PUF). On Norway, see Holm and Lorentzen 2010.

27. When approached by the Open Book Alliance, consisting of Microsoft, Yahoo! and Amazon (http://openbookenalliance.org) and allied with the Authors' Guild (http://authorsguild.org) and the Association of American Publishers (http://www.publishers .org), the U.S. Department of Justice was sensitive to the argument that Google, under the guise of a digital library, was actually building a large monopolistic "department store" (see Cypel 2010). On March 22, 2011, the U.S. Department of Justice broke the agreement that had been signed between the firm and the Association of American Publishers concerning the copyrighted works (information published in *Le Monde* on March 23, 2011, under the title "La justice américaine rejette l'accord entre Google et les éditeurs" [US Justice invalidates the agreement between Google and publishers]). Moreover, we know that in December 2009, the French La Martinière/Le Seuil publishing group had won its case against Google in its proceedings with the French Justice Department in connection with the French National Publishing Association and the French Association of Writers. The arguments used during the case were based on the counterfeiting of copyrighted works and the noncompliance with the moral rights of authors. (See, for example, Artus 2009a and 2009b).

28. The wording here is from standard contracts proposed to authors by this publisher.

29. In the standpoint already quoted, Antoine Gallimard does not question so much the production costs of the files than the costs for protecting and distributing "on complex platforms varying according to the technological environment" (2011). An independent study commissioned by *le Motif* (Observatory of Books and Written texts of the Île-de-France Region (hhtp://lemotif.fr) confirms the relative expensiveness of a distributing platform (the minimal investment would be EUR 500,000). However, it estimates the digital conversion costs of a novel of 256 pages at the ridiculous amount of EUR 151, setting the balance point at forty-six copies for a selling price of EUR 12.99. ("Livre électronique" 2010). Except perhaps a small additional cost to facilitate the to-ing

and fro-ing between text and critical apparatus at the end of the volume, the case of the conversion of a critical edition already published on paper is, of course, comparable to that of a novel with a similar number of pages.

30. See the case of the Bergen Electronic Edition of Wittgenstein's *Nachlass* produced at the Wittgenstein Archives at the University of Bergen (WAB; http://wab.aksis.uib .no/index.page), which seems to be withdrawing from the commercial market. Also see the French case of the exhaustive corpus of Montaigne's works and their editions up to the twentieth century at Electronic Champion, renamed since 2008 as Garnier Digital Classics. The prohibitive selling price is not within the reach of institutions. In 2005 the price of the first edition on CD-ROM began at £600 (without the facsimiles) and at £1,000 (with the facsimiles) for individuals (£1,600 and £2,400, respectively, for institutions). Presently, the the edition with the facsmiles seems to be available only through subscription.

31. These productions include the Norwegian Research Council (NFR) and Ministry of Culture for *Henrik Ibsen's Writings*; French National Research Agency (ANR) for Molière and for Flaubert's *Bouvard et Pécuchet* (de Flaubert) records; Deutsche Forschungsgemeinschaft (DFG, German Research Community), the German Federal Research Fund, and an also public but regional foundation, the Kunstiftung NRW (North Rhine–Westphalia Foundation for Art), for the Heinrich-Heine-Portal; the European Commission, the French Ministry of Research, and the French National Scientific Research Center (CNRS) for Nietzsche Source (formerly HyperNietzsche); the Ministry of Culture, the city of Rouen, the Regional Council of Haute-Normandie, the Béthancourt-Schueller Foundation, the University of Rouen, and the research unit Centre d'Études et de Recherche Éditer/Interpréter (CÉRÉdI) of the same university for *Madame Bovary*, and others.

32. See http://fr.wikipedia.org/wiki/La_Princesse_de_Montpensier_(film).

33. See http://stendhal.armance.com/?cat=8.

34. A number of companies worldwide, in fact, practice a business model invented by Henri Le More (see above) and offer reprints on demand. On the website Books2Anywhere.com, a French amateur in the little English town of Fairford can buy a book published in 1839, which is generally as impossible to find as the narrative by the Saint-simoniens Edmond Combes and Maurice Tamisier of their *Voyage en Abyssinie, dans le pays des Galla, de Choa et d'Ifat, précédé d'une excursion dans l'Arabie-Heureuse* (Paris, 1859).

35. See the survey by Eudes 2009.

36. Directive 96/9/CE of the European Parliament and of the Council of March 11, 1996, concerning the legal protection of databases.

37. Basic information on the *copyleft* and the *Creative Commons* licenses can easily be found on the Internet by using search engines. For an in-depth reflection, see Lessig 2001.

38. See http://www.opensource.org; http://www.soros.org/openaccess; and http://www.forumsocialmundial.org.br.

39. See the UNESCO website and the website of Intangible Cultural Heritage maintained by this international authority.

40. For reference, see note 36 above.

41. Interview with Chartier published under the title "Le droit d'auteur est-il une parenthèse dans l'histoire ?" [Is copyright a parenthesis in history?], *Le Monde*, December 18–19, 2005.

42. See http://www.toutmoliere.net/moliere-et-pezenas.html (accessed May 20, 2011).

43. For reference see note 41.

44. Racine 2007, 147f. The disagreement is essentially tactical, the president of the BnF having also shared his feeling of a "challenge" and his fear of a deletion of civilization: "I believe that those cultures that will not have engaged by due time in mass digitizing will be marginalized" ("Le droit d'auteur est-il une parenthèse," 42).

45. See the common project created in 2006 by the Library of Congress and the BnF under the title "La France en Amérique/France in America" (full reference to this website in the bibliography). See also its description at http://www.bnf.fr/documents/dp_france_amerique.pdf.

46. This project is mentioned without further details by B. Racine (2007, 41).

47. The site claims "to make hundreds of thousands of ebooks available for purchase" and "offer nearly 3 million free ebooks from the public domain" (http://books.google.no/help/ebooks/content.html).

Bibliography, Online Sources, and Software Tools

Books and Articles

Aarseth, Espen. 1996. "Text, Hypertext, or Cybertext? A Typology of Textual Modes Using Correspondence Analysis." In *Research in Humanities Computing 5: Selected Papers from the ACH/ALLC Conference. University of California, Santa Barbara, August 1995,* edited by Giorgio Perissinotto. Oxford: Clarendon Press.

———. 1997. *Cybertext: Perspectives on Ergodic Literature.* Baltimore: Johns Hopkins University Press. [Introduction available online at http://www.hf.uib.no/cybertext/ Ergodic.html.]

———. 1999. "From Humanities Computing to Humanities Informatics: Creating a Field of Our Own." Part of the interdisciplinary seminar "Is Humanities Computing an Academic Discipline?" University of Virginia, October 22. http://www.iath.virginia .edu/hcs/aarseth.html.

Adam, Jean-Michel, and Jean-Marie Viprey, eds. 2009. "Corpus de textes, textes en corpus." *Corpus* 8 (November). http://corpus.revues.org/1670.

Agathon [pseud. of Henri Massis and Alfred de Tarde]. 1911. *L'Esprit de la nouvelle Sorbonne: la crise de la culture classique, la crise du français.* Paris: Mercure de France.

Aland, Barbara, Kurt Aland, Johannes Karavidopoulos, Carlo M. Martini, and Bruce M. Metzger. 2000. *The Greek New Testament.* 4th rev. ed. Stuttgart: United Bible Societies.

Aland, Kurt, and Barbara Aland. 1982. *Der Text des Neuen Testaments. Einführung in die wissenschaftlichen Ausgaben sowie in Theorie und Praxis der modernen Textkritik.* Stuttgart: Deutsche Bibelgesellschaft.

———. 1987. *The Text of the New Testament: An Introduction to the Critical Editions and to the Theory and Practice of Modern Textual Criticism.* Translated by Erroll F. Rhodes. Grand Rapids, MI: Eerdmans.

Angenot, Marc. 1985. *Critique de la raison sémiotique. Fragment avec pin up.* Montréal: Presses de l'Université de Montréal. [English translation: *Critique of Semiotic Reason,* with an introduction by Marie-Christine Leps. Collection "Language, Media, and Education Studies" 2. New York: Legas, 1994.]

Angenot, Marc, and Régine Robin. 1985. "L'inscription du discours social dans le texte littéraire." *Sociocriticism* 1 (July): 53–82.

Apollon, Daniel. 1985. *Le noyau marcien de Luc dans le Codex Bezae.* Vol. 1, "Critique textuelle et méthodes quantitatives dans l'étude des rapports de Luc 6,1-11 D à la tradition parallèle de Marc"; Vol. 2, "Index des sources et apparat critique," PhD diss., University of Bergen.

Artus, Hubert. 2009a. "Google fait appel contre La Martinière." *Rue89* (December 21). http://blogs.rue89.com/cabinet-de-lecture/2009/12/21/google-fait-appel-contre-la -martiniere-130821.

———. 2009b. "La Martinière fait condamner Google pour contrefaçon." *Rue89* (December 18). http://blogs.rue89.com/cabinet-de-lecture/2009/12/18/google-perd-contre -la-martiniere-130589.

Azoulay, Jack, Maud Jutteau, Aurélie Lapidus, and Jean Richard de Latour. 2009. "Rapport sur la Bibliothèque nationale de France." Inspection générale des finances No. 2008–M-065-02. (January). http://www.enssib.fr/bibliotheque-numerique/document-40688.

Barbrook, Adrian C., Norman Blake, Christopher J. Howe, and Peter Robinson. 1998. "The Phylogeny of the Canterbury Tales." *Nature* 394 (August 27): 839.

Barthes, Roland. 1968. *La mort de l'auteur. Le bruissement de la langue.* Paris: Seuil.

———. 1984. *Le bruissement de la langue. Essais critiques IV.* Paris: Seuil.

Bassnett, Susan. 2002. *Translation Studies.* 6th ed. New York: Routledge. [Original publication London: Methuen, 1980.]

Bazin, Patrick. 1996. "Vers une métalecture." *Bulletin des bibliothèques de France* 41 (1). Available as a PDF file at http://bbf.enssib.fr/consulter/04-bazin.pdf. [English translation: "Towards Metareading." In *The Future of the Book,* edited by Geoffrey Nunberg, 153–68. Berkeley: University of California Press.]

———. 2009. "Les termes de notre contrat avec Google sont équitables. Le projet de la Bibliothèque municipale de Lyon ne sacrifie pas la culture." *Le Monde* (September 12).

BBC News. 2007. "Harry Potter finale sales hit 11m." (July 23). http://news.bbc.co.uk/go/pr/fr/-/2/hi/entertainment/6912529.stm.

Bédier, Joseph. 1890. *Jean Renart. Le Lai de l'Ombre.* Fribourg: imprimerie et librairie de l'œuvre de Saint-Paul, 1890 [new edition: Paris, Société des anciens textes francais, 1913.]

———. 1913. *Jean Renart. Le Lai de l'Ombre.* Paris: Société des anciens textes français.

———. 1928. "La tradition manuscrite du *Lai de l'Ombre*: réflexions sur l'art d'éditer les anciens texte." *Romania* 54: 161–96, 321–56. [Reprint, Paris: Librairie Honoré Champion Editeur, 1970.]

Beißner, Friedrich, ed. 1943–1985. *Friedrich Hölderlin. Sämtliche Werke.* Große Stuttgarter Ausgabe. Edited by Friedrich Beißner and Adolf Beck. 8 vols. Stuttgart: J. G. Gottasche Buchhandlung Nachfolger.

———. 1964. "Editions methoden der neueren deutschen Philologie." *Zeitschrift für deutsche Philologie* 83: 72–96.

Bélisle, Claire, ed. 2004a. *La lecture numérique: réalités, enjeux et perspectives.* Coordonné par Claire Bélisle, Préface de Bertrand Legendre. Collection "Références." Lyon-Villeurbanne: Presses de l'ENSSIB.

———. 2004b. "Lire avec un livre électronique: un nouveau contrat de lecture?" Chap.

9 in *Les défis de la publication sur le Web: hyperlectures, cybertextes et méta-éditions,* edited by Jean-Michel Salaün and Christian Vandendorpe, 167–86. Lyon-Villeurbanne: Presses de l'ENSSIB.

———, ed. 2011. *Lire dans un monde numérique.* Textes de Claire Bélisle, Philippe Bootz, Raja Fenniche, Eliana Rosado, Alexandra Saemmer, Christian Vandendorpe. Collection "Papiers." Lyon-Villeurbanne: Presses de l'ENSSIB.

Bell, Daniel. 1973. *The Coming of Post-Industrial Society: A Venture in Social Forecasting.* New York: Basic Books.

———. 1980. "The Social Framework of the Information Society." In *The Microelectronics Revolution,* edited by T. Forrester. Oxford: Basil Blackwell.

Benjamin, Walter. 1936. "The Work of Art in the Age of Its Technological Reproducibility." http://www.marxists.org/reference/subject/philosophy/works/ge/benjamin.htm (translated from German). [Original work, "Das Kunstwerk im Zeitalter seiner technischen Reproduzierbarkeit," published in *Zeitschrift für Sozialforschung,* 1932–1941. Available online as PDF file from Ex Centro Studi Walter Benjamin at http://walterbenjamin.ominiverdi.org/wp-content/kunstwerkbenjamin.pdf.]

Bergmann, Elizabeth, and Neil Fraistat, eds. 2002. *Reimagining Textuality: Textual Studies in the Late Age of Print.* Madison: University of Wisconsin Press.

Berne, Mauricette, ed. 2005. *Sartre.* Bibliothèque nationale de France. Paris: Gallimard.

Berners-Lee, Tim, James Handler, and Ora Lassila. 2001. "The Semantic Web. A new form of Web content that is meaningful to computers will unleash a revolution of new possibilities." *Scientific American* (May 17). http://www.cs.umd.edu/~golbeck/LBSC690/SemanticWeb.html.

Berry, Gérard. 2008. *Pourquoi et comment le monde devient numérique.* Collège de France. Collection "Leçons inaugurales du Collège de France." Paris: Fayard. Text of inaugural lecture on January 17, 2008, of the Liliane Bettencourt Chair of Technological Innovation (2007–2008), at Collège de France. [Video available online at http://www.college-de-france.fr/default/EN/all/inn_tec2007/lecon_inaugurale_.htm.]

Biasi, Pierre-Marc de. 1996. "What Is a Literary Draft? Toward a Functional Typology of Genetic Documentation." Drafts. Spec. Issue. *Yale French Studies* 89: 26–58.

Biggs, Michael, and Claus Huitfeldt. 1997. "Philosophy and Electronic Publishing: Theory and Metatheory in the Development of Text Encoding." *Monist* 80 (3): 348–67. http://www.philo.at/mii/mii/node5.html.

Birkerts, Sven. 1994. *The Gutenberg Elegies: The Fate of Reading in an Electronic Age.* London: Faber and Faber.

———. 2003. "Stage 2." *AGNI Online.* http://www.bu.edu/agni/essays/online/2003/birkerts-stage2.html.

Blanchot, Maurice. 1942. *Comment la littérature est-elle possible?* Paris: Corti.

———. 1955. *L'Espace littéraire.* Paris: Gallimard.

Blasselle, Bruno. 1997. "Le livre à la carte." *Bulletin des bibliothèques de France* 42 (6): 26. http://bbf.enssib.fr/consulter/bbf-1997-06-0029-005.

Bloch, Marc. 1995. "Critique historique et critique du témoignage." *Histoire et historiens.* Paris: Armand Colin. Discours prononcé en 1914, *Annales. Économies, Sociétés, Civilisations* 5, no. 1 (1950): 1–8.

Blosen, Hans, ed. 1979. *Das Wiener Osterspiel. Abdruck der Handschrift und Leseausgabe.* Texte des späten Mittelalters und der frühen Neuzeit 33. Berlin: Schmidt.

Böhme, Gernot, and Nico Stehr, eds. 1986. *The Knowledge Society.* Sociology of Sciences, Yearbook 1986. Dordrecht: D. Reidel.

Bolter, Jay David. 2001. *Writing Space: Computers, Hypertext, and the Remediation of Print.* 2nd ed. Mahwah, NJ: Lawrence Erlbaum Associates.

Bolter, Jay David, and Diane Gromala. 2003. *Windows and Mirrors: Interaction Design, Digital Art, and the Myth of Transparency.* Cambridge: MIT Press.

Bolter, Jay David, and Richard Grusin. 2000. *Remediation: Understanding New Media.* Cambridge: MIT Press.

Bon, François. 2006. "Si la littérature peut mordre encore." *Le tiers livre.* First online version September 26; last accessed version April 12, 2011. http://www.tierslivre.net/spip/spip.php?article519.

Bordalejo, Barbara, ed. 2003. *Caxton's Canterbury Tales: The British Libraries Copies.* Leicester: Scholarly Digital Editions.

Borgman, Christine L. 2007. *Scholarship in the Digital Age: Information, Infrastructure, and the Internet.* Cambridge: MIT Press.

Bowers, Fredson. 1964. "Some Principles for Scholarly Editions of Nineteenth-Century American Authors." *Studies in Bibliography* 17: 223–28.

Brossaud, Claire, and Bernard Reber, eds. 2006. "Les TICs pour soutenir le pluralisme des interprétations?" In *Humanités numériques* 1, chapter 5, "Nouvelles technologies cognitives et épistémologie." Série "Cognition et Traitement de l'information." Paris: Éditions Hermès/Lavoisier.

Bruns, Axel. 2005. *Gatewatching: Collaborative Online News Production.* New York: Peter Lang.

Burnard, Lou, Katherine O'Brien O'Keeffe, and John Unsworth, eds. 2006. *Electronic Text Editing.* New York: Modern Language Association. [Also published online as *Electronic Textual Editing,* TEI, Text Encoding Initiative Consortium. http://www.tei-c.org/Activities/ETE/Preview/index.xml.]

Busby, Keith, ed. 1993a. *Towards a Synthesis? Essays on the New Philology.* Amsterdam: Rodopi.

———. 1993b. "Variance and the Politics of Textual Criticism." *Towards a Synthesis?: Essays on the New Philology,* 29–45. Amsterdam: Rodopi.

Buzzetti, Dino. 2002. "Digital Representation and the Text Model." *New Literary History* 33 (1): 61–88.

Buzzetti, Dino, and Jerome McGann. 2006. "Electronic Textual Editing: Critical Editing in a Digital Horizon." Collection and Preservation of Electronic Editions. In *Electronic Textual Editing,* edited by Lou Burnard, Katherine O'Brien O'Keeffe, and John Unsworth. New York: Modern Language Association of America. http://www.tei-c.org/About/Archive_new/ETE/Preview/mcgann.xml.

Calabretto, Sylvie, Andrea Bozzi, and Jean-Marie Pinon. 1999. "Numérisation des manuscrits médiévaux: le projet européen BAMBI." *Actes du colloque Vers une nouvelle érudition: numérisation et recherche en histoire du livre.* Rencontres Jacques Cartier,

Lyon, décembre. Downloadable in PDF format at http://www.enssib.fr/bibliotheque -numerique/document-1509.

Carlton, William J. 1940. *Biblioth. Pepysiana.* Vol. 4. *Shorthand Books.* London: Sidgwick & Jackson.

Carr, Nicholas. 2008. "Is Google Making Us Stupid? What the Internet Is Doing to Our Brains." *Atlantic Monthly* (July). http://www.theatlantic.com/doc/200807/google.

Carter, Henry H., ed. 1941. *Cancioneiro da Ajuda: A Diplomatic Edition.* New York: Modern Language Association of America.

Castells, Manuel. 1996. *The Information Age: Economy, Society, and Culture.* Vol. 1. *The Rise of the Network Society.* Cambridge, MA: Oxford: Blackwell [2nd ed., 2010].

———. 1997. *The Information Age: Economy, Society, and Culture.* Vol. 2. *The Power of Identity.* Cambridge, MA: Oxford: Blackwell [2nd ed., 2004].

———. 1998. *The Information Age: Economy, Society, and Culture.* Vol. 3. *End of Millennium.* Cambridge, MA: Oxford: Blackwell [2nd ed., 2000].

———. 2004. "Informationalism, Networks, and the Network Society: A Theoretical Blueprint." *The Network Society: A Cross-Cultural Perspective.* Cambridge, MA: Edward Elgar.

Catach, Nina, ed. 1988a. *Les éditions critiques. Problèmes techniques et éditoriaux.* Annales Littéraires de l'Université de Besançon. Paris: Les Belles Lettres. [Also published as *Les éditions critiques. Problèmes techniques et éditoriaux.* Les Annales Littéraires de l'Université, Besançon: Publication GTM-CNRS-HESO, 1988.]

———. 1988b. "L'édition critique: un projet multiple." In *Les éditions critiques. Problèmes techniques et éditoriaux.* Les Annales Littéraires de l'Université de Besançon, 20–26. Paris: Les Belles Lettres.

Cavallo, Guglielmo. 2001. "Les bibliothèques monastiques et la transmission des textes en Occident." In *Des Alexandries I. Du livre au texte*, edited by Luce Giard and Christian Jacob, 264. Paris: Bibliothèque nationale de France.

Cavallo, Guglielmo, and Roger Chartier, eds. 1997. *Histoire de la lecture dans le monde occidental.* Paris: Editions du Seuil.

Caxton, William, ed. ca. 1476. *The Canterbury Tales,* by Geoffrey Chaucer. Westminster: William Caxton. [Online critical edition available at http://molcat1.bl.uk/treasures/ caxton/search.asp.]

———. ca. 1482. *The Canterbury Tales,* by Geoffrey Chaucer, with woodcut illustrations. Westminster: William Caxton. Online critical edition available at http://molcat1.bl.uk/ treasures/caxton/search.asp.

Cazalé Bérard, C., and R. Mordenti. 1997. "La costituzione del testo e la 'comunità degli interpreti'": libertà e responsabilità del critico/editore/ermeneuta in ambiente elettronico inter-attivo, in Internet e le Muse, a cura di P. Nerozzi Bellman. Milano: Mimesis, 1997.

Cerquiglini, Bernard. 1983. "Éloge de la variante." *Langages* 17 (69): 25–35. http://www .persee.fr/web/revues/home/prescript/article/lgge_0458-726x_1983_num_17_69_1140.

———. 1989a. *In Praise of the Variant: A Cultural History of Philology.* Translated by Betsy Wing. Baltimore: John Hopkins University Press, 1999. [Originally published as *Éloge de la variante. Histoire critique de la philologie.* Collection "Des travaux" 8. Paris: Seuil, 1989.]

———. 1989b. "Variantes d'auteur et variance de copiste." In *La naissance du texte, ensemble réuni par Louis Hay,* edited by Louis Hay, 119. Paris: José Corti.

———. 2000. "Une nouvelle philologie?" *Communication au Colloque international "Philologie à l'ère de l'Internet."* Budapest. http://magyar-irodalom.elte.hu/colloquia/000601/cerq.htm.

Chandler, Daniel. 1995. *The Act of Writing: A Media Theory Approach.* Aberystwyth: University of Wales. http://www.aber.ac.uk/media/Documents/act/act-of-writing.doc.

Chartier, Roger. 1995. *Forms and Meaning: Text, Performances, and Audiences from Codex to Computer.* Philadelphia: University of Pennsylvania Press.

———.1997. *Le livre en révolutions. Entretiens avec Jean Lebrun.* Paris: Textuel.

———. 2008. *Ecouter les morts avec les yeux.* Collège de France. Collection "Les leçons inaugurales." Paris: Fayard.

Chossegros, Aurélia. 2007. "'The William Blake Archive.' Le Site à la loupe." Observatoire critique: des ressources numériques en histoire de l'art et archéologie. With abstract in English. (January 17). http://www.observatoire-critique.org/article.php3?id_article=103.

Colwell, Ernest C., and Ernest W. Tune. 1963. "The Quantitative Relationships between MS Text-Types." In *Biblical and Patristic Studies in Memory of Robert Pierce Casey,* edited by J[ames] Neville Birdsall and Robert W[illiam] Thomson, 25–32. Freiburg: Herder. [Reprinted as "Method in Establishing Quantitative Relationships between Text-Types of New Testament Manuscripts," in *Studies in Methodology in Textual Criticism of the New Testament* (1969): 56–62.]

Combes, Edmond, and Maurice Tamisier. 1859 [1838]. *Voyage en Abyssinie, dans le pays des Galla, de Choa et d'Ifat: Précédé d'une excursion dans l'Arabie-Heureuse.* 4 vols. Paris.

Compagnon, Antoine. 1995. "Introduction." *Romanic Review* 86 (3): 393–401.

Comte, Auguste. 1830a. *Cours de philosophie positive. Tome premier contenant les préliminaires généraux et la philosophie mathématique.* Paris: Rouen frères. http://gallica.bnf.fr/ark:/12148/bpt6k76267p/f4.image.

———. 1830b. *Cours de philosophie positive. Tome premier contenant les préliminaires généraux et la philosophie mathématique.* Paris: Bachelier, Libraire pour les mathématiques. http://books.google.fr/books?id=9-qP2aFJFfcC&pg=PA746&dq=Cours+de+philosophie+positive+Stanford&hl=fr&ei=ElibToT1LeTO4QTm-rn-Aw&sa=X&oi=book_result&ct=result&resnum=1&ved=0CEMQ6AEwAA#v=onepage&q&f=false ("The Stanford Edition").

———. 1838. *Cours de philosophie positive. Tome troisième contenant la philosophie chimique et la philosophie biologique.* Vol. 3. Paris: Bachelier, Imprimeur-Libraire. http://books.google.fr/books?id=F-PUZGekS1YC.

———. 1839. *Cours de philosophie positive. Tome quatrième et dernier content la philosophie sociale et les conclusions générales. Première partie.* Paris: Bachelier, Imprimeur-Libraire. http://books.google.fr/books?id=s63fCXM7Ay4C.

———. 1864. *Cours de philosophie positive. Deuxième édition augmentée d'une préface par É. Littré.* Tome deuxième. Paris: J. B. Baillère et Fils. http://books.google.fr/books?id=HisCAAAAQAAJ.

Coombs, James H., Allen Renear, and Steven J. DeRose. 1987. "Markup Systems and the Future of Scholarly Text Processing." *Communications of the ACM* 30 (11): 933–47.

Corpus Codicum Islandicorum Medii Aevi. 1930–1956. Edited by Einar Munksgaard, Jón Helgason, et al. 20 vols. Copenhagen: Munksgaard.

Corpus Codicum Norvegicorum Medii Aevi. Folio serie, 2 vols. 1950–1960. Quarto Series, 10 vols., 1952–2002. Oslo: Selskapet til utgivelse av gamle norske håndskrifter.

Corpus Codicum Americanorum Medii Aevi: Litterarum Monumenta in Lingua Nahuati et Maya etc. 1942–1952. Edited by Ernst Mengin et al. 4 vols. Copenhagen: Munksgaard.

Cypel, Sylvain. 2010. "Numérisation des livres: report de la décision de justice dans l'affaire Google." *Le Monde* (February 19), 22.

Dacos, Marin. 2010. *Manifeste des Digital humanities.* THATCamp Paris. http://tcp.hypotheses.org.

Dacos, Marin, and Pierre Mounier. 2010. *L'édition électronique.* Collection "Repères." Paris: La Découverte.

Dahlerup, Verner, ed. 1880. *Ágrip af Noregs konunga sögum.* Samfund til udgivelse af gammel nordisk litteratur 2. København: Møller.

Dain, Alphonse. 1975. *Les manuscrits.* Collection "D'études anciennes." 3rd ed. Paris: Belles-Lettres. [1st ed. 1949; 2nd ed. 1964]

Darnton, Robert. 1990. *The Kiss of Lamourette: Reflections in Cultural History.* New York: W. W. Norton.

———. 1999. "The New Age of the Book." *New York Review of Books* 46 (5). http://www.nybooks.com/articles/archives/1999/mar/18/the-new-age-of-the-book.

———. 2010. *The Case for Books: Past, Present, and Future.* New York: Public Affairs. [French translation: *Apologie du livre.* Paris: Gallimard, 2011.]

Daudet, Alphonse. 1878. *Les femmes d'artistes.* Paris: Lemerre.

Dehaene, Stanislas. 2009. *Reading in the Brain: The Science and Evolution of a Human Invention.* New York: Viking Penguin. Translated from Stanislas Dehaene, *Les Neurones de la lecture,* préface de Jean-Pierre Changeux. Paris: Éditions Odile Jacob, 2007.

Delany, Paul, and George Landow, eds. 1994. *The Digital Word.* Cambridge: MIT Press.

———. 1995. *Hypermedia and Literary Studies.* Cambridge: MIT Press.

Dembowski, Peter F. 1996. "Towards a Synthesis: Essays on the New Philology." Edited by Keith Busby. Book review. *Romance Philology* 49 (3): 301–307.

Deppman, Jed, Daniel Ferrer, and Michael Groden, eds. 2004. *Genetic Criticism: Texts and Avant-Textes.* Philadelphia: University of Pennsylvania Press.

DeRose, Steven J. 2004. "Markup Overlap: A Review and a Horse." Proceedings of Extreme Markup Languages 2004, Montréal, August. http://conferences.idealliance.org/extreme/html/2004/DeRose01/EML2004DeRose01.html.

DeRose, S. J., D. G. Durand, E. Mylonas, and A. H. Renear. 1990. "What Is Text, Really?" *Journal of Computing in Higher Education* 1 (2): 3–26.

de Vasconcellos, Carolina Michaëlis, ed. 1904. *Cancioneiro da Ajuda.* 2 vols. Halle: Niemeyer. [Reprint, Lisbon: Impr. Nacional-Casa da Moeda, 1990.]

D'Iorio, Paolo, ed. 2000a. *HyperNietzsche.* Collection "Écritures électroniques." Paris: PUF.

———. 2000b. *HyperNietzsche. Modèle d'un hypertexte savant sur Internet pour la recherche en sciences humaines. Questions philosophiques, problèmes juridiques, outils informatiques.* Collection "Écritures électroniques." Paris: PUF. http://www.hypernietzsche .org/doc/puf/book/hypernietzsche/le-livre.htm.

———. 2002a. "Eine Forschergemeinschaft im Internet." Aus dem französisch übersetzt von Inga Gerike. In *Tagungsakten HyperNietzsche. Modell eines Forschungshypertextes im Internet,* edited by Paolo D'Iorio, *Philosophie, Textkritik, Softwareinstrumente, rechtsfragen.* http://www.hypernietzsche.org/events/lmu/diorio.html (in German).

———. 2002b. "Principles of HyperNietzsche." *Diogenes* 196 (49), fasc. 4: 58–72.

"Directive 96/9/EC of the European Parliament and of the Council of the 11 March 1996 on the legal protection of databases." 1996. *Official Journal* L 077, 27/03/1996: 0020–0028. http://eur-lex.europa.eu/LexUriServ/LexUriServ.do?uri=CELEX:31996 L0009:EN:HTML.

Driscoll, Matthew James. 2010. "The Words on the Page: Thoughts on Philology, Old and New." In *Creating the Medieval Saga: Versions, Variability, and Editorial Interpretations of Old Norse Saga Literature,* edited by Judy Quinn and Emily Lethbridge, 85–102. Odense: Syddansk Universitetsforlag.

Ducourtieux, Christine. 2004. "L'édition électronique en quête de définitions(s)." *Le médiéviste et l'ordinateur,* Histoire médiévale, informatique et nouvelles technologies 43. http://lemo.irht.cnrs.fr/43/43-02.htm.

Duggan, Hoyt N. 1994. "The Electronic *Piers Plowman* Archive and SEENET." *European English Messenger* 3: 86–87. http://www.ucalgary.ca/~scriptor/papers/duggan.html.

Eco, Umberto. 1996. Afterword to *The Future of the Book,* edited by Geoffrey Nunberg. Berkeley: University of California Press.

Eisenstein, Elizabeth L. 1979. *The Printing Press as an Agent of Change: Communications and Cultural Transformations in Early Modern Europe.* 2 vols. Cambridge: Cambridge University Press.

———. 2005. *The Printing Revolution in Early Modern Europe.* 2nd ed. Cambridge: Cambridge University Press. [1st ed., 1983]

Eklund, Sten. 1977. "On Errors and Contamination." *Kungliga Humanistiska Vetenskaps-Samfundet i Uppsala: Årsbok* (1975–1976): 73–83. [Printed in Uppsala: Almqvist och Wiksell.]

Espagne, Michel. 1990. "La référence allemande dans la fondation d'une philologie française." In *Philologiques I. Contribution à l'histoire des disciplines littéraires en France et en Allemagne,* edited by Michel Espagne and Michaël Werner. Paris: Maison des Sciences de l'Homme.

———. 1998. *De l'archive au texte. Recherches d'histoire génétique.* Collection "Perspectives germaniques." Paris: PUF.

Eudes, Yves. 2009. "Les pirates à l'assaut du livre numérique." *Le Monde* (October 23).

Farley, Abraham, ed. 1783. *Domesday-Book, seu liber censualis.* 2 vols. London.

Felsenstein, Joseph. 2004. *Inferring Phylogenies.* Sunderland, MA: Sinauer Associates.

Ferrer, Daniel. 2002. "Production, Invention, and Reproduction: Genetic vs. Textual Criticism." In *Reimagining Textuality: Textual Studies in the Late Age of Print,* edited by Elizabeth Bergmann and Neil Fraistat, 48–59. Madison: University of Wisconsin Press.

———. 2008. "La représentation hypertextuelle des manuscrits: quelques leçons de douze années d'expériences." In *L'édition du manuscrit. De l'archive de création au scriptorium électronique,* edited by Aurèle Crasson, 189–208. *Au cœur des textes* 10. Louvain-la-Neuve: Academia-Bruylant.

———, ed. 2010. Dictionnaire de critique génétique. Entry: "AVANT-TEXTE." http://www.item.ens.fr/index.php?id=577463.

Fischer, Steven Roger. 2004. *A History of Reading.* London: Reaktion Books.

Floridi, Luciano. 2005. "Semantic Conceptions of Information." In *The Stanford Encyclopedia of Philosophy,* edited by Edward N. Zalta. Stanford, CA: Stanford University Press. http://plato.stanford.edu/entries/information-semantic.

Foucault, Michel. 1969. "Qu'est-ce qu'un auteur?" *Bulletin de la Société française de Philosophie* 63 (3): 73–104. [Also published in Michel Foucault, *Dits et Écrits.* Paris: Gallimard, 1994.]

Foulet, Alfred, and Mary Blakely Speer. 1979. *On Editing Old French Texts.* Lawrence, KS: Regents Press.

Fourier, Charles. 1832. *Prospectus général du Phalanstère, 1st of June–30th of August 1832* (I, no. 1–4). Exemplary consulted at Bibliothèque de l'Arsenal. Paris, FE 2093.

Frobert, Ludovic, ed. 2010. *L'Écho de la fabrique: naissance de la presse ouvrière à Lyon.* Paris: ENS Editions/Institut d'histoire du livre.

Froger, Jacques. 1968. *La critique des textes et son automatisation.* Collection "Initiation aux nouveautés de la science" 7. Paris: Dunod.

Gabler, Hans-Walter. 1993. "What Ulysses Requires." *Papers of the Bibliographical Society of America* 87 (2): 187–248.

———. 1995. "Optionen und Lösungen: Zur kritischen und synoptischen Edition von James Joyce Ulysses." *Editio. Revue internationale des sciences de l'édition critique* 9: 179–213.

———. 2003. "Textkritik und Texttheorie." Schwerpunkt: Editionskritik, *Text* 8: 127–30.

———. 2007. "Textkritikens uttydningskonst." In *Filologi og hermeneutikk,* edited by Odd Einar Haugen, Christian Janns, and Tone Modalsli, 57–80. Nordisk nettverk for edisjonsfilologer. Skrifter 7. Oslo: Solum.

———. 2010. "Theorizing the Digital Scholarly Edition." *Literature Compass* 7 (2):43–56. Special issue on"Scholarly Editing in the 21st Century." http://www3.interscience .wiley.com/journal/117994384/home and http://lmu-munich.academia.edu/ HansWalterGabler.

Gabler, Hans Walter, Wolfhard Steppe, and Claus Melchior, eds. 1984. *James Joyce: Ulysses. A Critical and Synoptic Edition.* 3 vols. New York: Garland.

Gallimard, Antoine. 2011. "L'édition numérique accorde les mêmes droits d'auteur que le livre imprimé." *Le Monde* (January 21).

Ganascia, Jean Gabriel, Irène Fenoglio, and Jean-Louis Lebrave. 2004. "Manuscrits, genèse et documents numérisés. EDITE: une étude informatisée du travail de l'écrivain." *Document numérique* 8 (4). http://www.cairn.info/article.php?ID_ ARTICLE=DN_084_0091.

Gaskell, Philip. 1978. *From Writer to Reader*. Studies in Editorial Method. Oxford: Clarendon Press.

Genette, Gérard. 1982. *Palimpsestes: La littérature au second degré*. Paris: Seuil.

George, Andrew R. 2003. *The Babylonian Gilgamesh Epic: Introduction, Critical Edition, and Cuneiform Texts*. 2 vols. Oxford: Oxford University Press.

Gilman, William, et al., eds. 1960–1982. *The Journals and Miscellaneous Notebooks of Ralph Waldo Emerson*. 16 vols. Cambridge: Harvard University Press.

Goldfarb, Charles F. 1993. *The SGML Handbook*. San Jose: IBM Almaden Research Center.

Girard, Luce, and Christian Jacob, eds. 2001. *Des Alexandries I: Du livre au texte*. Paris: Bibliothèque nationale de France.

Goody, Jack. n.d. "Technologies of the Intellect and the Future of the Humanities." *International Journal of the Humanities* 2 (3). Available online as PDF file at http://ijd.cgpublisher.com/product/pub.26/prod.609.

———. 1986. *The Logic of Writing and the Organisation of Society*. Cambridge: Cambridge University Press. [Reprinted 1988, 1989, 1992, and 1996.]

Goody, Jack, and Ian Watt. 1963. "The Consequences of Literacy." *Comparative Studies in Society and History* 5 (3): 304–45.

Grange, Juliette, Pierre Musso, Philippe Régnier, and Frank Yonnet, eds. 2012. *Œuvres complètes Henri Saint-Simon (coffret de 4 volumes)*. Première édition critique intégrale. Introduction, notes, et commentaires par Juliette Grange. Paris: Presses Universitaires de France.

Greetham, David C. 1994. *Textual Scholarship: An Introduction*. New York: Garland. [1st ed., 1992]

Greg, Walter Wilson. 1927. *The Calculus of Variants: An Essay on Textual Criticism*. Oxford: Clarendon Press.

———. 1950–1951. "The Rationale of Copy-Text." *Studies in Bibliography* 3: 19–36. [Reprinted in *Art and Error*, edited by Ronald Gottesman and Scott Bennett, 17–36. Bloomington: Indiana University Press, 1970.]

Grésillon, Almuth. 1994. *Éléments de critique génétique. Lire les manuscrits modernes*. Paris: PUF.

———. 1995. "Critique génétique et 'Textual Criticism': une rencontre." *Romanic Review* 86 (3): 595–98.

Griesbach, Johann Jakob, ed. 1774. *Synopsis evangeliorum Matthaei, Marci et Lucae*. Halle.

———. 1797. *Synopsis evangeliorum Matthaei Marci et Lucae una cum iis Joannis pericopis*. Halle.

Griffith, John G. 1968. "A Taxonomic Study of the Manuscript Tradition of Juvenal." *Museum Helveticum* 25: 101–38.

———. 1969. "Numerical Taxonomy and Some Primary Manuscripts of the Gospels." *Journal of Theological Studies N.S.* 20: 389–406.

Gröber, Gustav. 1869. *Die handschriftlichen Gestaltungen der chanson de geste "Fierabras" und ihre Vorstufen*. Leipzig: Vogel.

Groß, Nathalie. 2005. "Der digitale Heine—ein Internetportal." *Jahrbuch für Computerphilologie* 6: 60–73. http://computerphilologie.uni-muenchen.de/jg04/gross/gross.html.

Gulbrandsen, Ib T., and Sine T. Just. 2011. "The Collaborative Paradigm: Towards an

Invitational and Participatory Concept of Online Communication." *Media Culture Society* 33 (7): 1095–1108.

Gunkel, Hermann. 1967. *The Psalms: A Form-Critical Introduction*. Philadelphia: Fortress Press. Translation of *Die Religion in Geschichte und Gegenwart*. 2nd ed. Tübingen: Mohr Siebeck, 1930.

———. 1998. *Introduction to Psalms: The Genres of the Religious Lyric of Israel*. Completed by Joachim Begrich. Macon, Georgia: Mercer University Press. Translation of *Einleitung in die Psalmen: die Gattungen der religiösen Lyrik Israels*. Zuende geführt von Joachim Begrich. 4th edn. Göttingen: Vandenhoeck & Ruprecht, 1985. [First edition published in W. Nowack, ed. *Göttinger Handkommentar zum Alten Testamen. Ergänzungband zur II. Abteilung*. II/2 1933.]

Gunnlaugsson, Guðvarður Már. 2003. "Stafrétt eða samræmt? Um fræðilegar útgáfur og notendur þeirra." *Gripla* 14: 197–235. (Stofnun Árna Magnússonar á Íslandi, Rit 60.)

Hagen, Friedrich Heinrich von der. 1816. *Der Nibelungen Lied*. Breslau: Max und Komp.

Hamman, Adalbert-Gautier. 1985. *L'Épopée du Livre. La transmission des textes anciens, du scribe à l'imprimerie*. Paris: Perrin.

Hardy, Thomas. 1896. *The Woodlander*. London: Osgood, McIlvaine.

Harvey, P. D. A. 2001. *Editing Historical Records*. London: British Library.

Haugen, Odd Einar. 1992. "Stamtre og tekstlandskap. Studiar i resensjonsmetodikk med grunnlag i Niðrstigningar saga." 2 vols. PhD diss., University of Bergen.

———. 2004. "Parallel Views: Multi-Level Encoding of Medieval Primary Sources." *Literary and Linguistic Computing* 19 (1): 73–91.

———, gen. ed. 2008. *The Menota Handbook: Guidelines for the Electronic Encoding of Medieval Nordic Primary Sources*. V. 2.0. Bergen: Medieval Nordic Text Archive. http://www.menota.org/MenotaHandbook-2-0-text.pdf.

———. 2009. "An Apology for the Text That Never Was: Reconstructing the King's Mirror." In *Medieval Texts—Contemporary Media: The Art and Science of Editing in the Digital Age*, edited by Maria Grazia Saibene and Marina Buzzoni, 57–79. Pavia: Ibis.

———. 2010. "Stitching the Text Together: Documentary and Eclectic Editions in Old Norse Philology." In *Creating the Medieval Saga: Versions, Variability, and Editorial Interpretations of Old Norse Saga Literature*, edited by Judy Quinn and Emily Lethbridge, 39–65. Odense: Syddansk Universitetsforlag.

Heikkilä, Tuomas, Petri Myllymäki, and Teemu Roos, eds. 2010–2012. *Studia Stemmatologica: A Series of International Workshops on Stemmatology*. Organizers: T. Heikkilä, P. Myllymäki, and T. Roos. Helsinki. http://cosco.hiit.fi/stemmatologica.

Henriet, Ottilia, Marie-Laure Malingre, and Alexandre Serres. 2008. "Enquête sur les besoins de formation des doctorants à la maîtrise de l'information scientifique dans les écoles doctorales de Bretagne. Analyse et synthèse des résultats." *Form@doct* ("FORMation à distance en information DOCumentation pour les docTorants"). Rennes: Services communs de documentations de Bretagne et de l'URFIST. http://memsic.ccsd.cnrs.fr/docs/00/52/63/25/TXT/Former_etudiants_RI_Olivier_Honore.txt.

Hertzberg, Nathaniel. 2011. "Numérisation: Google et Hachette s'entendent." *Le Monde* (July 30), 2.

Hillesund, Terje. 2005. "Digital Text Cycles: From Medieval Manuscripts to Modern

Markup." *Journal of Digital Information* 6 (1). http://journals.tdl.org/jodi/article/view/62/65.

Hoeningswald, Henry M. 1960. *Language Change and Linguistic Reconstruction.* Chicago: University of Chicago Press.

Hoeningswald, Henry M., and Linda F. Wiener, eds. 1987. *Biological Metaphor and Cladistic Classification.* Philadelphia: University of Pennsylvania Press.

Hölderlin, Friedrich. See editions by Beißner (1943–1985) and Sattler (1975).

Holm, Magnus, and Jørgen Lorentzen. 2010. "Er Google-avtalen en trussel for bokbransjen?" ["Is the Google agreement a threat to the book industry?"]. *Bok og Bibliotek* (February 6). http://www.bokogbibliotek.no/index.php?option=com_content&view=article&id=1290:er-google-avtalen-en-trussel-for-bokbransjen&catid=73:nr-1-2010.

Holm-Olsen, Ludvig, ed. 1945. *Konungs skuggsiá.* Utgitt for Kjeldeskriftfondet. Oslo: Dybwad.

Honigman, Sylvie. 2003. *The Septuagint and Homeric Scholarship in Alexandria: A Study in the Narrative of the "Letter of Aristeas."* London: Routledge.

Housman, Alfred Edward. 1962. *Selected Prose.* Edited by John Carter. Cambridge: Cambridge University Press.

Huitfeldt, Claus. 1994. "Multi-Dimensional Texts in a One-Dimensional Medium." *Computers and the Humanities* 28 (4/5): 235–41.

Ibsen, Henrik. 1866. *Brand. Et dramatisk Digt i 5 Akter.* København: Gyldendal.

———. 1867. *Peer Gynt: Et dramatisk Digt.* København: Gyldendal.

———. 1898–1902. *Samlede Værker.* København: Gyldendalske Boghandels Forlag.

———. 2005–2010. *Henrik Ibsens skrifter.* Edited by Vigdis Åse Ystad, Daniel Apollon, Thoralf Berg, Christian Janns, Jon Gunnar Jørgensen, Tone Modalsli, and Asbjørn Aarseth. 33 vols. Oslo: Aschehoug. (See also below under "Digital Critical Editions.")

Icher, Bruno. 2009. "Lyon transfère son fonds." *Libération* (August 29 and 30): 4.

IFLA [International Federation of Library Associations]. 1998. *Functional Requirements for Bibliographical Records: Final Report.* München: Saur. Available in PDF format at http://www.ifla.org/publications/functional-requirements-for-bibliographic-records.

Irigoin, Jean, and Gian Piero Zarri. 1979. *La pratique des ordinateurs dans la critique des textes.* Colloques internationaux du CNRS, no. 579. Paris: CNRS Éditions.

Jacob, Christian, 1987. "La lecture érudite." *Préfaces. Les idées et les sciences dans la bibliographie de la France* 1 (March/April): 89–93. Paris: Cercle de la Libraire/Éditions Professionnelles du Livre.

———. 1996. "Lire pour écrire: navigations alexandrines." In *Le pouvoir des bibliothèques. La mémoire des livres en Occident*, sous la direction de Marc Baratin et Christian Jacob. Bibliothèque Albin Michel Histoire. Paris: Éditions Albin Michel.

———. 2003. *Des Alexandries II: Les metamorphoses du lecteur.* Paris: Bibliothèque nationale de France.

Janns, Christian. 2005. "Friedrich Hölderlins verker—en prøvesten for ulike utgavetyper." In *Læsemåder: Udgavetyper og målgrupper,* edited by Per Dahl, Johnny Kondrup, and Karsten Kynde, 90–123. København: Reitzel.

Jeanneney, Jean-Noël. 2007 [2005]. *Google and the Myth of Universal Knowledge: A View from Europe.* Chicago: University of Chicago Press, 2007. Translated from *Quand Google défie l'Europe. Plaidoyer pour un sursaut.* Collection "Mille et une nuits." Paris:

Fayard, 2005. [Reprinted September 2006, 3rd reprinting. Rev., augmented, and updated March 2010.]

Jeanneret, Michel. 1995. "L'École de Genève." Colloque du Centenaire "L'histoire littéraire hier, aujourd'hui et demain, ici et ailleurs." Supplement to *Revue d'histoire littéraire de la France* 6: 59.

Jehasse, Jean. 1976. *La Renaissance de la critique. L'essor de l'Humanisme érudit de 1560 à 1614.* Saint-Étienne: Publications de l'Université de Saint-Étienne.

Johansson, Karl G. 2010. "In Praise of Manuscript Culture: Texts and Editions in the Computer Age." In *Creating the Medieval Saga: Versions, Variability, and Editorial Interpretations of Old Norse Saga Literature,* edited by Judy Quinn and Emily Lethbridge, 67–85. Odense: Syddansk Universitetsforlag.

Jónsson, Finnur, ed. 1912–1915. *Den norsk-islandske skjaldedigtning.* 2 vols. in 4 parts. København: Gyldendal.

Junack, Klaus. 1986– . *Das Neue Testament auf Papyrus.* Collection "Arbeiten zur neutestamentlichen Textforschung." Berlin: W. de Gruyter.

Kalifa, Dominique. 2005. *Crime et culture au XIXe siècle.* Collection "Pour l'Histoire." Paris: Perrin.

Kernan, Alvin. 1987. *Printing Technology, Letters, and Samuel Johnson.* Princeton, NJ: Princeton University Press.

Konungs-skuggsjá. Konge-speilet. Udgivet efter Foranstaltning af det akademiske Collegium ved det kongelige norske Frederiks-Universitet. Christiania: Werner.

Kiernan, Kevin. n.d. "Electronic Textual Editing: Digital Facsimiles in Editing." TEI, Electronic Textual Editing. http://www.tei-c.org/Activities/ETE/Preview/kiernan.xml.

Kratz, Reinhard G. 1997. "Redaktionsgeschichte/Redaktionkritik I." In TRE, *Theologische Realenzyklopädie,* 36 Bde. u. 2. Reg.-Bde 367–378. Berlin 1997–2007.

Kristeva, Julia. 1969. *Sèméiôtikè.* Paris: Seuil.

Kuhn, Thomas. 1962. *The Structure of Scientific Revolutions.* 1st. ed. Chicago: University of Chicago Press.

Labrousse, Élisabeth, and Antony McKenna, eds. 1999–2005. *Correspondance de Pierre Bayle.* 4 vols. Oxford: Voltaire Foundation.

Lachmann, Karl. 1826. *Der Nibelunge Not mit der Klage.* [*Niebelungen Lied*]. 1st ed. Berlin. [2nd ed., 1841; 3rd ed., 1851]

———, ed. 1831. *Novum Testamentum Graece.* Berlin. ["Editio minor."]

———. 1833. *Wolfram von Eschenbach.* Vol. 1, *Lieder, Parzival und Titurel.* Berlin: Reimer.

———. 1850. *Lucretii de rerum natura libri VI.* Berlin.

"La justice américaine rejette l'accord entre Google et les éditeurs." 2011. *Le Monde* (March 23).

Lalou, Élisabeth. 2004. "Les contes de Canterbury: une édition savante électronique." *Le Médiéviste et l'ordinateur* 43. http://lemo.irht.cnrs.fr/43/43-05.

Landow, George P. 1992. "Annotation in a Print Text." Chapter 1 (online) in *Hypertext and Critical Theory. Hypertext: The Convergence of Contemporary Critical Theory and Technology.* http://www.cyberartsweb.org/cpace/ht/jhup/contents.html.

———. 2006. *Hypertext 3.0: Critical Theory and New Media in an Era of Globalization.* Baltimore: Johns Hopkins University Press.

Landow, George P., and Paul Delany. 1991. "Hypertext, Hypermedia, and Literary Studies: The State of the Art." In *Hypermedia and Literary Studies*, edited by Paul Delany and George Landow, 3–50. Cambridge: MIT Press.

Lanson, Gustave. 1984. *Histoire de la littérature française*. Paris: Hachette.

"La Numérisation de masse à la BnF. Numérisation de masse: de la sélection de l'original au document numérique." 2008. DCO/DSR, version du 19/02/08. Bibliothèque nationale de France. PDF file downloadable online from http://www.bnf.fr/documents/numerisation_masse_bnf.pdf.

Laufer, Roger. 1988. "Édition critique synoptique interactive sur écran: l'exemple des maximes de La Rochefoucauld." In *Les éditions critiques. Problèmes techniques et éditoriaux*, edited by Nina Catach, 115–25. Les Annales Littéraires de l'Université. Besançon: Publication GTM-CNRS-HESO.

Lavagnino, John. 1995. "Reading, Scholarship, and Hypertext Editions." *TEXT* 8: 109–24. http://www.stg.brown.edu/resources/stg/monographs/rshe.html.

Lawall, Sarah. 1988. "René Wellek and Modern Literary Criticism." *Comparative Literature* 40: 3–24.

Lebrave, Jean-Louis. 1997. "Hypertexte et édition génétique. L'exemple d'Hérodias de Flaubert." In *Banques de données et hypertextes pour l'étude du roman,* edited by Nathalie Ferrand. Collection "Écritures électroniques." Paris: PUF.

———. 2006. "La critique génétique: une discipline nouvelle ou un avatar moderne de la philologie?" (November 9). http://www.item.ens.fr/index.php?id=14048.

Lebrave, Jean-Louis, and Almuth Grésillon. 2009. "Linguistique et génétique des textes: un décalogue." (February 16). http://www.item.ens.fr/index.php?id=384099.

Leclerc, Yvan. 2006. "L'édition intégrale en ligne des manuscrits de Madame Bovary." In *De l'hypertexte au manuscrit. L'apport et les limites du numérique pour l'édition et la valorisation de manuscrits littéraires modernes*, edited by Françoise Leriche and Cécile Meynard, 237. December 6–9, Université Stendhal Actes du colloque "Éditer et valoriser des manuscrits et des archives littéraires," Recherches & Travaux 72, Grenoble, ELLUG, 2008.

"Le droit d'auteur est-il une parenthèse dans l'histoire ?" 2005. Interview with Roger Chartier, *Le Monde* (December 18–19).

Lefèvre, Raoul. n.d. *Le Recueil des histoires de Troyes* [English: *Recuyell of the historyes of Troye* (Translated by William Caxton). Bruges: William Caxton, 1473?]. Detailed shelf reference available at http://www.bl.uk/treasures/caxton/references1.html#15.

Leitch, Caroline, Ray Siemens, et al. 2008. "Digital Humanities 'Readership' and the Public Knowledge Project." *Digital Humanities 2008: Book of Abstracts*. University of Oulu. http://www.ekl.oulu.fi/dh2008/Digital%20Humanities%202008%20Book%20of%20Abstracts.pdf.

Le Médiéviste et l'ordinateur. 1979–2007. Journal published by the IRHT (Institut de recherche sur l'histoire des textes). The journal deals with medieval history, informatics, and new technologies. Two paper volumes are available: no. 1–10, 1979–1983, and no. 11–20, 1984–1988. Issues from 1989 (no. 20) to 2007 (45) are archived on the website of IRHT at http://lemo.irht.cnrs.fr/archives.htm.

Le Men, Ségolène, ed. 2002. "Ceci tuera cela: autour de Hugo. L'avènement de nouveaux supports de la pensée." Colloque organisé par Ségolène Le Men (Univ. Paris X). Paris (May 24). http://www.diffusion.ens.fr/index.php?res=cycles&idcycle=69.

Lessig, Lawrence. 2001. *The Future of Ideas.* New York: Random House.

Levinson, Paul. 1998. *Soft Edge: A Natural History and Future of the Information Revolution.* London: Routledge.

Levy, David M. 2001. *Scrolling Forward: Making Sense of Documents in the Digital Age.* New York: Arcade.

Library of Congress. 2012. "Standards at the Library of Congress." http://www.loc.gov/standards.

Lisowsky, Gerhard. 1958. *Konkordanz zum hebräischen Alten Testament.* Edited by H. P. Ruger. 3rd ed., corrected. Stuttgart: Deutsche Bibelgesellschaft.

"Livre électronique: un coût peu élevé." 2010. memoclic. http://www.memoclic.com/1735–barometre/11912–cout-livre-electronique.html.

Lochard, Éric-Olivier, and Dominique Taurisson. 2001. "Le monde selon Arcane: un paradigme instrumental pour l'édition électronique." *Cahiers Gutenberg* (May): 39–40. http://www.gutenberg.eu.org/pub/GUTenberg/publicationsPDF/39–lochard.pdf. See also http://arcanews.univ-montp3.fr/arcane.

Lyotard, Jean-François. 1984. *The Postmodern Condition: A Report on Knowledge.* Translated by Geoffrey Bennington and Brian Massumi. Minneapolis: University of Minnesota Press, 1984. [Originally published as *La Condition postmoderne: Rapport sur le savoir.* Paris: Éditions de Minuit, 1979.]

Maas, Paul. 1960 [1927]. *Einleitung in die Altertumswissenschaft*, vol. 2: "Textkritik." Leipzig: Teubner, 1927. [4th ed., Leipzig: Teubner, 1960]. [English translation: *Textual Criticism.* Translated by Barbara Flowers. Oxford: Clarendon, 1958.]

Mabillon, Jean. 1681. *De re diplomatica libri VI. Ed. 2 ab ipso auctore recognita, emendata et aucta.* Paris, [1681] 1709.

Macé, Caroline, Philippe Baret, Andrea Bozzi, et al., eds. 2006. *The Evolution of Texts: Confronting Stemmatological and Genetical Methods.* Proceedings of the International Workshop held in Louvain-la-Neuve on September 1–2, 2004 (Linguistica Computazionale 24). Pisa: Instituti editoriali e poligrafici internazionali.

Manguel, Alberto. 1996. *A History of Reading.* New York: Viking.

Markaryk, Irena R., ed. 1993a. "Sociocriticism." In *Encyclopedia of Contemporary Literary Theory: Approaches, Scholars, Terms.* 189–93. Toronto: University of Toronto Press.

———. 1993b. *Encyclopedia of Contemporary Literary Theory: Approaches, Scholars, Terms.* Toronto: University of Toronto Press.

Marshall, Catherine C. 2004. "Reading and Interactivity in the Digital Library: Creating an Experience That Transcends Paper." Redmond, WA: Microsoft Corporation. http://citeseerx.ist.psu.edu/viewdoc/download?doi=10.1.1.76.7532&rep=rep1&type=pdf.

Martin, Henri-Jean. 1996. *Histoire et pouvoirs de l'écrit, avec la collaboration de Bruno Delmas.* Collection "Bibliothèque de l'Évolution de l'Humanité." Paris: Albin Michel.

Martinet, André. 1965. *La linguistique synchronique. Études et recherches.* Paris: Presses de Universitaires de France.

Masai, François. 1950. "Principes et conventions de l'édition diplomatique." *Scriptorium* 4: 177–93.

McGann, Jerome J., ed. 1992. *The Complete Writings and Pictures of Dante Gabriel Rossetti: A Hypermedia Archive.* www.rossettiarchive.org.

———. 2004. "Marking Texts in Many Dimensions." In *A Companion to Digital Humani-*

ties, edited by Susan Schreibman, Ray Siemens, and John Unsworth, 198–217. Oxford: Blackwell. http://jefferson.village.virginia.edu/~jjm2f/blackwell.htm.

———. 2006. "From Text to Work: Digital Tools and the Emergence of the Social Text." *Text* 16: 49–62. http://www.jstor.org/stable/30227956.

———, ed. 2010. *Online Humanities Scholarship: The Shape of Things to Come.* Proceedings of the Mellon Foundation Online Humanities Conference at the University of Virginia, March 26–28, 2010. Houston: Rice University Press.

McKenna, Antony, and Annie Leroux. 2003. "L'édition électronique de la correspondance de Pierre Bayle." *Revue d'histoire littéraire de la France* 103 (2): 365–73.

McKenzie, D. F. 1991. *Bibliography and the Sociology of Texts.* The Panizzi Lectures 1985, London: British Library, 1986. [French translation: *La bibliographie et la sociologie des textes.* Paris, 1991. Preface by Roger Chartier.]

McKerrow, Ronald B., ed. 1904. *The Works of Thomas Nashe.* London: Sidgwick & Jackson.

McLuhan, Herbert Marshall. 1962. *The Gutenberg Galaxy: The Making of Typograpic Man.* Toronto: University of Toronto Press.

Menzer, Melinda. 2001 [1999]. "Review of Bernard Cerquiglini, *In Praise of the Variant: A Critical History of Philology.*" Baltimore: Johns Hopkins University Press. [Also published in *Bryn Mawr Review of Comparative Literature* 2, no. 2 (2001).] http://www.brynmawr.edu/bmrcl/Spring2001/Cerquiglini.html.

Meschini, Federico. 2007. "Scholarly Editions: Does Form Matter?" Paper delivered at the Humanities Postgraduates Conference, De Montfort University, October 31. http://dspace.unitus.it/handle/2067/244.

Modalsli, Tone. 2005. "Utblikk over forskjellige utgavetyper." In *Læsemåder: Udgavetyper og målgrupper,* edited by Per Dahl, Johnny Kondrup, and Karsten Kynde, 13–28. Nordisk Netværk for Editionsfilologer Skrifter 6. Copenhagen: C. A. Reitzel.

Molière [Jean-Baptiste Poquelin]. 2010. *Œuvres complètes.* Bibliothèque de la Pléiade. Paris: Gallimard.

Mollier, Jean-Yves. 1984. *Michel et Calmann Lévy ou la naissance de l'édition moderne (1836–1891).* Paris: Calmann-Lévy.

Mozet, Nicole. n.d. "Pourquoi une édition électronique de La Comédie humaine?" http://www.v1.paris.fr/commun/v2asp/musees/balzac/furne/presentation.htm.

Müllenhoff, Karl, ed. 1876 [1969]. *Kleinere Schriften zur deutschen Philologie von Karl Lachmann. Kleinere Schriften von Karl Lachmann,* 1. Berlin, 1876. Reprint, Berlin, 1969.

Müllenhoff, Karl, and Johannes Vahlen, ed. 1876. *Kleinere Schriften von Karl Lachmann,* 2 Bde., herausgegeben von K. Müllenhoff und J. Vahlen. Berlin: G. Reimer.

Munk-Olsen, Birger. 1969 [1968]. "Revue de DOM JACQUES FROGER: La critique des textes et son automatisation." *Revue Romane* 4 (1): 94–102. [Originally published in *Initiation aux nouveautés de la science* 7. Paris: Dunod].

Najock, Dietmar. 1973. "Automatic Classification of Texts by Methods of Multivariate Statistics." *Revue: Laboratoire d'Analyse Statistique des Langues Anciennes* 2: 31–54.

Nichols, Stephen G. 1990a. "Introduction: Philology in a Manuscript Culture." *Speculum* 60 (1): 1–10.

———, ed. 1990b. "The New Philology." Special issue of *Speculum* 65 (1): 1–108.

———. 1994. "Philology and Its Discontents." In *The Future of the Middle Ages: Medieval Literature in the 1990s,* edited by William D. Paden, 113–41. Gainesville: University Press of Florida.

———. 1997a. "Why Material Philology? Some Thoughts." In *Zeitschrift für Deutsche Philologie* 116. Sonderheft: *Philologie als Textwissenschaft. Alte und neue Horizonte,* edited by Helmut Tervooren and Horst Wenze, 10–30.

———. 1997b. "Why Material Philology? Some Thoughts." Special issue of *Zeitschrift für Deutsche Philologie* 116: 1–21.

Niehoff, Maren. 2007. "Homeric Scholarship and Bible Exegesis in Ancient Alexandria. Evidence from Philo's 'Quarrelsome' Colleague." *Classical Quarterly* 57 (1): 166–82.

Nunberg, Geoffrey. 1996. *The Future of the Book*. With an Afterword by Umberto Eco. Berkeley: University of California Press.

Olson, David R. 1994. *The World on Paper: The Conceptual and Cognitive Implications of Writing and Reading*. Cambridge: Cambridge University Press.

Olson, David R., and Michael Cole, eds. 2006. *Technology, Literacy, and the Evolution of Society: Implications of the Work of Jack Goody*. Mahwah, NJ: Lawrence Erlbaum Associates.

Ong, Walter. 1986 [1985]. "Writing Is a Technology That Transforms Thought." Wolfson College Lectures at Oxford University, Opening Lecture. In *The Written Word: Literacy in Transition*, edited by Gerd Baumann, 35–41. Oxford: Clarendon Press.

———. 1997. *Interfaces of the Word*. Ithaca, NY: Cornell University Press.

———. 2002. *Orality and Literacy: The Technologizing of the Word*. 2nd ed. New York: Routledge.

Paris, Gaston, and Léopold Pannier, eds. 1872. *La Vie de Saint Alexis.* Bibliothèque de l'École des Hautes Études. *Sciences philologiques et historiques 7*. Paris.

Pauphilet, Albert. 1923. *La Queste del Saint Graal, roman du XIIIe siècle*. Paris: Champion.

Perrin, Norman. 2002. *What Is Redaction Criticism?* Eugene, OR: Wipf and Stock Pub.

Petit, Michèle. 2008. *L'art de lire, ou, comment résister à l'adversité*. Paris: Belin.

Phalèse, Hubert de. n.d. *Dictionnaire de l'édition*. Paris: Centre Hubert de Phalèse. http://www.cavi.univ-paris3.fr/phalese/desslate.

Pichler, Alois. 1995. "Transcriptions, Texts, and Interpretation." In *Culture and Value: Beiträge des 18. Internationalen Wittgenstein Symposiums,* edited by Kjell S. Johannessen and Tore Nordenstam, 690–95. Kirchberg am Wechsel: ALWS.

———. 2004. *Wittgensteins Philosophische Untersuchungen: Vom Buch zum Album*. Studien zur Österreichischen Philosophie 36. Amsterdam: Rodopi.

Pichler, Alois, and Odd Einar Haugen. 2005. "Fra kombinerte utgaver til dynamisk utgivelse. Erfaringer fra edisjonsfilologisk arbeid med Wittgensteins filosofiske skrifter og nordiske middelaldertekster." In *Læsemåder: Udgavetyper og målgrupper*, edited by Per Dahl, Johnny Kondrup, and Karsten Kynde, 178–224, 241–49. København: Reitzel.

Piégay-Gros, Nathalie, ed. 2002. *Le lecteur*. Paris: Édition GF Flammarion.

Pike, Kenneth Lee. 1967. *Language in Relation to a Unified Theory of the Structure of Human Behavior*. Janua Linguarum, Series maior, vol. 24. 2nd ed. The Hague: Mouton.

Prensky, Mark. 2001a. "Digital Natives, Digital Immigrants, Part I." *On the Horizon,* October 2001, 9 (5).

———. 2001b. "Digital Natives, Digital Immigrants, Part II." *On the Horizon,* December 2001, 9 (6)

Propp, Vladimir. 1968 [1927]. *Morphology of the Folktale.* Translated by Laurence Scott. 2nd ed., 1927. Austin: University of Texas Press.

Proust, Marcel. 1971. *On Reading.* Translated by Jean Autret and William Burford. New York: MacMillan.

———. 2000. *Sur la lecture.* Paris: Editions Flammarion. Collection "Librio." [Text originally written as the foreword written by Marcel Proust in 1905 for his translation of *Sesame and Lilies* by John Ruskin.]

Quentin, Henri. 1926. *Essais de critique textuelle (Ecdotique).* Paris: Picard.

Quinn, Judy, and Emily Lethbridge, eds. 2010. *Creating the Medieval Saga.* Viking Collection. Vol. 18. Odense: Syddansk Universitetsforlag.

Rabardel, Pierre. 1995. *Les hommes et les technologies. Approche cognitive des instruments contemporains.* Paris: Armand Colin Éditeur.

Racine, Bruno. 2007. Interview published in *L'Archicube, Revue de l'Association des anciens.*

"Reclaim the Commons." *Manifesto: Reclaim the Commons.* http://bienscommuns.org/signature/appel/?a=appel&lang=en.

Redeker, Robert. 2004. *Nouvelles figures de l'homme: Inhumain, déshumain, néghumain.* Latresne: éditions Le Bord de l'eau.

Reenen, Pieter van, and Margot van Mulken, eds. 1996. *Studies in Stemmatology.* Vol. 1. Amsterdam: Benjamins.

———. 2004. *Studies in Stemmatology.* Vol. 2. Amsterdam: Benjamins.

Rehbein, Malte. 1998. "Die dynamische digitale Textedition: Ein Modell." In *Vom digitalen Archiv zur digitalen Edition,* edited by Hans-Heinrich Ebeling, Hans-Reinhard Fricke, Peter Hoheisel, Malte Rehbein, and Manfred Thaller, 5–21. Göttingen: Max-Planck-Institut für Geschichte.

———. 2010. "The Transition from Classical to Digital Thinking: Reflections on Tim McLoughlin, James Barry, and Collaborative Work." *Jahrbuch für Computerphilologie* 10: 55–67. [Also available online at computerphilologie.tu-darmstadt.de/jg08/rehbein.pdf.]

Reinhard G., and Otto Merk. 1997. "Redaktionsgeschichte/Redaktionskritik I. Altes Testament II. Neues Testament." In *Theologishe Realenzyklopädie* 28: 367–78, 378–84.

Ricklefs, Ulfert. 1999. "Zur Systematik historischer-kritischer Ausgaben." *Editio. Internationales Jahrbuch für Editionswissenschaften* 3: 1–22. Downloadable as PDF file from http://www.reference-global.com/doi/abs/10.1515/9783484604278.1.

Robinson, Peter, ed. 1996. Geoffrey Chaucer. *The Wife of Bath's Prologue on CD-ROM.* Cambridge: Cambridge University Press.

———. 2004. *The Miller's Tale on CD-ROM.* Leicester: Scholarly Digital Editions.

———. 2006. "Electronic Textual Editing: *The Canterbury Tales* and Other Medieval Texts." In *Electronic Text Editing,* edited by Lou Burnard, Katherine O'Brien O'Keeffe, and John Unsworth. New York: Modern Language Association. [Also published online as *Electronic Textual Editing,* TEI, Text Encoding Initiative Consortium. http://www.tei-c.org/Activities/ETE/Preview/index.xml.]

———. 2009. "Towards a Scholarly Editing System for the Next Decades." In *Lecture Notes in Computer Science: Sanskrit Computational Linguistics,* edited by Gérard Huet, Amba Kulkarni, and Peter Scharf, 346–57. Berlin: Springer.

Robinson, Peter, and Robert J. O'Hara. 2003 [1992]. "Report on the Textual Criticism Challenge 1991." *Bryn Mawr Classical Review* 03.03.29. http://bmcr.brynmawr .edu/1992/03.03.29.html.

Roos, Teemu, and Tuomas Heikkilä. 2009. "Evaluating Methods for Computer-Assisted Stemmatology Using Artificial Benchmark Data Sets." *Literary and Linguistic Computing* 24 (4): 417–33.

Roques, Gilles. 1995. "L'édition des textes français entre les deux guerres." In *Histoire de la Langue française (1914–1945),* edited by Gérald Antoine and Robert Martin, 993–1000. Paris: CNRS-Éditions.

Rosen, Christine. 2008. "People of the Screen." *New Atlantis* 22 (Fall): 20–32. http:// www.thenewatlantis.com/publications/people-of-the-screen.

Rubow, Paul V. 1938. *Den kritiske kunst. En afhandling om filologisk litteraturforskning.* København: Gyldendal.

Rychner, Jean, ed. 1958. *Marie de France. Le lai de Lanval.* Textes littéraires français. Genève: Droz.

Sampson, Geoffrey. 1980. *Schools of Linguistics: Competition and Evolution.* London: Hutchinson.

Sanger, Larry. 2008. "On 'Is Google Making Us Stupid?'" by N. Carr." *Edge, The Reality Club.* http://www.edge.org/discourse/carr_google.html.

Sattler, Dietrich E., ed. 1975. *Friedrich Hölderlin. Sämtliche Werke. "Frankfurter Ausgabe."* Frankfurt am Main: Roter Stern.

Schlyter, Carl Johan, and Hans Samuel Collin, eds. 1827. *Westgöta-lagen. Samling af Sweriges gamla lagar.* Vol. 1. Stockholm: Haeggström.

Schnell, Rüdiger. 1997. "Was is neu an der 'New Philology'? Zum Diskussionsstand in der germanistischen Mediävistik." *Alte und neue Philologie 9,* edited by Martin-Dietrich Glessgen and Franz Lebsanft, 61–95. (Beiheft zu Editio, vol. 8.) Tübingen: Niemeyer.

Seim, Karin Fjellhammer. 2007. "Runologie." In *Altnordische Philologie: Norwegen und Island,* edited by Odd Einar Haugen, 147–222. Berlin: de Gruyter.

Sgard, Jean, and Catherine Volpilhac-Auger, eds. 1999. *La notion d'œuvres complètes.* Oxford: Voltaire Foundation.

SGML: Information Processing—Text and Office Systems—Standard Generalized Markup Language (SGML). ISO 88791986. International Organization for Standardization. Geneva. http://www.iso.org/iso/catalogue_detail.htm?csnumber=16387.

Shelton, Thomas. 1635 [1626]. *Tachygraphy.* London.

Shillingsburg, Peter. 1989. "An Inquiry into the Social Status of Texts and Modes of Textual Criticism." *Studies in Bibliography* 42: 55–78.

———. 2006. *From Gutenberg to Google.* Cambridge: Cambridge University Press.

Siemens, Ray, Cara Leitch, Analisa Blake, Karin Armstrong, and John Willinsky. 2009. "It May Change My Understanding of the Field: New Reading Tools for Scholars." *Digital Humanities Quarterly* 3 (4). http://www.digitalhumanities.org/dhq/ vol/3/4/000075/000075.html.

Siemens, Ray, Meagan Timney, Cara Leitch, Corina Koolen, and Alex Garnett. 2012a. "Understanding the Electronic Scholarly Edition in the Context of New and Emerging Social Media: Selected, Annotated Bibliographies." *Digital Humanities Quarterly* 6 (1). http://www.digitalhumanities.org/dhq/vol/6/1/000111/000111.html.

Siemens, Ray, Meagan Timney, Cara Leitch, Corina Koolen, Alex Garnett, and the ETCL, INKE, and PKP Research Groups. 2012b. "Toward Modeling the Social Edition: An Approach to Understanding the Electronic Scholarly Edition in the Context of New and Emerging Social Media." *Literary & Linguistic Computing* 27 (4): 445–61.

Siemens, Ray, John Willinsky, Analisa Blake, and Greg Newton. 2006. *A Study of Professional Reading Tools for Humanists.* http://etcl-dev.uvic.ca/public/pkp_report.

Simon, Eckehardt. 1990. "The Case for Medieval Philology." In *On Philology,* edited by Jan Ziolkowski, 16–19. University Park: Pennsylvania State University Press.

Sirinelli, Jean. 2001. "Alexandrie, royaume du livre." In *Des Alexandries I. Du livre au texte,* edited by Christian Jacob and Luce Giard, 46–47. Paris: Bibliothèque nationale de France.

Solopova, Elizabeth, ed. 2000. *Geoffrey Chaucer: "The General Prologue" on CD-ROM.* Cambridge: Cambridge University Press.

Sperberg-McQueen, C. M., and Lou Burnard. 2002. *TEI P4: Guidelines for Electronic Text Encoding and Interchange.* Text Encoding Initiative Consortium. XML Version. Oxford, Providence, Charlottesville, Bergen. [The latest edition, TEI P5, is available from http://www.tei-c.org.]

Stackmann, Karl. 1979. "Die Klassische Philologie und die Anfange der Germanistik." In *Philologie und Hermeneutik im 19. Jahrhundert,* edited by Hellmut Flashar, Karlfried Grunder, and Axel Horstmann, 240–59. Gottingen: Vandenhoeck und Ruprecht.

———. 1994. "Neue Philologie?" In *Modernes Mittelalter. Neue Bilder einer populären Epoche,* edited by Joachim Heinzle, 398–427. Frankfurt am Main: Insel.

Stauffer, Andrew M. 1998. "Tagging the Rossetti Archive: Methodologies and Praxis." *Journal of Electronic Publishing* 4 (2). University of Michigan Press. Reprint. [Initally published in *Revue Informatique et Statistique dans les Sciences Humaines,* Université de Liège, Belgique.] http://dx.doi.org/10.3998/3336451.0004.209.

Stehr, Nico. 1994. *Knowledge Societies.* London: Sage.

Stewart, Philippe. 2002. "L'Encyclopédie éclatée." In *Recherches sur Diderot et sur l'Encyclopédie* 31–32. L'Encyclopédie en ses nouveaux atours électroniques (April): 189–97. PDF file downloadable at http://rde.revues.org/document3133.html.

Stock, Brian. 1993. Afterword. In *The Ethnography of Reading,* edited by Jonathan Boyarin, 270–75. Berkeley: University of California Press.

Stubbs, Estelle, ed. 2000. *The Hengwrt Chaucer Digital Facsimile: Research Edition.* Leicester: Scholarly Digital Editions. Updated version 2012: http://www.sd-editions.com/AnaAdditional/HengwrtEx/images/hgopen.html.

Tanselle, G. Thomas. 1976. "The Editorial Problem of Final Authorial Intention." *Studies in Bibliography* 29: 167–211.

———. 1991. *Textual Criticism and Scholarly Editing.* Charlottesville: University Press of Virginia.

TEI Text Encoding Initiative Consortium. 2011. *Electronic Textual Editing: Guidelines for Scholarly Editions.* http://www.tei-c.org/About/Archive_new/ETE/Preview/

guidelines.xml. [Preview from 2004 at http://www.tei-c.org/About/Archive_new/ETE/Preview.]

The Canterbury Tales Project. 2006. "The Open Transcription Policy." http://www.canterburytalesproject.org/OTP.html.

Thomas, Paul. 2006. *The Nun's Priest Tale on CD-ROM*. Birmingham: Scholarly Digital Editions.

Tisseron, Serge. 2001. *L'intimité surexposée*. Paris: Ramsay.

Unger, Carl Richard, ed. 1877. "Niðrstigningar saga." In *Heilagra manna sögur*. Vol. 2, 1–20. Christiania: Bentzen.

Valéry, Paul. 1928. *La conquête de l'ubiquité*. In *De la musique avant toute chose* (textes de Paul Valéry, Henri Massis, Camille Bellaigue, etc.). Editions du Tambourinaire. Paris, 1928. [Reprinted in Paul Valéry, *Oeuvres*. Vol. 2, Coll. "La Pléiade." Paris: Gallimard, 1960, 1284–87.]

van Arkel-de Leeuw van Weenen, Andrea, ed. 1987. *Möðruvallabók: AM 132 Fol.* 2 vols. Leiden.

Vandendorpe, Christian. 2009. *From Papyrus to Hypertext: Toward the Universal Digital Library*. Champaign: University of Illinois Press. [Translated from the original French edition: *Du papyrus à l'hypertexte: essai sur les mutations du texte et de la lecture*. Paris: La Découverte, 1999.]

"Vente Berès des manuscrits stendhaliens." 2006. *Stendhal, l'actualité stendhalienne*, 28/03/2006. http://stendhal.armance.com/?cat=8.

Viprey, Jean-Marie. 2005. "Philologie numérique et herméneutique intégrative." In *Sciences du texte et analyse de discours: Enjeux d'une interdisciplinarité. Études de lettres*, edited by Jean-Michel Adam and Ute Heidmann, 51–68. Revue de la faculté des Lettres de l'Université de Lausanne 270 (1/2), Lausanne.

Virilio, Paul. 1986 [1977]. *Speed and Politics: An Essay on Dromology*. Translated by Mark Polizzotti. New York: Semiotext(e).

Wagner, Andreas. 1996. "Gattung und 'Sitz im Leben'. Zur Bedeutung der formgeschichtlichen Arbeit Hermann Gunkels (1862–1932) fur das Verstehen der sprachlichen Große Text." In *Texte—Konstitution, Verarbeitung, Typik*. Hrsg. von Susanne Michaelis und Doris Tophinke, 117–29. Edition Linguistik 13. Munchen: Newcastle.

Wellek, René. 1955–1993. *A History of Modern Criticism, 1750–1950*. 8 vols. New Haven, CT: Yale University Press. Vol. 1, *The Later Eighteenth Century*, 1955; Vol. 2, *The Romantic Age*, 1955; Vol. 3, *The Age of Transition*, 1965; Vol. 4, *The Later Nineteenth Century*, 1965; Vol. 5, *English Criticism, 1900–1950*, 1986; Vol. 6, *American Criticism, 1900–1950*, 1986; Vol. 7, *German, Russian, and Eastern European Criticism, 1900–1950*, 1991; Vol. 8, *French, Italian, and Spanish Criticism, 1900–1950*, 1993.

Wellek, René, and Austin Warren. 1949. "The Nature of Literature." *Theory of Literature*. 1st ed. [3rd ed. New York: Harcourt, Brace & World, 1956]. http://www.plu.edu/~jensenmk/271wellek.html.

Welshons, Marlo, ed. 2006. *Our Cultural Commonwealth*: The Report of the American Council of Learned Societies Commission on Cyberinfrastructure for the Humanities and Social Sciences. New York. http://www.acls.org/cyberinfrastructure/OurCulturalCommonwealth.pdf.

West, Martin L. 1973. *Textual Criticism and Editorial Techniques Applicable to Greek and Latin Texts*. Stuttgart: Teubner.

Williams, Peter, and Ian Rowlands. 2007. *The Literature on Young People and Their Information Behaviour*. Work Package II. "Information Behaviour of the Researcher of the Future: A British Library/JISC Study." (October 18) Final draft. Available as a PDF file at http://www.jisc.ac.uk/media/documents/programmes/reppres/ggworkpackageii.pdf.

Witt, Andreas, Harald Lüngen, Felix Sasaki, and Daniela Goecke. 2005. "Unification of XML Documents with Concurrent Markup." *Literary and Linguistic Computing* 20 (1): 103–16.

Wittgenstein, Ludwig. 2000. *Wittgenstein's "Nachlass": The Bergen Electronic Edition*. Edited by Wittgenstein Archives at the University of Bergen. Oxford: Oxford University Press.

Wolf, Jürgen. 2002. "New Philology/Textkritik. A. Älteres deutsche Literatur." In *Germanistik als Kulturwissenschaft. Eine Einführung in neue Theoriekonzepte*, edited by Claudia Benthien and Hans Rudolf Velten, 175–95. Rowohlts Enzyklopädie. Reinbek bei Hamburg: Rowohlt.

Wolf, Maryanne. 2008. *Proust and the Squid: The Story and Science of the Reading Brain*. London: Icon Books.

Zapf, Volker. n.d. "HNML HyperNietzsche Markup Language." PDF file available at http://www.hypernietzsche.org/events/sew/post/Slides%20and%20Texts_files/HNML.pdf.

Zeller, Hans. 1958. "Zur gegenwärtigen Aufgabe der Editionstechnik: Ein Versuch, komplizierte Handschriften darzustellen." *Euphorion* 52: 356–77.

———. 1975. "A New Approach to the Critical Constitution of Literary Texts." *Studies in Bibliography* 28: 231–63.

Zumthor, Paul. 1972. *Essai de poétique médiévale*. Paris: Seuil.

Online Bibliographies and Websites with Scholarly Articles

Digital Scholarship. Web portal at http://www.digital-scholarship.org. Provides a series of digital bibliographies at http://www.digital-scholarship.org/about/dsdigbib.htm covering:

- Digital Curation and Preservation Bibliography (1/17/11)
- Scholarly Electronic Publishing Bibliography (12/13/10)
- Electronic Theses and Dissertations Bibliography (11/30/10)
- Institutional Repository Bibliography (11/15/10)
- Transforming Scholarly Publishing through Open Access: A Bibliography (10/12/10)
- Open Access Journals Bibliography (8/23/10)
- Google Books Bibliography (4/12/10)
- Scholarly Electronic Publishing Weblog
- Reviews of Digital Scholarship Publications

Digital Studies/Le champ numérique (DS/CN). A refereed academic journal serving as a formal arena for scholarly activity and as an academic resource for researchers in the digital humanities. DS/CN is published by the Society for Digital Humanities / Société pour l'étude des médias interactifs (SDH/SEMI), a partner in the Alliance of

Digital Humanities Organizations (ADHO). DS/CN was founded for SDH/SEMI at the Electronic Textual Cultures Lab, University of Victoria, in 2008 by Ray Siemens and Christian Vandendorpe. http://www.digitalstudies.org.

Editio: Internationales Jahrbuch für Editionswissenschaft [International Yearbook for Scholarly Editing] Revue internationale des sciences de l'édition critique. Tübingen: Max Niemeyer Verlag, 1987– . More information online at http://www.degruyter .com/view/serial/35478?rskey=n7KGZ7&result=1.

INKE: Implementing New Knowledge Environments. A project funded by the SSHRC Major Collaborative Research Initiatives Program Implementing Knowledge Environments. Web portal at http://journals.uvic.ca/index.php/INKE/article/view/168.

MLA. *Annotated Bibliography: Key Works in the Theory of Textual Editing.* http://www .mla.org/cse_guidelines#doe2067.

TEI. Text Encoding Initiative. *Electronic Textual Editing: Annotated Bibliography: Key Works in the Theory of Textual Editing* [compiled and annotated by Dirk Van Hulle]. http://www.tei-c.org/Activities/ETE/Preview/vanh-bib.xml.

A Few Blogs about Digital Humanities

Blogo-Numericus: Le Blog d'homo-Numericus. http://blog.homo-numericus.net (in French).

Digital Scholarship in the Humanities: Exploring the Digital Humanities. Blog authored by Lisa Spiro, NITLE Labs. http://digitalscholarship.wordpress.com. Its purpose is to "explore how digital resources and tools are affecting scholarship in the humanities and consider the potential for digital scholarship."

Hyperstudio: Digital Humanities at MIT. "HyperStudio explores the potential of new media technologies for the enhancement of education and research in the humanities." http://hyperstudio.mit.edu.

Hypothèses.org: *plate-forme de carnets de recherche en sciences humaines et sociales proposée par le Centre pour l'édition électronique ouverte* (Cléo). Laboratoire du CNRS, EHESS, Université de Provence et l'Université d'Avignon. http://hypotheses.org (in French).

Insula: Le blog de la Bibliothèque des Sciences de l'Antiquité. "Antiquité et humanités numériques." Edited by Christophe Hugot, Bibliothèque des sciences de l'Antiquité de l'université Lille 3. http://bsa.biblio.univ-lille3.fr/blog/2011/01/antiquite-et-humanites-numeriques (in French).

Les petites cases. Blog held by Gautier Poupeau, editor of electronic documents at École des Chartes (French Library School) about digital critical edition. http://www .lespetitescases.net/index348 (in French).

Philologie à venir. Digital humanities website run by specialists of the Hellenistic and Roman world. http://philologia.hypotheses.org (in French).

Scholarly Digital Editions

The list of digital editions listed below is only indicative and not exhaustive.

African-American Women Writers of the 19th Century. The New York Public Library

Digital Library Collections. Digital Schomburg. New York: New York Public Library, 1999. http://digital.nypl.org/schomburg/writers_aa19.

ARTFL Encyclopédie Project. The ARTFL Encyclopédie. Robert Morrissey, gen. ed.; Glenn Roe, assoc. ed. *The Encyclopédie ou Dictionnaire raisonné des sciences, des arts et des métiers,* par une Société de Gens de lettres, was published under the direction of Diderot and D'Alembert, with 17 volumes of text and 11 volumes of plates between 1751 and 1772. Containing 74,000 articles written by more than 130 contributors, the *Encyclopédie* was a massive reference work for the arts and sciences, as well as a machine de guerre that served to propagate the ideas. Description available online at http://encyclopedie.uchicago.edu (in French and English). [The old URL—http://www.lib.uchicago.edu/efts/ARTFL/projects/encyc—still points to the same page.] Details about the CD-ROM version available at http://atilf.atilf.fr.

ARTFL. American and French Research on the Treasury of the French Language. "The Project for American and French Research on the Treasury of the French Language (ARTFL) is a cooperative enterprise of the Laboratoire ATILF (Analyse et Traitement Informatique de la Langue Française) of the Centre National de la Recherche Scientifique (CNRS the Division of the Humanities, and Electronic Text Services (ETS) of the University of Chicago." ARTFL offers a specialized intratextual and intertextual search engine and text analysis tool PhiloLogic exploiting an extensive database of French texts, ARTFL-FRANTEXT. http://artfl-project.uchicago.edu (in French and English).

[Austen] *Jane Austen's Fiction Manuscripts Digital Edition.* Edited by Kathryn Sutherland and Elena Pierazzo. Joint project of the University of Oxford and King's College London. Available online through a link at http://www.elenapierazzo.org.

[Balzac] *La Comédie humaine.* Édition critique en ligne. Integral online text of the original Furne edition, 1842–1855. Nicole Mozet, ed. (undated). http://www.v1.paris.fr/commun/v2asp/musees/balzac/furne/presentation.htm.

[Bayle] *The ARTFL Project. Dictionnaire de Bayle.* Online version is a copy of the 1740 edition (5th ed., Amsterdam, Leyde, La Haye, Utrecht; 4 vols. in folio) of Pierre Bayle's *Dictionnaire historique et critique.* Chicago: University of Chicago. http://artfl-project.uchicago.edu/node/60. [The old URL—http://www.lib.uchicago.edu/efts/ARTFL/projects/dicos/BAYLE—still points to the same page.]

[Bayle] *Corpus des oeuvres complètes de Pierre Bayle.* Paris: Classiques Garnier Numérique. Available online under the title "Corpus Bayle—Oeuvres completes" at http://www.digento.de/titel/104849.html.

[Bentham] *Transcribe Bentham.* The project's Transcription Desk is the heart of a major crowd-sourcing initiative to transcribe the manuscripts of Jeremy Bentham from the archives of University College London. Edited by Philip Schofield, Tim Causer, et al. The project was established under funding from the AHRC (2010–2011) and managed by UCL Bentham Project and UCL Digital Humanities, with the support of the University of London Computer Centre. http://www.transcribe-bentham.da.ulcc.ac.uk/td/Transcribe_Bentham.

[Blake] *The William Blake Archive.* Morris Eaves, Robert Essick, and Joseph Viscomi, eds. A hypermedia archive sponsored by the Library of Congress and supported by the University of North Carolina at Chapel Hill, the University of Rochester, and the Scholarly Editions and Translations Division of the National Endowment for the Humanities. November 13, 1997. http://www.blakearchive.org/blake.

[Boccaccio] *Decameron Web.* Co-edited by Michael Papio and Massimo Riva. Brown University. April 25, 2010. http://www.brown.edu/Departments/Italian_Studies/dweb/index.php.

BVH: Les Bibliothèques Virtuelles Humanistes du CESR is published by the Centre d'études supérieurs de la Renaissance, Tours, France. This virtual library was started in 2002 in collaboration with the humanities department of IRHT (Institut de recherche et d'histoire des textes). It provides access since 2008 to a variety of digital documents; e.g., facsimiles of Renaissance works from the French Centre Region, a repository for textual resources Epistemon, transcriptions and analyses of historical legal records and numerous other manuscripts, and pictures. It aims to provide lemmatization and statistical tools in the future. http://www.bvh.univ-tours.fr.

[Cervantes] *Biblioteca Virtual Miguel Cervantes.* http://www.cervantesvirtual.com.

[Cervantes] *Cervantes Project. L'Edición Variorum Electrónica del Quijote du Proyecto Cervantes.* Electronic variorum edition of the *Quixote.* Eduardo Urbina, ed. Cervantes Project, Texas A&M University and Cátedra Cervantes, Universidad de Castilla-La Mancha 2005–2008. http://cervantes.tamu.edu/V2/CPI/variorum/index.htm and http://cervantes.tamu.edu/V2/CPI/index.html.

[Chaucer] *The General Prologue on CD-ROM.* Elizabeth Solopova, ed. Cambridge: Cambridge University Press, 2000.

[Chaucer] *The Canterbury Tales Project.* New Canterbury Tales Project website. http://www.itsee.bham.ac.uk (ITSEE) at the University of Birmingham. Edited by Peter Robinson and Barbara Bordalejo. http://www.canterburytalesproject.org.

[Chaucer] *The Hengwrt Chaucer Digital Facsimile: Research Edition.* Edited by Estelle Stubbs. Leicester: Scholarly Digital Editions, 2000. Updated version 2012: http://www.sd-editions.com/AnaAdditional/HengwrtEx/images/hgopen.html.

[Chaucer] *The Miller's Tale on CD-ROM.* Edited by Peter Robinson. Leicester: Scholarly Digital Editions, 2004.

[Chaucer] *The Nun's Priest Tale on CD-ROM.* Edited by Paul Thomas. Birmingham: Scholarly Digital Editions, 2006. http://www.cambridge.org/us/academic/subjects/literature/anglo-saxon-and-medieval-literature/chaucer-general-prologue-cd-rom.

[D'Alembert] *Les Œuvres Complètes D'Alembert (1717–1783). Série I-V.* A companion site to the complete edition of the works of D'Alembert. http://dalembert.academie-sciences.fr/.

[Dante] *The World of Dante.* A multimedia research tool intended to facilitate the study of the *Divine Comedy* through a wide range of offerings. These include an encoded Italian text that allows for structured searches and analyses, an English translation, interactive maps, diagrams, music, a database, timeline, and gallery of illustrations. Edited by Deborah Parker (gen. ed., 1996–), John Unsworth (1996–1997), Daniel Pitti (1997, 2006–2008), and Martin Worthy (2006–2008). Institute for Advanced Technology in the Humanities, University of Virginia. http://www.worldofdante.org.

[de Scudéry] *Artamène, ou, le Grand Cyrus.* This site, maintained by Claude Bourqui and designed by Alexandre Gefen, offers the entire text of the largest novel of French literature (13,095 pages!) and figures available as "bubbles" while reading the text. http://www.artamene.org. "*Artamène, ou, le Grand Cyrus,*" written by Mlle de Scudéry. The site offers various tools, such as a hyperlinked web of references, summaries, and articles.

[Dumas] *Les Journaux d'Alexandre Dumas.* Sarah Mombert, ed. This site at http://alexandredumas.org presents the various activities and writings of Alexandre Dumas's days as chief editor of various newspapers. Lyon: ENS, 15 août 2008.

[Dumas] *Le Mousquetaire,* No. 1 (November 12, 1853). http://alexandredumas.org/eJ/journal/Le_Mousquetaire/1853-11-12-.

[d'Urfé] *Le règne d'Astrée,* roman d'Honoré d'Urfé (1607–1627). This web portal, produced and curated by Delphine Denis and d'Alexandre Gefen in collaboration with the ARTFL project, offers the complete text of Honoré d'Urfé fabulous work *L'Astrée* (1607–1627). It is presented as a hypertextual critical edition compliant with the *TEI Guidelines* and with access to all variants. http://www.astree.paris-sorbonne.fr (in French).

Édition "en ligne" de la Queste del saint Graal. Trancription et traduction par Isabelle Vedrenne-Fajolles, Marchello-Nizia, Christiane et Serge Heiden. http://txm.bfm-corpus.org/?command=documentation&path=/GRALL.

electronic Enlightenment—letters & lives online. A digital database formed from the correspondence of Voltaire, Rousseau, Franklin, and Jefferson. Edited by Robert Darnton, Voltaire Foundation, University of Oxford. http://www.e-enlightenment.com.

ELEC. Publications électroniques de L'École des chartes. The ELEC collection offers freely available textual corpuses, educational resources, and online demonstrations of computer-based methods and tools developed at ELEC. http://elec.enc.sorbonne.fr (in French).

[Flaubert] *Édition numérique des "Dossiers de Bouvard et Pécuchet" de Flaubert.* Stéphanie Dord-Crouslé, ed. http://lire.ish-lyon.cnrs.fr/spip.php?article130&lang=fr and http://dossiers-flaubert.ish-lyon.cnrs.fr.

[Flaubert] *Gustave Flaubert, Madame Bovary, Mœurs de province 1857* (Édition Conard, 1910). Published online at http://fr.wikisource.org/wiki/Madame_Bovary.

[Flaubert] *Gustave Flaubert, Madame Bovary, Mœurs de province,* Édition définitive, Paris: G. Charpentier éditeur, 1877. Published as black-and-white facsimile by Gallica at http://gallica.bnf.fr/ark:/12148/bpt6k80210g (title page).

[Flaubert] *La Génèse de Madame Bovary.* L'Atelier Bovary. Bibliothèque de Rouen–Centre Flaubert de l'Université de Rouen. Danielle Girard, Yvan, Leclerc, et al., eds. Centre d'Études et de Recherche Éditer/Interpréter (CEREdI, EA 3229), 2004–2008. http://flaubert.univ-rouen.fr/bovary/atelier/atelier.php.

[Flaubert] *Les manuscrits de Madame Bovary, édition intégrate sur le web.* Bibliothèque municipale de Rouen. Édition électronique de Madame Bovary. Editors: Danielle Girard and Yvan Leclerc. Based on the édition of Charpentier in 1873. http://www.bovary.fr/.

[Flaubert] *The Gustave Flaubert (1821–1880) portal* published by Cérédi at the University of Rouen (Centre d'étude et de recherche Éditer-Interpréter) in close collaboration with the Municipal Library of Rouen offers digital editions of Flaubert, bibliographies, and doctoral theses. http://www.univ-rouen.fr/flaubert.

Gazette d'Amsterdam. 12 CD-ROMs. Images of 78,000 pages covering the years 1691–1796. http://www.voltaire.ox.ac.uk/www_vf/gazette_a/gazettea_index.ssi.

[Heine] *Heinrich-Heine-Portal.* Nathalie Groß, ed. http://www.hhp.uni-trier.de.

[Holberg] *Ludvig Holbergs Skrifter* [*Ludvig Holberg's Writings*]. A Danish-Norwegian co-operative project to edit the works and correspondence of Ludvig Holberg (1711–1754). Eiliv Vinje and Karen Skovgaard-Petersen, eds. In development. See beta website in Danish and Norwegian at http://holbergsskrifter.dk or http://holbergsskrifter.no.

[Ibsen] *Henrik Ibsen's Writings.* [*Henrik Ibsens Skrifter.*] Text archive and printed edition edited by Vigdis Åse Ystad (gen. ed.), Daniel Apollon, Thoralf Berg, Christian Janns, Jon Gunnar Jørgensen, Tone Modalsli, and Asbjørn Aarseth. Forthcoming electronic edition under the auspices of the University of Oslo, Henrik Ibsens Skrifter and Eining for digital dokumentasjon. *Electronic version Beta 1,* edited by Stine Brenna Taugbøl., in Norwegian. http://www.ibsen.uio.no.

[Kierkegaard] *Søren Kierkegaards Skrifter (the Writings of Søren Kierkegaard). Electronic version 1.5.9.* Edited by Karsten Kynde, Niels Jørgen Cappelen, et al. Søren Kierkegaard Forskningscenteret. Copenhagen, November 2010. http://sks.dk.

L'Écho de la fabrique, Journal industriel et littéraire de Lyon. Ludovic Frobert, ed. This web portal offers a critical edition of newspapers published by the silk workers (*canuts*) of Lyon during the two uprisings of 1831 and 1834. http://triangle.ens-lyon.fr/spip .php?article1644 (undated, in French).

La France en Amérique/France in America. Conceived in partnership with France's national library, the Bibliothèque nationale de France, France in America/France en Amérique is a bilingual digital library made available by the Library of Congress. http://international.loc.gov/intldl/fiahtml.

Le Cartulaire blanc of the Abbey of Saint-Denis. ELEC, Chartes de l'abbaye de Saint-Denis (VIIe-XIIIe siècle). Edited by Olivier Guyot-Jeannin. Last version: Paris: Sorbonne, October 2011. http://saint-denis.enc.sorbonne.fr.

Liverpool Online Series: Critical Editions of French Texts. The aim of this series is to establish a resource bank of critical editions and/or translations of French texts. These are available in electronic form, with parallel paper publication of a small number of copies of each item. Online versions of items in the series are designed to be viewed as exact replicas of the printed copies. Each item in the series has its own ISBN and is lodged in hard copy with the major copyright libraries. http://www.liv.ac.uk/modern-languages-and-cultures/french/liverpool-online-series/.

MathML, W3C MathML Home. http://www.w3.org/Math.

[Molière] *Molière 21.* A companion site to the new complete learned edition of Molière's work published by La Pléiade (Molière. Œuvres complètes. Bibliothèque de la Pléiade. Paris: Gallimard, 2010). http://www.moliere.paris-sorbonne.fr.

[Molière] *Site-Molière.* Philippe Parker offers online text access to all Molière's plays (1622–1673) in hypertextual version, with musical excerpts from his comédies-ballets, a biography, biographical information's about his contemporaries, and a concordance of his works. http://www.site-moliere.com. Another site, curated by Gabriel Conesa, Université de Reims, targets a broader public. See also www.toutmoliere.net.

[Molière] *Tout Molière*. Le site de référence sur l'œuvre de Molière. Created by the municipality of Pézenas, Hérault, France. http://www.toutmoliere.net.

[Montesquieu] *Montédite. Édition en ligne des pensés de Montsequieu.* General editors: Carole Dornier and Pierre-Yves Buard. UMR 6583. Centre de recherche d'historie quantitative (CRMQ), CNRS. Université de Caen Basse-Mormandie, axe "Cultures et politiques à l'époque moderne et contemporaine." https://www.unicaen.fr/services/puc/sources/Montesquieu.

[Montesquieu] *Montesquieu.* A companion site to the ongoing edition of the complete works of Montesquieu (*Œuvres complètes de Montesquieu.* 22 volumes. Vols. 1–4, 8–9, 11–13, 16, and 18 jointly published by the Voltaire Foundation, Oxford and l'Istituto italiano per gli Studi Filosofici, Naples); since 2010 the remaining volumes are published by ENS Editions, Lyon, and Classiques Garnier, Paris). http://montesquieu.ens-lyon.fr/spip.php?rubrique5.

[Munch] *eMunch. Edvard Munch's Writings.* An electronic archive of Edvard Munch's written material. [In Norwegian: eMunch, Edvard Munchs tekster, Digitalt arkiv.] Edited by Hilde Bøe. Oslo: Munchmuseet. First beta version January 20, 2011. http://www.emunch.no. [There is also an English edition at http://www.emunch.no/english.xhtml.]

[Nietzsche] *HyperNietzsche.* Provides access in German, English, French, and Italian to *Friedrich Nietzsche's Digitale Kritische Gesamtausgabe*, a digital version of the German critical edition of the complete works of Nietzsche edited by Giorgio Colli and Mazzino Montinari, and to the *Digitale Faksimile Gesamtausgabe*, a digital facsimile reproduction of the entire Nietzsche estate, including first editions of works, manuscripts, letters, and biographical documents. HyperNietzsche proposes also a new hypertextual model allowing a widely geographically dispersed community of scholars to collaborate on the analysis of the works of Nietzsche. Online at http://www.nietzschesource.org (redirected from http://www.hypernietzsche.org). See also NietzscheSource.

[Parzival] *Parzival-Project. Wolfram von Eschenbach, "Parzival." Eine überlieferungskritische Ausgabe in elektronischer Form.* Ein project des Schweizerischen Nationalfonds. Edited by Michael Stolz. http://www.parzival.unibe.ch/home.html.

[Perseus] *Perseus Digital Library.* Gregory R. Crane, editor in chief, Tufts University. Version Perseus 4.0, also known as the Perseus Hopper. Tufts University, September 2011. http://www.perseus.tufts.edu/hopper.

[Phénix] *Phénix. Bibliothèque libertaire et anarchiste,* collection of reprints from the Phénix editions: http://cgecaf.ficedl.info/mot90.html. See also *Bianco: 100 ans de presse anarchiste,* online presentation of the thesis of René Bianco (1941–2005): *Répertoire des périodiques anarchistes de langue française: un siècle de presse anarchiste d'expression française, 1880–1983* (*100 Years of Anarchist Press*). Aix-Marseille, 1987. http://bianco.ficedl.info/.

PhiloSource. Discovery Project. Philosophy in the Digital Era. Read, study, cite and publish in a semantic web environment. Supported from 2006 to 2009 by the eContentPlus programme. Coordinated by ITEM, Paris. Paolo D'Iorio, coordinator. http://www .discovery-project.eu/home.html.

[Plowman] *The Piers Plowman Electronic Archive*. Robert Adams, et al., eds. A hypermedia archive supported by the National Endowment for the Humanities, the University of Virginia Institute for Advanced Technology in the Humanties. Forthcoming. Charlottesville,VA: 2005. http://www3.iath.virginia.edu/seenet/piers.

The Princeton Charrette Project Le Projet Charette. Alfred Foulet (1900–1987) *In memoriam.* http://www.princeton.edu/~lancelot/ss. The Princeton Charrette Project is a complex, scholarly, multimedia electronic archive containing a medieval manuscript tradition—that of Chrétien de Troyes's *Le Chevalier de la Charrette* (Lancelot, ca. 1180). It was developed and maintained by Karl Uitti (Princeton University, Dept. of French and Italian) from 1994 to 2003. From October 2003 through July 2006 the web presence of the project was maintained by the editorial board of the project under the general direction of Gina Greco (Portland State University), Sarah-Jane Murray (Baylor University), and Rafael Alvarado (Dickinson College). A new version called *The Charrette Project 2* is available at http://lancelot.baylor.edu. [The French version called *Le Project Charette,* described at http://meet.tge-adonis.fr/projet/le-projet -charrette, is currently unavailable.]

[Rossetti] *The Complete Writings and Pictures of Dante Gabriel Rossetti: A Hypermedia Archive*. Edited by Jerome J. McGann. Charlottesville, VA: IAHT-University of Virginia, 1992. http://www.rossettiarchive.org/index.html.

SEENET. The Society for Early English & Norse Electronic Text. John A. Burrows, et al., editors. Society for Early English and Norse Electronic Texts (SEENET), Charlottesville: University of Virginia Institute for Advanced Technology in the Humanities, 2007. http://www3.iath.virginia.edu/seenet.

[Shakespeare] *The Complete Works of William Shakespeare*. MIT's public domain non-scholarly electronic edition based on the Complete Moby Shakespeare. http://shakespeare.mit.edu.

[Shakespeare] *Internet Shakespeare Editions*. http://internetshakespeare.uvic.ca.

[Shakespeare] Links to Shakespeare's work online. http://pages.unibas.ch/shine/ linkssourcesshworks.htm.

[Shakespeare] *The Shakespeare Quartos Archive*. http://www.quartos.org/index.html.

[Shakespeare] Cambridge World Shakespeare Online. Covers the historical William Shakespeare (THWS) and the world he inhabited as well as the collected works of William Shakespeare (CWWS). http://cwso.blogs.brynmawr.edu.

[Stendhal] *Les Manuscrits de Stendhal.* Les manuscrits de Stendhal conservés à la Bibliothèque municipale de Grenoble: vues numérisées des pages, transcriptions et descriptions. Site conçu par les chercheurs de l'équipe Traverses 19–21 et du laboratoire LIDILEM (Université Stendhal–Grenoble 3) et par la Bibliothèque municipale de Grenoble. http://www.manuscrits-de-stendhal.org.

[Strindberg] *Nasjonalupplagan av August Strindbergs Samlade Verk [National edition of August Strindberg's complete works]*. Last updates September 11, 2006. Per Stam (chief editor). http://www.strind.su.se.

[Twain] *MTPO. Mark Twain Project Online. Authoritative Texts, Documents, and Historical Research.* Edited by Anh Q. Bui, Victor Fischer, Michael B. Frank, Sharon K. Goetz, et al., Mark Twain Papers, the Regents of the University of California. California Digital Library, UC Press, 2007–2013. http://www.marktwainproject.org.

[Voltaire] *Voltaire intégral.* This site offers many texts of Voltaire (1694–1778) online, a complete edition available as CD-ROM, some critical studies, and links to other related sites. It aims to evolve as an "extensive encyclopedia about the XVIIth century and French literature." [The site was accessible online at http://www.voltaire-integral .com but is currently unvailable(in French).]

[von Sternberg] *The Sternberg Project: Commented Edition of the Correspondence to and from Kaspar Maria von Sternberg (1761–1838).* Edited by Claudia Schweizer. Wien: University of Vienna. Described at http://www.fwf.ac.at/en/finals/final .asp?L=E&PROJ=P14773 [the project's website was unavailable on October 15, 2011]. http://www.univie.ac.at/sternberg/contents.

[Wittgenstein] *Wittgenstein's "Nachlass": The Bergen Electronic Edition (BEE).* Oxford: Oxford University Press, 2000. *Wittgenstein's "Nachlass". Text Only Version: The Bergen Electronic Edition.* Oxford: Oxford University Press, 2000. *Wittgenstein's "Nachlass": The Bergen Electronic Edition* (BEE) is a joint publication by the Wittgenstein Archives at the University of Bergen (WAB) and Oxford University Press. Publication of the edition, which was initially intended to consist of four separate volumes, began in April 1998. After publication of volume 2 it was decided to publish one final, complete title. The complete edition was released in 2000 on six CDs (one CD with edited *Nachlass* texts and software, and five CDs with facsimile files). BEE is available online in the Past Masters series from InteLex Corporation. See http://http://wab.uib.no/wab_BEE. page for a bibliography of reviews of BEE.

[Wittgenstein]. *Wittgenstein Archives at the University of Bergen (WAB)* is a research infrastructure and project platform bringing together philosophy, editorial philology, and text technology. WAB published *Wittgenstein's "Nachlass": The Bergen Electronic Edition* (Oxford: Oxford University Press 2000). This edition contains all the manuscripts of Wittgenstein's *Nachlass* on six CDs in facsimiles and both normalized and diplomatic versions. The edition is equipped with a range of search and analysis functions. http://wab.uib.no.

[Woolf] *Woolf Online: An Electronic Edition and Commentary of Virginia Woolf's "Time Passes."* Initiated by Julia Briggs (1943–2007). Edited by Peter Shillingsburg. NJH/ Faculty of Humanities at De Montfort University 2008. http://www.woolfonline.com.

Software Tools, Resources, and Infrastructures for Digitization

Adonis/Huma-Num. TGE Adonis is a very large networked infrastructure established by the French National Research Council CNRS (TGE: Très Grand Equipement) targeting the humanities and social sciences. Adonis pools together different services, resources, and networks for the research community through a freely accessible web portal. A specialized infrastructure for the humanities called Huma-Num replaced the original TGE Adonis. [The original website—http://www.tge-adonis.fr—now points to http://www.huma-num.fr (in French).]

Arcane. Software for collaborative scholarly text editing. Description available in French at halshs.archives-ouvertes.fr/halshs-00004716.

BAMBI. Better Access to Manuscripts and Browsing of Images. See description in Andrea Bozzi, ed. *Better Access to Manuscripts and Browsing of Images: Aims and Results of a European Research Project in the Field of Digital Libraries.* BAMBI Lib-3114. CLUEB: Bologna 1997. See also Sylvie Calabretto, Andrea Bozzi, and Jean-Marie Pinon, "Numérisation des manuscrits médiévaux: le projet européen BAMBI." Actes du colloque Vers une nouvelle érudition: numérisation et recherche en histoire du livre, Rencontres Jacques Cartier, Lyon, décembre 1999. A description of Bambi is now available at http://journals.tdl.org/jodi/index.php/jodi/article/view/10/20.'

[BnF] La numérisation de masse à la BnF. Bibliothèque Nationale de France. The video can be watched online at http://www.bnf.fr/fr/collections_et_services/bibliotheques_ numeriques_gallica/a.numerisation_masse_bnf.html.

centerNet. An international network of Digital Humanities Centers. "centerNet is an international network of digital humanities centers formed for cooperative and collaborative action to benefit digital humanities and allied fields in general, and centers as humanities cyberinfrastructure in particular." http://digitalhumanities.org/ centernet/about.

CHAIN: The Coalition of Humanities and Arts Infrastructures and Networks. "The aim of CHAIN is to support and promote the use of digital technologies in research in the arts and humanities. Bringing together members with experience in creating and operating digital infrastructure, we aim to create a shared environment where technology services can interoperate and be sustained, thus enabling new forms of research." http://mith.umd.edu/chain.

CHCI: Consortium of Humanities Centers and Institutes. "The Consortium of Humanities Centers and Institutes serves as a site for the discussion of issues germane to the fostering of cross disciplinary activity and as a network for the circulation of information and the sharing of resources within the humanities and interpretive social sciences." http://chcinetwork.org.

CORPUS: Coopération des Opérateurs de Recherche Pour un Usage des Sources numériques. A research infrastructure for human and social sciences. This platform for cooperation gives access to the main collections of documents (images, sounds, and texts) produced within the human and social sciences research framework generally, and more specifically to those in linguistics, psychology, history, archaeology, philosophy, anthropology, geography, humanities, and the arts. CORPUS is also a funding mechanism, a cooperation and sharing framework for resources and know-how through labeled consortia in order to accompany and foster learning effects and synergies for the constitution and the development of the use of digital sources by human and social science researchers. A general description is available at www .cnrs.fr/inshs/recherche/journee-entrants-2012/pouyllau.pdf. [The original project site—http://www.corpus-ir.fr/index.php?—points now at http://www.huma-num .fr/index.php?] (See the entry Adonis above.)

DARIAH: Digital Research Infrastructure for the Arts and Humanities. "The mission of DARIAH is to enhance and support digitally-enabled research across the humanities and arts. DARIAH aims to develop and maintain an infrastructure in support of ICT-based research practices." http//www.dariah.eu.

DEBORA. Digital Access to the Books of the Renaissance. Description available as PDF file at http://www.enssib.fr/bibliotheque-numerique/document-995. DEBORA, funded by the EU Telematics for Libraries, aimed to provide public access to rare sixteenth-century literary resources that are currently inaccessible for reasons of preservation, and in doing so to investigate the costs and techniques involved in digitizing this type of material, analyze the requirements of users working with these resources, and develop tools to allow international access and collaboration.

Digital Archives of Early Scholarly Journals. Situated at the University of Waterloo, this site offers a repository of scientific journals published by learned societies from 1323 to 2009, with many links providing access to texts. http://www.scholarly-societies.org.

EMMA: Edition de Manuscrits Modernes Assistée. Software to support transcription of authors' manuscripts. Laboratoire "Perception Systèmes Information" (Laboratoire PSI CNRS FRE 2645), Université de Rouen. http://thierry.paquet.free.fr/thesestephanenicolasilitis.pdf

Gallica. Bibliothèque numérique. http://gallica.bnf.fr. English description at http://gallica.bnf.fr/?&lang=EN.

Google eBookstore/Google Books. "Search and preview millions of books from libraries and publishers worldwide using Google Book Search. Discover a new favorite or unearth an old classic." http://books.google.com.

Gutenberg-e. American Historical Association and Columbia University Press. http://www.gutenberg-e.org/index.html.

IDE: Institut für Dokumentologie und Editorik. Offers a catalog of Digital Scholarly Editions with links to English and German sites. http://www.uni-koeln.de/~ahz26/vlet/index.html.

IMPACT. A project funded by the European Commission. It aims to significantly improve access to historical text and to take away the barriers that stand in the way of the mass digitization of the European cultural heritage. http://www.impact-project.eu.

ISIDORE. A research platform integrated into the ADONIS infrastructure providing access to digital resources in the humanities and social sciences. http://www.rechercheisidore.fr (in French).

JSTOR. A not-for-profit service that helps scholars, researchers, and students discover, use, and build upon a wide range of content in a trusted digital archive of over one thousand academic journals and other scholarly content. http://www.jstor.org.

Ministère de l'éducation nationale. There are also a number of websites run by the French Ministère de l'éducation nationale offering links to virtual municipal libraries and freely accessible online text resources (in French). E.g., Portail national educhol at http://www.educnet.education.fr/lettres/pratiques5675/college/lecture-culture-humaniste/?searchterm=lettres%20textimage.

Munich Digitization Center (MDZ)/Münchener Digitalisierungszentrum, Digitale Bibliotek. Available in English at http://www.digitale-sammlungen.de/index.html?c=startseite&l=en&projekt=.

Norsk Aviskorpus. The Norwegian Newspaper Corpus. A large and self-expanding corpus of Norwegian newspaper texts. The collection of this dynamic and continually growing corpus began in 1998. The corpus is automatically updated by means of w3mir, which is an all-purpose http copying and mirroring tool. On a daily basis, the mirroring tool retrieves recently published texts from a set of remote websites, specifically the entire Internet version of ten major Norwegian newspapers. English description available at http:/avis.uib.no/.

Norton Critical Editions. Online catalog of scholarly editions on paper available through W. W. Norton & Company, Inc. http://books.wwnorton.com/books/subject-detail .aspx?tid=11202.

Numilog. La librairie numérique. French site available at http://www.numilog.com/ accueil.aspx. English site. Ebook store is at http://www.numilog.net.

Observatoire critique des ressources numériques en histoire de l'art et archéologie. The old website maintained from 2006 to 2008 contains numerous articles, directories, and students' works. It is still accessible online at http://www.observatoire-critique.org. The new website, created by CLEO (Centre pour l'édition électronique Ouverte), is accessible online at http://observatoire-critique.hypotheses.org.

PROBADO. Innovative digital library services for nontextual documents. The project PROBADO aims to overcome these limitations by developing content-based access and presentation methods for specific, selected types of non-textual documents. http://www.probado.de/en_home.html.

Public Knowledge Project. A partnership between Simon Fraser University British Columbia and Stanford University, individual university teachers, librarians, and postdoctoral researchers aiming to improve the professional and public value of academic research. http://pkp.sfu.ca/research.

Sartre. Virtual exhibition. http://expositions.bnf.fr/Sartre/ (in French and English).

Sartre. Mauricette Berne, ed. Bibliothèque nationale de France. Paris: Gallimard, 2005.

Summit on Digital Tools for the Humanities. "Report on Summit Accomplishments." Conference held at University of Virginia, Charlottesville, in September 2005. PDF file available at from http://www.iath.virginia.edu/dtsummit/SummitText.pdf.

TEI: Text Encoding Initiative. "The Text Encoding Initiative (TEI) is a consortium which collectively develops and maintains a standard for the representation of texts in digital form. Its chief deliverable is a set of Guidelines which specify encoding methods for machine-readable texts, chiefly in the humanities, social sciences and linguistics. Since 1994, the TEI Guidelines have been widely used by libraries, museums, publishers, and individual scholars to present texts for online research, teaching, and preservation. In addition to the Guidelines themselves, the Consortium provides a variety of supporting resources, including resources for learning TEI, information on projects using the TEI, TEI-related publications, and software developed for or adapted to the TEI." http://www.tei-c.org.

Theleme: Techniques pour l'Historien en Ligne: Études, Manuels, Exercices. This is an educational resource published by ELEC offering various educational resources about historical methods, commented analysis of sources, transcriptions, repertories, lectures, etc. http://theleme.enc.sorbonne.fr (in French).

TLF: Trésor de la langue française. This online dictionary, run by CNRS teams and an heir to Littré, is the result of advanced linguistic research on the history and contemporary usage of the French vocabulary. It exploits a powerful search engine and is now acknowledged as a standard reference. http://atilf.atilf.fr.

Contributors

DANIEL APOLLON, Digital Culture Research Group, Department of Linguistic, Literary, and Aesthetic Studies (LLE), University of Bergen, PhD, is an associate professor of Digital Culture (Humanistic Informatics) at UiB and former head of the research group for Text Technologies at Aksis Unifob AS (2003–2009). He is presently leading the Digital Culture Research Group at LLE. He also has considerable experience in coordination of lifelong learning and digital media European projects as well as a long track record serving as an expert for the EU Commission, Agence Nationale de la Recherche (ANR), CRE (now EAU), and other international organizations. He has also taken part in diverse COST Actions, among them *Interedition*. He is presently part of the international interdisciplinary Studia Stemmatologica team. His research interests focus on digital text, general text evolution and reconstruction, and cross-cultural and cross-linguistic aspects of digital media.

CLAIRE BÉLISLE is a consultant and researcher and is presently working on digital reading. She holds a doctorate in cognitive psychology and has worked as a human and social sciences research engineer for the National Scientific Research Centre (France) for most of her career, focusing on training and research in digital environments. She has conducted user studies on reading and digital corpuses, cognitive navigation in hypermedia contents such as online encyclopedias, managed several international research projects (for example, on telepresence, digital campus), and published numerous articles and edited books. Her latest contributions are in *Lire dans un monde numérique* (Presses de l'ENSSIB, 2011), of which she was also editor. She does consulting work for educational organizations and the European Commission and is an associate researcher at LIRE-CNRS, Lyon.

TONE MERETE BRUVIK, Norwegian State Archives, Bergen, is a former executive director of the Text Encoding Initiative and a text encoder at the Text Technology Research Group Aksis Unifob, Bergen.

ODD EINAR HAUGEN is part of the Old Norse philology research group, in the Department of Linguistic, Literary, and Aesthetic Studies, at the University of Bergen. He has worked on textual criticism in a number of contexts, including his doctoral dissertation on qualitative and quantitative methods of recension (using an Old Norse text as a case study), and in a number of articles, and in the edition of the handbook *Altnordische Philologie* (de Gruyter Lexikon, 2007).

TERJE HILLESUND is an associate professor of media and communication at the University of Stavanger, Norway. He has a master's degree in sociology from the University of Oslo and a PhD in media and communication theory from the University of Bergen. His main research interests have been in printed media—newspapers, journals, and books—and their transformation in the age of computers and the Internet. From 2000 to 2002 he led a project for Arts Council Norway in which a research team studied the potential impact of e-books on the Norwegian book industry. The results were presented in three reports in 2002. Since then Dr. Hillesund has published several scholarly articles on subjects such as e-books, digital reading, XML, digital text editions, and open access.

CLAUS HUITFELDT has been an associate professor of philosophy in the Department of Philosophy of the University of Bergen since 1994. His research focuses on the ontology, epistemology, and semantics of markup languages and digital documents. He was founding director (1990–2000) of the Wittgenstein Archives at the University of Bergen, for which he developed the text encoding system MECS as well as the editorial methods for the publication of *Wittgenstein's "Nachlass": The Bergen Electronic Edition* (Oxford University Press 2000). He was research director (2000–2002) of Aksis (Section for Culture, Language, and Information Technology at the Bergen University Research Foundation). In 2003 he returned to his position in the Department of Philosophy, where he teaches modern philosophy and philosophy of language and also teaches frequent courses in text technology in the the Department of Humanistic Informatics. He has been active in the Text Encoding Initiative (TEI) since 1991 and was centrally involved in the foundation of the TEI Consortium in 2001. His research interests are in philosophy of language, philosophy of technology, text theory, editorial philology, and markup theory. He is currently involved in the project Markup Languages for Complex Documents (MLCD).

SARAH MOMBERT is an associate professor of nineteenth-century French literature at ENS de Lyon (École Normale Supérieure) and senior researcher at CNRS. A specialist of swashbuckling romance, her literary and historical research investigates nineteenth-century French popular literature and press as multiple windows on society opened to readers during this period. At ENS de Lyon she heads a research group within LIRE (Littérature, Idéologies, Représentations) and is responsible for the digital edition of Alexandre Dumas's periodical publications written after 1848 during the last period of his literary and journalistic career. She has authored many scholarly articles on Théophile Gautier, Victor Hugo, Michelet, and especially, Alexandre Dumas. She has co-edited with Pascal Durand and published in 2009 *Entre presse et littérature: Le Mousquetaire, journal de M. Alexandre Dumas (1853–1857)*, Bibliothèque de la Faculté de Philosophie et Lettres de L'universite de Liège: (Diffusion Droz).

ALOIS PICHLER is director of the Wittgenstein Archives at the University of Bergen (formerly at Aksis Unifob AS, now Uni Digital AS) and an associate professor in philosophy. He has been involved in a number of editions of Wittgenstein, both on paper and in digital form, the most prominent being the Bergen Electronic Edition (Oxford University Press 2000). His research interests include philosophy, editorial philology, literary studies in philosophy, and recently the Semantic Web.

PHILIPPE RÉGNIER is research director of the CNRS and head of the UMR LIRE (Lyon 2–CNRS) research lab team in Lyon. He is a specialist of the history of nineteenth-century French literature with particular interest in ideas, opinion, and literary practices among French Republicans and Socialists since 1820. His main research and publication area is about mapping Saint-Simonism from all possible angles of views as the co-editor of the complete works of Saint-Simon (*Œuvres complètes Henri Saint-Simon*, 4 volumes), completed in 2012.

Index

The University of Illinois Press
is a founding member of the
Association of American University Presses.

University of Illinois Press
1325 South Oak Street
Champaign, IL 61820-6903
www.press.uillinois.edu